EASILY LED

To my long-suffering best friend, my wife

EASILY LED

A HISTORY OF
PROPAGANDA

OLIVER THOMSON

SUTTON PUBLISHING

First published in the United Kingdom in 1999 by
Sutton Publishing Limited · Phoenix Mill
Thrupp · Stroud · Gloucestershire · GL5 2BU

Copyright © Oliver Thomson, 1999

British Library Cataloguing in Publication Data
A catalogue record for this book is available from the British Library

ISBN 0 7509 1965 5

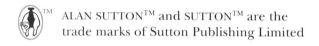
Typeset in 10/12 pt New Baskerville
Typesetting and origination by
Sutton Publishing Limited
Printed in Great Britain by
Biddles Ltd, Guildford, Surrey.

Contents

Preface

'The power of the glittering phrase'

Boris Pasternak

Among the most remarkable and least studied aspects of world history are the many examples of how easily led human beings can be. Over substantial periods we have been cowed by the blatantly artificial images of kings and tyrants, so that we meekly supported the most pernicious regimes. With amazing credulity we have been lulled into idolizing conquerors, applauding genocide, upholding persecution and condoning exploitation. We have happily been drilled by religious fanaticism into worshipping cruel gods, fearing strange hells, blessing human sacrifice or torture, admiring self-mortification and obeying the oddest of moral codes. We have been willing to believe the silliest myths, we have let our senses be ruled by martial music, poetic slogans, absurd prophecies and exotic images. We may now claim to be more sophisticated and less easily manipulated than our ancestors, but there is little evidence of this. From the awesome ceremonials round Stonehenge or the Temple of Karnak right through to the Romans, the Crusades, Napoleon, Hitler, Kennedy or Yeltsin the ability to deploy propaganda skills has been one of the major determinants of historical direction. This has not just been true of political power but of religion, morality and to some extent economics. The purpose of this book is to examine the variety of techniques used for propaganda in different periods and to demonstrate the extent to which such techniques influenced the course of events over the past five millennia.

For convenience this book is divided into two main parts: first a broad review of all the types, skills, tools and themes of propaganda throughout the ages, then a historical narrative picking out the highlights of propaganda over a roughly 5,000-year period from ancient Egypt to the end of the twentieth century.

'Philosophy is a battle against the bewitchment of our intelligence by means of language.'

Ludwig Wittgenstein

PART ONE
Analysis

'Lies are the mortar that binds the savage individual man into
the social masonry.'

H.G. Wells, 1900

Introduction

Defining Where Propaganda Begins and Ends

There is a tendency to think of propaganda as a relatively recent development and to associate it with the appearance of modern media. Yet propaganda does in fact have an extremely long history. Thousands of years before the invention of mass media in the modern sense, the ancient civilizations and their successors could use the communications channels of their own particular era with skill, cunning and effect.

Before moving on to an analysis of techniques it is important to arrive at an acceptable definition of the term propaganda. The word was originally part of the heading of a sixteenth-century papal bull directed against Protestantism. Partly, perhaps, because of this Catholic connection, the term acquired the overtones of a black art early on. On the one hand, the practitioners of literature, music and the visual arts tended to look down on those of their colleagues who overtly aimed for political or religious influence in their work, ignoring the fact that their own efforts inevitably also had some kind of message, albeit less obvious. On the other, democratic politicians and reforming priests tended to condemn the propaganda activities of reaction, forgetting their own reliance on very similar techniques. Hence the all-round tendency arose for propaganda to be thought of as a technique used by the other side, rather than what it is – the range of skills used by all sides, consciously or subconsciously, to put across their own point of view.

Harold Lasswell, the American pioneer of propaganda studies in the 1930s, defined it as 'the management of collective attitudes by the manipulation of significant symbols'. The Institute of Propaganda Analysis, founded in 1937, defined it as 'the expression of opinion or actions by individuals or groups deliberately designed to influence the opinions or actions of other individuals or groups with reference to determined ends'. Similarly, the American scholar Leonard Doob defined it as 'a systematic attempt by an individual or individuals to control the attitudes of groups of individuals through the use of suggestion and consequently control their actions'.

All these definitions are helpful, but there remains some confusion. First of all, there is the question of whether propaganda always has to be deliberate or planned, excluding, as Lasswell did, what he called the 'unpremeditated contagion of ideas'. In a historical review of the spread of political and religious ideas we will find many examples of where this dispersal has happened without much planning or premeditation: the spread of anti-Semitism, of witch persecution, of some aspects of nationalism, has often been a communal knee-jerk reaction to shared pressures, in which one group has set about persuading and influencing the rest of the population without any clear understanding of what it was doing. If the vast number of individual contributions and skills involved in such extempore campaigns were excluded from the umbrella concept of propaganda, then its study would be very one-sided. It is suggested, therefore, that it is unwise to insist on the words 'deliberate' or 'systematic' in any definition of propaganda. Too many great movements of mass persuasion have begun and continued without any master plan, although they were often eventually exploited by factional groups who did have a set agenda. The definition of propaganda formulated by H.J. Gans is broader and overcomes this difficulty: 'each group in society tries to get its own particular values legitimated by the media and they affect the distribution of wealth, power and prestige by controlling the symbols, myths and information'. Marshall McLuhan put it quite neatly when he described how a 'new message system dunks the entire population in a new imagery'. Roland Barthes also encapsulated the main idea well with his summing up as 'the myriad rites of com-munication which rule social appearances'. Group pressure, whether organized from above or simply based on peer group clannishness and competition, can achieve remarkably thorough and rapid spread of ideas, exploiting sarcasm, ridicule, harassment, guilt, competition for approval, and many other forms of bullying to achieve conformity to a new cult or fashion.

A second problem over the definition of propaganda lies in the common assumption that mass persuasion is only propaganda when it uses mistruth and deception or emotional manipulation. Plato contributed to this idea by advocating the use of lies – white lies – to pacify the population in his *Republic*. Kautilya, the Indian pioneer writer on propaganda of roughly the same period, followed similar lines. More than 2,000 years later Richard Hoggart expressed alarm that 'advertising, propaganda, most religious proselytising and many other forms of emotional blackmail . . . exploit human inadequacy'. Vance Packard also in the 1950s shocked Americans with the idea that in the era of mass media 'the manipulation of the people by a tyrant with a controlled society is now a fairly simple matter'. We shall see many historical examples which show that there is nothing particularly new about such manipulation, nor is there any particularly valid division between the use of lies and the use of truth to achieve propaganda results. If anything, it is easier for propaganda to be effective if it is based on the truth. Any definition of propaganda which emphasizes a reliance on untruth would be naive and would exclude too many important campaigns of mass persuasion which did not have to resort to any deception. News, information, facts are often a major component of propaganda. Goebbels wrote 'objectivity has nothing in common with propaganda, nothing in common with truth', but this typifies the essentially short-term view of propaganda prevalent among the Nazis.

A third confusion arises over whether agitation is part of or separate from propaganda. Lenin in particular drew attention to the perceived difference in his mind and many writers have tended to look on terrorist campaigns, mob manipulation, ceremonial, cell-networking and stunts as a separate subject. But the distinction is somewhat artificial. Most campaigns of mass persuasion have contained significant elements of public performance and agitation, used not just in their own right but as a means of attracting media exposure and myth building.

A fourth difficult confusion lies in the overlap between propaganda and education. Of all forms of communication, education ought in some respects to be the most free of factional or sectional propaganda, yet clearly this has hardly ever been the case throughout history. The fact that one function of education has usually been to produce citizens useful to and cooperative with the state, obeying its moral parameters, responsive to its corporate objectives, means that even regimes which have regarded themselves as above the use of propaganda have, in fact, been using many aspects of the education process to mould the young religiously, morally, economically and politically. The Nazis, Communists, Jesuits and Spartans were all groups who drew particular attention to the value of early training as part of long-term propaganda. Educational subjects like history, literature, religion, geography have nearly always been taught in a biased manner, bringing up new generations to have attitudes compatible with the dominant group in society. Sports training too has very often been used as part of the moulding process to achieve compatibility for political control or military response.

One final confusion must be faced over the definition of propaganda, and that lies in the supposed distinction between pure art, or pure literature, and propaganda. This view sees great works of art, creative writing or music on one side and propaganda on the other as an automatically second-rate level of art just because of its overt political or religious patronage. It implies that great artists in any medium are unlikely to stoop to working for sectional paymasters or to devote their talents to putting across a sectional viewpoint, whereas second-raters who do take on such tasks will produce work that is ephemeral and flawed. Again, the distinction lacks credibility. While many works of art may be produced with no conscious desire to proselytize or convert and with no obvious patronage from paymasters with a clear agenda, the vast majority do contain an element of attitudinal positioning and many a great deal more than that. Beethoven's *Fidelio*, Shakespeare's *Macbeth*, Michelangelo's *Pieta*, Picasso's *Guernica*, Dante's *Inferno* and Pope's *Epistle II of Horace Imitated* are just a few masterpieces which fall into this category. Beyond that nearly all the great creative talents in every era have devoted at least some of their output to political, religious or moral propaganda, have received appropriate patronage or commercial success and the work, no whit artistically inferior to the rest of their output, has achieved permanent respectability because the propaganda content is not really noticed by later audiences.

So we come to a broad definition or propaganda suitable for analysing it in a historical context. The phrase 'manufacturing of consent' favoured by Walter Lippmann and Noam Chomsky captures almost all that is necessary, but to cover all eventualities let us settle for the definition of propaganda as: the use of communication skills of all kinds to achieve attitudinal or behavioural changes among one group of people by another.

How Do We Know It Works?

The Evidence

Sadly, the archaeology of propaganda suffers from considerable gaps. The first requirement, for instance, for the analysis of contemporary propaganda campaigns is audience statistics. Even in the present day these are not totally reliable, since there is little correlation between standard measurements such as OTS (Opportunities To See) or TVRs (Television Ratings) and the number of messages actually absorbed. Awareness- and attitude-tracking studies are conducted, but again the relationship to media exposure and message content is remote. Going back into history it is even harder to quantify the population's exposure to media and messages – the number of times an average Roman saw the emperor's face and slogan on coins, the number of times a medieval peasant saw representations of St Francis or the Virgin Mary, how many actually read the works of Martin Luther, or how many citizens of the Third Reich listened how often to Adolf Hitler on the radio. Nevertheless there are at least some statistics on edition numbers of books, pamphlets and newspapers which can be related to literacy and population levels. There is even fair circumstantial evidence as to the numbers of statues, inscriptions, paintings, symbols, buildings and public ceremonies which helped influence humans in all areas throughout history.

Also to be taken as evidence is recorded mass attitude change on numerous occasions. We can cite the remarkably rapid initial spread of Christianity and Islam; the mass motivation by men like Cromwell, Mussolini or Hitler; the level of multiple motivation achieved by the American and French revolutionaries; the acquiescence and cooperative loyalty achieved by the pharaohs, the Roman emperors, Alexander the Great, Henry V of England or Frederick Barbarossa. In each case we observe the media utilization practised by the leaders, the level of cooperation achieved and, though there is no accurate syllogism to prove cause and effect in precise relationship, it is possible with the benefit of numerous examples to draw at least some broad conclusions: particularly that a leader, religious or political, with skill and sensitivity in the patronage and use of the media available was more likely to be successful than one without.

The third and by far the largest body of evidence is the surviving content of propaganda material: poems, novels, plays, statues, paintings, musical scores, buildings. Because of our lack of detailed awareness of contemporary taste, manners, acceptable imagery and innuendo, some of the force of this original material may be lost on us, but with careful interpretation and imagination we can still appreciate the effect which it once had.

What Was It All For?

Analysis by Objectives

For the sake of convenience it is useful to divide propaganda into seven main categories, according to the objectives for which it is used.

POLITICAL

This covers the whole gamut of communication skills, manipulation and event management which lead to the acquisition or sanctification of political power. It includes not just the rival electioneering and rhetoric of opposing parties, but the subtler forms of image projection which lie at the base of all political power. Tribal loyalty, patriotism, nationalism, respect for authority are both the tools and the end products. Flags, anthems, crowns, ceremonial parades, palaces, arches of triumph, pyramids, panegyric poems, equestrian statues are just some of the ancillary techniques available. The building of myths and images with fable and symbol are all part of the process of giving a particular individual or group the authority to command obedience and support. Self-made or otherwise insecure rulers from Rameses to Napoleon, from Caesar to Gorbachev, have always tended to be the most innovative and active practitioners because they needed the extra help. But throughout history virtually every government which wanted to survive has had to make at least some effort to cultivate its image and reputation. Significantly, as we shall see, nearly every dynasty and most elected regimes have cheated at least some of the time both in inventing their own pedigrees, denigrating their predecessors and exaggerating their own achievements.

RELIGIOUS

This is at once the most exciting and sometimes most dangerous form of propaganda, in that it tends to rely the most heavily on emotional manipulation. It is neither sacrilege nor an insult to suggest that founders of great religions and sects must have been very able communicators. Even those who, like Christ and Mohammed, left behind only a relatively small number of converts when they died, clearly had inculcated such a strong message system that the conversion process accelerated rapidly after their deaths. Several of the old testament prophets and semi-mythical figures in other religions such as Buddha, Zoroaster or the Guru Nanak, as well as more recent sect founders such as Martin Luther, Calvin, Ignatius Loyola, John Wesley, Charles Taze Russell, the Imams of Iran or Sun Myung Moon, all had a range of skills in communication which occasionally came close to misusing human inadequacy and yet at the same time often achieved results which undoubtedly benefited large numbers. Religious propaganda is more inclined than political, if only marginally so, to make use of irrational, mystical and unprovable statements, of emotive images and crowd manipulation. It can be shown that most religions, even those, perhaps especially those, classified as higher have used devious techniques to enhance their promotion. The temptation to prove the unprovable by resorting to miracles, dreams, prophecies and forged documents has been too strong. But religion has played a vital and more often constructive than destructive role in the development of mankind. Its propaganda techniques merit serious study.

ECONOMIC

This covers all propaganda aimed at persuading people to spend more or less money, to work harder for less, to have confidence in paper currency or precious metals, to conserve fuels, land, water or other materials, to put a high valuation on anything, to buy or sell shares, to have confidence in an economy, not to panic. It includes the whole creation and maintenance of belief in some form of economic equilibrium, a house of cards built on confidence which has proved to be the magic placebo of capitalist economies. It is important in the modern world particularly in relation to deflation or inflation, boom or slump, confidence or panic, where currency or share values can be talked up and talked down for the benefit of speculators. In the broader sense it covers the whole projection of acquisitive materialism as a human objective which governs the spiral of work, competition, wages, saving and the survival of a workable system. It also covers the projection of alternative attitudes like the reverence for mendicancy or poverty put forward by such groups as the Franciscans and Hindus, or of economic equality, put forward by the early Communists, or the concept of austerity as often required by governments in financial trouble.

By its nature, economic propaganda tends to be more long term and less obvious than political or religious, and it is often carried out almost subconsciously by large amorphous sections of each society, yet its influence is very considerable and the method of its operation is deserving of close study. The eco-propaganda of the 1980s and '90s with its attack on CO_2 emissions and the use of the global warming scare is a variant form of economic propaganda.

MORAL

The communication of codes of moral behaviour is a massive subject in its own right.* Clearly, moral codes have been created or modified to suit

---

*   See my *History of Sin*, Edinburgh and New York, 1991.

different eras and regions, as well as the objectives of the dominant sections of the population in each case. Many propaganda *tours de force* have been achieved by some of the great originators of ethical systems like Moses, Confucius, Lycurgus and others. There have also been a number of great packagers and communicators of existing moral systems such as Erasmus, Castiglione and Franklin.

But throughout history there have also been amorphous groups of minor communicators whose combined efforts to project various types of moral conformity have been critically important. Typical examples would be the Stoics, the Puritans, the campaigners against the slave trade, evangelical Victorians and the human rights activists of the twentieth century. Whether their motivation was the introduction of new ideas or simply the effort to maintain a traditional moral code among a new generation, these campaigners and others have often made use of the skills of propaganda to achieve acceptance of their ideas. As Rousseau wrote in connection with Poland, 'Whoever makes it his business to give laws to a people must know how to sway opinion and govern the passions of men.' Two remarkable instances of targeted moral propaganda have been the early Christian promotion of celibacy and the success of Islam in projecting temperance.

Throughout history there has been a massive role for popular literature in promoting easily digestible moral norms, such as the unitary family, while at the same time also fostering racial prejudice, inequality and intolerance of abnormal behaviour. Moral propaganda is often extremely long term, with opinion leaders gradually achieving changes in attitudes towards behaviour patterns such as celibacy, adultery, promiscuity, monogamy, sexual inequality and so on. Long-term attitudes on loyalty, honour, pride and revenge have been particularly important.

Moral propaganda also covers the use of messages by governments or pressure groups to achieve specific behavioural objectives such as family planning, prevention of disease, protection of the environment, better treatment of children or minorities, accident prevention and so on. Notable examples would be the modern Chinese campaign for the one-child family (pl. 18), the worldwide battle against the AIDS virus or the twentieth-century urban campaigns against litter.

SOCIAL

Socio-economic propaganda covers the techniques of mass persuasion which have been used over the millennia to project the superiority of classes, castes, races and usually the male sex. Mythology, graphic symbolism, event management and other techniques have been used to present as natural laws the concepts of landowning primogeniture, warrior or priest superiority, male dominance at the expense of female subjection, slave ownership and racial élitism. While all these ideas sometimes overlap with other forms of propaganda, they have nevertheless been of huge influence on the history of the world and general attitude formation. Again it can be seen that many aspects of social propaganda are extremely long term. The decline in the image of women and, to some extent, conventional marriage which began with the Christian fathers was not seriously reversed for 1,000 years. The favourable view of slavery was remarkably deep and difficult to dislodge. Many feuds between races, nations or sects can last for centuries after the propaganda and the events which first gave rise to them and bubble up to the surface at the first hint of the propaganda being reused – anti-Semitism is the classic example.

DIPLOMATIC

This is a specialist form of international propaganda mainly used before or during periods of warfare. It tends to involve organizing an appeal to other governments or peoples to take specific sides in international disputes or civil wars. In 1549 the Venetian pamphleteer Pietro Aretino (1492–1556) planted a false rumour that Venice was aiding the Protestants of Germany. Other classic examples have been the English putting the French in the wrong during the Hundred Years' War, Bismarck manipulating the Ems Telegram incident to put his own people in the mood for war and the French into a state of mind in which they could not withdraw from conflict, the German Kaiser's support of Kruger in the Boer War, Lenin's campaign to get the Germans to make peace with him in 1917, Hitler's campaign in Argentina or Saddam Hussein's worldwide effort to gain respectability for his invasion of Kuwait in 1990. The encouragement of inter-ethnic hatred and tit-for-tat xenophobia – one of the easiest of all propaganda techniques – has been one of the huge tragedies of human history. Equally dangerous are the exhibitionistic displays of armaments like competitive peacock displays indulged in by countries which want to overawe their neighbours. Underground nuclear testing by India on the Pakistan border in 1998 was a particularly risky example.

MILITARY

This is a kindred specialist form of propaganda mainly geared to the demoralization of enemies or the boosting of allies during wars. It includes the dispersal of surrender leaflets to opposing troops – on the end of bayonets during the Napoleonic Wars or dropped from the air by balloons over Paris in 1870, or aircraft from 1916 onwards. It includes the spreading of atrocity stories to harden troop morale and discourage surrender, the adoption of terrifying displays on ships, flags, shields, aircraft, buildings and everything which may be seen by the other side.

With the advent of the new media, blitzkrieg films of Poland were used to terrify the Norwegians in 1939, numerous radio stations were used for troop and non-combatant demoralization of the opposing side and encouragement of those at home. Music too has played an important part in the motivation of fighting peoples from Tyrtaeus of Sparta and the 'Song of Deborah' in ancient Israel right through to the 'Marseillaise', the 'Battle Hymn of the Republic', 'Lili Marlene' and 'We'll Meet Again'. Legend building round military heroes is also an age-old technique, used for Rameses II, Julius Caesar, Charlemagne, Genghis Khan, Nelson, Rommel and numerous others.

Military propaganda also embraces the vast volume of material which has glorified the idea of war itself over the last 5,000 years; from the epics of Homer and the carvings of the pharaohs, through Norse sagas and the *Song of Roland*, to the arts of the Napoleonic Empire, the posturings of Prussian militarists, the cinema of the Third Reich and the exploitation of state television by the Serbs. In almost every era the available techniques of propaganda have always tended to make it easier to promote the idea of war than that of peace. The role of all media in supporting various cultures of violence has been critical: it has promoted gun cultures, swordplay, the tournament, vendetta, duelling, affairs of honour, avenging insults, conquering heathens or barbarians for their own good and it being an admirable ambition to rule the world.

DIVERSIONARY

As a shadow eighth form of propaganda it is worth including the widespread use of media throughout the ages to divert populations away from questioning their rulers. One specific example was the 1902 Russian campaign which used the forged *Protocols of the Elders in Zion* to divert the Russian middle class towards hating the Jews instead of their government. The 'panem et circenses' policy of the Roman emperors was a prime example; the encouragement of corporate demonstrations of hysteria for gladiators, bull fighters and football teams or the mass absorption in escapist soap operas are all part of similar opiate strategies utilized consciously or unconsciously by dominant minorities. Another opiate function of propaganda is the general reinforcement of current norms, contributing to the maintenance of mass self-esteem. This is not to suggest any organized conspiracy, just to recognise the commercial reality of most artistic endeavour.

One of the common characteristics which becomes evident in all seven types of propaganda is the urging of people to sacrifice their own personal comfort, pleasure, liberty or even lives for the sake of the greater good. This involves a consistent level of moral if not physical intimidation which has induced a remarkable mass docility and obedience to norms from an early age in the vast majority of societies over most of the last 5,000 years. We can recognize that this is not of itself necessarily a bad thing, but in the wrong hands it is very prone to being abused. And it has almost always been in suspect hands.

Whereas most propaganda initiatives commence with the ambitions of a political or religious leader we have to recognize that the vast bulk of propagandists were simply following a lead which they hoped would enhance their career or financial prospects as writers, artists, musicians or potential leaders themselves, and that this grouping has included many of the most talented people throughout history.

Tentacles

The Range of Media Used

There are various ways of classifying propaganda media and considering their development. The first is quantitative or by method of transmission. It starts with the direct one-off exposure, involving single works of art, single speeches, performances, ceremonies or events seen once by a single audience. This is a basic primitive situation, but given a strong message content it may be very effective.

Beyond this stage there are two strands of development. One is the human chain emanating from the first experience, the retelling of the message to another group, who can then pass it on to a third and so on. Such crude message chains have been responsible for the spreading of oral traditions among illiterate peoples, indeed, for the growth and spread of most of the world's great religions. It was, for instance, truly remarkable how the message structures of the Jewish religion, or Hinduism, or the primitive ethics of Homer were passed on and remembered by considerable numbers over very long periods before written copies were possible, using devices like rhyme and professional reciters to spread the word. The Arabs gave the word 'ijaza' to the concept of the certified handing on of ideas from one generation to the next. The second parallel development from the original one-off exposure is the capacity to replicate the message in modest quantities, the hand copying of manuscripts, the multiple imitation of paintings like icons or statues and images, the repeat performances of plays, pieces of music or ceremonies so that by a geometric progression fairly large numbers of repetitions are eventually achieved. Thus in ancient Egypt, classical Rome or medieval India and China we find fairly substantial penetration both of visual images and literary works.

The next development in transmission comes with the mass production of messages, the earliest example of which, in the propaganda sense, was probably the coinage in the Macedonian and Roman Empires. This was followed by the invention of printing in the fifteenth century (earlier in China), albeit on a relatively modest scale until steam and rotary presses made possible genuine mass production in the nineteenth century. Then the twentieth brought the new electronically based media: film, radio, television and their offshoots.

Another broad classification of propaganda media is by the type of creative skill or craft which is used to communicate the message. Basically these are three: the visual arts, including graphic design, painting, caricature, architecture and sculpture with all their subdivisions; then the literary, including poetry, drama, the novel, oratory, philosophy, history and various other academic subjects which can be used to dress up a propaganda message; and finally music. There are also mixtures created from these three basic skills, together with a fourth, very important skill in terms of propaganda: that of the event manager. This skill, akin to that of the producer of a play, is in the organization of artistic performances or ceremonial, or variations of both, so that audience response and penetration is maximized.

The remainder of this chapter will give preliminary examples of each of the media categories and begin to develop some of the themes which will be reviewed in the historical narrative.

VISUAL ARTS

Taking the visual arts in more detail, one of the oldest and most important has been the ability to draw, design or make recognizable corporate symbols. The Star of David, for instance, a hexagram signifying fire and water, is of great antiquity yet still functions as the corporate identity for Jewry. It had the advantage of simplicity of reproduction, uniqueness and recognizability. The lions of Assyria were from the same era. Most civilizations from the earliest times have made use of one or more symbols which became identified with specific dynasties or gods. The Christian cross in all its many different forms is another excellent example – it had a real meaning yet was also easy to reproduce and distinctive. The three gold balls of the Medici, Napoleon's bee, the fasces of Rome which were revived by Mussolini and Hitler, the falcon of the Plantagenets, the greyhound of the Tudors, the wheel of Buddhism have all been very important. This leads to a further subcategorization. We see the use of animals like the white horse of Hanover, the eagles of Germany and the elephant of the American Republican party, of flowers like the blue cornflower for the French anti-Semites, the 'rose without thorns' for the Virgin Mary, the red rose for Lancaster and the British New Labour Party of the 1990s, of semi-realistic symbols like sun, stars or crescent moons, the skull and crossbones used by the Gestapo or the stylized Pillars of Hercules for the Emperor Charles V which still survive as the dollar sign. There is also a wide variety of national or regional identities relying on blocks of colour like the French tricolor – the first national flag was introduced by King Valdemar II of Denmark in 1219 and flags have been a dangerous focus for identity ever since. Colour became a regular component of corporate identity at an early stage. In Islam for example green was the colour for the Prophet, white for the Umayyads, black for the Abbasids and red for the Kharijites. The ideas of the 'yellow streak', 'white feather', 'red peril or 'black Pope' have all been examples of colour-coded propaganda tools.

There are then extensions of design into the semi-abstract, like the powerful swastika or *hakencreuz*, or complex coats of arms – the first royal coat of arms was that of Richard I of England. Also useful as the raw material for corporate identities have been initials, such as SPQR (Senatus Populusque Romanus) or GOP (Grand Old Party), the SS for Hitler's Schutzstaffel, or the ☧ chi-rho for Christ. Sometimes visual metaphor takes over as with the warming pan, which was a symbol of ridicule for the Stuart dynasty for at least a century after the odd circumstances surrounding the birth of the Old Pretender in 1687 were publicized, or wooden shoes, which for at least two centuries in Britain were a symbol of oppressed Catholic peasantry. Sometimes an important figure would be projected by groups of symbols, like the Indian god Vishnu who was known by a footprint, a conch and a wheel. Finally there have been a number of caricature figures as corporate symbols, like John Bull or Uncle Sam, or sometimes as just stereotypes of a race, like the Irish ape-man or the Nazi stormtrooper and the Jewish capitalist, or as idealized figures like Britannia, the French Marianne or the Winged Victory.

Corporate identity may also take the form of an item of dress, like the Phrygian cap of the French revolutionaries, the plain black garb of the puritan or Jesuit, the Safawid white turban with twelve white layers for the twelve imams wound round a red spike, the habit of a monk, or the elaborate robes, sceptre and crown of a medieval king. The uniform clothing and style of Sikhs or Ku Klux Klan members similarly had distinctive qualities. Equally, corporate symbols may be applied to numerous artefacts or items likely to have frequent exposure. Coinage is the classic example, prime propaganda medium of the Roman Empire and quite often thereafter. Medals were often a popular medium too. For example they were used by the absurd King Alfonso of Naples to project his aspirations as a would-be emperor. In subsequent periods symbols were applied to carriages, engines of war, mugs, fans, playing cards, postage stamps – an almost infinite number of items. Playing cards encouraged Queen Elizabeth I to topple the Earl of Essex, teapots carried the slogans of the Boston Tea Party, there were buttons boosting Napoleon, anti-slave trade Wedgwood cameos and umbrellas bearing the words 'Down with the Jews' in France in 1898. The Hungarians had cake moulds with images of Christ, the Indians playing cards with the exploits of Krishna, the Anti-Dreyfusards of France a vast range of propaganda board games, toys, sweet wrappers and kaleidoscopes with anti-Semitic slogans. The Unionists produced Gladstone chamber pots so that supporters of the cause could urinate on their opponent's face. Individually, these ambient media may seem to have played only a trivial part in human history, but in their own time, as small pieces of a coordinated message system, they were a significant component in the thrust of leadership. A classic example of effective image coordination was the Hitler regime with its corporate colours of red and black displayed with high frequency and the standard swastika applied to uniforms, vehicles, buildings, flags, artefacts, documents, film, ships, planes, so that the Third Reich's subjects were constantly reminded and overawed.

An adjunct of developing visual identity is the cultivation of regular props by individual leaders as permanent trade marks, as with Baldwin's pipe, Churchill's cigar or Kenyatta's fly switch. In some cases the prop can be added posthumously as with St Peter's keys, Christ's lamb or St Catherine's wheel. Sometimes even the removal of an expected prop can be the sign of a significant change of image as when Yeltsin's daughter persuaded his aides to discard their dark glasses.

Clothing and other forms of body decoration themselves became a medium of propaganda when used in unison to project a common identity, thus overawing opponents. This was true of numerous forms of military uniform or war paint, of priestly robes whether ostentatiously rich or ostentatiously poor, of common forms of dress for aristocrats, politicians, merchants, sports fanatics, or numerous other groups. Special haircuts and tattoos fulfilled the same purpose as did other artificial physical features: a classic example was the Jewish habit of circumcision which came to symbolize an ethnic divide.

Architecture may not be one of the more obvious propaganda media, but it is nevertheless of great importance. Buildings are capable of communicating awe, size, assurance, power and munificence. If in a central or imposing position, they can do this to a fairly large audience over a long period. As Louis XIV's minister Colbert put it, 'Kings are judged by the size of their monuments', and most of the world's great architecture owes its existence to that fact. The pyramids and temple complexes of ancient Egypt, the ziggurats of Babylon, the arches of triumph throughout the Roman Empire, the fortresses of the Normans, the massive palaces of the eighteenth century, were all designed to communicate the strength and permanence of rulers and their dynasties. Even the majority of great temples and cathedrals have been erected with the same objective, although their nominal task was to convey the image of and respect for their particular religion. Height and size have always been a major factor, from ancient Egypt to Communist Russia; domination in architectural terms has been a persistent theme and an objective. Semi-functional monuments like tombs, triumphal arches and war memorials have been designed to impress, sometimes simply as a demonstration of an ability to outspend. Dynastic dwelling places have been endowed with exhibitionistic security, with successions of intimidating ante-rooms, high ceilings, elaborate decoration and dynastic focal points. Places of entertainment like ancient amphitheatres or Enlightenment opera houses have had the royal box as a subtle secondary focus, and the whole as an advertisement for munificence and patronage. Even places of worship, for the most part built also as dynastic advertising, have been constructed with extravagant height and decoration. In the last few centuries, democratic parliaments and court houses have also been designed with the appropriate images of power and authority.

The other feature of propaganda architecture is its adherence in each case to a corporate style which is then repeated, beginning as early as the Stone Age circle or henge, in many parts of Europe. The Buddhist stupa, the Roman forum and the medieval Gothic church each had an individuality unique to the message system of which it was a part, yet by repetition it was able to stamp its meaning over wide areas. Architecture also had the capacity to create focal points for national and dynastic, or religious and sectarian message systems. St Paul's Cathedral was designed by Christopher Wren as the central symbol of the new British Empire, just as the new St Peter's in Rome was commissioned from Bramante by Pope Julius II to give a heart to reformed Catholicism, the Capitol was built to be the epicentre of the United States, Versailles to be the embodiment of 'le roi soleil', the Parthenon, literally, the high point of Athenian culture. It is hardly surprising that nearly all the most active despots and dynastic heads in world history have been extravagant builders who, at whatever cost, have left the world remarkable monuments, and that most of the great religions, although they usually started with far too inadequate resources to be great builders, have each rapidly come to appreciate the value of architecture as soon as they had the necessary funds. This art form could also be extended to include some of the more ephemeral structures used at times to convey a public message: royal coaches with elaborate decor, temporary triumphal arches, royal trains and yachts.

In addition we should recognize the way in which primitive societies adopted pieces of the natural landscape as visual furniture for their propaganda: mountains like Olympus or Fuji, rivers like the Ganges or the Nile, caves like Eleusis, sacred groves and pools like Nemi, islands as with the Celtic hermits, even mere springs or trees became manifestations of religion. There have also been theories that prehistoric monoliths were lined up to point at certain star formations on key festival days, so that early religions were able to claim control over the stars as part of their event management.

Sculpture as a propaganda art form is one which lends itself particularly to the idealization of dynastic leaders and religious figureheads (pls 1–3). There are three broad categories of propaganda sculpture, the first being the creating of human images. The Egyptians devoted substantial resources to this, with the massive Rameses II of Abu Simbel as a classic example. The other ancient civilizations followed suit, with the Assyrians specializing in bas-relief, the Chinese in modelling, the Greeks in idealized portraiture and the Romans in mass production of images of their gods and emperors. The two great exceptions were the Jews and Muslims who disapproved of religious sculpture. Standards dipped somewhat in the Middle Ages though not in narrative sculpture (see below) and a new development was the brass tomb, for example that of King Eric VIII of Denmark in 1319. Then came the revival in the Renaissance with Donatello's *Pope John XXIII*, the great equestrian statues of Italian princelings like Leonardo's *Sforza* which took twelve years, and Verrocchio's *Colleoni*, both conveying aggressive power. The increased use of bronze at this period made possible more dramatic monuments than could easily be achieved in stone. Roubillac and Rysbrack between them made a pantheon of British heroes for Westminster Abbey. The Catholic world was filled with stone and wooden Virgin Marys, Christs and saints, the British Empire had stone Victorias in every major city, the United States had its presidential apotheosis in stone on Mount Rushmore, and every twentieth-century dictator ordered his massive stone effigy to be placed prominently in city squares until most were toppled by revolution or disgrace.

The second type of propaganda sculpture is the symbol: the lion of Assyria in Babylon or of England in Trafalgar Square, statues of victory, peace, mercy and other abstract qualities, of which Michelangelo's *Pieta*, Gregor Erhart's carving of *Vanitas* and the French-donated Statue of Liberty in New York are great examples. King Edward VII commissioned the *Quadriga of Peace* by Adrian Jones for Hyde Park, the French the pierced German eagle at Compiègne or Dalou's *The Triumph of the Republic* in Paris.

Thirdly, there is narrative sculpture, the telling of propaganda stories in sculptural relief. The Egyptians, Assyrians and Aztecs were all expert in gory battle scenes sculpted to demonstrate the military prowess of their leaders and the awful fate of their enemies. The Column of Trajan in Rome is a more constructive example, with a stone narrative of the Emperor's campaigns, including bridge building and other activities. Other well-known pieces of narrative sculpture are Chartres Cathedral, with its many thousands of carved figures illustrating almost the whole Bible, and the Temple of Konarak in India, with its stone illustrations of the permissive Tantric teachings of Hinduism. Even the Elgin marbles from the Parthenon fall into this category, as do the sculptural tableaux organized by Friar Caimi at Varallo in 1565 or the Foolish Virgins of Magdeburg Cathedral.

Before leaving sculpture, we should recognize the wide range of mass-produced artefacts under its aegis. Seals carried corporate messages in ancient Crete, and coins have been a significant propaganda medium in almost every society. Miniature crucifixes, mass-produced brass heads of Disraeli or Gladstone, bronze Buddhas by the thousand, china kings and queens, duplicated busts of heroes . . . in all these the industrialized sub-culture of sculpture has played just as important a propaganda role as the major megaliths in city centres. In the sadistic make-up palettes of ancient Egypt, the anti-slavery cameos of Wedgwood, the teapots of Boston, the buttons of Napoleon, each age had its ancillary media.

Painting in all its forms and derivations has been a major propaganda medium almost from the dawn of history. The earliest examples were probably the wall paintings or frescoes of Egypt and Crete which were used for both dynastic and religious image building. Court painting continued with the Greeks and Romans, though too little has survived to estimate its real importance; certainly Alexander the Great had his tame painter, Apelles (fl. 325 BC). The Dark Ages offer a predictable lapse in the genre, but the Christian churches, both East and West, gradually improved their estimate of the value of pictures in the conversion process. Pope Gregory I gave his blessing to painting, although it was some time after his pontificate before the art reached maturity. Meanwhile the Byzantine icon led the way as a major artistic infrastructure for the Eastern empire. The serious contribution of Western painting to propaganda began with a succession of artists who devoted much of their time to the promotion of St Francis of Assisi: Giotto di Bondone (1267–1337) began work sixty years after the saint's death, with Simone Martini (1284–1344) following on, particularly with his *Annunciation* and the patronage of the friars during the fourteenth century was a major factor in the development of European painting. Giotto went to work for the King of Naples and Martini for the Popes in Avignon. Fra Angelico (1387–1455), himself a Dominican friar employed by a succession of Popes, developed similar themes with his *Coronation of the Virgin* and *Glory*, all aimed at arousing acute devotional feeling. Yet another monk-painter, Fra Filippo Lippi (1406–69), helped project the Carmelites in the same way, so that overall the Catholic Church became a major patron of art and used it to develop its image. Often paintings like the Black Madonnas of Poland were used for veneration like relics, and the concept of the icon as a two-dimensional idol with miraculous powers added considerably to the propaganda power of the painter.

Others of the new breed of Italian artists worked for the glorification of various rulers and city states: Lorenzo Ghiberti (1378–1455) for the dreaded Malatesta of Rimini, Paulo Uccello (1397–1475) for the city of Florence. Both Botticelli (1444–1510) and Fra Bartolommeo (1475–1517) were followers and supporters of the reforming Florentine monk Savonarola, while Raphael (1483–1520) and Michelangelo (1475–1564) painted for the aggressive Pope Julius II and Lorenzo de Medici. Raphael's *St George* was sent as a suitable diplomatic gift by the rulers of Urbino to the King of England.

Several painters in the sixteenth and seventeenth centuries combined careers as major artists, diplomats and event organizers for their rulers, the three jobs sitting quite comfortably with each other. Rubens (1577–1640) acted as an image maker for Marie de Medici, Vincenzo Gonzaga, Duke of Mantua, the Jesuits in Flanders and Philip III of Spain whose envoy he was in 1629 to King Charles I of England, where he produced his picture *Peace and War* as part of the diplomatic effort. Similarly, Holbein (1497–1543) did woodcuts for Luther's Bible before becoming court painter and pageant organizer for Henry VIII of England, whose wives he painted. Van Eyck (1390–1441) painted for the Duke of Burgundy, Philip the Good. Albrecht Dürer (1471–1528) not only designed copper plates developing the courtly image of the

Emperor Maximilian I, such as his *Triumphal Car* and *Triumphal Arch*, and generally contributed to the visual image of the Habsburgs, but organized the actual triumphal processions for the emperor. His contemporary Lucas Cranach (1472–1553) acted as court painter for the Elector Frederick I, was ambassador to the Emperor Maximilian and was later associated with work for the reformers Luther and Melancthon. Titian (1490–1576) spent a large part of his career as the chief painter for that most exhibitionistic of all Habsburg emperors Charles V, while Velasquez was both court painter and event organizer for the regime of Olivares. So while it could not be suggested that all the great masters of the Renaissance were mere producers of propaganda, it is clear that much of their creative skill was expended in that area, and that painting owed much in its development to the need for dynastic and religious images. It was the sight of Domenico Fetti's *Ecce Homo* which inspired Count von Zinzendorf to refound the Moravian Brethren.

This is not the place to delineate the propaganda connections of every great painter, as many will appear in our historical narrative, but before leaving the subject, it is worth hinting at the breadth of the material: it ranges from the dynastic image painters of the seventeenth and eighteenth centuries like Van Dyck (1599–1641) for the Stuarts or Le Brun for the Bourbons, to the continuing visual efforts on behalf of the Counter-Reformation by Correggio (1494–1534) or Tintoretto (1518–94) and from the revolutionaries like David (1748–1825), chief painter for the French Revolution and Napoleon, to the patriots like Goya (1746–1828) with his *Caprichos* and the *Shooting of the Madrid Patriots*, or even Picasso with his influential *Guernica*, symbol of Fascist bombing of helpless civilians. Less talented but none the less skilled painters have done the routine projection of every empire and faith; the professional battle painters like Wootton and Monamy developed special genres for the display of imperial heroics, followed by such stalwarts as Lady Butler with her *Roll Call*. Considerable propaganda use has often been made of idealized war pictures: the huge sale of prints of Samuel Scott's *Capture of Portobello by Admiral Vernon* in 1739 is just one example, while the visualization of the Battle of the Boyne became a whole industry which survived for centuries. Hack painting of this type has been a potent tool at many stages in history. The post-Reformation Catholic Church developed new images such as the Sacred Heart and the Immaculate Conception which lent themselves as themes for constantly repeated and copied pictures which were to be hung in almost every home, just as Greek Orthodoxy had its relatively easily copied icons of St George and the Dragon. Similarly, the Mogul emperors of India encouraged the development of large numbers of fairly cost-effective miniatures, while nineteenth-century Bengal produced the Kalighut style of popular Hindu religious images; brightly coloured and romantic, they were copied on a huge scale until the job was overtaken by printing in the 1930s. Though the study of propaganda thus leads often to reviewing paintings of a quality which might not merit entry in a normal art history, the contribution of both geniuses and hacks is equally relevant.

Other techniques of visual propaganda included the use of mosaics, pioneered by the Macedonians, extended by the Roman and Byzantine Empires, particularly by Justinian at Ravenna and elsewhere, and revived for example by Stalin for the huge propaganda mosaics in the Moscow underground. With the invention of the flying buttress which made the construction of bigger windows possible, stained glass became an even more exciting medium for religious propaganda, and in the early Renaissance tapestry versions of dynastic paintings provided kings with a portable form of wall propaganda to carry with them as they visited the scattered parts of their realms.

This then leads finally to the utilization of painting and illustration by printing techniques. The one-off mural was succeeded by the mass-produced poster campaign. The skills are not totally different. Lithographic printing was invented in 1798 by Alois Senefelder and by 1848 could produce 10,000 sheets per hour, with colour too by 1856. Similarly, the woodcuts of the Lutheran period soon developed into copper plates, then the mechanically produced letterpress and litho plates of the present day. Posters became a serious mass medium in the late nineteenth century but simple examples had been known earlier, such as the edicts posted by Francis I round Paris in 1539, announced by trumpets and gunshot, or the Golden Rump campaign against Walpole in 1737, or the placarding of Paris in 1789. The new style political poster designers were Alfred Leete, who was responsible for 'Your Country Needs You', Hohlwein, his opposite number in Germany, Jules Abel Faivre the creator of 'On les aura', Xanto who worked for Mussolini and Mayakovsky for Lenin, and the artists behind Hitler's massive 'Ja' campaigns. Later came the sophisticated electioneering posters of the later twentieth century – Saatchi and Saatchi's notorious 'Labour isn't working' campaign of 1979 or the US Presidential posters from the 1960s onwards. A recent addition to the forms of poster replication has been the use of one-off posters for a backdrop against which politicians can launch campaigns on television, giving the impression that the posters are spread over a country or area when in fact perhaps there is only one on a mobile trailer, arranged specially for the photo-opportunity.

PHOTOGRAPHY

By the 1860s illustrative propaganda also utilized photography, which offered special advantages in terms of realism. In particular, photography enabled the unvarnished truths of warfare and slum living to be displayed to populations which had never been close to either. From the American Civil War onwards photography portrayed the full horrors of military conflict and by the time of the Boer War it could be mass-produced in newspapers by the half-tone process and shown at high speed in the fast-expanding chains of cinemas. Great photographers, like Robert Capa with his *Moment of Death* from the Spanish Civil War, raised the medium to new heights of emotive communication.

Heinrich Hoffman was the photographer responsible for the presentation of Hitler, for many of his posturings and for developing the concept of photo opportunities as a tool of fascism. Similarly Alexander Rodchenko was the leading propagandist photographer of Stalinist Russia and Dorothea Lange of 1930s USA. In Russia particularly, photographic retouching to rearrange the truth also became a significant propaganda skill, removing one Soviet hero and adding another.

MUSIC

Music has the capacity to contribute to propaganda penetration in a variety of different ways, but most are based on its ability to change the pulse rate of the listener and gain a physical response. Thus it can generate belligerent feelings – as Plutarch put it 'music and valour are allied' – helping to inspire nations to go to war. At the same time it can create an atmosphere of pomp and glory which is extremely useful for both political and religious manipulation – the sostenutos and arpeggios of the great emotive anthems. Allied to this quality is its ability to provide an emotional focus or group identifier as is the case with national anthems or other group loyalty songs. Music can also perform a mnemonic role, a reminder of specific emotions in its own right or alongside words which do not necessarily even have to be repeated with it every time to be effective. Additionally music can have a cathartic quality designed to convey a sense of awe and submission to fate, again useful to the propagandist in certain situations. Finally, music can in a different context be used to help ridicule, as an adjunct to parody or satire as for example in 'We'll hang out our washing on the Siegfried Line' of 1939.

Military music with its power to help troop morale was a feature of the very earliest civilizations, with King Nebuchadnezzar's military bands, the 'Song of Deborah' for the Hebrew warriors, the marches written by Tyrtaeus for the Spartan army and the marching songs for Julius Caesar like 'The bold adulterer' or the hugely effective music of the Turkish janissaries. Right through from the anthems of the crusaders to 'Colonel Bogey' and Glen Miller, music has been a significant tool for military motivation and war has been a great patron of tunes.

Religious music too has a very long history with the chanting of the Rig-Veda beginning at least 3,000 years ago in Hindu temples and King David's psalm writers from about the same period using the Levites as a caste of sacred musicians. Music also had a significant role in the early propagation of Buddhism, Japanese Shinto with the *kagura* and in China with the Sung Chin. In classical Greece Plato analysed the different effects of music, the morally debilitating F Minor key, the Phrygian for military, the Dorian for chastity, the Ionian for permissive and so on.

Religion and military leadership were again the mainstays of music in the Middle Ages. The Gregorian chant with its mnemonically powerful stepped notes was an important part of the armoury of Catholicism and St Ambrose converted Italian folk tunes into popular hymns, introducing the antiphonal method of chanting. Venantius Fortunatus, Bishop of Poitiers (540–609) wrote a hymn which later became a popular anthem for the crusaders. Other successful monk composers included Huchbald (840–950) and Adhelm, Bishop of Sherborn. Their contemporaries in Islam at first rejected music as an aid to propaganda, as Mohammed himself had forbidden its use, but within a few generations Muslims too came to appreciate its value.

Among medieval royal and military leaders, the utility of music was understood early on. Taillefer was court musician to William the Conqueror, before and after 1066, projecting his master's image in song. The *Song of Roland* and many other ballads produced by the troubadours of Provence or the *minnesinger* of Germany, were extremely popular throughout Europe, projecting the heroic duties of feudalism and the images of kings. 'Now the day dawns' for King Robert the Bruce or Henry V's 'Agincourt Song' are examples from a long line of popular war songs in each period.

In England from 1400 the Chapel Royal became the headquarters for national music, but by this time music was also finding a role as a propaganda tool of opposition. The 'Song against the retinues of great people' for instance made its appearance in the campaign against the Gaveston clique under Edward II and 'The song against King of Alamaigne' came from the unrest against Henry III. 'Chevvy Chase', destined for long-term popularity, came from the English defeat at Otterburn in 1388.

Most new developments in Christianity were accompanied by new styles of promotional music which contributed to their success. The Franciscan friars developed attractive carol-type tunes and 'The Canticle of Creatures' of 1223 was the first hymn in Italian. Guillaume de Machaut (1300–77) was priest and court poet-musician in Bohemia, Navarre, then Paris. Martin Luther was a particularly skilled musician who appreciated the value of good tunes – 'I wish after the example of the prophet to make German psalms for the people by means of song.' He has also encouraged the development of good Czech hymns and while John Calvin discouraged music as unnecessary his Huguenot and Scottish followers soon found a use for melodies like 'The Old Hundred' and Marot's French translations of the psalms. Thomas Beze's 'Battle Hymn' of the Huguenots was later used as a war anthem by Oliver Cromwell in 1643. A final excellent example of the use of music for propagating new Christian sects was the huge hymn writing output of Charles Wesley (1707–88), brother of John the founder of Methodism. He produced a massive collection of hymns including 'Jesu lover of my soul' and 'Love divine all loves excelling' which were important tools for the promotion of the sect over a long period.

Returning to the secular, Renaissance rulers in general placed a great deal of importance on good dynastic music. In England Henry VII increased the size of the court orchestra for his staff composer Robert Fayrfax and his son Henry VIII was associated with popular tunes such as 'The Hunt is up' and 'Greensleeves'. Queen Elizabeth had a quite prolific group of court composers such as William Byrd (1543–1623) and Thomas Morley (1557–1603) who produced 'The Triumphs of Oriana' as part of the post-Armada image campaign. John Bull, a court composer under Elizabeth's successor James I, is credited with the original version of 'God Save the King'. Elsewhere Palestrina (1525–94) was chief composer for Pope Julius III and involved in the musical projection of the Counter-Reformation while Monteverdi (1567–1643) was hired by the Duke of Mantua.

The dynastic struggles of the Stuart royal family in Britain produced some exciting propaganda music on both sides: the 'Cavalier Song' on one, 'The Triumph of the Roundheads' on the other during the Civil War. There was also the superb court music of Purcell (1659–95), with gems like the 'Prince of Denmark's March', the unattributed 'Trumpet Voluntary', and the devastatingly successful 'Lilliburlero' with its rousing chorus of anti-Catholic passwords put together by Lord Wharton to foster panic about Catholic conspiracies – in Winston Churchill's words this song 'cost James II three kingdoms'. Thereafter a succession of great Jacobite songs such as 'Bonnie Dundee' and 'Heh Johnnie Cope' were ultimately met by the awesome musical power of Handel (1685–1759) who projected redcoat success with his *Te Deum* of 1713, *Zadok the Priest* for the coronation of George II in 1727, 'See the conquering hero comes' for Cumberland's defeat of the Pretender in 1746 and the 'Fireworks Music' for the end of war in 1749. The build up of British nationalist and later imperialist music can be seen with Arne's 'Rule Britannia' in 1740, the Boyce/Garrick 'Hearts of Oak' in 1769, the naval war songs of Dibdin, Charles Burney's patriotic music, McDermott's 'Jingo' song of 1877 – 'The Russians shall not have Constantinople', Stanford's 'Revenge' and Elgar's 'Land of Hope and Glory'. After that came Parry's 'The Glories of our Blood and State', Novello's 'Keep the home fires burning' in 1915 and Vera Lynn in 1940. These examples are only part of a vast connected but ever changing mosaic which helped shape the corporate mind of one country over several centuries. In other parts of the world similar trends were evident. The glories of Louis XIV were expressed in music by Couperin and Lully but with the deluge in 1789 came more popular works such as the French revolutionary 'Ça ira' which swept Europe, the Carmagnole and the superb anthem the 'Marseillaise' (pl. 8). The great revolutions of the period 1776 to 1917 all had strong musical support. In the United States there were 'Yankee

Doodle', John Dickinson's 'Liberty Song' of 1762, and later Adair's 'Liberty' and the 'Star Spangled Banner'. The Irish had 'The wearing of the Green' from 1798, Tom Moore's 'Minstrel Boy' and 'The Battle of the Boyne'.

While Chopin (1810–49) with his Polonaises and Liszt (1811–86) with his Hungarian Dances championed the musical cause of two underdog nations and Beethoven (1770–1827) switched allegiance from Napoleon in his pan-European Ninth Symphony, Haydn (1732–1809) produced 'Gott erhalte Franz der Kaiser' in 1797 which was rewritten as 'Einigheit und Recht und Freiheit' in 1848 and again as 'Deutschland über Alles' in 1922, one of the world's great anthems which was recycled each time with a different propaganda objective. *Ma Vlast* by Smetana (1824–84) and Sibelius's (1865–1957) *Finlandia* are two other outstanding examples of a musical stimulus to national feeling.

Socialism also at times made effective use of music. The Chartists had their own hymns as did many of the world's labour movements and minorities. The Paris Commune of 1871 produced the popular 'Internationale' – 'debout les damnés de la terre' – by Poitiers which was adopted by the Russians and international Communism as its anthem, while other tunes like 'Tannenbaum' made popular working class rally songs.

The major wars of the nineteenth and twentieth centuries produced their popular rallying tunes: the 'Blue Danube' came out of the Sadowa crisis in Austria in 1866, while the American Civil War had powerful melodies on both sides, 'Yankee Doodle Lincoln' in 1860, Grant's version of 'Champagne Charlie', Julia Ward Howe's 'Battle Hymn of the Republic', and Daniel D. Emmett's 'Dixieland'. The Boer War had 'We're Soldiers of the King' and 'Goodbye Dolly', the First World War 'Tipperary', the original of the Horst Wessel tune and 'Over there', while the Second World War had 'La Giovinezza' for Mussolini's Italy, 'Lili Marlene', 'We'll Meet Again' and a host of others. From 1880 John Philip Sousa (1854–1932) had been conductor of the US Marines band and produced a considerable output of militant nationalist music, just as Johann Strauss (1804–49) had done for the ailing Habsburg empire with scores like 'Imperial Echoes' and the 'Radetzky March' of 1848. Throughout the world music was a minor but significant nutrient for peoples being encouraged to make war, just as it was used both by establishments to try to keep loyalty and by revolutionaries to try to change it. The introduction of a number of new or more developed musical instruments was associated with innovative image projection by a number of rulers or institutions – the organ with the Benedictine monks, the virginals with Queen Elizabeth I, the cornet with the Emperor Charles V, the modern harp with Charles VI of France, and the pianoforte with Frederick the Great of Prussia. The distinction between popular and classical composers is almost irrelevant; success lay in the ability of tunesmiths and sometimes lyricists to capture the desired mood of the people.

The propaganda power of music was significantly enhanced by its reproduction through radio, gramophone, tape and disc. An example of the effect of technological change was the role of illicit cassette tape copying in the spread of anti-Communist folk songs and poetry in Russia under Brezhnev, specifically the songs of Vladimir Vysotsky as a national figurehead.

OPERA

The extension of music to opera, despite its relatively low audience penetration due to the huge expense of production, has also at times made a significant contribution to propaganda over the past four centuries. On the establishment side, Charles II's reign saw a number of political operas, notably Purcell's *Arthur* with libretto by Dryden, which contained what was to be Britain's leading patriotic tune for half a century: 'Britons strike home'. Davenant's *The Cruelty of the Spaniard in Peru* (1658) had an obvious xenophobic theme and Arne's masque *Alfred* of 1740 was also anti-Spanish in its motivation. Lully's (1632–87) operatic prologues on behalf of Louis XIV were backed up by Cavalli's (1600–76) operas like *Ercole Amante* composed for the 'Sun King's' wedding. Mozart's *Idomineo* glorified the enlightened despotism of his patron Joseph II of Austria and his *Clemenza di Tito* was produced for the coronation of the Emperor's brother Leopold II of Bohemia. Glinka's (1803–57) *Life of the Tsar* helped promote Nicholas I of Russia as a national figurehead. In America the pro-British ballad opera *The Disappointment* of 1767 attacked the rebel colonists and featured the song 'Yankee Doodle', subsequently purloined by the other side.

In a compromise for the Lutheran churches which distrusted opera, J.S. Bach, Schutz and Handel developed the oratorio, as a more discreet vehicle for ecclesiastical propaganda. Anti-clerical opera too had its place, for example Antonio Salieri's (1750–1825) *Tartare* was highly popular during the French Revolution while the following generation enjoyed François Berton's *Les Rigueurs du Cloître*.

Three operas stand out on the anti-establishment side. Pepusch's (1667–1752) score for John Gay's ballad opera *The Beggar's Opera* played to packed houses in London in 1728; it substantially assisted and inspired the opposition against the administration of Sir Robert Walpole. A performance of *La Muette de Portici* or *Masaniello* (pl. 9) by Daniel François Auber (1782–1871) in Brussels in 1829 inspired the audience to rise up and start a nationalist revolution against the alien Dutch rule over the Belgians. A third anti-establishment opera, *Taking Tiger Mountain by Strategem*, was part of the build-up to the Cultural Revolution in China. Verdi (1813–91) may not originally have seen himself as overtly political but the banning of one of his operas in Naples made him almost accidentally a hero with the Italian patriots and the 'Chorus of the

Hebrew Slaves' from his *Nabucco* was instantly adopted as one of the anthems of the Risorgimento and nearly as the new Italian national anthem, while his *Rigoletto* was seen as openly anti-aristocratic and liberal. Verdi's contemporary Richard Wagner (1813–83) was probably the most politically motivated of all composers of opera, although in a very mixed up way. He resented the failure of the liberal revolution in Germany in 1848 which led to his exile, yet that year he began his vast *The Ring of the Nibelungen* which carries a message of unique German values and predestined eminence. As Malherbe put it the *Ring* 'is so deeply steeped in poetry and dreams that its dangerous significance may not be noticed. Thus its subterranean message full of imagery can permeate the souls with greater ease.' Wagner looked back to Frederick Barbarossa as the ideal German emperor, evincing in his speeches, newspaper articles and pamphlets his belief in the superior destiny of the German 'volk' to which the presence of Jews, if not also Catholics because of their multi-national allegiances, was a serious threat.

Propaganda content can also be seen in many other operas. Beethoven's *Fidelio* is a moving plea for liberty, Smetana's *Bartered Bride* for Czech nationalism, and Kurt Weill's (1900–50) *Threepenny Opera* of 1928 is an attack on crude capitalism. Francis Poulenc's (1899–1963) *The Breast of Tiresias* of 1941 also has a strong moral message. Thus though opera has always been élitist in its audience penetration it does have a record of leaving a deep propaganda impression – at least on middle-class audiences – which has at times been significant. Lighter weight musicals have also had propaganda significance, Harold Rome's *Pins and Needles* of 1947 supported trade unionism and Gershwin's *Porgy and Bess* of 1935, the southern black community.

DANCE AND BODY LANGUAGE

It would be wrong totally to ignore dance as a persuasive medium. Certainly in eastern religions it has been significant; Hinduism had an elaborate sign language of hand and arm movements which enabled dancing to play a promotional role and there are numerous other examples of where even the simple choreography of rites, processions and ceremonials to music has had virtually the same impact. Ballet as a means of projecting the prestige of monarchs became very fashionable from around 1580 onwards – one example was the Medici wedding of 1617 which was celebrated with the ballet *La liberazione*, based on Ariosto's *Orlando* with added elements of Florentine history. Another example of the use of dance for propaganda was the staging by Cardinal Richelieu in 1641 of the *Ballet de la Prosperité des Armes de la France* with music, dance and elaborate scenery to celebrate the victories of Louis XIII over Spain.

As an extension of dance we could include other aspects of corporate body language which became visual symbols: the Nazi salute, the 'V' sign,

the Serbian three fingers or the black fist. Most extensive were the
elaborate hand signals of Buddha statues, one of which 'Forget Fear' was
adopted later by Gandhi. Military drill movements, pioneered for
example by Frederick I of Prussia, can also be seen as corporate
manipulation of body language to enhance a totalitarian image. In 1997
the public playing of an imaginary flute by the footballer Paul Gascoigne
was censured as an incitement to anti-Catholic hysteria. But perhaps most
important of all has been the range of body signals developed over the
years to instil an attitude of submission – bowing, saluting, standing and
all other variations on forelock-touching.

LITERATURE

The next broad category of media is the spoken or written word.
Certainly the oral tradition of memorizing and reciting long legends or
poems over many generations was remarkable. It accounts for the early
progress of the Jewish Pentateuch and the Hindu Rig-Veda, of Homer's
epic poems, Norse sagas and many other great works which were carried
down from one generation to the next with remarkable accuracy despite
the absence of written text. For the next 2,000 years or so texts could be
written but not printed – except in China – so penetration was severely
restricted. It is noticeable that most of the early civilizations made
substantial use of the carved inscription for propaganda purposes, for
example, dynastic statements in stone at strategic parts of the empire, as
in Egypt, Assyria, Rome, and Ashoka's India. Similarly the Muslims
turned mural calligraphy into an art form, decorating mosques and
palaces with quotations from the Koran. Many ancient and medieval
societies also devoted huge resources to book production. The early Jews
had a hereditary sect of copiers who were important for the survival of
Jewish ideas. The medieval Catholic Church and contemporary Islam
regarded manuscript copying, combined with magnificent artistic
embellishment, as an important calling. Oral recitation of texts in many
forms also played a key part in the pre-printing period propaganda; so
that though overall penetration of written text remained low, the spread
of verbal message material in the pre-print era was remarkably thorough.
  The Chinese introduced printed propaganda material much earlier
than any other nation (see p. 131), but it is easy too to exaggerate the
initial difference which primitive printing made when it arrived in
Europe. Luther's *Sermon of Indulgence and Grace* sold 25,000 copies in two
years, Erasmus's *Enchiridion* was an international best-seller with 100,000
copies in twenty-two languages, Columbus's account of America also ran
to more than twenty editions, but by modern standards such numbers
were relatively low. By the time of Hannah Moore and her cheap tracts,
or the works of popular revolutionaries like Tom Paine, printing
techniques had improved somewhat but the real breakthrough towards

mass circulation came with the introduction of rotary printing powered by steam in 1811, plus continuous belt paper-making in 1817. Linotype and photo-engraving followed towards the end of the century by which time print could be regarded as a mature medium capable of mass penetration at low cost.

We can now start a preliminary survey of the main literary genres which have been used for propaganda purposes at different levels in different periods and areas.

POETRY

The advantages of poetry – its mnemonic qualities due to rhyme, rhythm and imagery – were recognized at a very early stage, particularly for the retention of didactic myths among illiterate peoples. The tradition of epic oral poetry in illiterate societies was an important element in the attitude coordination of many early nations. The *Iliad* and *Odyssey*, Icelandic sagas and Indian religious epics are all examples of this category. The Eddic *Havamal* was a kind of poetic guide to moral behaviour. Some long poems like the *Epic of Pabuji* survived in their oral form into the late twentieth century, despite the huge requirement for the learning by heart of thousands of lines as compared with the easier resort of reading or recording now available. The importance of semi-professional groups of learner reciters was enormous in many early societies, perhaps most of all in the first 2,000 years of Judaism; but also for example in the preservation against all the odds of the Serbian epic in Turkish-ruled Bosnia.

The propaganda use of poetry falls into four main categories: the versified myth such as the *Mahabharata*, or the *Song of Roland* putting across courtly values and loyalty to king, nation or god; the panegyric or rather more elaborate and artificial court poems of dynastic glorification; the lyric exploited for the sudden incitement of warlike or religious feelings; and verse satire as a potent tool for the humiliation of political enemies. In addition there were substantial quantities of simple verse or even doggerel used to inculcate good behaviour, prayer, regard for leaders, disrespect for enemies. From the earliest times there are examples of all four types. Among the Greeks Solon was the political poet putting across ideas of justice; Tyrtaeus was the war poet of Sparta, and Pindar the panegyric specialist who produced public relations poetry for various cities and towns. Of the Romans Virgil was the most powerful propagandist poet, building the image of the Emperor Augustus while Juvenal created the genre of satire. Poetry persisted in the Dark Ages: even Attila had his bards in 448 and Widsith was the poetic promoter of Anglo-Saxon patriotism. Every respectable dynasty had its court poets, like Amoros dau Luc who worked for Henry III of England and Lawrence

Minot who created war propaganda in verse for Edward III. Ludovico Ariosto (1474–1533) was employed by the Este family of Ferrara to develop the image of the Emperor Charles V as the new Charlemagne in his *Orlando Furioso*. Pierre de Ronsard (1524–85) did the same for Charles IX of France, attacking the Huguenots in his *Discours des misères de ce temps* and *La Franciade*. Edmund Spenser (1552–99) contributed to the anti-Catholic propaganda of the Elizabethan era with his *Theatre of Worldlings*, his idealization of Sir Philip Sidney in *Astrophel* and his nationalist epic *The Faerie Queen*, supporting Queen Elizabeth I with the new concept of maritime empire. Thereafter almost every generation in British history produced at least one significant poet with strong propaganda motivation. Andrew Marvell (1621–78) was a friend of Cromwell and political satirist against the Stuarts, while his colleague John Milton (1608–74), the outstanding poet of his age, was a masterly writer of prose propaganda on behalf of the Cromwellian regime. John Dryden (1631–1700) produced a series of verse satires – *Absalom and Achitophel*, *The Medal* and *MacFlecknoe* which contributed much to the political failure of the Whigs in the early 1680s. His description of Shaftesbury was particularly telling:

> Stiff in opinions, always in the wrong
> Was everything by starts and nothing long
> Was chymist, fiddler, statesman and buffoon . . .

Joseph Addison (1672–1719) a literary all-rounder was the poetic supporter of Queen Anne and Marlborough with his *Campaign* to celebrate the Battle of Blenheim. The group of poets who assisted Viscount Bolingbroke in his opposition to Walpole was probably the most brilliant ever employed to conduct poetic propaganda. Headed by Alexander Pope (1688–1744) and Jonathan Swift (1667–1745) it also included James Thomson (1700–48) with Samuel Johnson (1709–84) on the fringe. These plus a number of less well-known colleagues produced a blistering barrage of poetic innuendo against Walpole and his allegedly corrupt, appeasing foreign policy. Thomson in particular concentrated on the imperialist theme which became a major strain in British poetry until at least 1914, with Robert Southey (1774–1843) the projector of Nelson and Wellington and Alfred Tennyson (1809–92) also promoting the Tory theme published in *The Times* in 1859:

> Better a rotten borough or two
> Than a rotten fleet and a city in flames.

Rudyard Kipling (1865–1936) maintained the same tradition with his 'Recessional' as did a number of lesser jingoistic poets of the period. From Ebenezer Eliot with his verse for the repeal of the Corn Laws to Matthew Parker and his for the Temperance movement and the Victorian work ethic, almost every cause had its poet, some indifferent, some ephemeral but most quite effective in their own day. Poetry also played a major role among the oppressed nationalities of Europe. Camoens's (1524–80) 'Lusiads' was the distillation of Portugal's entrepreneurial spirit. Serbian oral poetry survived the loss of their freedom to the Turks and the Kosovo cycle of 1389 remained an inspiration. During the Greek wars of independence each of the guerrilla Kephts had a public relations poet, most notably Kissabos with his 'Glory to Death'. The upsurge of German patriotic poetry with Ernst Arndt (1769–1860) and Ludwig Uhland (1787–1862) played a major role in creating the climate for unification and the *Kalevala*, the national epic of Finland which was written down in 1835, became a major influence in the nineteenth century. Even in the twentieth century Gabriele D'Annunzio (1863–1938), the Italian poet-advocate of the new Renaissance, felt inspired to seize the city of Fiume in 1919 and left the beginnings of an image for Mussolini (see pp. 38 and 267). In 1920 the poet Sheikh Mohammed of Somalia led a rebellion against the Christians, making extensive use of poetry as a political weapon. In the 1970s poetry was still the most influential medium in Somalia; political poems would be transmitted across the country within days by professional reciters travelling around a largely illiterate population. Mao Zedong (1893–1980) the Chinese Communist leader used verse to put across his ideas as had so many of his predecessors. Remarkably poetry was also a significant medium in the lead up to the Iraqi revolution of 1952 as, for example, with Abdul Wahhab al Bayati's 'Intifadhah':

> Our slogans were like the sky
> Drenched with the blood of comrades.

And the living tradition of epic poetry was a key factor in the revival of Serbian nationalism in 1990.

For want of a better categorization we could also include here the sort of short memorable phrases that become mottos, a common vehicle for dynastic and other propaganda, and proverbs, short sharp memorable sentences usually with a moral. They are often helped by some form of rhyme or alliteration. Clearly the musicality of some languages leads more naturally to the popularity of poetry than others. Particularly in Africa and Asia there is still more of a major role for the medium than in the West in propaganda terms.

THEATRE

While drama has undoubtedly been used by many regimes and their opponents for propaganda purposes, most plays which were heavily political have not survived in the literary canon because they are boring or unintelligible to a modern audience. It is well known that Shakespeare's *Macbeth* had a short eulogy for the Stuart dynasty in the witches' scene, but the plays performed for some of those leaders who made great propaganda use of the theatre like Cromwell, Robespierre and Mao Zedong were destined to be ephemeral – this does not mean that they were ineffective in their own day. The best known propaganda plays have always been those of oppositions, usually satires. The greatest ancient practitioner was Aristophanes (*c.* 448–388 BC) whose cutting *Clouds* and *Wasps* still have a contemporary ring. In the same mould was Henry Fielding (1707–54) whose burlesques at the Little Haymarket Theatre were so powerful that Walpole passed the Licensing Act to stop performances of all plays of that kind. In the years which followed there were vivid examples of the propaganda use of theatre, now with subtly hidden political innuendo, in plays like Mallet's *Mustapha* and James Thomson's *Edward and Leonora* causing a major furore in their own time. The most influential play in the preparations for the French Revolution was without question *The Marriage of Figaro* by Beaumarchais which opened in 1784, while Victor Hugo's *Hernani* enjoyed a similar influence before the revolution of 1830. Two of the most effective political playwrights of the twentieth century were Bertolt Brecht (1898–1956) with his *Mann ist Mann* and *Mutter Courage* and George Bernard Shaw (1856–1950) a socialist pamphleteer who kept the propaganda content of his plays low key to avoid diminishing their dramatic worth. In 1961 the play *Hai Rui Dismissed from Office* by Wu Han was seen by Mao Zedong as an attack on his reputation: he exploited the play by counter-attacking with the preliminary stages of the Cultural Revolution.

Theatre has played an even more important role in religious than political propaganda, perhaps because the medium was well suited to the re-enactment of religious events almost as a variant on ritual. Medieval morality plays, the Passion play of Oberammergau, even the standard nativity plays, are all examples of the didactic value of the re-enactment of biblical stories. Similarly the modern Shi'ites in Iran have massive theatres such as the huge one at Isfahan, capable of holding 20,000 people, where mass hysteria and masochism could be induced by the staging of Shi'ite legends. Most recently Vaclav Havel (1936–), the Czech subversive playwright, became national leader and president in 1989 largely because of the profile of his views created by his theatrical career.

THE NOVEL

The novel has on the whole been more successful as a propaganda medium of oppositions than of establishments. As prose took over from poetry as the natural idiom for storytelling, the novel came into its own. It has a relatively recent history compared with other propaganda media, the first great example probably being John Bunyan's (1628–88) *Pilgrim's Progress*. Yet in sixteenth-century Ming China the romantic novel was already widely used for promoting Buddhist values and Ming policies. British opposition politics produced the outrageous anti-Marlborough *New Atlantis* by Mrs Mary de la Rivière Manley (1672–1724) and *Gulliver's Travels*, with its disguised attack on Walpole, by her journalistic colleague Jonathan Swift (1667–1745). In the following century there was a strong liberal element in many of the works of Charles Dickens (1812–70) and of Christian Socialism in those of Charles Kingsley (1819–75).

The novel has been particularly important in the propaganda history of Russia. The very influential attack on serfdom by Ivan Turgenev (1818–83) in *The Sportsman's Sketches* was matched by the vigorously political *What is to be done?* by Tchernyshevsky (1828–89) which became a rallying call for revolution. More recently Boris Pasternak (1890–1960) and Alexander Solzhenitsyn (1918–) have had much the same force while Anatoly Rybakov's *Children of Arbat* sold seven million copies in 1985 and was plainly seen as supporting the Gorbachev reforms.

Other great novelists who injected a strong propaganda content into their work include Emile Zola (1840–1902), who paralleled Dickens in France, and one of the most influential of all nineteenth-century novels was *Uncle Tom's Cabin* by Harriet Beecher Stowe (1811–96). The novel is a naturally good medium for exciting patriotism and military enthusiasm, since military exploits lend themselves well to being exploited through it. Thus G.A. Henty, P.C. Wren, John Buchan and Rudyard Kipling all helped build up the image of the British imperialist, and similar groupings can be found in most other countries. This tendency is at its most dangerous in children's literature where the Biggles attitude of evil Huns and sporting British heroes is the pernicious junior version of the *Four Feathers*. Aesop's *Fables* were the model for many generations of children's moral tales, the Brothers Grimm made their contribution to juvenile German patriotism and Enid Blyton to the worldwide promotion of middle-class values. Junior and senior fiction, particularly when regurgitated in film or television scripts forms a substantial part of the total didactic message system in terms of attitude formation, value creation and role models. Though it is dangerous to deduce too much from the symbolism of fairy stories, it is certainly clear that they have been used over the years to project the moral views which suited the majority or sometimes the dominant minority.

The novel, apart from *Pilgrim's Progress*, has perhaps played a less prominent part in religious propaganda, partly because it is by definition fiction and religions need facts. However, there is room for the mixed approach as in *Ben-Hur* and *The Robe*. Salman Rushdie's *Satanic Verses* was taken as such a virulently anti-Islamic novel that it almost had the opposite effect in creating a rallying point for fundamentalist Muslim hysteria. The novels of Vir Singh (1872–1952) could be seen as a major contribution to the self-image of the modern Sikhs.

HISTORY

The writing of history has been a propaganda tool from the earliest times. The ancient civilizations soon grasped the value of dynastic histories which traced the ruling family back to a god or other hero, ignored previous dynasties and exalted the current regime. This technique was used by the writers of the Jewish *Chronicles* and the *Anglo-Saxon Chronicle*, by Chinese emperors, Norman kings, the Bourbons, the Habsburgs and virtually every major dynasty. Once beyond merely using history to seek credibility through the 'discovery' of divine ancestors, there was a tendency for rulers to look for legitimacy by clinging to the reputations of particular admired regimes of the past. Hence Charlemagne's desire was to recreate the Roman Empire and then establish his historical connection with it; this was followed by subsequent rulers' desire to claim the image of Charlemagne and establish a historical connection with him. The same idea is seen in the idea of the First Reich, the Second and the Third.

The second trait of propaganda history is to exaggerate military success and ignore failure, painting the picture of warlike superiority as a justification of effort for future conquest. This is seen in the histories written for Edward III and Henry V of England and even for Queens Elizabeth I and Victoria. It is also very evident in the work of the Roman historian Livy who charted the seemingly inevitable expansion of Rome. It is at its most fanatical in historians like the German Treitschke who wrote how Teutonic providence led the Germans to defeat the godless Gauls in the distant past and would do so again in the future. Even in the 1990s three totally different versions of their national history were taught to Serb, Croat and Muslim children in Bosnia, with the failures and atrocities always on the other side.

Religious bias in history made it a particularly useful propaganda medium in that area. Walter Raleigh's *History of the World* had its explanation of how a Protestant God helped the English to defeat the Armada and then lay the foundations for a Protestant transatlantic empire. The highly influential *History of England* by Rapin de Thoyras (1661–1725) dwelt on the disastrous drift of the Stuart dynasty towards Catholicism, the glories of 1688 and the Protestant succession, a theme essentially carried on by Thomas Macaulay (1800–59)) in his classic Whig version of British progress towards parliamentary empire.

Histories by imperial powers have often been derogatory and unappreciative of their new subjects. The Romans damned 'barbarians', the Jews damned Canaanites, the British painted a poor picture of the Indians, among others. It often took a long time for the victims of this vitriolic writing to have the capacity to respond with their own version of the truth. The vital importance of historians in packaging national credibility, dynastic legitimacy, political values, and religious loyalties cannot be over-emphasized. The delusions which a fairly mild bias is enough to create and the manipulation of factual material which it is difficult to see through without independent research, have been responsible in part for a number of very dangerous acts of national posturing.

As a similar discipline biography naturally also has made its contribution, particularly in the creation or demolition of heroes, and again only mild distortion of the facts can be enough to make all the difference. Almost all major rulers and religious leaders have had their contemporary hagiographers who have thus contributed to positioning them, enhancing their image and their influence.

Sometimes biography can be used later to draw comparisons, as with Samuel Johnson's *Drake* which was a deliberate effort to cast doubt on Walpole's ability to defeat the Spaniards. Similarly Ludwig Quille's best-selling *Caligula*, a study of Roman imperial madness, was a thinly disguised attack on Kaiser Wilhelm II. Hitler's identification with Frederick II, Mussolini's with Julius Caesar, Saddam Hussein's with Nebuchadnezzar are just further examples of historical similes fostered by biased biography.

Idealized biographies of role models for particular ways of behaving have had considerable importance from the Chinese canal builder Yu (tenth century BC), the primeval workaholic, onwards. The Byzantines in particular turned hagiography into an industry. Foxe's *Book of Martyrs*, numerous lives of saints, the cherry-tree childhood of George Washington, the log-cabin origins of Abraham Lincoln, the narratives of Joan of Arc or Florence Nightingale, all have been used and reused as role model material for countless generations, with emphasis on the appropriate character features. In due course damning biography can be exploited for the opposite effect. It was in the interest of Henry VII for Richard III's biography to be as uncomplimentary as possible, just as Stalin's under Gorbachev or Kennedy's under Nixon. Seeley's biography of Christ *Ecce Homo* is just one example of the late Victorian trend in debunking biographies, many of which had a point to make for their own time.

Others of the humanitarian disciplines can also be exploited for propaganda purposes. Economics is an obvious example; it is so subjective in its deductions that it is particularly easy to manipulate. In the eighteenth century mercantilist tracts constantly pressed the case for conquering overseas colonies and fed the enthusiasm for competitive wars between the imperial nations. Adam Smith's theory of free trade was quarried as the basis for *laissez-faire* political programmes. Then in 1848 Karl Marx constructed an entire world system based on his economic ideas and expectation of the self-destruction of capitalism. More recently economic concepts such as monetarism have been used to bolster party political campaigns.

Philosophy too can become propaganda: this was certainly the case with Aristotle, Locke, Hobbes, Rousseau and Tom Paine. The theory of human liberties and rights was used to make political points. From this it is evident that the abstract discussion of the meaning of terms such as justice, liberty, equality and democracy has to be regarded as tainted by the emotive connotations of all such terms, which have no proven existence beyond the language of propaganda.

Travel and geography have also been given a propaganda slant as for instance by Richard Hakluyt (1552–1616) whose *Principal Navigations, Voyages and Discoveries of the English Nation* was part of the Elizabethan drive for empire. Maps and the use of place-names have been a regular vehicle for racist or imperialist propaganda, many nations in succession positioning themselves as the centre of the world and spreading their version of place-names as a form of linguistic colonization. The Anglicization of American place-names, the Germanicization of Czech town names, the Catholicization of South American geography and the Stalinization of Russian city names are all examples.

Biology and anthropology have often also been misused for propaganda purposes. Joseph Gobineau (1816–82) produced his *Inequality of Human Races*, a textbook for white superiority, just as William Petty (1623–87) and Lahoutan had earlier projected the inferior black, on an anatomical basis. Even more dangerous were the pseudo-academic treatises like John Nider's *Formicarius* and the *Malleus Malleficarum* of Kramer and Sprenger in 1486 which based on apparently factual information a complete edifice of witch-phobia to help justify the continued power of the Inquisition.

THE PRESS AND PRINT

The delivery of written messages before the invention of type in Europe was relatively limited. The first mechanical duplication of a propaganda message was the use of seals in the Middle Eastern civilizations, particularly the clever cylindrical seals of Mesopotamia. The classical world developed this technique into the printing of messages on coins, and the Emperor Constantine added the ingenious idea of bread stamps so that his 'Conquer in Christ' slogan appeared on millions of loaves. From around AD 200 ink rubbings were taken from stone carvings of the Confucian classics as a primitive form of paper printing. The first mass printing of propaganda was the leaflet distribution by the Emperor Wen Ti of the Sung Dynasty in AD 589 (see p. 131). The missionary I'Ching claimed that Buddhists in India were making use of woodcuts in the late seventh century and in 770 in Japan it was recorded that the Empress Shotoku had a million leaflets distributed showing Buddhist charms and symbols. By comparison the pamphlet wars of the Holy Roman Empire and the papacy were based on a tiny circulation among a small number of key opinion formers.

Luther was the first propagandist to make serious use of larger quantities of printed pamphlets and from the mid-sixteenth century onwards printed broadsheets or newspapers played a growing part in the promotion of political causes at least to the literate classes. Newspapers played a major role in the posturings of both sides in the English Civil War of 1640. The press grew in size and sophistication thereafter with a major period of advance in propaganda terms in 1728 when Bolingbroke brought out the brilliantly written *Craftsman* and again with John Wilkes's *North Briton.* These two publications created new standards of partisan journalism and planned manipulation of a wider public.

The last half of the eighteenth century saw two major developments in press propaganda: firstly, the simultaneous multi-regional attacks made by a succession of creatively aggressive newspapers in the American colonies in the period leading up to Independence, probably the most important historical event since the Reformation to which the printed word had contributed; secondly, the French Revolution, which particularly in its later stages produced a number of highly innovative newspaper proprietors such as Marat and Hébert.

The nineteenth century witnessed accelerated growth in literacy, newspaper circulation and political influence, at least in the so-called civilized world. British prime ministers began to cultivate the journalist. In Prussia Bismarck founded and wrote for two newspapers, regarding the press as a significant tool, despite his stated preference for pure power. In Italy, the Piedmontese leader Cavour was editor of the newspaper *Risorgimento* which gave its name to the entire movement towards Italian reunification which he masterminded. Lenin spent seventeen years as editor of his paper *Iskra*, the newspaper which more than any other developed the infrastructure for the Communist takeover of Russia. Although by the time of Hitler other alternative media of major importance were becoming available, the press of the Third Reich was still very significant. Remarkably in the totalitarian states with tight control over their mass circulation newspapers, there came a reversal to semi-primitive technology, as in the period of the *samizdat* or privately duplicated newspapers of the revolutionary movements in Russia and its satellites during the 1980s.

LEAFLET DISTRIBUTION

Other methods of distribution of the printed word have been significant at different times. Post offices, particularly those controlled by the government, have played a key role in the distribution of propaganda material, as for example with Robert Walpole's exploitation of his control over the British postal system in the 1730s. Ultimately house-by-house distribution is one of the few ways of achieving saturation coverage. The organization of good mailing lists was the key to success for Lenin, F.D. Roosevelt and John F. Kennedy. The first of these had his wife to do the donkey work, the second two had the money to pay for large numbers of secretaries to do it for them. In 1948 Italian Americans were encouraged to undertake a mass letter-writing campaign to their relations back home to discourage them from becoming Communists. This kind of mass-mailing was made faster by the development of computer software which could target large numbers of individuals of specific types by name. This had novelty value when first used by Western politicians and again when used by Boris Yeltsin in Russia in 1996, helped by his daughter who was a computer specialist. The development of database mailing and address segmentation greatly increased the cost-effectiveness of leaflet distribution.

The development of aerial propaganda drops began when Victor Hugo's leaflets were dropped on the streets of Paris from a balloon during the Prussian siege in 1871. In 1915 the Italian poet soldier D'Annunzio dropped 200,000 leaflets on Vienna. The Germans dumped vast numbers of surrender leaflets on Poland in 1939 and anti-Semitic jigsaw puzzles on France in the same year. British planes from HMS *Illustrious* bombed French Dakar with surrender leaflets, as the Japanese did in Hong Kong and Singapore. The Germans' main leaflet effort was on front-line troops, though they dropped symbolic autumn leaves on the Maginot Line in 1939, only to have oak leaves with a similar meaning dropped on them by the British during the siege of Stalingrad. Cherry blossom cast out of aeroplanes on to the Japanese in Burma had to be accompanied by the explicit wording 'cease resistance, now surrender'. By the 1950s leaflet bombing had vastly expanded: the Americans dropped 28 million leaflets a week on Korea, including the successful cash offer of $100,000 for a MiG fighter plane flown to the American side.

CINEMA

Cinema first became a serious propaganda medium in the 1890s and its power even without sound was early appreciated. In Britain this development coincided with the Boer War, during which three companies, including British Mutoscope, made a major effort to put across the heroic cause of the imperial armies. Films such as *The Entry of the Scots Guards into Bloemfontein* and *Setting to between John Bull and Paul Kruger* had a dramatic effect. Many of these films were mixtures of genuine documentary footage and scenes shot with actors. Doctored film of the bombing of Red Cross tents by Boers was used to spread the atrocity myth which was being officially encouraged by the British government.

Significantly one of the first German films was *Life in the German Navy* of 1902 sponsored by Kaiser Wilhelm, confirming the special value of film as a medium for conveying war propaganda of almost every kind. The German films *Call of the Fatherland* and *Watch on the Rhein* of 1914, were matched by a plethora of biased film from all sides in the First World War, culminating in the crudities of the American *Beast of Berlin*.

In just the same way the first Russian film shown in the first Russian cinema in 1896 was Tsar Nicholas II's *Coronation*, followed later by such vague efforts to arouse nationalist feeling as the *Stenka Rasin* of 1910, *Down with the German Yoke* and *The Holy War* of 1914. Perhaps significantly Kerensky and the Russian social democrats of the March 1917 revolution failed to appreciate the value of film and cut the electricity supply to cinemas, whereas Lenin and his colleagues in the October revolution made a point of rapidly harnessing cinema, making special use of the *agitki* or short films and organizing mobile cinemas in trains, lorries and steamers to help spread the word of Communism (see pl. 6). Trotsky even made the comment that film would 'take the place of religion and vodka'.

During the interwar period film, both as conscious and unconscious propaganda, grew in sophistication. John Grierson (1898–1972) the Scottish documentary pioneer saw its value. 'Hollywood was one of the greatest potential munitions factories on earth . . . it could make people love each other or hate each other . . . a key to the mass will.' His own films such as *The Night Mail* were much more subtly persuasive just as the more self-deprecating war films of the 1940s such as *London Can Take It* had moved on a generation. Meanwhile, Sergei Eisenstein (1898–1948) had been advancing techniques in Russia with major propaganda films like *The Battleship Potemkin* and *October* which were works of art in their own right, and in his wake Leni Riefenstahl (1902–) was doing the same for the Third Reich. With its combination of picture quality, sound, music, darkness and audience closeness, cinema was the most powerful medium the world had known. The showing in Norway in 1939 of Hitler's blitzkrieg film had a totally demoralizing effect.

At its height in the late 1940s the worldwide penetration of films reached huge proportions, with weekly cinema attendance in the USA at 90 million and in the UK at 30 million. This peak penetration lasted longer in countries where television was introduced more slowly, but by the 1950s film had lost its peak audience penetration levels and in particular its propaganda influence was seriously diminished. Cecil B. de Mille's (1881–1959) production of the *Korea Story* for Eisenhower was to be the apogee of cinema before the much greater potency of television. However, commercial film making, due to its repeat audiences on television, remained a very influential medium in the final years of the second millennium. Apart from war and politics its greatest strength lay in its capacity to project moral norms, the ethics of work, niceness, monogamy and conformity to the current values of each society. The possibilities of film as an underground medium were shown by film makers like Arkady Ruderman who carried round his projector to show films secretly to private audiences in the final years of Soviet Communism.

RADIO

Radio, like cinema, was a medium which peaked early in its history and because of the rapid advance of technology had a relatively short period in the premier rank of world propaganda. But it does retain certain advantages over cinema and television: its very lack of picture, its disembodied character means that it can have an unexpected realism and urgency, as with the famous Orson Welles broadcast of *The War of the Worlds* which led to panic in the streets of New York where it was actually believed that an invasion from outer space had taken place. Radio also has a unique capacity to cross frontiers – although the spread of satellite television has eroded this advantage – so it has a special value in war or diplomatic propaganda. Its first single great contribution was the spreading of the Communist revolution in October 1917 when Lenin made use of the military network: ironically a makeshift illicit radio transmitter was also a key medium in the fall of Soviet Communism in 1991. Radio's main influence as a propaganda medium fell into the thirty-year period from 1930 to 1960 in the Western democracies with another half century of influence in less developed parts of the world. Early on the value of political broadcasting was appreciated throughout Europe and further afield. In 1924 radio was first used to heighten the adversarial tension of the US presidential conventions and Rudyard Kipling wrote scripts for the first royal broadcast by King George V to the peoples of his empire. In 1932 the first British royal Christmas broadcast was heard by 20 million people and from the 1940s the radio soap opera *The Archers* was used to promote good farming practice and other virtues in Britain.

Without question the most provocative user of radio propaganda was Adolf Hitler. He used it in his remarkable trickery during the plebiscite vote in the Saar, where the immediacy of radio was exploited to cast a slur over the pro-French party which no other action had the speed to counteract. He also used here the idea of cheap or free *Volksempfangsanlage* (VE) sets, with limited frequencies which restricted listening to Hitler's own wavelengths. By 1942 there were 16 million VE sets and radio wardens were appointed to ensure good listening habits in all public buildings and private homes.

Meanwhile the propaganda use of radio expanded elsewhere. Japan's national radio station began broadcasting in 1928. Roosevelt had great success with his fireside chats, just as Churchill proved a penetrating if unorthodox broadcaster, and Stalin evinced similar skills. The Cold War period witnessed a vast expansion in the multilingual trans-frontier radio propaganda stations: the Voice of America (VOA), Radio Moscow and the Chinese stations which by 1961 were broadcasting 600 hours per week in twenty-four languages. Much of the material from all sides was doctrinaire or naive, so that its effectiveness in even the most gullible of Third World countries was questionable. There have been numerous local success stories for radio – the BBC effort in India during the early 1940s was quite effective, as was Nazi-inspired radio in Argentina.

There were also a number of examples of the effective use of radio to propagate or revive interest in religions: the Radio Church of God owed its entire existence to radio, and several other US sects made use of it.

Particularly important in the late twentieth century have been the Arab and African radio stations. The Voice of Cairo, Voice of Libya and Voice of Palestine have all had a major effect in reaching scattered semi-literate ethnic groups with versions of the Arab nationalist, anti-Semitic message which nurtured various revolutionary movements. Similarly the Voice of Zambia helping Robert Mugabe's ZANU movement across the border in Rhodesia or the Voice of Tanzania helping FREMLO in Mozambique. Throughout the Third World radio was a medium of profound importance with its advantages of relatively low cost for both transmitters and receivers, easy range over national borders and circumvention of literacy problems. The ethnic conflict in Rwanda in 1994 was exacerbated by high-pitched racist propaganda on the national radio station, Radio-Television Libre des Mille Collines. The way various points of view can be presented by radio is well illustrated by the Afghan civil wars in the 1970s: Radio Kabul put out heavy propaganda denigrating the mujahidin, including broadcasting a lot of fake material; international services like the BBC and VOA tried to contradict it; eventually the rebels got their own lightweight transmitters and launched Radio Free Kabul in 1981/2.

As a minor variant gramophones and tape recorders have also been used to distribute propaganda. Gramophone records of political speeches or rallies were useful on occasions; one classic example was the long-playing record of Nelson Mandela's early speeches which helped to keep alive his image during his long captivity. Use of cassette tapes was probably at its greatest in Poland, Russia and other East European states during the build-up of anti-Communist propaganda in the 1980s. Cassette tapes of Afghan patriotic epics were produced in the 1970s by the mujahidin to be played in local bazaars and in the same period tapes of Somali nationalist poetry were distributed secretly at a time when the population was still largely illiterate.

TELEVISION

Television was introduced in 1936 but the Second World War delayed its expansion and it was the 1950s before it began to explode rapidly into a world force. Technologically it became able to transmit worldwide instantly and with remarkable quality. Like cinema it could capture crowd reaction, turn drama into melodrama, project personality, expose weakness, enthuse and motivate, terrify and involve. It was prone to certain visual clichés: the political handshake, the standing ovation without end, violence, fire at night, spectacle. In the USA Eisenhower and his successors adapted the techniques of commercial advertising for electoral campaigns and bought time from private sector stations. In 1952 the drama of the party conventions was first exploited on TV. De Gaulle saw to it that French television was rigidly pro-government and Harold Macmillan had himself interviewed by Ed Murrow as his means of scoring an advantage on the British, non-commercial, non-partisan BBC. The 1970s and 1980s were a period of steady expansion in television penetration worldwide and the development of techniques for the spreading of political standpoints. Charles Guggenheim had pioneered the idea of the filmed walkabout for the 1956 presidential elections. Television training for politicians became essential, as was demonstrated in the Kennedy defeat of Nixon. As a medium it was unforgiving of amateurishness and of penny-pinching, it was a medium for political parties or religious sects with the time and resources to exploit it effectively.

Just as political packaging on television was initially developed in the United States, partly because the buying system there favoured it, so in the same way television evangelism had its origins there, with some sects exploiting the medium to raise substantial funds, some of which were recycled to buy further television time. The power of television to persuade audiences to make wrong political or religious decisions because of their susceptibility to the superficial techniques of the medium as opposed to the pure message, soon caused concern, but in effect there was nothing really new about this situation.

State run television stations have tended to be unexciting in terms of propaganda innovation, but commercial stations owned by politicians have been more effective. Two examples were Bertolucci's in Italy and Collor's in Brazil while in Russia when stations were privatized a major one came under the control of Boris Berezovsky, a millionaire newspaper owner who was also briefly Yeltsin's deputy secretary of the Security Council up to 1997. One of the most damning results of the propaganda use of television was the stirring up of Serb nationalism by the Serb-dominated Yugoslav broadcasting system in the 1990s and the Bosnian Serb station at Pale was built ironically with equipment stolen from the BBC. Meanwhile in 1998 the Australian media owner Rupert Murdoch was building up a major share in the Communist Chinese cable television network as ideology became less important than finance.

The techniques too developed rapidly. The introduction of smaller video cameras led to much more immediate and evocative coverage of wars, violence and other disasters, all material geared to have a much stronger emotive effect on audiences. For example camcorders were distributed to the Afghan rebels in the 1980s to encourage anti-Russian footage. Similarly politicians tended to cut back on direct camera confrontation, realizing more than a couple of minutes would breach the boredom threshold: they relied more on artificial interviews, staged public meetings, carefully planned walkabouts or pure speech interspersed with atmosphere and lifestyle material borrowed from the techniques of advertising.

The ability of television to jump frontiers came with the development of satellite. This undoubtedly contributed to the collapse of Soviet Communism and to the international image, both good and bad, of Saddam Hussein. Television generally is now established as the most important medium for political persuasion in virtually all parts of the world.

TELEPHONE AND INTERNET

The telephone is not normally considered a propaganda medium, since it is not truly a mass medium, only a means of individual communication. However, it is possible to organize the multiple use of telephones on a planned basis and the classic example was the 'Calling for Kennedy' campaign organized to conduct systematic telephone canvassing in 1960. Fax machines, cable, e-mail and other technologies add marginally to the armoury but are likely to remain minor media. In 1995 there came the first signs of alarm about the use of Internet, or direct computer transfer, to distribute racist propaganda. In 1998 the Internet showed its propaganda value as a vehicle for the trickle release of damaging information about US President Bill Clinton, but as a medium it lacks the emotive power of most of is competitors.

EVENT MANAGEMENT

One of the oldest of all propaganda techniques and the most versatile is the area of event management, spectacle and crowd control. Very often this can involve an amalgam of other media such as music and the graphic arts. For example, the organization of coronations has been perfected over 4,000 years, but even before that the pharaohs were handling it in a remarkably sophisticated way. The detailed symbolism, mystery and message repetition evolved by French and English royalty, the great efforts made by men like Charlemagne and Napoleon, the huge mobilization of resources to put across primogeniture, legitimacy, divine descent, holy powers, and untouchable superiority combined to create one of the most remarkable confidence tricks in the history of mankind. The triumphs or postwar processions of the Caesars, the rallies of Adolf Hitler, the amazing royal tours of the Holy Roman emperors are further outstanding examples. Both the weddings and funerals of the great have been similarly exploited for dynastic image-making and political exhibitionism. Also of key importance in the propaganda of labour has been the event management of strikes, walk-outs, pickets and sit-ins. And in the twentieth century one of the most active areas for propaganda through event management has been the exploitation of internationally competitive sports with their heavy use of military images such as 'victory' or 'battle'.

Also important, particularly in religious propaganda, have been the great ritual anniversaries; Christmas and Easter have been superbly orchestrated mass ceremonies of participatory propaganda, as have Passover and Ramadan. The whole history of relic presentation has been on the same lines. Louis IX of France used the acquisition of relics from the true cross to persuade his people to support him in the organization and funding of an extravagant and dangerous crusade. The preservation of relics and the cult of pilgrimages have been major components in loyalty building. The development of the pilgrimages to Santiago de Compostella, Lourdes, Mecca or the Ganges are examples. The Indians in particular saw the use of pilgrimages as a means of message inculcation and reinforcement, which could be enhanced by appropriate poems and ritual. The organization of Pope effigy burning in seventeenth-century England was a major focal point for maintaining anti-Catholic prejudices as subsequently were re-enactments of the Battle of the Boyne. It is possible that animal or human sacrifice should also be seen partly as components in the management of intimidation and therefore as propaganda. Certainly organized demonstrations of asceticism such as flagellation, walking on hot coals or beds of nails are useful tools both to heighten awareness and impress doubters.

The techniques of event management, the use of painted scenery, statues, arches, flags, drapes, drill, dramatic lighting, music, fireworks, tableaux, exotic costumes and a whole range of mnemonic symbols, go back to the earliest civilizations. The individual was deliberately made to feel inferior to the mass, to feel tense, threatened and trapped. Considerable organization was required and the event managers were often distinguished court artists: Dürer for Maximilian, Titian for Charles V, Holbein for Henry VIII, the architect Speer for Hitler. Once conceived many such events had the advantage – like the Passover, Easter, Guy Fawkes Night, Orange Days, Independence Day and Bastille Day – of being self-perpetuating. Birthdays from that of Jesus Christ to Hitler's have been the focus for celebrations, as have numerous other kinds of anniversary.

In addition to their capacity to persuade by size, spectacular sights and sounds and well-staged rhetoric, event managers also have the opportunity to exploit emotional crowd characteristics, the response to music, dramatic involvement, sensation, mass grief, anger, affection and frustration. Certainly there are some key ancillary tools for event management such as the use of candles or torches for creating atmospheric lighting, censers for a linked purpose but also as a symbol of prayers rising to heaven, and background sound effects like drumbeats or fanfares. The ability simply to gather a large crowd has been regularly used as a visible means of demonstrating power and raw material for further propaganda. The use of extorted public confessions, phoney volunteers, isolation of objectors and other techniques of psychological stampeding can all be made to contribute. Perhaps the ultimate in the use of event management skills for mass intimidation has been the spectacle of public execution and human sacrifice. From the mass sacrifices of Aztec Mexico to the *auto-da-fé* of the Spanish Inquisition or the ritual floggings of the Royal Navy, violence is the ultimate technique for crowd control. Psychological violence such as the mass ridicule of Chinese intellectuals during the Cultural Revolution is another facet of the same technique.

In our review of propaganda history we will come across a number of situations where new media developments have both contributed to and been encouraged by major propaganda campaigns. The spread of the Reformation by the new invention of movable type is a classic example, as was the spread of Buddhism in ninth-century China by wood block printing. Other instances include the contribution of radio and cinema to the spread of Fascism in the 1920s and '30s, the role of satellite and handheld video in the fall of Communism and the use of database marketing for the promotion of Yeltsin in 1996.

Tricks of the Trade (1)

Heart Rather Than Head

There are three broad types of propaganda – the purely rational, the quasi-rational/half emotional and the purely emotional – which, as it were, provide a complete spectrum between fact and fiction. In the case of propaganda using purely rational material the style is factual, informative or logical, and the act of persuasion lies mainly in the selection of facts favourable to the argument and the leaving out or discounting of those which are not. Much routine political propaganda falls into this category and if the presentation is reasonable or logical, then it can be effective; but it does demand quite high levels of audience attention, a requirement which its dull content may make difficult to achieve; and it does suffer from the problem that opponents may come back with an equally cogent argument for the opposite case, resulting often in an advantage for the side having the last word. Modern research indicates that this type of propaganda is not particularly popular with audiences, and that the percentage of people who change attitudes as a result of it tends to be quite low. By nature it is often best presented within one of the conventional disciplines such as history, economics or anthropology. The low boredom threshold for this style of propaganda is one of the big problems of rational democracy. However, in the 1990s it was made more exciting by the use of computers allowing instant retrieval of damaging response material, the so-called rebuttal units, with 'spin doctors' assisting in short, sharp exchanges which enhanced the gladiatorial aspect of political rivalries. The use of just-in-time releases for key media deadlines meant that structured leaks of both bad and good news could catch attention, including leaks of deliberately exaggerated bad news designed to take the sting out of the full story which followed later, or alternative scandals to distract attention, eleventh-hour compromises and other methods of positive headline grabbing.

The second style category, following the quasi-rational approach, uses allusions and associations to lend force to an otherwise weak argument. In an analysis of propaganda devices for the American Institute of Propaganda Analysis in 1937 Doob listed seven: name calling, image transfer, the testimonial, the 'plain folks approach', card stacking or the piling up of apparently bad information, the band-wagon or exploitation of herd instinct and what he called 'the glittering generality'. These are indeed the hallmarks of the cruder forms of propaganda, but the concept of image association has very much wider implications. The use of visual symbols, music and metaphor covers a large area of quasi-rational propaganda, gradual acts of mass manipulation which are often not recognized as propaganda at all. Unjustifiable persecution has often been based on smear campaigns using these techniques: examples appear down the centuries including the campaign of Philip the Fair of France against the Knights Templar who were accused of bestial practices and homosexuality, the campaign against the Albigensians, the development of hysteria about witches in the sixteenth century with a pseudo-factual explanation presented as if it was proven fact, the build-up of anti-Semitism in the twentieth century using fake texts like the *Protocols of the Elders of Zion* and the case built up by Senator Joseph McCarthy against suspected American Communists. In each of these cases a tiny factual base was extended by innuendo and exploitation of prejudice, allowed to simmer over a period, then transmuted into violent action. The atrocity myths at the centre of most cases of inter-ethnic hatred are an unfortunately common symptom of the same process.

The third style category of propaganda, the purely emotional, relies on the use of subjective ideas projected with a high level of emotive force accompanied probably by an exploitation of some or all of the techniques of event management. The common ingredients tend to be music, a large crowd space, some preconditioning, some elements of visual imagery and a speech drawing forth strong emotions such as hate, fear, religious or racial prejudice. A good medieval example would be the techniques used for persuading people to join the Crusades. Humbert of the Romans (1210–77) the Master General of the Dominicans wrote his treatise *On Preaching the Cross* for this purpose. Large evangelical camp meetings were summoned at which the preacher called all his audience sinners who should repent and make the decision for Christ. Crosses were presented, hymns sung, collections taken, the event well managed and deliberately made to last quite a long time, so that the audience almost had to agree to the crusade as a relief from the ordeal of the meeting. The faint-hearted were lambasted with insulting innuendo: reluctant soldiers were compared to 'fat palfreys' who spent their time in ostentatious parades instead of real fighting. Those slow to volunteer were compared to 'hens or placid cows tethered to the houses of Flanders'. This moral blackmail was exacerbated by crowd hysteria induced by the presence of self-flagellating monks and in some cases by inflammatory anti-Semitism. The recruitment rate was high. In the sixteenth century St Ignatius Loyola practised similar techniques on a smaller scale, with vigils in cold, dark chapels and other intensifying factors leading up to the moment of surrender to Jesuit commitment at the level for which he was looking.

John Wesley 200 years later was an outstandingly able practitioner of the techniques of emotive propaganda, with large crowds reduced to sobbing, fainting and hysteria by the vehemence of his hell-fire preaching and his promise of salvation. And 200 years after Wesley, Adolf Hitler was one of the most effective political exploiters of such techniques, with his mass rallies held by torchlight, with vast numbers of swastikas, music, artificial tension while he deliberately kept them waiting, and then hysteria when he at last spoke in short sharp sentences of venomous hate. Lord Northcliffe, founder of the *Daily Mail* in 1896, commented that his readers 'relished a good hate'. Many of these practitioners of emotive propaganda came close to multiple brainwashing, creating a shared psychological experience for their audiences in which they were first reduced to anger, despair and pent-up frustration, then offered an easy solution – conversion to whatever was on offer. The ultimate in the use of sensory deprivation to induce mental change might well be the 'lung gom pas' of Tibet, where trainees would be exposed to seclusion for three years and three months, sitting most of the time cross-legged in total darkness doing breathing exercises and jumping from this position, apparently achieving remarkable resistance to cold, hunger and tiredness as well as deep levels of spiritual indoctrination.

There is always a question mark over the permanence of conversions achieved under emotional duress, but the history of the world is full enough of groups which lasted long enough in their new beliefs to act on them. There were hundreds of thousands of unsuitable crusaders who went off to die *en route* to the Holy Land; there were large numbers of committed Jesuits to be persecuted and persecute, large numbers of convinced Nazis whose obedience was solid enough for them to help push millions through the gas chambers. Even in the 1970s the converts of Jonestown were so beyond recall to reason that they accepted the order to commit mass suicide. David Koresh (1960–93) achieved similar results on a smaller scale in Waco, Texas. Shoko Asahara of the Japanese doomsday cult Aum Shinri Kyo used the same kind of methods before the Tokyo underground poison attacks of 1995. The susceptibility of the young in particular to these techniques is not to be underrated, even in a so-called sophisticated, well-educated society. The use of semi-hypnosis for what is loosely termed brainwashing by religious cults and extreme political groups has been widely discussed and as a result there is a parallel study of the techniques of 'deprogramming'.

Of all the emotions exploited by propaganda the most powerful has been fear, with the ability to spin dangers almost out of thin air – the torments of hell, devils, Napoleons in the cupboard, witches, phantom armies and millennial cataclysms, all dressed up and given fearsome attributes. Equally the release from fear, the promise of paradise, of resurrection, of reward for martyrdom has been almost as pernicious.

Tricks of the Trade (2)

Devices Used to Achieve Effect

There are available to the propagandist a large number of structural tools, linguistic, musical and visual which make the task of persuasion easier.

Rhyme has been recognized for thousands of years as having the capacity to make simple phrases more memorable, more exciting and apparently more significant. There have been numerous rhyming moral or legal codes such as the Norse *Havamal* and rhyme has been almost universally used to help with behavioural training of the young:

Coughs and sneezes spread diseases.

It also made its appearance early on in political slogan writing, for instance in the English Peasants' Revolt of 1381:

When Adam delved and Eve span,
Who was then the gentleman?

while one of the main slogans of the Crusades was:

Dieu le veut [God wishes it].

In eighteenth-century England there was the popular cry of:

No Jews, no wooden shoes

and when the government needed a scapegoat for the capture of Menorca by the French in 1757 the crowds were given:

Hang Byng, and take care of your king.

From the American Revolution, probably from Samuel Adams, came:

Rally, Mohawk, bring your axe
And tell King George we'll pay no tax

while the French Revolution had its incomparable:

Liberté, égalité, fraternité.

American elections have often produced good examples – from 1840:

We'll beat little Van, Van, Van (Van Buren)
He's used up man

from 1948:

Dewie, Dewie, Halleluia

and from 1952 the magnificently succinct:

I like Ike.

In the 1960s it was either:

All the way
With L.B.J. (Johnson)

or:

Hey, hey, hey L.B.J.
How many kids have you killed today?

From the British naval build-up of battleships in 1903 came:

We want eight, and we won't wait.

From Germany in the First World War came the crude:

Jedem Russ, ein schuss [One bullet per Russian]

and from Britain in the Second World War there were a succession of mnemonics such as:

Lend to defend

and:

Save wheat, help the fleet.

The approach of the Common Market in the 1960s called forth:

The EEC is not for me

while the Cold War had its:

Reds under the bed

and:

Better red than dead.

These little rhymes were not great poetry, but often ingeniously effective like the initially powerful:

Thatcher the milk snatcher.

or the sarcastic:

Tony's Cronies – for New Labour

Rhythm, particularly repetitive rhythm, was a quality which lent itself to propaganda from the earliest times, particularly as it provided a vehicle for crowd participation and had its own inherent capacity to motivate. The endless hypnotic repetition of mantras like:

Hare Krishna, Hare Krishna

or the Shi'ite Muslim chants of the Berbers:

O Hassan, O Hussein . . .

the American:

Nixon out, Nixon out

the Germanic:

Sieg Heil, Sieg Heil

taken advantage of by Hitler or the Crusaders' emotive:

Peccavi, peccavi, peccavi [I have sinned, I have sinned, I have sinned]

or the Polish:

Solidarnośc, solidarnośc.

Subtle, almost accidental scansion is a feature of memorable slogans which otherwise seem to have little meaning such as Ronald Reagan's iambic:

You ain't seen nuthin' yet

or the Nazi tag, also iambic:

Das ganze Volk sagte ja [The whole people says 'yes']

and the American:

Avenge the *Lusitania.*

Then there is the trochaic:

Adolf Hitler ist der Sieg [Adolf Hitler is Victory]

or the more or less dactylic:

Workers of the world unite; you have nothing to lose but your chains

the American independence slogan:

Give me liberty or give me death

and the Romanian revolution of 1989:

Ole, ole, ole, Ceauşescu Nu mai e. [Ceauşescu out]

The ultimate use of rhyme and rhythm occurs when almost meaningless chants are used repetitively to induce semi-hypnotic surrender as in the Buddhist use of mantras:

Om Tare tutare ture swaha.

With its early vibrating 'm', this is typical of the modified sanskrit rhymes chanted in the Buddhist rite.

In the same family of techniques is alliteration. Without question one of the world's most ingenious slogans was Julius Caesar's:

Veni, vidi, vici [I came, I saw, I conquered]

which is alliterative, rhymes and, by the luck of Latin verb construction, is amazingly short. Similarly from Germany there is the male chauvinist motto:

Kinder, Küche, Kirche [Children, kitchen, church]

which has some of the same quality, or Kaiser Wilhelm's:

Das Gelbe Gefahr [the Yellow Peril]

or the slogan of the German peasant party in the 1870s:

Junker und Juden [Junkers and Jews].

From Britain there is the temperance ditty, alliterative and dactylic in rhythm:

Lips that touch liquor shall never touch mine

or the pre-1914 military slogans:

For King and Country –
Fight to the Finish –
Butcher and Bolt –

and the Lloyd George election slogan of 1921:

Homes fit for heroes

which like 'Fight to the finish' equates to the last five syllables of a classic hexameter, or the 1940s:

Careless talk costs lives.

The Americans, as was to be expected, extended the art with gems like Polk's presidential slogan:

Fifty-four forty or fight [referring to the degree of latitude, cf. the 38th Parallel]

or the obscenely trite:

Kill the Kikes, Koons and Katholics

from the late nineteenth-century Ku Klux Klan. The Russian Communists had:

Vsya Vlast Sovietam [All Power to the Soviets]

Alliteration has played its part too in highlighting sections of political speeches so that phrases were remembered and repeated, such as 'bag and baggage' from one of William Gladstone's Midlothian speeches on the Bulgarian atrocities. His regular opponent Benjamin Disraeli had a gift for this type of structure with his:

dethroning this dynasty of deception

against Derby and the similar:

ministry of mandarins.

A prohibitionist slogan was borrowed by F.D. Roosevelt:

Bread not booze

while the British Labour Party of 1996–7 had:

Twenty-two Tory tax increases.

Alliteration is also a popular way of developing nicknames which have their own special part to play in political image building or destruction:

The Welsh Wizard – Lloyd George
Glorious Gloucesters
The Wavy Navy
The Tamil Tigers.

In many respects the poetry of primitive peoples often had even more ingenious mnemonic tricks than that of later periods. For example, ancient Jewish poetry used to teach the religion relied on couplets with thought rhymes, word repetition and association, chiasm (the A–B, B–A pattern) and the acrostic (each line starting with the next letter of the alphabet).

Moving to figures of speech, the metaphor has always been a useful aid to effective propaganda. One of the most outstanding exponents of appropriate metaphor was Jesus Christ, a master of the use of simple but very effective images:

the house built on sand,
new wine in old bottles,
the seed falling on stony grown,
the shepherd and his sheep

or some fine similes such as:

like the lilies of the field

and the supremely evocative:

like a camel through the eye of a needle.

Mohammed too was a good practitioner of this form with his regular use of nature as a symbol of divine benefit and his:

narrow bridge over the abyss of hell

an image also used with a slightly different slant by Buddha. Mahatma Gandhi, sharing the need of some of these early prophets to communicate vividly to an illiterate people, often used his 'Banyan tree' and other images.

Political propaganda has always been rich in metaphor; there is for instance the regularly used:

ship of state

with many variations of the steersman theme, of which, among others, Chairman Mao Zedong was very fond. The dismissal of Bismarck was memorably portrayed as:

The dropping of the pilot.

Nixon had his sarcastic anti-Kennedy:

Nobody drowned at Watergate

and Harold Wilson used the flippant:

rearranging the deck-chairs on the *Titanic*.

Kaiser Wilhelm II had his famous:

A place in the sun

which was reused for forty years.

With the advent of television metaphors became more visual as when Hubert Humphrey had Nixon pictured as a weathervane in his 1968 campaign and then Nixon used the same image against McGovern in his 1972 publicity.

Papal propaganda used a variety of similes but was particularly fond of 'the seamless robe', an image of the apostolic inheritance of St Peter which was crucial to its credibility. Similar was the *pré carré* the 'square paddock' of the French natural frontiers, a metaphoric shape lending authenticity to a nationalistic objective – similar to Theodore Roosevelt's 'Square Deal' of 1901 which gave visual form to a political promise and the size of cake metaphor used to give a confusing image of British economic policy.

A number of other dimensional similes have had long-term propaganda exploitation. The most obvious is comparison of size where bigness of empire has been made the most desirable image and has been used with disastrous consequences. The identification of size as a virtue is a frequently dangerous propaganda extension of innate human competition. There has also been the recurrent image of going forwards rather than backwards – in other words the strange idea of progress created by many nameless propagandists – to bigger empires, greater democracy, freedom, faster transport, higher buildings or whatever else could be painted as evolutionary advance. Frequently this has been a motivational illusion useful to those with a vested interest. Another shape metaphor is the left, right and middle between two extremes, the concept of a spectrum which can be used for political or religious labelling (e.g. right-wing, broad church, etc.) and moral promotion as with Buddha's middle road and Aristotle's golden mean which partially gain credence from an imaginary geometric position. Again, this is just a handy image for justifying a complex stance.

Vivid pictorial metaphors have often been used to achieve a memorable focal point for political orations, such as Harold Macmillan's:

Wind of change

about the dangers of apartheid in South Africa, or Pitt the Elder's devastating comparison of Fox and Newcastle with the Rivers Saône and Rhone:

languid but not deep

or Disraeli's description of the Whigs as:

flies caught in amber

or again how he:

caught the Whigs bathing and walked away with their trousers.

Churchill produced both:

The Iron Curtain

and:

The soft underbelly of Europe.

Two final and extremely vivid examples are the American description of President McKinley as:

having no more backbone than a chocolate éclair

and the Meiji Japanese idea of Japan's former attitude to the world as being:

the frog looking at the world from the bottom of a well.

The embellishment of myths with additional dramatis personae – a chorus of ogres or angels, monsters or elves – becomes a kind of baroque elaboration of religious propaganda concepts on the basis that one major unsupported statement may be more credible if surrounded by further unsupported statements. The elaboration of heaven and hell with detailed cameo images follows the same formula, whether in the Koran, Dante, the Book of Revelation, or the paintings of Hieronymus Bosch.

The force of most of these images is undeniable and the importance of the technique lies in the fact that by this means people can be persuaded to change attitudes by long-term mythical precedent without pausing to consider whether the image is actually truthful.

Personification is a verbal trick which also has visual implications making it a useful tool for propaganda purposes. It is regularly used to produce a kind of shorthand for the objects of hate or love, turning an abstract idea into a visible symbol. Thus were born both the Statue of Liberty and Uncle Sam, John Bull and Britannia, Marianne in France, and Satan or the Devil. A variant on this concept is the use of relationship terms to add emotive quality as in 'fatherland', 'mother country', Uncle Sam, Brother Francis or Sister Earth. The use of animals to personify causes is also common, allowing as it does a variety of pictorial uses and further metaphors – lions and unicorns; the bald-headed or the double-headed eagle; the bear of Russia; the bulldog of Britain; the serpent of Eden; the dove of peace; the peacock for god among the Kurds. The mythological battles between heroes and dragons have been a vital part of many regimes and religions. Plants also provide raw material – the lotus in ancient Egypt; the oak for glory and the Stuart dynasty; the fleur-de-lis for life, France and Bosnia; the laurel for victory; the olive branch for peace; the poppy for sleep. From this we can pass to the codification of colours – green for hope and the environment; orange for Protestantism; red for danger and revolution; blue or purple for empire. There follows a whole variety of easily recognizable shapes or everyday objects which acquire a special meaning – the Buddhist wheel meaning transmigration of souls and other ideas; spurs meaning chivalry; skull and crossbones meaning death and ruthlessness; scales meaning justice; or specific objects connected with saints like St Lawrence's grill or St Catherine's wheel. More complex visual constructions were, for example, the medieval depiction of chastity as a veiled female figure holding a palm and trampling on a pig. Other important symbols included the chalice or holy grail symbolizing the Last Supper and the chariot denoting military triumph. The importance of all these myriad images lies in their capacity to make the message shorter, more easily grasped and more adaptable to almost any medium.

The use of puns and word play is really just an extension of these figures of speech, but again has the advantage of strong mnemonic quality. Nuances of language are important here and one famous pun or deliberate ambiguity arose from the fact that in Russian the word 'mir' means both peace and world, so when Lenin said I want 'mir' it had two meanings. The same sort of use was made by the pre-Christian rabbis of the similarity in Aramaic of the name Eve and the word for serpent, thus creating a peg for an anti-feminist stance. Perhaps the world's most successful propaganda pun came from Christ's changing the name of Simon to Cephas or rock (=Peter in Greek). More recently we have the pun on King Henry VII as Earl of Richmond referring to him as Richmount, with jewelled mountain as a symbol of his wealth. From the German Reformation there was the useful pun on Pope Leo X as a ravenous lion (=Leo). 'Bottomless Pitt' was applied to Pitt the Younger in 1790. The series of pun posters produced by Saatchi and Saatchi to help Mrs Thatcher win her first British election in 1979 included 'Labour isn't working', followed by 'The Foot Pump' (Michael Foot and inflation), from 1983 and for John Major in 1991 they created 'Labour's going for broke'. From the Middle Ages came 'Domini canes' [dogs of god] sounding like Dominicans, who were also known as Dalmatians. The Jacobites had their symbolic butler, which represented James Butler, Duke of Ormond. In Florence in the 1430s a pun was used to link Cosimo de Medici with the concept of cosmo, meaning world. The French Revolution had 'Autri-chienne' [the Austrian bitch] for Marie Antoinette, and earlier there had been a pun on Cardinal Richelieu as a 'rich place' meaning the coveted La Rochelle, as well as the witty 1787 word-play against the tariff system:

> Le mur murant Paris/Rend Paris murmurant. [The walls surrounding Paris/Make Paris complain]

In the USA the Kennedy election campaign of 1960 produced:

> Let's put a new John in the White House

and later the anti-Vietnam campaigners used:

> Johnson's baby powder.

While in Arkansas Governor Clinton was referred to as:

> Billion Dollar Bill.

Even medieval heraldry made significant use of puns as, for example, with the cumin plant for the ambitious Comyn family in Scotland.

The introduction of numbers into propaganda messages has mnemonic qualities: it provides packaging concepts, dresses up otherwise dry ideas and provides an identity. Thus for example:

Zero Tolerance

Three Fates
Three Graces
The Trinity
Three wise men
Three worlds – of Hinduism
Three Jewels of Jainism
The Third Reich
The third way – Tony Blair, etc.

Four horsemen of the Apocalypse
Four Absolute Virtues
Four Gospels
Four Books of China

Five Sikh virtues (all beginning with K)
Five Classics – Confucian canon
Five Points of Calvinism
Five crosses of the Franciscans – and Kingdoms of Outremer

Five Wounds of the Redeemer
Five Talismans of Tao

Six pillars of wisdom
Six, the symbolic number of the Chi'in
Six spokes of Jainism

Seven heavens of Islam
Seven Sages of Greece
Seven deadly sins
Seven days of creation
Seven graces
Seven Bibles
Seven ages
Seven stars
Seven candlesticks (Menorah)
Seven wonders of the world
Seven ears of corn
Seven sorrows of the Virgin
Seven sacred planets of Egypt
Seven virtues of Zoroaster

Eight paths of virtue (Buddha)
Eight beatitudes
Eight Immortals of Tao

Nine orders of angels
Nine muses
Nine gods
Nine worthies
Nine books
Nine Rings of Odin

Ten commandments

Twelve apostles
Twelve Follies
Twelve imams of the Shia's

Thirteen – Last Supper and other traditions

Fourteen Stations of the Cross – and generations of House of David

Fifteen O's of St Bridget

Twenty-one Taras

Twenty-four Fordmakers
Thirty-nine Articles of 1551
Forty days and forty nights (Noah, Moses, Elijah, Jesus, St Swithin)

Forty-five – the number of a famous edition of John Wilkes's paper the *North Briton* was used symbolically by the American colonists in the War of Independence

Eighty-four and 8,400,000 forms of life in Sikhism

Ninety-five Theses – of Martin Luther

Hundred days – used by Napoleon and Harold Wilson

Hundred-and-fifty moral habits

318 (TIH) the mystical number of the cross used by Constantine

Four hundred – New York 1892

Garibaldi and his thousand

Thousand pilgrimages of the Shi'ites

Death by a thousand cuts

100 million (Ichioku) various slogans for Japanese defiance in 1945.

In each of these examples the number is used simply to make the concept more vivid, more unique. There have also been more obscurely symbolic numbers like from the Book of Revelation 'six hundred three score and six' i.e. 666 supposed to be evil and used for Julian, Luther and Napoleon. To this should be added the use of dates to symbolize movements like 4 July in the USA, 26 July for Castro's Cuba and 18 May for Argentina.

Another technique, both for shortening messages and providing a peg for memory or visual identity is the use of initials.

SPQR [Senatus populusque Romanus]

became widely known because the lettering could be easily carved or applied to objects. The same is true of the extremely effective chi-rho symbol ☧ (Christ) used by the early Christians. There was also the Greek pictorial acronym I CH THUS meaning fish – but the initials stood for Jesus Christ Son of God and Saviour. More obscure was the origin of the anti-Semitic chant of the crusading period:

HEP, HEP, HEP Hurrah [Hierosolymnus est perdita – Jerusalem is lost]

or the long-lasting slogan for the Democrat Martin Van Buren known as:

OK (Old Kinderhook)

which became part of the world's language or many simple slogans such as from the British war effort of 1940:

my girl's a WOW (Woman Ordnance Worker).

The Austrian motto AEIOU (Austria Est Imperare Orbi Universo – It is for Austria to rule the entire world) also had an ingenious quality. Initials have always been a popular way of shortening the names of leaders such as J.F.K. and L.B.J. or parties like GOP and CDU to make them more acceptable.

Nicknames are an art form in their own right, but divide neatly into the derogatory and the affectionate. Derogatory include:

The bold adulterer (Julius Caesar)
Boney (Napoleon)
Tricky Dicky (Richard Nixon)
Bluff Harry (Henry VIII)
Bloody Mary (Queen Mary)
Bloody Castlereagh
The Grand Vizier (Duke of Marlborough)
His Highness (Duke of Marlborough)
Madame Veto (Marie Antoinette)
Madame Deficit (Marie Antoinette)
Bob of Lynn (Robert Walpole)
Sir Blue Ribband (Robert Walpole)
Lady Cheatem (= Chatham, Pitt's wife)
Jack Boot (The Earl of Bute)
the desiccated calculating machine (Hugh Gaitskell)
Krokotilly (Marshall Tilly)
Artful Joe (J. Chamberlain)
Sham-Berlin (N. Chamberlain)
Boneless Wonder (R. MacDonald)
King Arthur (Arthur Scargill, National Union of Mineworkers)
Attila the Hen (Margaret Thatcher)
Dragon Lady (Nancy Reagan)
In yenzi = cockroaches (the Tutsi people of Rwanda)
Krauts (Germans)
Nemets (German in Russian = dumb)
Nips (Japanese)
Poms (British in Australia)
Frogs (French)
Slick Willy (Bill Clinton)

The affectionate number for instance:

Good Queen Bess (Elizabeth I)
Great Billy (Pitt the Younger)
Winnie (Winston Churchill)
Uncle Joe (Joseph Stalin)
Teddy (President Roosevelt)
The lady with the lamp (Florence Nightingale)
Gorby (President Gorbachev)
Ike (Eisenhower)
Old Hickory (President Jackson)
Dev (Eamon de Valera)
Black Pimpernel (Nelson Mandela)
Sunny Jim (James Callaghan)
Paddy (Irish)
Taf (Welshman)
Comeback Kid (Bill Clinton)

Parody names can also be very effective like Ignoramus of Ole for Ignatius Loyola, Black Pope – for Grand Master of the Jesuits – as opposed to White Pope. Name substitution has also been a standard technique, for example making a film about Frederick the Great when the real subject was Adolf Hitler, Peter the Great when the beneficiary was Stalin, tapestries of Hercules standing in for Charles V, Theseus instead of Richelieu, Demosthenes instead of a Whig politician, Charlemagne instead of a contemporary Habsburg or King Arthur for King Henry VIII. Another technique of word substitution has been used for shock effect, such as the Quaker use of 'steeple house' for a church and 'hireling' for a priest to downgrade their opponents, or the dramatic French revolutionary shift from 'vous' to 'tu'.

Altering familiar quotations or proverbs is yet another way of attracting attention. For example the surprisingly well-remembered misquotation by Margaret Thatcher in 1982:

The lady's not for turning (instead of burning – title of play by Fry)
A sheep in sheep's clothing (Denis Healey)
The incredible sulk (instead of Hulk – title of a TV programme – used for Edward Heath)
Cool Britannia – from 1997 New Labour
Which Twin is the Tory? (1970 Liberal poster with Tory replacing Tony, a much advertised shampoo)

or Disraeli's

Sanitas, sanitatum [vanitas, vanitatum, from Ecclesiastes]

Even odder was the early medieval fascination with the fact that the first word of 'Ave Maria' spelt backwards was Eva, Latin version of the first woman and epitome of evil, Eve. Irangate, Travelgate, Koreagate, Zippergate and Monicagate, all developments from the original Watergate scandal, provided a generic suffix for all Washington scandals and a useful shorthand to aid political attack.

Among the armoury of verbal techniques is the deliberate cultivation of often repeated clichés used like a comedian's catchphrase and trotted out at regular intervals so that audiences do not even have to pay attention to what is being said. Thus the Communists used phrases like 'Trotskyist, deviationist imperialistic pigs' and 'imperialist lackeys' without having to think, just as Hitler constantly repeated his 'Versailles traitors', 'master race', 'Lebensraum', 'thousand-year Reich', 'November traitors', etc. Harold Wilson had his 'thirteen years of Tory misgovernment', Mao his 'Capitalist roadrollers'. The 'winter of discontent', a frequently repeated Shakespearian quotation, was used by the British Conservatives in 1978/9. Another useful tool is the rhetorical question such as 'Would you buy a used car from this man?' used with reference to Richard Nixon; this kind of phrase can be stronger than a mere statement with the same basic content.

There are certain words given a kind of icon status by carefully hallowed usage over long periods so that they acquire an inbuilt awesomeness for all but the least cowable – words like god, fatherland, sovereignty, country and royal. The mere use of such words can trigger a submissive reflex. The reverse of this, though strangely some of the same words may appear again, is shown in the emotional relief people feel in speaking taboo words or the shock in hearing them (e.g. 'Christ!').

Many of these essentially linguistic techniques for easing the transmission of messages have their equivalent in the visual arts and taken as a whole have played a major role in most propaganda exercises. The slaying of fearsome dragons, the symbolism of mother feeding child, the overflowing fruit bowls of mercantile Holland, the idealized shepherds with their flocks are some of many examples of the visual metaphor. The empty lamp in Martin Schongauer's (1450–91) *Foolish Virgins* was shorthand for selfishness to a contemporary audience and an example of thousands of visual emblems which in each generation have enabled artists to convey specific messages more easily.

Tricks of the Trade (3)

The Uses of Fantasy and Fable

In addition to the armoury of word and visual image techniques used by propagandists over the centuries there is also a whole range of narrative themes, which in the same way, because they have a regular pattern with an expected conclusion, form part of the shorthand for the route of least resistance to communication success. For example, knight hears of maiden held captive by monster, slays monster, wins hand of maiden. These themes work because they fit an existing niche of understanding and have a proven track record of winning the sympathy and attention of populations in all eras. The propagandist simply has to fit his objectives round such a theme to take advantage of the consequential benefits. And it is remarkable how different combinations of the same old concepts have worked time and again throughout history to create obedience.

A first obvious theme, often relevant to propaganda situations, is that of the hero and the heroic struggle against difficult odds. Perseus and the Gorgons, George and the dragon, David and Goliath – there are numerous allied myths which have been used to shape dynastic attitudes, creating credibility for a monarch or religion. Homer, the Norse sagas, the Hindu *Mahabharata* are full of such material. The images of Julius Caesar, King Arthur, King Alfred, Charlemagne, Napoleon, Hitler have all been built up using this type of cliché material. Mohammed had the same kind of struggle against the wealth and power of Medina, Abraham Lincoln had it against his humble origins, John Kennedy against the Republican establishment, Fidel Castro against the Batista dictatorship. Often rulers short of such myth material could create it: many medieval rulers, for example, offered single combat with their opposite numbers, as Robert the Bruce did before Bannockburn – Disraeli did the same in the nineteenth century. Chairman Mao Zedong whose early period of power followed such genuine heroic acts as the Long March of 1934, in his declining years tried to recreate that image by restaging the Long March and participating in his long geriatric swim in the Yangtze.

There has always been an inevitable trend for the image of heroes to be embellished and elaborated, often into the fantastic. Such sub-themes include, for example, the extraordinary circumstances of the hero's birth, as with Moses, Romulus and Remus, Hercules, Jesus Christ and many others. Amazing achievements as youngsters form the next sub-theme, feats which gave clues to subsequent greatness, as with Kings David, Arthur and Alfred and many more who thus became men of destiny.

Symbolic visions or dreams were part of the image of Constantine, Robert the Bruce and Joan on Arc. Symbolic acts of bravery were part of the build-up of Nelson, Napoleon and many others, and superhuman acts or miracles for that of Christ, the kings of England (curing the kings' evil) and numerous saintly miracles. Spectacular acts of self-denial were attributed to the Jains, the pillar saints or Gandhi and of course extraordinary deaths were common to Elijah, John the Baptist or John F. Kennedy. The personality cult of heroes is frequently projected by the heroes themselves in their own lifetimes, but sometimes by later figures who find it easier to create the image of a dead hero with whom they can be identified as with Frederick the Great by Hitler or St Francis by Gregory IX.

One of the more subtle aspects of hero-projection is the use of false modesty, the deliberate disguising of dictatorial power with a show of humility, as demonstrated by the Emperor Augustus who did everything to hide his real powers with a show of republicanism, the Medici in Florence who had to try the same technique, or the first Ming emperor who emphasized his reluctance in having to accept the throne.

The obverse of the hero-worship theme is the tall poppy syndrome, where the media are used to exploit the fact that crowds soon tire of heroes and want to see them toppled – *Schadenfreude*. One clever example of the propaganda usage of this idea was the undermining of Krushchev by both Brezhnev and Bulganin: both deliberately overdid the personality cult of their superior as a prelude to their coup against him.

The step from heroic to supernatural achievement is not massive and propaganda over the ages has not been shy in flouting the laws of nature. The attribution of miracles and magic powers, the creation of supernatural beings and worlds, the immortality of mortals, have all been frequent elements in religious teachings and obvious lack of credibility has rarely stood in the way of effectiveness; in fact often the more extreme the claim the stronger the belief, reinforced by the standard jibe of 'doubting Thomas' which can shame the hesitant into acceptance. Even in the late twentieth century fundamentalists often found it easier to gain acceptance than those who tried to expurgate the supernatural from sacred texts.

The ultimate in hero worship is when kings come to be treated as gods and magicians. This was a common feature of early kingship, but became more sophisticated and powerful with Alexander of Macedonia and again from Augustus onwards in the Roman Empire. This pagan notion was subtly transferred to the monarchs and emperors of Christian Europe who claimed the divine right of kings and could cure scrofula to prove it, a good, long-lasting propaganda concept.

A connected theme is that of suffering and martyrdom. The classic example here is the crucifixion of Jesus Christ, an act of martyrdom which forms a central plank in the promotion of the Christian message. Many other early saints who suffered terrible deaths – medieval martyrs like Joan of Arc or Savonarola, Jesuit and Protestant martyrs after the Reformation – all contributed to the same build-up of credibility.

Similarly the martyrdom of the third imam, Husayn contributed particularly to the spread of the Shi'ite sects of Islam (see p. 125). Again, as a substitute for genuine martyrdom many religious figures have artificially exposed themselves to pain in order to add credibility to their message: the ascetic masochist monks like Simeon Stylites or St Antony, the flagellant monks of the Middle Ages who whipped each other's backs raw to help create crowd empathy, or the Shi'ite flagellants and Berber fakirs, Hindus walking on hot coals or Buddhist monks eating dog flesh for effect. There have been numerous examples too of the exploitation of political martyrs for propaganda purposes. Cato, William Wallace, King Charles I, Gordon of Khartoum, Abraham Lincoln, Horst Wessel, Che Guevara, Sandino, have all received post-mortem treatment for the benefit of their successors. Martyred military heroes are particularly valuable for preaching the lessons of loyalty, patriotism and steadfastness, so Leonidas of Sparta, General Wolfe, Admiral Nelson have been used for this purpose. Numerous lesser warriors have also been exploited as role models, as have groups of soldiers like the Thermopylae 300, the paladins of Charlemagne, the martyrs of Ireland, the defenders of Alamo, the Light Brigade, the Glorious Gloucesters and the Japanese kamikaze, even the unknown soldiers. A classic example of milking the advantages of a war wound for propaganda purposes was that of the Mexican leader Santa Anna (1797–1876) who was president on eleven occasions from 1833 to 1854. He had his amputated leg paraded through the streets and buried ceremonially on each occasion he was elected, but disinterred ready for the next comeback whenever he was defeated.

Mass martyrdom has also been frequently exploited, from the defendants of Massada to the captives in the Black Hole of Calcutta, the victims of the Bulgarian atrocities, the Armenians, the Jews and the Kurds. The image of imprisonment as proof of a leader's credentials has been used only slightly less frequently: certainly Lenin's period in Siberia, Hitler's in Munich prison, George Fox's nine spells in prison cells, Kenyatta and Banda's imprisonment, Mandela's incarceration on Robben Island, the sufferings of Suffragettes were all used to good effect. A spell in prison can be used to enhance the reputation of a prospective leader, religious or political. Similarly a fast to death or near death as practised by Gandhi, the Suffragettes, Danilo Dolci and members of the IRA could be used for the same effect. Even second-hand disasters can be used to enhance the gravitas of leaders as with Ronald Reagan after the *Challenger* rocket explosion, Bill Clinton after the Oklahoma bombing or Tony Blair after the death of Princess Diana.

After the theme of the hero comes that of the anti-hero. Demonology has been a useful part of propaganda going back to the Zoroastrians in the second millennium BC and probably earlier. To have a frightening figure of wickedness, devil, demon or witch helps to focus motivation.

Another narrative theme of fundamental importance throughout the history of propaganda is group distinctiveness. The classic example is the

self-image of the Jews; they distinguished themselves from others by
projecting themselves as the chosen people, by their special traits of
circumcision, diet, moral code and religious belief, to some extent also by
dress and other habits. Thus they established a unique corporate image
which has been crucial to their self-preservation as a race and ultimately
to their resurrection as a nation. Different tribes and peoples have
chosen different postures and techniques for asserting their similar
individuality, but the basic common denominators have always tended to
be a fostering of group loyalty round a visual image made up of costumes,
flags, emblems and architecture, backed up by slogans, music, poetry and
folk myths. Some have demonstrated particular confidence and
aggression like the Romans, who regarded most other nations as
barbarians, and the Germans, who styled themselves a master race. Some
like the Cossacks, Kurds, Scots, Armenians and Basques have successfully
projected their corporate image over many centuries, without achieving
the military infrastructure needed to turn it into practical independence.
Others like the Serbs, Irish and Palestinians demonstrate the very great
power of the image to survive crushing defeats. In some cases the image
differentiation has become so important in its own right that members
cannot bear to surrender their imagined superiority, hence the
emergence of groups like the Ku Klux Klan and right-wing political
parties who take the fight for image reality to absurd lengths. The same is
true of religious sects whose self-image is so powerful that they regard all
others as heathens. It is also true of the whole concept of rank, especially
hereditary rank, which is after all only the artificial creation of image
making, particularly when a rank grouping adopts elaborate trappings of
self-imagery, in other words the propaganda scheme necessary to
persuade their inferiors to be appropriately submissive.

Linked to the theme of differentiation is the theme of authenticity.
There is pressure on prospective leaders, political or religious, to create a
narrative of credentials, a task most brilliantly accomplished as early as
around 1100 BC by the *Chronicles* of Judah. Another good example of this
is the papacy which in its early propaganda went to great lengths to
establish the legitimacy of the apostolic succession and created a Petrine
mythology which was crucial to its claims to primacy of the Christian
world. In the same way Charlemagne's propaganda concentrated on his
picking up the trappings of the Roman Empire, and later Charles V used
his artistic propaganda machine to present himself as the new
Charlemagne, as did Napoleon and Charles de Gaulle. In England
a number of kings modelled themselves in the same way on Arthur
and his Round Table: both Edward III and Henry VII did this. Later
John F. Kennedy did the same with his Camelot image. The invention of
ancestors was always a common feature of dynastic propaganda:
Alexander the Great, the dukes of Burgundy and the Habsburg emperors
all traced themselves back to Heracles. For Roman consuls or Chinese
emperors and many other self-made rulers the creation of an impressive

family tree was an important exercise. Classic examples in this field include the invention of the Apostle Peter's daughter St Petronella to provide a saintly ancestor for King Pippin of the Franks, the efforts of Aelred of Rievaulx (1109–66) to show that Henry II of England was descended from both the Nordic god Woden and Noah. The most popular ancestors for European monarchs were Brutus, Aeneas of Troy, King David and Japheth. The Chinese Empress Wu forged a family tree showing descent from Buddha. The new Russian empire of Ivan IV (the Terrible) was based on a forged document by a monk Gerasimov and the forged 'Fifth Epistle of Clement' by Pseudo Isidore of AD 850 was used later to give a biblical justification for the abolition of private property. The images of primogeniture and patrilinear descent were of the utmost importance to many nations, causing a significant number of wars throughout history. Pedigree documents for Popes, emperors and lesser rulers were regularly forged. One classic minor example was Bishop Aldric of Le Mans (fl. 832–51) who had created a whole false history, a make-believe saint, poetry and eighty forged documents all to help extend the boundaries of his see.

The credentials of being descended from a goddess were sought by Julius Caesar and many other self-made monarchs. Tricks used to achieve false authenticity include the forging of imaginary testaments like the 'Will of Constantine' used by the papacy or the 'Will of Peter I' used by Napoleon against the Russians, or the forging of letters from imaginary supporters as used by Napoleon and Bismarck. In some cases the credentials of previous heroes were lifted in their entirety as when Pugachev, the Cossack rebel, assumed the identity of the dead Tsar Peter III, Perkin Warbeck posed as the murdered Richard, Duke of York, and there have been numerous would-be reincarnations of Jesus Christ. Religious leaders required other types of credential narratives, for example, the performance of miracles as with legions of medieval saints, the possession of vital relics from previous saints, the hearing of voices like Joan of Arc or Bernadette, the collecting of tablets of stone like Moses or Joseph Smith of the Mormons, the accomplishment of a great journey which could then be repeated as an act of pilgrimage or the suffering of a great deprivation which could be re-enacted as a festival of abstinence. Lesser prophets resorted over the years to crystal balls, animal entrails, smoke, pebbles or star movements to give credibility to their pronouncements and gained awe by living in remote sacred places.

Yet another useful narrative strain throughout the history of image-making was the whole idiom of prophecy. From Joseph and Moses through to the Messiah, the Jews maintained a constant apocalyptic cycle which was a cornerstone of their entire propaganda scheme, often dreaming up prophecies to fit current situations. The Gospel writers took pains to add to the authenticity of Jesus as a Messiah by arranging evidence to show how his life had fulfilled prophecies from the Old Testament – birth in Bethlehem, the appearance of stars, descent from

David and so on. Subsequently the Messianic concept of a new day of judgement followed by a new resurrection has often been an important platform for Christianity, particularly for the Crusaders, the Anabaptists and more recently sects like Jehovah's Witnesses, Pentecostalists, Moonies and the Seventh Day Adventists. Numerous other sects have focused on the idea of a prophet who has died and will eventually return, like the Mahdi or the Caliph al Hakim who disappeared in AD 1021 and whom the Druze expect to return. Many other religions have also thrived on their floods and Armageddons with the promise of a heaven for the elect. Prophecy was also used by both the Greeks and Romans for political propaganda. Alexander the Great used it extensively; for example he invented an Egyptian prophecy to encourage the surrender of Egypt to him in 332 BC. In Rome the prophecies of the Sibylline books were endowed with fake charisma so that they could then be used to create artificial credibility for the political decisions of each new generation. They had such respect that they were even recycled by the early Christians with a new version backing the Jewish Messiah. Astrology, prophetic oracles, and seers have all played their part in providing the raw material for the tools of mass conversion. The Florentine friar Savonarola achieved huge prominence by making a number of correct prophecies, such as the fall of the Medici, thus adding to his stature as a political figure.

Similarly prophecies of doom were used to undermine unpopular rulers; there were many examples of such protest songs under the Chow and Han dynasties in China, where forecasts of downfall were often used to accelerate the reality, as with the rebellion of the future Emperor Wang Mang. The concept of nemesis, of 'the higher they stand, the harder they fall', is an acceptable propaganda theme because it panders to the jealousy of majorities. This also allowed for the reinterpretation of past disasters like floods and plagues as if they were acts of punishment, making them useful propaganda materials. The Jews were particularly adept at structuring their judgemental disasters linked to human underperformance, plus odd confirmatory miracles to reward virtue as with Daniel in the fiery furnace. In the Middle Ages whenever an army was defeated the church could announce that this was due to unchristian behaviour or occasionally a victory was due to the opposite: Wulfstan's public condemnation of Ethelred the Unready comes into this category. In the late twentieth century global warming was presented as the next judgemental disaster to justify an attack on energy waste and pollution.

To some extent millennia – like centuries, decades and other anniversaries – provide a peg upon which propagandists can hang predictable structures for promoting their own value systems or ideas. In politics too the idea of the millennium has been frequently exploited. Hitler formulated his idea of the Third Reich which followed two previous failed German empires, the Third being the Reich that would last for 1,000 years; his philosophy produced a neat piece of propagandist packaging, not dissimilar to what Charlemagne and the Habsburgs did with the idea of the Roman Empire. The vision of a second-rate period to be followed by the dawning of a golden age was popular too with the propagandists of Augustan Rome and with the British during the age of Walpole. The Fatimids won control of Egypt in 969 by forecasting the return of the Mahdi. In the English Civil War both sides used popular almanacs to prophesy events and victories as a means of strengthening morale.

The concept of mystery has always been an asset to propaganda, half-truths often more effective than truths, obscurity an advantage rather than a disadvantage. The mysterious, inexplicable quality of many higher religions is a classic example, the deliberate secrecy of groups like the Freemasons, Eleusinian Mystery cultists, the Ismailis or the Carbonari illustrate the attractiveness of avoiding obviousness. A specific example of this is the use of dreams in propaganda. Joseph's dreams in Egypt, Constantine's dream at the Mulvian Bridge, Joan of Arc's dreams, the 'I have a dream' speech of Martin Luther King all illustrate the value of the mysterious in creating an exciting message. Similarly the mystical novel *Zohar* written in the thirteenth century by Moses de Leon to inaugurate the Kabbalah was a lastingly effective piece of propaganda.

One of the oldest and most common of propaganda narrative themes is the idea of the scapegoat. Many regimes, particularly if they have problems, wish to find someone else to take the blame. For at least 2,000 years the Jews have very often been picked for this role, in Roman Alexandria, Visigothic Spain, crusading Germany, and in almost every country in Europe from 1880 to 1945 particularly. By their self-differentiation they laid themselves open to this, but they were not unique. The papacy made an example of the Albigensians by encouraging the French to commit genocide against them, picking on them not just because they were heretics but because they were odd, because they could be turned on with some kudos accruing to the persecutors. The same principle attached to the Inquisition's creation of the topic of witchcraft, which provided both Europe and the American colonies with a scapegoat formula for 200 years, and to the Turks picking on the Armenians and Hitler on Jews, Communists, homosexuals and gypsies. Joseph McCarthy was the classic example of a politician trying to establish his career by this technique. It lent itself to event management, to effigy burning, howling mobs and stage-managed confessions. Mao used it most effectively during the Cultural Revolution. Newcastle had used it with the unfortunate Admiral Byng. Throughout history finding a scapegoat has been the last resort of weak-minded regimes and exploiting a common hate figure has been one of the lowest forms of creating mass camaraderie.

Another popular story theme is the concept of reward or punishment. The moral legend of the fall of Adam and Eve is a classic example found in most of the Middle Eastern religions. Most national mythologies are

packed with narratives of sin and retribution which form an important
strand for behavioural control (pl. 23). The reward and punishment
theme also covers the nemesis of upstart subjects or unjust rulers, the
penalties of greedy priests, disloyal soldiers or cruel masters. It paid
Henry VII of England to paint the picture of his predecessor Richard III
as an evil king who met his just comeuppance, just as it was part of Pope
Julius II's propaganda to distance himself from the corruption and
downfall of his predecessor Alexander Borgia. The first tactic for every
Ottoman Sultan faced with unpopularity was to execute his vizier.

The final narrative idiom popular with propagandists over the
centuries is the irreverent joke, the mocking of opponents. The satirical
undermining of the Earl of Shaftesbury by Dryden, the mockery of the
Duke of Marlborough by Jonathan Swift and Mrs Manley, of Walpole by
Pope, Johnson and Whitehead are examples of the use of satire as a
vehicle for destructive propaganda. The same idiom has been successfully
used in magazines like *Private Eye, Le Canard Enchainée* and *Krokodil,* by
British television programmes like *Spitting Image* and *That Was the Week
That Was.* The techniques of irony and satire have been usefully
employed by numerous politicians in their own speeches, notably Pitt the
Elder and Disraeli. The use of spiteful innuendo is seen in Teddy
Roosevelt accusing Woodrow Wilson of lack of manhood in 1915 because
he refused to go to war, or the British nineteenth-century smear that all
Indians were effeminate. Similarly Thomas Jefferson before he became
president was accused of 'a womanish attachment to France'.

All these themes reveal the fact that propaganda, like most forms of
literary entertainment tends to use a relatively limited number of popular
story lines, most of them first used at least 4,000 years ago, which are
known from experience to retain the reader or listener's attention, and
which are sufficiently commonplace for him to grasp without having to
concentrate and to have a good idea of the outcome before it is finished.
The rises and falls of different nations or dynasties, the victories and
defeats of great leaders, the miraculous survivals or martyrdoms of
prophets, the switch from fear to mockery of tyrants, all are themes which
audiences find entertaining and which will encourage people
subconsciously to take sides. The history of mass persuasion is almost
entirely made up of variations on these themes, decorated with the
idioms and symbols already discussed.

It is one of the hallmarks of clever propaganda that it offers a credible
ideology, specifically an answer to human worries about the cosmos, death
and the purpose of life. There is a reassuring quality about providing
people with an explanation of creation, rewards for good behaviour and
continuity after death, with a god in control of all these aspects, so any
mythology based on these ideas tends to be readily acceptable.

As we have seen different media dominate the world of propaganda in
different eras. Inevitably, as a result of this, the skill characteristics of the
main propagandists also vary in each period. In the ancient civilizations

the key skills were probably mnemonic poetry, relief sculpture and a talent for ecstatic prophecy. In the Greco-Roman world the emphasis moved towards creative chroniclers, court poets, event management and the decorative arts. In the Middle Ages propaganda was centred on the writing ability of the priesthood, ritual and architecture. The Renaissance was the great age of artist event managers from Rubens, Dürer, Velasquez and Holbein right through to David. Pamphlet writing had begun seriously at least as early as the time of the Lollards in the late fourteenth century, came into its own during the Reformation and graduated into the populist propaganda journalism of Lord Bolingbroke, Wilkes and Marat by the mid-eighteenth century, with a first great climax in the revolutions of 1776 and 1789, and further periods of prominence between 1848 and 1933. Meanwhile, advancing techniques of picture reproduction gave a new lease of life to the visual arts from the 1890s onwards, followed rapidly by the growth successively of cinema, radio and television. Thus the twentieth-century propagandist had essentially to be versatile and managerial rather than specialist, with increasing emphasis on precision-timed campaigns, tightly controlled presentation and planned manipulation of all available media. But beyond the general categories in every age there are always outstanding practitioners who defy the current media fashion. The effectiveness of the unusual, of surprise and the flouting of normality always remains potent.

The motives of propagandists have always been varied and complex. Often their work has been simply an avenue to quick promotion or easy cash, but often also they have been half-unwitting components in an ideological stampede in which by seeking popularity they pushed the causes which seemed easiest to push at the time. Myriad popular writers and artists have promoted variants of totalitarian or revolutionary dogma, cults and fads, nationalism, racism, sexism and class, just because it seemed the better way to get commercial acceptance for their work or attention for themselves. Thus they have been no more than the leading lemmings, speeding up the process of self-destruction.

The Dangers of Not Going Far Enough

In analysing the likely reasons for failure in propaganda campaigns there are three main areas to consider: message structure, media and audience factors. On the message side the most likely factors are that the propaganda material is boring, unintelligible or incredible. These criticisms in fact apply to a remarkably large proportion of all propaganda output, political, moral and religious. Sincere politicians and dogmatic priests have always spent a great deal of effort attempting to project rational arguments or deeply held beliefs which lose their audiences within seconds. One research project showed that after two years of patient mass media explanation a large percentage of the postwar German population still did not understand their parliamentary system. A test campaign explaining the functions of the United Nations Organization in Cincinnati only succeeded in lowering the level of ignorance from 30 per cent to 28 per cent. Unadorned factual argument often leads to the failure of many worthwhile political arguments. Similarly, religious proselytizing which assumes that the audience is as spiritually receptive as the preacher is often wasted effort. Arguments which do not evince a real sensitivity to the attitudes and aspirations of the recipients almost inevitably fail. The French war slogan of 1940 'We shall win because we are stronger' was uninspiring because it was unconvincing. Logically argued campaigns against racial hatred in both India and the USA have had poor results, just as a rational message of peace in Northern Ireland or the Lebanon in the 1980s had no meaning. Equally there is public resistance to too much propaganda that is obvious. In Great Britain in 1940 Mass Observation reported that there were forty-eight different government poster campaigns all up at the same time covering every subject from carrying a gas mask to saving scrap metal. The cumulative effect was to increase resistance to the propaganda and reduce its credibility. Majorities, as Viscount Bolingbroke had observed in 1728, are manipulated through their emotions and instincts rather than reason. Only tiny minorities, already interested in the subject or half converted to the point of view, are likely to be influenced by protracted rational explanation.

In terms of media utilization it is clear that established governments or religions have a major advantage. Their power or money give them ready access to all available media and so long as they pay reasonable attention to message structure and the artistic or entertainment quality of its presentation their results should be adequate. Media access for opposition throughout the ages has been difficult. The use of many visual messages like coins, seals, public buildings, is out of the question as are many state-controlled or high-cost media. New parties and new religions therefore need to have significantly more skill than their established opposite numbers to win through. However, the history of the world is full of great ideas which have triumphed over all the odds of poor access to media: Christianity and Islam in their early stages, the French Revolution, the movements against slavery in the USA and serfdom in Russia. If the message is exciting enough, difficulty of media access becomes almost unimportant.

With regard to the third area of difficulty, audience factors, there are a number of significant considerations. As G. Miller put it 'man is a miserable component in a communications system. He has a narrow bandwidth, is expensive to maintain and sleeps eight hours out of twenty-four.' Not only are there limits on literacy, intelligence and memory to overcome but also high levels of apathy with regard to numerous issues which the propagandist may wish to address. One significant inhibiting factor is scepticism, often induced by previous propaganda from another point of view. Maguire did research on the effects of propaganda on a prejudiced audience. He found that basically it either ignores the messages or distorts their meaning to fit in with its preconceived ideas. This points to the considerable difficulty of putting over ideas which conflict with beliefs and attitudes created by successive generations of previous propaganda. After all, tradition is no more than second- or third-hand propaganda. Ideas on race, nationality or sectarian allegiance particularly are inculcated over several generations and therefore instilled in each audience from an early age: this makes them especially difficult to combat – hence the difficulty of projecting toleration between Hindus and Muslims, Catholics and Protestants, Serbs and Croats, Arabs and Israelis, Sunnis and Shi'ites, Kurds and Iraqis.

There are some other general anomalies such as the fact that some groups very good at internal propaganda are bad at external; a classic example would be the Jews who have been so brilliant at maintaining their own ideologies but little interested in projecting them to others. The obverse is those ideas which have appealed better outside their own country of origin, particularly Christianity and to a lesser extent Buddhism. In general it can be seen that dull, hectoring propaganda even for the worthiest causes can be counter-productive, so that worthwhile concepts and institutions are left undersold. Peace, racial harmony, religious toleration, family values and pro-social behaviour are the messages which often in history have had the least effective propaganda with very damaging consequences. The poor effect of negative drug propaganda is a classic example.

The Dangers of Going Too Far

A number of factors both of message presentation and media usage have tended to improve propaganda performance down the ages. The value of repetition has been recognized subconsciously from the earliest times, particularly in terms of visual messages on coins or buildings, event management and music. More recently its efficacy for verbal propaganda has been more appreciated. Benjamin Franklin commented on the effects of frequent repetition on his pro-American campaign in France in 1776:

> It is only right to strike while the iron is hot, but it may be very practicable to heat it by continually striking.

Similarly Hitler's propaganda organizer Joseph Goebbels said:

> If you tell the same lie often enough people will believe it.

Research on the effectiveness of television advertising shows that a repetition of at least four times per person is on average the minimum required, but clearly rates vary for different messages, different media and different audiences. The value of multiple exposure of a coordinated message, using the same corporate identity, the same style down to the finest detail of typography, colour, wording, musical arrangement, style and tone is considerable. Really high frequency may begin to generate diminishing returns or even create antipathy through boredom, but the threshold for this is usually quite high.

A second known factor in message intensification is the source effect. Most great religions and many primitive ones have always projected their scriptures as having been written or dictated by their god – the Jews and ancient Egyptians as well as the Muslims did this. The stone-carved pillars showing the legal code of Hammurabi of Babylon (c. 1900 BC) were surmounted by a relief carving of the King receiving the code from the sun god Shamash. A message appears to have greater credibility and persuasive power if it comes from a prestigious or authoritative source. In an experiment by P.A. Sorokin Brahms's First Symphony was played twice identically to a large audience of students who were told a so-called expert view that one playing was much better than the other; 55 per cent accepted the expert view, only 16 per cent rejected it and the remainder hesitated. Similarly P.G. Zimbardo did experiments which showed that audiences paid more attention to the opinions of a well-dressed speaker than a dull or poorly dressed one, though conversely many ascetic saints commanded large audiences by deliberately dressing like beggars and the Jain gurus of early India achieved authority by preaching stark naked as did Isaiah occasionally. Equally, many politicians in the twentieth century, such as Castro and Saddam Hussein, have chosen to wear khaki fatigues as an image differential from the full dress uniform approach of more traditional dictators like Generals Pinochet or Galtieri.

In general terms the greater the perceived prestige or ability of a propaganda source, the more likely the message is to be accepted. Hitler had lost so much credibility by the last year of the Second World War that he resorted to the horoscopes of his newspapers to put propaganda material across to his people, since they were more likely to believe astrology than direct messages from the Führer. Similarly French television under de Gaulle was so tainted by its image of subservience to the government that it lost general credibility. At times also the Catholic Church has lost credibility because of its apparent support of unpopular political regimes. Thus overall the effectiveness of a poor message may be enhanced if it appears to come from a popular source, so John Wayne was asked to speak out for Richard Nixon, Hindenburg for Hitler, and it is now a standard procedure for political parties and religious sects to seek endorsement from celebrities. By contrast even a well-constructed message may be less effective if delivered by an unpopular or unrespected presenter. Von Bülow as propaganda assistant to Bismarck concocted fake letters from imaginary supporters in the provinces to help boost the Chancellor's case. A forged letter from the Sultan Khalil, boasting about atrocities in Palestine was used to help recruit crusaders. The opponents of Julius Caesar and the supporters of Napoleon resorted to the same technique.

Not so different psychologically were the fake confessions, testimonials extorted by torture or by intimidation in show trials. These were used to start the spread of apparently authentic myths about cannibalism among the early Christians about blood drinking by the Roman political rebel Catiline, sodomy among the Knights Templar, ritual murder by the medieval Jews, and devil worship among the so-called witches of the fifteenth century. Fake plot rumours were a standard technique used by both Napoleon and Hitler, and fake atrocity stories have been a standard ploy at the start of most wars; some of the manufactured anti-Iraqi stories after the invasion of Kuwait in 1991 were not untypical of the genre. Similarly, conspiracy phobia has always been easy to spread. There have been black perils in 1850s' USA and 1940s' South Africa, red terrors in Paris in 1871, Germany in 1933, Argentina in 1942, the Philippines in 1965 and many other places, yellow perils in Germany in 1905 and Japan in 1932, White Terrors in China in 1930 and Russia in 1919.

It is stating the obvious that intimidation is likely to improve the effectiveness of a propaganda message at least in the short term. The promotion of fear is one of the oldest of all forms of propaganda, from the period when Egyptian pharaohs hung defeated enemies from the prows of their ships or Assyrian monarchs had huge carved reliefs of the terrible fate suffered by their enemies. The Ottoman Turks used sadistic punishment as the focal motivation of their highly efficient empire. Horrific Aztec sculptures of torture, didactic paintings of the punishment of rebels or the pains of hell-fire (pl. 23) have contributed to what Foucault called the 'hundreds of tiny theatres of punishment'. The application of fear may be far more subtle, as in many forms of event management where the ceremonial is so elaborate, the music so powerful, the visual effects so strong that any rebellious participant has to risk not just physical punishment but the expected derision of his fellows. As Solzhenitsyn put it of Stalinist Russia:

> It is a brave man who is the first to sit down during a standing ovation.

Fear of ridicule or public humiliation has regularly been used as part of propaganda technique, with the French and Chinese revolutions as prime examples. There have also been numerous techniques of emphasis with the underlining of a person's or an institution's image by attention-commanding metaphor, anything from the trumpet fanfare to animal sacrifice, from architectural positioning to military drill movements.

The use of intimidation (pl. 24) may in due course stimulate a reaction simply because people ultimately resent having been influenced by it. In the same way studies of the impact of propaganda on some subjects show that fear can be counter-productive: too much emphasis on the horrors of lung cancer is not always the most effective way of persuading smokers to give up. Fear of humiliation or disapproval has, however, been regularly very effective with the white feather approach to military recruitment or slogans like 'Don't be half a man, join the Klan'. Accusations of national effeminacy were used by John Brown (1715–66) in the build-up of British nationalism and underlay the posturings of the German élite in 1914. Accusations of lack of patriotism, lack of courage, love, faith or imagination are standard jibes used in political and religious propaganda, usually when the case is weak. Almost every society has had its fearful dragons designed to instil obedience, from the Eskimo Adlet which lived on human blood to the boy/girl-eating Minotaur of Crete. Fear can be particularly potent if violence is combined with the claiming of divine authority for it as for instance with many Islamic insurgent groups such as the GIA in Algeria during the 1990s. In other words a propaganda theme is used to legitimize and encourage mass violence.

There is no doubt that it is easier for propaganda to project absolute good or evil, extremes of any kind, rather than moderate policies. Thus propaganda which is fed on extremist views is clearer, more confident and more evidently committed than propaganda for moderate causes like peace or sensibly restrained behaviour. Therefore, superficially at least, it is easier to promote uncompromising ideas like papal infallibility, the divine right of kings, biblical fundamentalism, or the sanctity of life, rather than fudged moral compromises.

The use of the techniques referred to as enthusiastic in the original meaning of that word – i.e. using possession by god – have been well analysed by the psychologist J.A.C. Brown: they include the softening up with a barrage of threats and insults, perhaps also accompanied by sensory deprivation – darkness, cold, hunger – followed by an orchestrated rise to a crescendo of relief when the audience is offered a solution to its problem, the promise of fulfilment and happiness in return for conversion to the cause. There are elements of hypnotic technique in the use of language rhythms and the building up of tension. It is clear that dramatic changes of mind can be achieved with surprising speed by these methods as practised by Peter the Hermit or John Wesley. The adoption of aspects of these techniques by political propagandists like Gladstone, Hitler, Gandhi, Kenyatta and Kennedy, for example, demonstrate the added value of the use of the emotions in mass persuasion. A classic example was the development of sophisticated emotive techniques for the recruitment of crusaders. Books like the *Ordinatio de predicatione Sancti Crucis* gave specific instructions on how to produce emotively effective sermons, using simple metaphors, exploiting obvious cults like that of the Virgin and using constant repetition of phrases such as 'Arise therefore, take up my cross and follow me', with variations on these words repeated frequently throughout the sermon to the point where, as Girald Cambrensis noted, a trance-like enthusiasm was induced. Similar techniques of extreme emotive preaching are found among the Buddhist monks of medieval China such as Huei Yan in the fourth century whose narrative style could reduce his audiences to paroxysms of weeping and trembling followed by kneeling and repentance. St Francis and his followers achieved the same effect in the twelfth century as did Chaitanya in India in the sixteenth, John Wesley in Britain in the eighteenth and General Booth in the early twentieth. Later American evangelists were even able to adapt the technique to radio and television. The Japanese used the techniques of seishin to indoctrinate the perfect business executive.

The most extreme extension of the exploitation of rhythm and crowd pressure is the addition of music and dance. The circular dancing processions of the Russian Dukhobors or the effect of the whirling dervishes on themselves and others illustrate the development of the primitive war dance to assist in mass persuasion. Props like flaming torches could be used to accentuate the effect still further.

Clearly it is often easier to achieve a propaganda effect if it is applied to a crowd as opposed to reaching individuals through media. Because of the dynamics of crowd psychology the less credulous in any group tend to be pressurized by the more credulous to conform with the master of the ceremony. This is the shaming of Doubting Thomas technique, where individuals in a crowd feel isolated and vulnerable and are made to feel afraid of ridicule if they confess that they are not patriots or true believers or do not accept whatever creed the master is aiming to project. Propagandists can thus use the pliant to intimidate the less pliant. This lemming factor is so significant that it can be translated through the mass media to a wider audience if the crowd reaction is described or shown. The effect of crowds is to diminish confidence in rational thinking, heighten leader-worship and eliminate conscience if that is useful.

An insidious variant on the emotive theme is the use of flattery to intensify propaganda effectiveness, calling the Jews or Aztecs 'the chosen people', Calvinists the 'elect' or the Germans the 'master race' and numerous other forms of flattery helped precondition various audiences. Concepts of racist superiority have always been useful material for national propaganda campaigns. By a strange anomaly propaganda of this kind can be enhanced sometimes by appearing to be secretive. The esoteric rites and exclusive image of secret societies can make them seem more interesting.

As propaganda is similar in many ways to, and sometimes even a form of, education (pl. 20), it is not surprising that audience participation, a recognized aid to educational learning, is also of value in persuasion by propaganda. Organizing crowds to shout slogans, carry banners, sing campaign songs, repeat the propaganda message in some form or another makes conversion more likely. In medieval China audiences had to chant their responses to imperial rescripts in unison. The concept of organized drill movements as part of a training for unquestioning obedience, or the use of compulsory hand salutes, the clenched fist or the Nazi 'heil', the regular recitation of scriptures from ancient Egypt onwards, the demand for 'Hail Marys' or 'amens' in churches or prostrations in mosques, are all examples of requests for fairly small acts of compliance, which become the psychological foot-in-the-door for acceptance of the whole ideology. Communal effigy burning as in anti-papal demonstrations is another participative focus for crowd manipulation. It can also often be demonstrated that propaganda is more effective when there is feedback and participation. In post-Stalinist Russia large volumes of correspondence to the newspapers were encouraged as a partial outlet for frustrations in a totalitarian state; phone-in radio programmes or audience participation on television can be used for the same effect in political broadcasting. The general rules seem to be that an audience kept involved can be more tractable than an audience allowed to become totally passive. Participation combined with repetition is seen in the frequent resaying of particular prayers emphasized by the mnemonic device of a rosary or abacus of beads. Participation can itself be enhanced when competition is introduced, to see who are the most flamboyant supporters and the best memorizers of the official mantras. The Chinese were always great advocates of enforced memorization of official propaganda texts, for instance Wang Mang's *Classic of Filial*

Submissions or the Empress Wu's rhyming *Rules for Subjects*. The Manchus in 1652 insisted on oral recitation of the *Six Maxims* twice a month on the 1st and 15th day.

It is obvious enough that when a majority in a crowd is seen to be favouring a propaganda message of any kind then the remainder will tend to be drawn along by the bandwagon effect. This acceleration of conversion can sometimes be artificially aided. The planting of knights already committed to go on a crusade in the front rank at the crusading rallies was an early example of exploiting this technique. The planting of compliant participators, primed cheer-starters or leading-question askers in audiences is all part of the same set of methods. A more sophisticated example is the use of carefully structured opinion polls to prove artificial majorities, or to use staggered elections like the US presidential primaries or the plebiscites of Napoleon III and Hitler to create bandwagon effects. These work on the principle of a popular vote organized so that it is very obvious that the answer expected is yes. Hitler happily reinforced this with bandwagon style poster slogans like: 'Ja, Führer, wir folgen dir' ['Yes, leader, we follow you.']. The concepts of participation and bandwagon effect can be linked and directed by the technique of the leading question expecting a specific answer. A loaded questionnaire used in an opinion poll produces an apparent popular endorsement which can then be recycled to reinforce subsequent propaganda. Boris Yeltsin helped his case with self-fulfilling opinion polls. A population offered a limited choice, for example conquest by another nation or war, will choose the lesser of the two evils and therefore apparently endorse the pro-war stance of its government. This extorted endorsement can then be used to feed a patriotic frenzy for greater war effort. Similar to this is the whole idea of deliberately publishing economic performance indicators like the Dow Jones Index by which capitalist systems feed their own need for speculative activity which is in itself a whole additional industry. This half-controlled nexus of economic propaganda is a significant component in the twentieth-century world system, relating to levels of confidence and the perceived value of money or other commodities.

Particularly extraordinary can be the lemming-like behaviour of whole populations when the appropriate emotional chord is struck by relevant media. The contagion of mass hysteria which can be induced for the multiple worship of heroes, dead or alive, for cult crazes or religious manias and fashions is perhaps most likely to be sparked off when groups of people are suffering from some sense of physical or emotional deprivation and an intense reaction can be triggered by the propagandist pushing the appropriate psychological buttons. This was true of flagellomania and millennial cults after the Black Death, of the French Revolution and of German Fascism. It has also been true of the worship of Elvis Presley or the mass mourning of Diana, Princess of Wales. In each case when the initial reaction reaches a critical mass, majority intimidation takes over to mop up the stragglers. The subsequent sense of security following previous uncertainty leads to new levels of conformity which may take in aspects of personal appearance and behaviour which match the new emotional fashion.

Propaganda tends to be most effective when it embodies meaningful rewards and punishments, rewards such as a sense of racial superiority, communal approval, the promise of immortality, a guaranteed passage to heaven or punishments such as eternal damnation, public disgrace and social ostracism.

A feature of the most effective propaganda empires, both political and religious has been that they early on established a decisive artistic identity, a significant style differential consistently applied; what in modern commercial terms would be described as strong branding. This is evident in the projection of the earliest empires such as Egypt and Assyria, each of which had unique and dominant styles. It is particularly true of the Romans who had a highly developed combination of ancestral images, self-made military symbols, uniquely characteristic shapes adapted from Greek models and a letter style of great dignity, all of which were applied with considerable consistency and cumulative impact to achieve deep impregnation of the Roman ethos over a wide area and time span. Christianity also developed a whole group of dominant styles which were consistent for many years, although many of them later subdivided. The combination of apse, mosaic and icon in Byzantium, of Romanesque architecture, illuminated lettering and hagiographic symbolism in the Middle Ages, of baroque architecture, painting and music in the Counter-Reformation are all examples of the establishment of a new and dynamic style spread over all available media. Islam with its combination of ritual, unique buildings, texts and calligraphy was projected with remarkable discipline. The French Revolution with its Napoleonic aftermath was an outstanding example of adding a new, distinctive and commercially viable style to an ideological stance, and commercial marketability is indeed an essential feature of the great propagandizing styles – the artefacts have to be bought. Fascist Germany with its Nordic symbols, Gothic script, racist folklore and total discipline in all art forms demonstrated the same principle. Thus it can be seen how originality and disciplined adherence to a new style can substantially enhance the impact of propaganda campaigns. Stalinist Russia on the other hand shows how a style which lacks creative elegance, even when it is executed with discipline, is in the end counter-productive, dull and unmarketable. An example of some style but little consistency would be the projection of Victorian British imperialism which was amateurish and undisciplined but remarkably effective. The United States has shown a lack of flair and inadequacies of style induced by over-reliance on short-term commercial criteria in the second half of the twentieth century, yet its version of cultural imperialism has been effective in many secondary areas of life.

One of the most important intensifying factors for propaganda is the concept of novelty or fashion. It appeals to the competitive and socializing sides of audiences, particularly the young. New fashions in art, music, literature or the media themselves have an inherent extra ability to win attention. Many specifically fashion-motivated ideas such as flagellation have spread and died again with remarkable speed. Sometimes even reversion to former fashion has a major effect. The removal of religious statues by the Byzantines or the Calvinists, their whitewashing of murals, had an effect almost as dramatic as the original art. The toppling of Stalin's statues was more noticeable than their erection.

The concept of branding is at its most literal when it includes the participating act of adherents wearing the badge of their cause on their clothing or even more so directly on their bodies. Thus Nazi uniforms or orange sashes both acquired and created repetitive impact. Cavalier or Jacobin hairstyles or tribal tattoos perhaps went even further, and the circumcision of Jewish males or Kikuyu females is perhaps an extreme form of corporate branding.

Ultimately the concept of branding and participation can be combined when the participants form a second layer of propagandists, paying for or conducting the propaganda themselves as a means of achieving favour from their leaders. This was the case with the numerous patrons of Christian art in the Middle Ages or with Mao's mass cloning of the Red Guard in the Cultural Revolution. Other examples include the competitive asceticism of medieval monkish orders or of the sixteenth-century Puritans.

Significantly one of the most potent aspects of successful propaganda lies in the age of the audience. Mass indoctrination of the very young is much easier than that of adults, reaches much deeper and is very much harder to erase. Among examples of this are the Spartans, the Jesuits, the Prussians under the inspiration of August Francke, the nineteenth-century British public school ethic and the Hitler Youth. In such situations youth can be programmed either to be deferential as in the case of the Christians or the opposite, for example in Mao's Cultural Revolution.

It is also important to recognize the special force of what we could call macro-propaganda, that which enjoys repetition not just over a short period but over successive generations, catching each at an early age. Ideas developed by such propaganda may appear to be so ingrained that they come to be regarded almost as natural laws, as has been the case over many centuries with several forms of inequality: race, sex, class and caste. Sometimes such attitudes originate from some past act of subjugation and are then perpetuated by the media without real thought, as was the case with slavery. Many other concepts have begun with force and been continued by persuasion, whereas the ideas of primogeniture, property ownership and inheritance, male authority, and vendetta have been sanctified by myth and ceremonial. Long-term ideas such as monogamy, the Protestant work ethic, Catholic priestly celibacy, homophobia, anti-Semitism, Muslim temperance or Hindu caste have been nurtured by the prevailing tones of art and literature for thousand-year periods to the point where changes of attitude become extremely difficult. The importance of such macro-propaganda and the deep impregnation of all forms of media underlies most prejudices and shifts of attitude. Many pernicious modern propaganda campaigns, such as those by Hitler or Jim Jones, have worked well because they simply recycled familiar themes in a new style.

BY-PRODUCTS

It is in the nature of propaganda to aim for total conversion and therefore because of media and audience variables to overshoot on many occasions. The nature of some types of conversion is such that there is a tendency to create a minority at least of over-converted fanatics. Thus in the aftermath of the Roman Empire when the Catholic Church waged a campaign in favour of clerical celibacy and asceticism, there were some who responded by self-castration and absurd extremities of mortification. Equally the Inquisition started the legend of witchcraft to help maintain its own usefulness but witch paranoia swept far beyond that level. The spread of the flagellant movement, the excesses of the Crusades, perhaps even of anti-Semitism and in certain areas Communism went beyond the intentions of the original activators of the propaganda. This same feature results in the development of deviations. Strong propaganda often achieves not only the desired effect but a deviant one – Mensheviks as well as Bolsheviks, Shi'ites as well as Sunni, Arians as well as orthodox Christians. Propaganda has therefore often been the indirect cause of substantial persecution, mainly the result of its own inefficiency, or over-efficiency or variations in efficiency.

A second side effect of propaganda is a high level of polarization. While it is commonly the intention both of religious sects and nationalist groups to establish their corporate individuality and differentiate themselves from other such groups – that is an acknowledged requirement of the process – the final situation can be quite the reverse with groups not only coming to regard themselves as different but also being paranoically hostile. Much political propaganda which exploits the route of patriotism or sectarian speciality can result in this kind of confrontational effect at a more intense and dangerous level than was required by the original objectives. The Ulster obsession with the Battle of the Boyne legend is an example, as is the survival ethos of the Maronite sect of Christians. The adversarial nature of Christian anti-Muslim propaganda had long-lasting serious effects as did the confrontational style of both sides after the Reformation. Because, too, propaganda relies on the entertainment theme of combat, it creates further tension and combat.

As a result of all this effort and of the contrary strain in human nature, most propaganda has a tendency to produce the total opposite of the effect intended among at least a small minority of its audience. Thus heavy democratic propaganda will encourage a small group of fanatical monarchists, or hearing Catholic propaganda will provide a spur to extreme Protestants, and exaggerated idol worship will induce some wayward iconoclasm. Anti-drug propaganda can make drug taking actually seem more exciting. This negative reaction to propaganda can be particularly noticeable in societies that become conscious of its cost. The promotional activities of the Renaissance Popes and Louis XIV were so extravagant as to invite protest, and this has often enough been the case with regimes which over-flattered their own images. The 'control freak' image of New Labour in Britain in the late 1990s is another example of propaganda becoming too obvious.

Propaganda also has a significant tendency to trivialize. Because to achieve its ends it uses the emotional more often than the rational, and aims for the lowest common denominator of audience response, it reduces issues to myths, oversimplifies complex problems and sometimes totally obscures the original issue.

Propaganda by its nature favours élites, the most powerful, richest, fastest and even the most fanatical self-deniers and this very competitiveness can at times contribute to a severe loss of corporate self-esteem among normal populations. Such low self-esteem may well create a healthy breeding ground for other less savoury propaganda like anti-Semitism, the right-wing poor white syndrome and suicide cults.

At the same time and for the same reason propaganda has a tendency to reduce the decision-making role of the individual. It feeds its audiences with ready-made answers, requiring no intellectual effort, only an emotive act of surrender. The concept of vast robotic masses, easily susceptible to new propagandists with irresponsible or virulent campaigns is a not entirely ridiculous spectre. Certainly reasonable levels of education and sophistication in terms of media perception are some safeguard, but by no means a total protection. Ultimately it has to be recognised that a so-called advanced society may not really be that at all if manipulation techniques have outdistanced popular education levels. Yet perhaps some freedom has to be sacrificed for the sake of a management system that takes away some of life's less pleasant uncertainties.

How Often Did It Work?

Response Analysis

In considering the ways in which people react to propaganda there are clearly a number of stages. The first is that the propaganda must initially command attention, consciously or unconsciously, otherwise nothing further will take place. This attention needs to be no more than the subliminal absorption of repeated visual symbols, walking past rows of swastika flags, posters and badges so that some cumulative awareness is created. The strength of the visual media lies in their ability to achieve this. Otherwise the concept of attention simply indicates the switching on of the brain to the beginning of a particular message, giving it the opportunity to go to the next stage if it is so motivated. Thus the characteristics required of a piece of propaganda to accomplish this part of the exercise are likely to be some exciting initial words, bold visual image, or loud music, something which strikes the necessary initial chord.

The second stage is attraction, the drawing in of the mind to absorb the main part of the message. Here continued motivation of the audience remains important, as does quality of presentation and interest of content. Then comes understanding or absorption of the meaning of the message where the deployment of themes and images is crucial.

At this point, as the message concludes, it is time to assess the immediate response. Ideally this might be some form of participatory or responsive act, an amen, an ovation, kneeling, standing, repeating, joining in a chorus vote. This in turn may lead to the final stage of response which is possible retention, either genuine remembering or semi-conscious absorption so that if the message is later repeated it contributes to the cumulative building of memory. In this context the mnemonic and motivational aspects of the content are all-important.

In historical terms hard evidence on the penetration of propaganda, both quantitative and qualitative, is almost non-existent, but what we do have is the record of innumerable acts of mass irrationality which can only be attributed to the fact that people have been so easily led by those who had that skill. The mute acceptance of crazy tyrannies, adherence to highly unlikely religions, loyalty unto death for worthless regimes and make-believe empires, outrageous persecution of other groups responding to someone else's propaganda, century upon century of mesmerized pursuit of blatantly non-beneficial ideas and policies, self-immolation and masochism for second-rate deities, acceptance of gross inequalities and totally infamous mass cruelty – all these things prove the remarkable effectiveness of quite modest exercises in propaganda. Certain mindsets have reappeared frequently in history in response to similar stimuli from leaders, as if, as Richard Dawkins has suggested, the idea patterns had a biological entity and could be made to replicate themselves in the same way as efficient species replicate in evolution. The basic ingredients of the most effective emotion and attitude management systems have altered very little over the last 5,000 years.

In general it is much easier to observe the more dramatic and often short-term effects of high-profile propaganda campaigns like the Reformation or the rise of Fascism than the much longer term and slower changes achieved by less superficially obvious ones. Examples of this are the long-term bad image of women which lasted in the West from about AD 200 to AD 1600 or the idolization of the duel to the death which started perhaps with the medieval tournament and trial by combat and survived through to the era of swordplay, duelling, affairs of honour, gunplay in Westerns and gun culture generally, all providing a background justification of war based on revenge and tit-for-tat vendetta.

What is also remarkable is the fact that throughout history audiences have often been quite cynical about the effect on them of propaganda to which they have been exposed, yet nevertheless have still been too intimidated or complacent to resist it. This has been true of many political and religious propaganda exercises which made extraordinary demands on the credibility of the recipients who still found it convenient not to reject them.

PART TWO

History

'. . . the plain truth will influence half a score of men at the most in a nation while mysteries will lead millions by the nose.'

Henry St John, Lord Bolingbroke, 1728

Introduction

Any relatively short history covering a long period and a wide area has to be selective, and such selection is always to some extent an act of bias. The pages which follow concentrate on those periods or events for which there is evidence of new propaganda skills or above average use of propaganda, or where propaganda played a significant role in the historical process. The choice of examples is by no means exhaustive, but perhaps sufficient to indicate some broad comparisons and trends.

The prehistory of propaganda is as obscure as most aspects of prehistory, if not more so. There can be no doubt, however, that a number of prehistoric nations devoted very considerable resources to putting across the image of their favoured dynasties and religious beliefs from the third millennium onwards. The 20-ton monoliths of Stonehenge, the 4-kilometre stone avenue of Carnac, the numerous circles and cairns scattered all over Europe were without question components in a hugely elaborate and expensively created environment for event management. Silbury Hill, a massive ceremonial platform for princes or priests in southern England, is reckoned to have taken 3 million man hours to construct. The details of how this construction project was achieved are unknown, but the level of social manipulation involved must have been high, given the effort to create such monuments and the huge impression that their surprising sophistication must have made in their own time. It is a reasonable assumption that grandiose funerals of dynastic princelings and other awe-inspiring rituals played a significant part in the primitive engineering of consent long before other media were invented. The standing stones of the Stone Age were therefore the first example of the use of visual propaganda techniques for crowd manipulation. Specifically the process resulted in the emergence of a neolithic élite, whose tombs, monuments and emblems of status, declared the importance of their ancestors and promoted the concept of hereditary power.

In the same period primitive societies could make use of their natural environment, adopting mountains as homes for their gods, sacred rivers, lakes and islands as a visible part of their myth infrastructure. It is argued by some that they also used the positions of the sun and stars to enhance their propaganda, placing their monoliths in line with expected stellar positions on certain days of the year to instil in their audience a sense of the omnipotence of the priests.

A key feature of even prehistoric propaganda was the remarkable standardization of monument styles and craftsmanship over very wide geographical areas and this sense of corporate identity among the neolithic élites demonstrates further their awareness of the power of images.

The recorded history of propaganda dates back to three specific features of the ancient civilizations: their dynastic empire building, their religions and their requirement for obedience to a moral code. Egypt, Assyria, Persia and China all to varying extents developed mass-persuasion techniques alongside, but not totally dependent on, the use of force. They harnessed myth and visual symbolism, architecture and ritual, poetry and music to generate respect for their rulers. Perhaps even more remarkable was the ability of a few early religions, Judaism, Hinduism and Buddhism in particular, to package a life proposition so precisely and so brilliantly that their propaganda rose above the inadequacy of the media available to achieve lasting authority and penetration.

Early Civilizations

THE JEWS

One of the earliest examples of innate propaganda skills producing lasting results was the remarkable achievement of the Jews. What distinguished them from any other nation in their own era, and most since, was their total contempt for the visual media, combined with an absolutely outstanding command of language and message structure. Almost their only visual symbols were the simple Ark of the Covenant which was eventually housed in the Temple of Solomon, and the six- or seven-branched candlestick, but long before these objects emerged they had built up a repertoire of superbly told historical anecdote, rich in images, sharp in characterization, gripping in dramatic narrative and always totally pointed in its nationalist message content. The themes of 'the chosen people', 'the promised land' guaranteed by the Covenant, the distinctive features like circumcision, the sabbath, and a single God with no graven images – were all so brilliantly expounded by a succession of prophet-teachers that many of them still appear fresh after 4,000 years. Didactic myths like Eden and the Flood were not unique to the Jews, so they should not get full credit for creating them, but the range of superbly crafted parables and the quality of language certainly were. Indeed, some of the long-term success of the Jewish myth system can be attributed to the fact that it often followed formulae tried and tested by other nearby peoples such as the Canaanites. For example, it is always underdog, younger sons who come out on top, human sacrifice is cancelled at the last minute, babies survive attempts at infanticide and so on.

The Pentateuch, the first five books of the Old Testament, is one of the richest, most effective propaganda works of all time. As well as literary prophets there were the writers of chronicles, psalms and proverbs, giving the Old Testament at least four styles of persuasive writing. In addition there were plenty of didactic folk tales with appropriate props like Leviathan the monster and plenty of metaphors and symbolism such as fire for God and the vine for Israel. Moses with his tablets of stone, his charismatic crowd-handling and his ability both to produce a comprehensive ethical code and a short well-packaged summary – the Ten Commandments – mark him out as one of the world's great communicators, despite his stutter. In addition he or his successors clearly had a good idea of the value of corporate identity with the detailed instructions for colour schemes and proportions for the tabernacle noted in Exodus. The precise use of blue, red and purple and the careful positioning of the gold cherubims show significant attention to detail.

The early Jews undoubtedly had some other propaganda techniques too including a sense of the value of the poetry and music as shown in the 'Song of Deborah', the fierce mystic female soldier, and the psalms of David. The value of ritual and event management was also appreciated as shown for instance by Moses' laying-on of hands for the succession of Joshua, by the re-enactment of the Covenant, Pentecost and the pilgrimage to Sinai. The Jews also produced a succession of folk heroes who provided material for their theme of didactic history. Each of the heroes, like Joseph, Samson, Samuel, Saul and David, had a mixture of semi-amiable faults or eccentricities to provide both credibility and involvement. Now lost histories like the *Book of the Chronicles of the Kings of Judah* demonstrated the outstanding Jewish ability to write very memorable and convincing historical myth, the cumulative effect of which was one of the most deep-seated ideologies in world history. The deployment of judgemental disasters like the Flood or the Plagues was complemented by that of confirmatory miracles like the burning bush or manna from heaven, all in effect natural occurrences adopted by a charismatic speaker as his own work.

In the period of decline after the death of Solomon there emerged a succession of further brilliant communicators like the desert fanatic Elijah, the excellent writer Hosea and the charismatic verbal image-maker Isaiah. The ethos was kept fresh by the addition of new ideas in each generation. Most of the prophets were wildly eccentric in appearance and ecstatic in their pronouncements. Habi or 'men entrusted with a message' were noted in Ebla, Syria, as early as 2300 BC and the idea passed to the Jews via the Canaanites. Groups of prophets, as seen by Saul, were intoxicated with music and wild dancing. Leaders like Samuel and Nathan began to use the techniques of forecasting judgemental disasters to position themselves above mere royalty and to enforce orthodoxy. Sometimes earlier prophecies were rewritten to fit subsequent events and boost the credibility of prophecy for the future. The memorability of their words was enhanced by dramatic delivery, for example Jeremiah wearing his iron yoke or Isaiah preaching naked. The concept of linking both past and future disasters to disobedient behaviour was to become a classic formula for centuries to follow. In addition all prophecies down to the Exile were in a verse format, using thought rhyme:

> In the place where dogs lick up the blood of Naboth
> Shall dogs lick up your own blood.

The Jewish propaganda technique was not particularly a model for other peoples, but it was profound and unique, an amazing *tour de force*, based almost entirely on a large number of brilliant, often repeated verbal images with virtually no technical embellishment. It was helped by the established themes of Ugaritic epic, by remarkably high levels of literacy for a primitive people and an outstanding ability among many practitioners to manipulate words. The Pentateuch and Torah had a fixed format by 622 BC and were frequently read in public, particularly at major ceremonies; Ruth at Pentecost, Ecclesiastes at the Tabernacles and Lamentations at the feast of the destruction of Jerusalem. This contributed to the deep inculcation of ideas as did the organization of generations of scribe families or masovetes to produce a steady supply of the sacred texts.

EGYPT

Though the ancient Egyptians had no technique of printing or other means of mass production of messages they had evolved an exceptional range of propaganda skills by about 3000 BC and for nearly three millennia kept tight psychological control over a substantial population. A make-up palette of carved slate from 3100 BC Hierakonpolis shows a royal victory with decapitated enemy soldiers and a prisoner led by a rope through his nostrils, a remarkable and by no means unique example of high quality craftsmanship dedicated to the promotion of a political message. The sophisticated use of intimidating images and the disciplined control of symbols shows very great understanding of the techniques of propaganda. The Victory Tablet of King Narmer from around 2900 BC is mature propaganda. The early kings encouraged superb levels of artistry but it was mainly directed at impressing their gods rather than their living subjects. However, after the Hyksos invasion, political unity, morale and national feeling became more important, so the Egyptian rulers began to project themselves more actively in this world.

The pharaohs of the 18th Dynasty were in fact the first to use this title. Individual pharaohs had their cartouches – stylized presentations of their name which were in effect corporate identities – and under Amosis developed the cult of the sun god Amon to help stir up an aggressive nationalism first against the Hyksos invaders and then against neighbouring countries. The close identification of god and pharaoh, the public use of the god as an oracle who shared major decisions with pharaoh, the development of the visual imagery of a dark blue god with the sun disc, ram emblems and sacred geese showed Amosis's grasp of visual charisma. The liturgy performed by shaven-headed priests in dimly lit, incense-filled temples showed his talent as an event manager. From this time Amon was linked with coronation ceremonies and with the idea of world conquest.

The successors of Amosis went even further. Tuthmosis I added 'Mighty Bull' to his own titles and developed the huge new temple complexes at Thebes and Luxor with avenues of ram sphinxes for the god's procession. Tuthmosis III (1490–1439 BC) developed his image as a particularly daring general – one of his victory carvings showed him defeating 330 kings. His subjects had to make seven prostrations as part of ceremonial designed to create additional awe for him. All this was portrayed on the walls of the Hall of Annals at Karnak, inserted on a black granite tablet 6 feet tall and it was sung in his 'Hymn of Victory'. Here he also showed his sixty-one predecessors, presented as a continuous dynasty. King Seti I did the same at Abydos in 1290 BC showing his seventy royal predecessors. Massive murals carved in relief or painted became a major feature of Egyptian promotion in all main cities, with inscribed stones or stelae to project the imperial message at border crossings and provincial towns. The superhuman deeds of Amenophis II were carved on tablets, the Syrian campaigns of Rameses II were cut into temple walls throughout Egypt and an epic poem on his touch-and-go victory at Kadesh was inscribed at Luxor, Karnak and Abydos. Rameses was an even more extravagant temple builder than his predecessors and with each reign before him the size of royal statues had become larger; the colossi of Memnon, statues of Amenophis III, were now surpassed by the massive likeness of Rameses II at the Temple of Abu Simbel. His obelisks at Luxor were even bigger than Tuthmosis II's at Thebes.

The breadth of Egyptian propaganda skills is shown even by one of its failures – the religious revolution initiated by Amenophis IV, who renamed himself Akenhaten in 1377 BC. He personally briefed his artists, including his main sculptor Bek, on the change of image and arranged elaborate new solar symbolism to project his replacement religion, including the 'Great Hymn of Aten', but it did not penetrate the psyche of the Egyptian population deeply or achieve much lasting effect. This was in part due to the counter-propaganda of his successors, particularly the self-made pharaoh Ay who took over from and had previously managed the image making of young Tutankhamun, and who conducted a smear campaign saddling the 'heretic pharaoh' with judgemental disasters, as shown on the Third Pylon of Karnak. Ay positioned himself as 'the powerful bull with wise dreams and countless miracles at Karnak'.

One of the remarkable features of Egyptian propaganda was the range and discipline of their corporate symbols. The use of the bee or lotus symbol for southern Egypt and its white crown, or the papyrus symbol and red crown of the north, plus the symbols, colours and flags of the various districts show the careful exploitation of regional loyalties. Numerous other symbols such as the royal cobra headdress, the knot of eternal life ☥, the dung beetle or scarab symbolizing re-creation, the countless animal images of gods, related in a disciplined visual hierarchy to the pharaoh himself, all show a high degree of artistic subtlety and political control of vast artistic output. The Egyptians made substantial use of animals as visual metaphors for divine powers, from the lion figure of Re to the ibis and raven. Other regularly used visual metaphors included the ladder of heaven, the aegis or collar of protection, the papyrus tent meaning much the same thing and the ring of eternity. In addition the Egyptians exploited the pun effect of certain hieroglyphs, many of which had double or treble meanings depending on the context in which they were used, as in the propaganda of Senuseret I in 1971 BC for the

unification of Upper and Lower Egypt where the same sign could mean
lungs or unite and the pun was enhanced by a symbolic carving of two
plants popularly associated with the two regions.

While dynastic grandeur was the dominating theme of Egyptian
propaganda and achieved an extravagance hardly equalled since, parallel
effort was put into religious promotion albeit perhaps mainly as a
contributory factor to the political. With the Book of the Dead and other
productions the Egyptians also showed their ability to package and
promote an ethical system – specifically, they were probably the first
people to introduce the concepts of heaven and hell as motivation.
Funerary papyri prepared for members of the upper classes in readiness
for their deaths and full of propaganda material were part of a major
industry in Egypt and would clearly enjoy a significant readership in their
pre-interment years. As with the Jews the sacred books had the extra
charisma of claiming to have been written by the gods themselves and
their message was reinforced by regular recitation, another technique
later adopted by most religions. Overall the Egyptians' investment in the
visual imagery of power was very substantial and its residual effectiveness
cannot have been totally unconnected with the longevity of their empire.

MESOPOTAMIA

As in Egypt the peoples of Sumer developed the basic media for
propaganda at an early stage. An alabaster vase of about 2800 BC from
Uruk portrays the local dynasty and its gods, whereas the Standard of Ur
decorative panel in shell mosaic from only a little later shows the King and
his followers celebrating a military victory. The elaborate inscriptions
organized in public places to boost new dynasties and damn their
predecessors are a standard feature of Sumerian propaganda, for example
those of Urukagina of Lagash from 2350 BC. The creation and projection
of images of great military heroes is shown with the story of Gilgamesh,
which was eventually formalized as an epic or the hymn of Sulgi from 2093
BC. The ability to promote legal codes came with Urnammu and later
Hammurabi when the technique of publicly installed stone inscriptions was
developed – the stone poster. In addition the Sumerians, like the Jews, had
their great flood myth with the pious king priest Ziusudra their equivalent
of Noah. The use of tales of past dooms and prophecies of future dooms
was a standard method of imposing moral conformity over a wide area.

The most active propagandists of this area were, however, the Assyrians
who were particularly obsessed by the need for an imperial image and
who, like the Egyptians, asserted a right to conquer the entire world (as
they knew it). King Ashur-nasir-pal II (883–859 BC), the real founder of
the new Assyrian empire, was concerned to create an image of
intimidating power (see pl. 1). Colossal statues of winged bulls and lions
guarded his palaces. Wall paintings glorified the victories of King Sargon,

showing the mutilated bodies of his enemies and linked the King with sacred symbols to create an image of royal divinity. Pictorial freezes on obelisks presented narratives of successful wars. Huge bas-reliefs showed the King heroically fighting lions, conducting sieges, winning battles or accepting tribute from the vanquished. The repoussé bronzes of his son Shamanasar's time showed naked prisoners of war totally demoralized, his chariot battalions scaling mountain ranges and bringing back large quantities of booty. Carved ivories and cylinder seals were all used to put across quasi-mythical images of the dynasty. Royal inscriptions on stones were placed on public buildings and at frontiers – the Annals of Tiglath Pilaser (1115–1077 BC) are the earliest surviving example, albeit this was for a limited literate audience. The Assyrian propaganda organization also made heavy use of omens and prophecies to reinforce royal decisions. Epic poems were composed to celebrate great victories like those of Adad Narari and Tukulti Ninurta (1222–1208 BC). At his new palace in Nineveh King Sennacherib (d. 681 BC) commissioned two miles of sculptured slabs extolling his exploits, including one chamber showing his conquest of Judaean Lachish. All in all the Assyrian monarchy demonstrated a shrewd ability to use visual intimidation, directional history writing, event management and poetic legend-making to impose an exceptionally aggressive image on its own population and its neighbours.

CRETE

The Minoan civilization spanning the years roughly 3000 to 1400 BC had extremely sophisticated monument styles to promote both civil and religious leaders. Their propaganda objectives were perhaps less obvious than in some of the other ancient civilizations but further research may make them clearer. As in Egypt animal symbols such as bulls, lions and snakes featured strongly in religious promotion, but unlike almost all the other pre-classical empires the Minoans alone do not seem to have made use of intimidatory propaganda. But it is probable that they did have an epic tradition such as the one which came to its peak with Homer and paralleled that of Phoenicia and the Jews.

CHINA

As with so many early civilizations, the main characteristics of ancient China's propaganda were myth, monument and ritual. Little is known of the promotional methods of the Shang (1500–1000 BC) or early Chou (1000–770 BC) dynasties, but both certainly projected the fact that they were descended from gods. They appreciated the value of ancestor-worship and to some extent fear. Even nobles visiting the king had to kneel, then knock their heads three times on the floor, repeating all this three times so that the ceremony was known as 'the three kneelings and nine knockings' or kowtow. Such an act of propaganda by enforced participation is enough to demonstrate their grasp of the value of indoctrination.

What is perhaps unique about early China is the huge and long-lasting influence of a number of literary propaganda works. The first and most influential of these was 'The Analects of Confucius' (551–479 BC), edited after the philosopher's death from notes of his teachings which he left behind. This was not only a collection of anecdotes culled from previous chronicles but a detailed working out of a total ethical system pre-packaged and immensely detailed. Confucianism was relatively slow to spread and certainly did not enjoy any rapid propaganda success for several centuries after the prophet's death, but it did have certain intrinsic qualities which made its ultimate successful projection likely and laid the foundations for its long predominance. Confucius did clearly understand the value of a multi-media approach. His works included a collection of *Odes*, poetic training using easily remembered parables and metaphors. It also included the *History*, as he saw the importance of a moralized tradition in helping to form attitudes, and the *Rites*, because of the perceived value of ceremonial for the same purpose. He also had a clear recognition of the power of music 'to refine or corrupt an audience'. His moral packaging which at its simplest was presented as 'the five virtues', but at its most complex comprised around 3,000 behavioural precepts governing every aspect of human life, was thus accompanied by an exceptionally clear understanding of promotional skills and media usage. As Confucius put it himself:

Education begins with the *Odes*, is confirmed by the practice of rites and completed by music

– a remarkable early description of the propaganda process. Confucianism was helped by its tolerant approach to the other great Chinese philosophy of the period, the Tao, the role of whose legendary founder Lao Tzu is much less clear-cut. The two dovetailed together quite satisfactorily in that Confucianism was primarily a moral system with a rational outlook, whereas the Tao was more of a religion, more emotional and provided an explanation of the world. As with the teachings of Confucius, those of the Tao were not so much original as a neat repackaging and tidying up of earlier prophets and traditions. The principle of Yin and Yang, the concept of opposites, used the analogies of the sexes, winter and summer, moods, colours, sky, earth and so on. It was not new but was presented more vividly with corporate symbolism based on the circle crossed by a wavy line, often surrounded by eight shapes for the eight immortals. This symbol was used on the robes of priests, gates of houses, temple objects, baby clothing and household ornaments, thus providing one of the first examples in history of the planned utilization of a corporate identity. In due course the Tao adopted its corporate colour, yellow, and it had its favourite number – five: the five elements of ritual, the five talismans. These were all signs of the effective packaging of ideas. While, like many early religions it avoided the visual representation of gods, it was strong on parable and verbal imagery such as its popular candle metaphor. It also happily made use of dance which was used to project the image of the work-ethic role model, the primeval canal-builder Yu.

Confucianism and to a lesser extent the Tao had one other feature which they shared with other successful religions in other parts of the world – the capacity to appeal to governments. The fact that the Han dynasty in particular found the teachings of Confucius compatible with its political objectives meant that it assisted with their propagation. Buddhism benefited from the same trend in Ashokan India and Christianity in Carolingian Europe.

INDIA

As with China the first major successes of propaganda in India were religious rather than political. Without acquiring written texts and with little interest in visual representation what was remarkable about early Hindu propaganda was the development of a tradition of memorizing massive sections of the early scriptural epics which could be recited aloud. A class of professional reciters which continued over three millennia was a key component in its continuity, backed up by the strong encouragement for music. The oral tradition of Rig-Veda provided a collection of hymns for use during official ceremonies. The deliberate complexity of these rites meant that event management was the other key skill in Hindu propaganda of the Vedic period, and the task was confined to expert priests following ceremony guides such as the Sama-Veda. The other great literary product of this early period was the Upanishads with their preoccupation with the endless circle of birth and rebirth to which the soul was subject until it could achieve liberation.

With the background of this effective tradition of oral scriptures and event management it is less surprising that so early in human history India produced two particularly remarkable communicators, the founders of Buddhism and Jainism, two religions whose message was to survive more than two and a half millennia right to the present day. In the case of Gautama Sidartha (*c.* 568–490 BC), none of his sayings were written down for about 400 years, so the tradition of memorization of the Sutras was essential. It is clear that the personal drama of his biography made a highly memorable piece of packaging in itself: he was the prince who voluntarily became a beggar, experimented for six years with self-mortification, then found enlightenment. The use of a monastic structure with cellular proselytization also helped the spread of

Buddhism as did the fact that Buddha managed to keep preaching for forty years until his death. His concept of the middle way between self-indulgent materialism and ostentatious austerity also had significant appeal and he kept the theology very simple by adding no new idea of god to the existing Hindu tradition. His great communication skill lay in the development of appealing or easily understood images. The 'eight-fold way' was represented by the eight-spoked wheel. His image of the three baskets, 'the night of the great going forth' and 'the night of the great awakening' all captured vivid images. Though the early Buddhists probably made no use of the visual arts, they did create visual images with words, the image of the Buddha himself meditating under his bo-tree, the wheel and the razor edge between the two types of evil. Certainly from very early on Buddhism had its corporate colour, yellow, adopted as the uniform for its monks. In due course Buddhism was to adopt all kinds of new propaganda techniques to enable it to spread through the East. In the short term, however, its initial spread can be attributed to the powerful communication techniques of its founder.

Jainism never spread into other countries, as Buddhism did, but it has lasted just as long and has survived in its own country whereas Buddhism in India never recovered from the wiping out of its professional monks by the Mogul invaders. The founder of Jainism Vardhamana Mahavira (599–527 BC) had, like Buddha, an authority won by imposing severe self-mortification on his body, the charisma of the ascetic. He and his followers believed in absolute nakedness which became as it were their uniform and corporate symbolism. Numerical packaging was a feature of Jain propaganda with their six spokes of the wheel of time, three jewels and twenty-four fordmakers. The use of metaphor was also significant, especially the ford metaphor which was a focal point for the sect. Again initially there were no artistic representations of any kind or written texts, only memorized sayings and very vivid verbal pictures. An example was the parable of the man halfway down a well with poisonous snakes at the bottom, a wild elephant at the top and a swarm of killer bees in the middle; he then enjoys a single drop of honey which falls on his face. This was not untypical of a faith which had a low view of life on earth, yet encouraged humans to become jinas or conquerors. Vardhamana Mahavira himself, known as the twenty-fourth fordmaker died by deliberate starvation, an act of martyrdom later adopted by others in his sect. He built up a solid group of lay supporters, primarily from the mercantile classes, who were able to survive Mogul purges in later years, enabling the faith to survive to modern times, a remarkable testimonial to the strength of the original communication skills. In due course the Jains gave up their contempt for graven images and developed their own unique iconography of naked stone priests with symbolic regal umbrellas. They also acquired literary back-up with works like Asaga's poetic biography of Mahavira himself.

IRAN

Iran also produced a major religion, Zoroastrianism, which was successfully propagated without the use of the written word or the visual arts, the latter regarded as alien to its principles. Again it relied primarily on the memorization of exciting parables which eventually, after about 1,200 years, were written down as the *Avesta*. The pieces most specifically identified with Zoroaster himself were the *Gathas*, a series of seventeen hymns. Poetry, imagery and good presentation were the keys to the spread of the religion which attracted the support first of north Iranian tribes, then of the new Persian empire under Cyrus the Great who adopted it as his official religion. Central to the teaching was the easily grasped image of the conflict of good and evil, light and dark. The number seven was a key component of the packaging: seven stages of development, seven regions, seven virtues, seven holy days. The main image was fire, a living corporate identity which was part of the visual atmosphere of the ritual and the temple. Symbolizing good, it was always kept alight during the five daily prayers which were preceded by ablutions. The other corporate symbol was the Kusti, a knotted rope, used for prayer participation. The personification of evil in a satanic figure to be hated was a specific achievement of the Zoroastrians, later borrowed by the Jews and Christians. The message overall was clear and appealing, the duties of the magi in event management, helped by the easy yet effective symbol of the burning fire, were sufficiently demanding for them to make the ritual interesting and involving. It was this strength that enabled Zoroastrianism to dominate the Middle East for 1,500 years (until it was sidelined by Islam), to influence significantly both the Romans and the Christians and still to survive today among the Parsi of Bombay.

After the death of Cyrus (529 BC) the new Great King Darius put up a massive propaganda inscription in three languages on the sides of the Behistan mountain, projecting both the imperial and Zoroastrian message.

AMERICA

In Central America by 1200 BC the civilization known as Olmec was producing huge stone heads of their gods or rulers, had evoked a complex image system of jaguars and dragons, pyramids and human sacrifice, all in a little understood control structure for their society which was later to be copied by the Mayans and Aztecs.

Overall, the early civilizations demonstrated an outstanding level of propaganda skill in many parts of the world and showed the ability of societies to put together highly effective communications packages which transcended the lack of genuine mass media.

13

Classical Period

GREECE

Despite their massive contribution to the development of art, literature and political ideas, the ancient Greeks (excluding the Macedonians) cannot really be described as original or dedicated propagandists. There are probably two main reasons for this: the fact that the Greeks guarded so conscientiously the idea of the city state which was such a small unit that mass persuasion was not particularly important and that the Greeks did not produce a religion which was of any depth or which they had any burning desire to propagate. Despite this the civilization did generate one or two interesting examples of propaganda technique.

For many centuries the city state of Sparta had such an unusual and artificial form of government that it needed to develop an exceptionally strong myth system to justify this method of rule to its population. While a tiny minority ruling class of Spartiates held down the huge majority of peasant Helots, the resultant imbalance meant there had to be an unusually high level of discipline, motivation and physical fitness among the Spartiates. The extraordinary ethos of cold baths, communal living, heavy exercise, removal of young boys from mothers at an early age, stealing in order to develop self-sufficiency, total dedication to military duties, was evolved by the legendary Lycurgus (*c.* 800 BC). It was given poetic form by the blind poet Tyrtaeus (685–668 BC) and it fed on the legends of mothers preferring their sons dead on their shields to returning with no shields. The martyrdom of King Leonidas and his 300 before Salamis was almost an act of propaganda in itself, encapsulated by the poet Simonides (556–468 BC) and the epitaph:

Stranger report to the Lacedaemonians that we lie obedient to their commands.

Spartan kings, who usually reigned in pairs, were particularly concerned with their image, asserting their descent from Heracles and a very special position among the other Greek leaders. Even the ordinary Spartiates, with their long hair and red cloaks were very image conscious. Even though their reputation was tarnished by a number of examples of corruption the Lycurgan propaganda concept remained remarkably effective for several centuries and while, not surprisingly, the ideas did not spread in their own time they did much influence the Victorian British and nineteenth-century Germans.

There were other isolated examples of ancient Greek propaganda skill. The two Homeric epics, the *Iliad* and the *Odyssey*, stand alongside the *Mahabharata* or some of the great Viking sagas as great poetic expositions of the warrior code and moralistic human behaviour. Hesiod's (*c.* 750 BC) *Works and Days* is a fine poetic projection of the work ethic. Another later Greek poet, Pindar (522–440 BC), was an early example of a city public relations officer and developed the concept of the panegyric poem for that purpose. The Parthenon stands out as one of the finest of architectural celebrations of the style and objectives of a particular state, but Athens' expenditure on the arts was so huge relatively speaking that in propaganda terms it was almost counter-productive, drawing attention to the heavy taxes levied by the Athenians on the members of their League.

As a would-be imperial city Athens essentially failed to project to its colonies any real benefits for being part of its empire, but earlier it had shown signs of propaganda skill. Solon (d. 564 BC) was both politician and poet – there is at least one example of him using his poetry to advertise a specific policy, the conquest of the island of Salamis. Later a specific campaign was organized to reduce the credit to the Spartans for helping restore democracy to Athens in 510 BC: the sculptor Antenor was employed to carve the idealized tyrant slayers Harmodius and Aristogeiton, songs were written and history adjusted to boost the idea that the Athenians had rescued themselves. In addition the Athenians did orchestrate a significant anti-Persian propaganda campaign in the arts and literature to justify their leadership of the Confederacy of Delos after 479 BC.

Equally remarkable was the self-promotion of the shrine of Apollo at Delphi which used a subtle mixture of carefully contrived myths, poetry, architecture and event management to establish itself as the chief centre of prophecy in Greece. Thereafter the use of Delphic pronouncements to give credibility to the policies of politicians become a regular feature of Greek city state propaganda. It is clear too that the cities did take pains to assert their image by creating little monuments for every victory. Athens in particular projected its success at Marathon, Cimon commissioning elaborate battle pictures by Polygnotus for the market place, and Pericles using captured Persian ship masts for the roof of his new concert hall.

Probably the ablest propagandist of the Greek way of life was not a Greek but a Macedonian, King Alexander the Great (356–323 BC). His forefathers had already demonstrated their appreciation of the uses of propaganda. King Archelaus of Macedonia had been of bastard birth and attracted to his court the greatest playwright of the day, Euripides (484–406 BC), whose play *Archelaus* helped legitimize his ancestry and whose *Bacchae* dwelt on the beauties of Macedonia. Archelaus also used sporting prowess – victory in the Olympic chariot races. Alexander's own father Philip II (382–336 BC) had also worked hard at his image, using a number of Greek writers to glorify the dynasty, including the historian Anaximenes, Callisthenes who produced the *Royal Journal* and Theophorus the *Philippica.* The philosopher Aristotle was employed as Alexander's royal tutor. Paintings, gold statues, fine silver coins showing Heracles as their ancestor, ivory miniatures, monumental tombs, the first mosaics and a dominant new building at Olympia all contributed to Alexander's image.

During Alexander's spectacular empire-building career he devoted some time for the development of imperial propaganda which, if he had lived longer, might have played some real part in preventing the break-up of his conquests. At an early stage he began to cultivate a personal image with the fostering of legends like the taming of his horse Bucephalus. Callisthenes was taken to Asia with the army to send back favourable accounts to the mainland Greeks. On the one hand Alexander sought to project himself as a superhuman hero, the successor of Achilles returning to Troy, the one person who could cut the Gordian knot, the conqueror of Darius great King of the Persians. As the conqueror of Egypt he could identify with their god Amon and exploited the classic technique of staging the fulfilment of an apparently ancient prophecy to justify his easy conquest of Egypt, where he posed as a liberator and had himself crowned pharaoh. On the other hand he projected the gentler side of his persona, the man who had allowed old Diogenes to be rude to him, who had spared the matrons of Thebes, and the widow and children of Darius.

With the collaboration of his court painter Apelles and his sculptor Lysippus it is clear that Alexander intended to start to make his physical image one of the focal points of his diverse empire. He had himself portrayed usually as Zeus with a thunderbolt, which the Persians could identify with their god Baal, and he controlled the way he was depicted very tightly by allowing no artists other than Apelles and Lysippus to portray him. His encouragement of mixed marriages – the mingling of the Greek and Persian cultures – was in itself to some extent a propaganda exercise to bring some semblance of unity to his empire and the mass wedding at Susa in 324 BC was a carefully staged example of event management. He continued to encourage theatre and panegyrics like the so-called *Alexander Romance*. With unity in mind he was one of the first rulers to have himself portrayed on his own coinage and for this he encouraged those who gave him a god-like status, promoting himself as Heracles or Zeus alongside personifications of Victory. He again showed skill in event management, for example with the triumphal entry into Babylon, projecting his image as a liberator of subject peoples from the Persian oppressors. Altogether his brief career shows many signs that he well understood the need for coordinated propaganda in order to attempt to consolidate such a multinational empire: but for his early death, his techniques might have achieved some longer-lasting results. In the end without him as a focal point his successors stood no chance of holding the disparate conquests together. However, the encouragement of king or emperor worship did intensify after the death of Alexander and the dynasty of the Ptolemies in Egypt encouraged a cult of their family as divine, a tactic later taken up by Augustus and subsequent Roman emperors.

The most effective religious propaganda in Greece at this period related to the various mystery cults where suspense was generated by

creating an atmosphere of strict and rather exclusive secrecy, which was
brought to a head when initiates at last qualified to the level of
revelation. By that time the tension and sense of achievement were so
great that the resultant emotional experience made up for the fact that
the secrets turned out in the end to be nothing desperately novel. This
technique was used to create mystery around the cults of Isis, Attis,
Mithras and others throughout the eastern Mediterranean and there are
even hints of it in Judaism in the same period, as for example in the story
of Daniel.

ISRAEL

Even after the destruction of the Jewish kingdoms by the Assyrians the
Israelites preserved their remarkable ability to produce images which
could transcend both time and suppression. Daniel and Jeremiah were
examples. Then after the collapse of the Assyrians Jewish propaganda
became more political. *The Book of Maccabees* was mainly directed to
boosting the morale of the Jews in their war against the Greek Seleucids,
particularly in projecting the image of Judas Maccabeus (*c.* 200–160 BC)
as a heroic national leader, exaggerating the strength of the enemy and
deliberately understating the size of the Jewish armies, so that defeats
would look less depressing and victories prove that God must be on the
side of the Jews.

One of the most remarkable propaganda writers of this period who can
be identified as a real, single individual was Ben Sira (Ecclesiasticus), who
wrote in about 132 BC and produced a mixture of proverbs, psalms and
homilies, brilliant emotive writing, some of it characterized by ingenious
poetic tricks such as the use of acrostics – poems with the first letters of
each line reading downwards to form the alphabet, a good aid to
learning by heart.

After Palestine's conquest by the Greeks, the Jews became part
Hellenized and produced numerous writings in Greek to defend and
perhaps extend their own religion. They even started to forge excerpts
from great Greek writers to try to put across an awareness of the Old
Testament stories and borrowed the Roman legend of the Sibylline
prophecies to predict in hexameter verse the doom of the pederastic
Romans. Most impressive of all was the translation of the Old Testament
into Greek, the Septuagint, which was given charismatic quality by the
legend of its production in seventy-two days by seventy-two translators,
and became an important tool in the propaganda of Judaism in the
western Mediterranean. The Jews' pertinacity helped provoke the growth
of anti-Semitic writing in which men like Mnaseas of Patra put out the
notion that the Jews kept an ass's head in the Holy of Holies. The
misrepresentations on both sides were to form the prelude to much ill-
fated propaganda in the future.

INDIA

Shortly after Alexander's death India produced its first great political propagandist, Kautilya, the chief minister of Chandragupta Maurya (*c.* 300 BC). Kautilya wrote at least the basis of the *Arthasastra*, a guide to government including mass persuasion, in about 322 BC although the complete book did not appear for another 500 years. The Emperor Ashoka (264–222 BC) was also an innovative user of propaganda. It is clear that after his expensive and bloody defeat of the Kalingas, Ashoka wanted a new image: his subsequent change of attitude and conversion to Buddhism was to be seen as a domestic turning-point. Secondly, almost unique among great empire builders, he purported to offer his subjects a philosophy of life, the Buddhist idea of Dharma or righteousness, a system of social justice, non-violence and personal fulfilment. Whatever his motives his adoption of Buddhism gave him a monastic field-force which shared his objectives. In addition to the monks he used stone inscriptions as a prime medium for his message. Rock edicts were inscribed on eighteen selected cliffs putting across his ideas and achievements; thirty pillar edicts with the same objective were put up at prominent places in each town. In literature, he had the Buddhist Pali canon or *Tipitaka* formalized.

The use of stone for building was introduced for monuments during Ashoka's reign and this was also the period of the first Buddhist stupas, which originally had carved umbrellas on top symbolizing sovereignty. Large numbers of them were built to house texts and relics, often on the sites of pre-Buddhist temples. Sculpture too began to be developed; although it did not yet show the Buddha himself, it did spread the visual symbols of his creed – the bo-tree, the footprints, the trident and the wheel. Overall Ashoka's successful combination of a religious and political propaganda message with a significant spread of media was a remarkable achievement.

CHINA

Almost contemporary with Ashoka was the first great Chinese political propagandist – Chin Shih (259–210 BC) who adopted the grandiose title Emperor-god (Huang Ti) in 221 BC after conquering a group of neighbouring states. With an eye to the overall unification of his huge new empire Chin coordinated the diverse variations of the Chinese alphabet, built a massive road system linking the main towns and constructed the Great Wall to define his territory's frontier on the north west. In addition, 3,000 scholars were hired to manage the literary output of his regime, but they proved hard to control and many were later executed. Above all he concentrated on projecting the image of his own dynasty, rewriting past histories to enhance its role. As well as the unbelievably massive deployment of resources on his Wall he also set about a huge palace-building programme at the capital Hsien Yang, including a massive mausoleum for himself. To this he added the skill of event management which included a new sacrifice ceremony for his dynasty and a series of well-orchestrated triumphal tours round his empire, marked by huge inscriptions at key sites using rhymed stanzas with messages such as:

> The August Emperor pitied the maltreated,
> The powerful and overbearing he boiled and exterminated
> The ordinary folk he lifted and saved. . . .

Often these sayings were inscribed on a massive scale on the sides of mountains such as Mount T'ai. As part of the packaging of his imperial propaganda he also had a number of symbols; water typified the huge canal-building programme, one of his major platforms. This went with black, the corporate colour of his regime which was used on flags and other insignia, while the number six was chosen as the symbolic number for his reign, all his acts and qualities being grouped in packages of six.

Chinese propaganda developed further a century later when the energetic Han Emperor Wu Ti (141–87 BC) encouraged poets and other writers to come to work in his court (pl. 21). The small moralistic tracts with a question and answer format known as 'fu' were given patronage as were dynastic propaganda poems and the massive new *History Record* of China by Ssuma Chien. The latter was to form an important basis for the Chinese mass personality and spawned numerous plays, operas and novels over subsequent centuries. Wu Ti also made use of high profile royal tours as a propaganda tool, making a point of visiting all the great mountains and rivers of his huge empire and having these occasions marked by poems, inscriptions or ostentatious ceremonial.

The Chinese also had a tradition of grass-roots opposition propaganda embodied in popular songs sold in the market places. Many of these took the form of prophecies of doom for unpopular rulers as with 'Stanza on the Red Cassia', cassia symbolism of the Han dynasty and yellow of the future Emperor Wang Mang:

> The cassia blossoms but bears no fruit
> A yellow sparrow nests in its crown.

Once in power Wang Mang organized the enforced memorization of standard texts such as the *Classic of Filial Submissions*, twenty-four salutary stories for children. Anti-war and anti-exploitation songs were also common such as:

> In the dawn you went out to glory
> At night-fall you did not return.

The use of paintings was also extending to put across the Confucian virtues. Under the Han dynasty in the first century AD many of these were formalized with stock pictures, like the son chewing food ready for his aged father – one of many illustrations of filial piety.

ROME

The republic of Rome founded in 510 BC developed a strong propaganda requirement from its earliest days. The first objective was to blacken the image of its former and still dangerous dynasty, the Tarquins, who had just been expelled. The very low opinion of monarchy resulting from this effort was to last many centuries and later was to cause difficulty for Julius Caesar and the early emperors. The other reason why Rome needed propaganda was because like Sparta it set itself ambitious targets of military prowess from a very small base; thus it had to project an exceptionally strong patriotic ethic to its own population. An armoury of didactic legends was built up from Horatius defending the bridge to the early consul Brutus who condemned his own two sons to death for treachery to the state. There was Mutius Scaevola thrusting his own hand into the fire to prove Roman fortitude, Cincinnatus returning to the plough to show how a successful general could be modest enough to go back to being a peasant, or Regulus returning voluntarily to the Carthaginian torturers to demonstrate good faith. This repertoire of patriotic fables was constantly recycled and updated to assist with the upbringing of virtuous new members of the military classes. The Sibylline books, a vague collection of prophecies, were promoted and exploited to give credibility to political decision making.

Most of these myths had little if any foundation. Romulus and Remus, for example, seem to have been a fourth-century invention and many of the legendary heroes of early Rome were fictitious creations to boost the reputations of later noble families. The historian Livy mentions the large number of forged inscriptions on monuments, creating imaginary ancestors for prominent political figures, and also the amount of sheer fiction in panegyric poems. Songs about early heroes were a standard form of Roman propaganda, adding layer upon layer to the remarkable mythology of the Roman motivational system. In addition military successes were boosted by a number of publicity techniques, including the staging of triumphal processions, carving lists of victories in prominent places, and flagrantly biased national epics like the *Punic War* by Naevius or the massive *Annals* of Ennius. The Romans also developed large-scale battle paintings; successful generals put them up outside the senate in the immediate aftermath of hostilities and then had them moved to permanent sites in temple galleries so that the Roman population was saturated with the visual images of victorious war and regaled with romanticized songs on the same subject. For example, in 167 BC the general Aemilius Paulus hired the painter Metrodorus of Athens to do the pictures for his triumph over Perseus and later Pompey had his portrait made in pearls. The Romans also proved quite adept at political sloganizing. Cicero, for example, had his neat rhyming slogan 'Concordia ordinum' [unity of the classes] and his 'salus publicus, suprema lex' [the safety of the people is the highest law] with its repeated alliterations.

The skill of the Romans in exploiting their own mythology to produce one of the most highly motivated and consistently disciplined peoples the world has ever known was matched only by their excellent military management so that their territorial power expanded steadily over a 500-year period and then survived a further 400 years. Despite spasmodic lapses into corruption the basic image of Roman discipline and efficiency remained intact for the entire period and indeed reappeared subsequently in Europe long after the empire's fall. The means to this success included early attention to external propaganda directed towards their newly conquered subjects. For example, in 196 BC Flaminius cleverly dressed up the conquest of Greece as an act of liberation and thereafter the Romans allotted significant budgets for Greek poets and dramatists such as Melinno to produce pro-Roman literary propaganda in their own language.

The two most active and successful individual practitioners of propaganda in Roman history were Julius Caesar and his nephew Augustus. Whereas previous great leaders of the republic like Sulla and Pompey had built their careers on genuine military success without much need for propaganda, Caesar's early career had been fraught with scandal, near bankruptcy and a real lack of military achievement. He saw the need not just for a rapid military success but also for ensuring it achieved wide publicity, so as part of his plan for rescuing his career he secured a military command in Gaul. He then sought to pick fights with the various Gallic tribes, whom he could defeat with substantial bloodshed, and sent home for publication in serial form the story of his conquests. Ghosted by a semi-professional writer, Gaius Oppius, Caesar's *Gallic Wars* have been described by Michael Grant as 'the most potent propaganda ever written', building up his image as a successful general like the legendary Pompey.

Meanwhile, Caesar had arranged for his political accomplice, Clodius, back in Rome, to organize a campaign of terrorism and uncertainty which would make the episodes of the successful general in Gaul even more appealing to a population rendered insecure and uncertain. The combination of an unnecessary but apparently glorious war abroad with an unnecessary panic at home has become a standard formula for preparing a *coup d'état*. But Caesar was amplifying his image by other techniques as well. At an early point he began to issue coins to celebrate his own victories, and coins became a standard propaganda medium thereafter for the Roman Empire. As Grant put it 'they were the only social documents which the Romans could be sure that many people would see'. Caesar was also taking steps to increase the level of pomp and ceremony associated with holding public office, circulating rumours about his own possible descent from the goddess Venus, and subsidizing massive gladiatorial shows in the Roman amphitheatres. In addition he had taken special lessons in oratorical technique from a Greek teacher after which he seems to have developed successfully an emotion-charged style of addressing his troops. He had a high-pitched voice with an intense manner, and cultivated vigorous use of gestures such as tearing open his tunic. The drama of his crossing the Rubicon speech with its vivid use of metaphor – the dye is cast – is still evident, and in public relations terms he easily outshone the more conventional Pompey.

Between 49 and 46 BC as Caesar consolidated his power, the truly masterly touch of his public relations was evident. This was the period of his massive triumphal processions – four within a single month at one point – each celebrating a different victory in the civil war against Pompey and his followers, each with a different style of presentation. The event management involved in the organization of these spectacles with vast numbers taking part and vast numbers watching must have been very considerable. The triumphs were described in some detail by the historian Suetonius; on one occasion Caesar had eighty elephants in two columns dressed overall; for another he had huge decorated floats with scenes from his battles carried on wagons. After his annexation of Egypt his prisoner guest Cleopatra was used in one of the tableaux and unusual captives provided part of the spectacle. Even in Rome, which had seen a lot of triumphal processions, the cumulative effect of four such massive ones in such a short space of time must have been considerable, accompanied as they were by substantial largesse. As a climax to the celebrations Caesar crowned one of his floats with what must rank as one of the most verbally clever political catchphrases in any language, the alliterating and rhyming 'veni, vidi, vici' ['I came, I saw, I conquered'] which has the additional merit in Latin of being incisively short. Meanwhile, the image of Caesar's only rival Pompey the Great was deliberately undermined, with crowds organized to chant insults outside his house.

Caesar had a good understanding of the traditional symbols of Roman greatness: the laurel of victory, the eagles of the legions, and the fasces or rods of authority. He reused these symbols adding his own personal mythology as he prepared the way for himself to assume the powers of a monarch. He exposed the weakness of the existing republican regime by publishing first the daily proceedings, then the correspondence of the senate.

The third and final period of Caesar's propaganda campaign covers the last three years of his life, during which he leaned towards overdoing the weight of his image projection to the point where it probably contributed to his own murder. As Oscar Wilde put it, paraphrasing the Latin, 'those whom the gods wish to destroy they first make them believe their own advertising'. Caesar certainly seems to have become isolated by his own propaganda and less sensitive to public opinion. He was over-embellishing his image with titles, many of them with deep significance in Roman eyes: first 'Imperator', a title originally awarded only temporarily to victorious generals, but transformed by Caesar into a permanent accolade, since even he dared not use the unpopular title 'rex' or king. Our word emperor derives from this moment of changeover, just as the titles Kaiser and Tsar derive ultimately from the junction of Caesar's name with the title 'Imperator'. He also called himself 'Father of the Fatherland' (Pater Patriae), 'Dictator', 'Censor', 'Chief Priest' and in most years 'Consul', thus combining in himself all the most revered positions in the Roman republican hierarchy. Adopting many of the outward signs of kingship, he put his own statue among those of the old kings, he had a golden throne, he wore a special white fillet and obtained an outstanding horse perhaps to recreate the image of Alexander the Great and his Bucephalus. All this may well have been part of the build-up to the final adoption of the title king. He had a senator briefed to publicize a quotation from the ancient Sybilline prophecies which said that 'only a king can conquer the Parthians'. This linking of Caesar with ancient legends or using astrological tricks was a particularly interesting aspect of the way in which he summoned up the mythical past to legitimize the present, but it was also a symbol of his increasing megalomania.

Meanwhile, there had been increasing pamphlet activity in Rome. Especially interesting was the cover-up of Caesar's affair with Cleopatra, where his publicist Gaius Oppius was employed to produce a pamphlet proving that her son Caesarion had not been fathered by Caesar. Sallust (86–34 BC) was at the same time publishing history books which denigrated the old senatorial form of government and there were at least two poets writing on Caesar's side: Bibaculus and Terentius Varro.

On the opposite side clearly it was difficult to match Caesar's huge-scale event management, his bribery, indeed his complete propaganda machine. But the senatorial party did make some effort. Caecina produced pamphlets and there were a number of underground poets attacking the eastern potentate image created by Caesar's behaviour in Egypt. Catullus, a lyric poet of real stature, and a number of his lesser colleagues produced a variety of lampoons caricaturing Caesar's bald head and alleging homosexuality while he was serving in the east. Often these lampoons could be chanted by troops disaffected with his leadership and there is also evidence of the use of hand-painted slogans and cartoons on walls making sarcastic comments on his policies.

One of the remarkable features of Caesar's propaganda – and a tribute to its depth – was the fact that it survived his murder and made it difficult for his murderers to achieve popularity. His aide Mark Antony had acquired many of the same skills as Caesar in crowd control and exploited the spectacle of Caesar's funeral to the full. There were groups of professional mourners, a dramatic pyre, the divine shrine in purple and gold, the 20-foot high monument to the Father of the Fatherland, the well-publicized sighting of meteors, all helping to add a quality of mysticism to his martyrdom and confirming his larger than life image. It also shows how masterly had been Caesar's tying together of the attitude-forming symbols of the Roman Republic with his own image. He had made use of what he needed in the old regime – the army, the state religion – and exploited every available art form, every communications medium and every popular superstition or fear to create a coordinated programme for attitudinal change. This was what gave his military dictatorship, which was really not so different from several which had gone before it, the power to outlive his death. In his total grasp of available media – coins his only mass medium, spectacle, his favourite, literary media including history and poetry, architecture and sculpture – Caesar has perhaps only been equalled by Napoleon and Hitler. His grasp of meaningful symbols and the psychological needs of all except the ruling class which he was supplanting, was quite remarkable. Above all in common with other parvenu dictators he had the ability to create events as legend fodder. The *Gallic Wars* was not only a book which he wrote but a war he created for his own benefit as the basis for his heightened image, which he then exploited to the full.

Julius Caesar's adopted heir and nephew, Octavian (63 BC–AD 14), displayed a maturity and subtlety of mass manipulation perhaps less original than Caesar's but in many ways more effective. Even his later choice of the epithet Augustus as his formal name was part of a propaganda plan. His ability to influence public opinion, coming as it did immediately after his uncle's campaign, provided an example of a sustained effort to achieve long-term attitudinal change in the Roman Empire. He was to create a climate which not only accepted the idea of monarchical rule but also had a new wider pride in imperial objectives.

Octavian's early propaganda efforts were mainly opportunistic in the power struggle after Caesar's murder, first with the murderers and later with his rival for the succession, Mark Antony. He used coin images to establish links with his uncle in the public eye. He fully exploited the astrological susceptibilities of the Romans with the idea of a new golden age and of a saviour about to appear, a theme which was worked on in that remarkable poem by Virgil, the *Fourth Eclogue*. Ultimately the propaganda value of astrology became so great that most practitioners were expelled from Rome in 33 BC to let the government publicize its own prophecies unchallenged. For the time being all reminders of the myth of Caesar's divine descent from Venus were useful to Octavian Augustus.

The other important aspect of Octavian's publicity was the campaign to destroy the image of Mark Antony, exploiting the errors into which the latter's infatuation with Cleopatra had led him. There were rumours started about the capital being transferred to Egypt, oriental tortures and the corruption of Roman men by exotic Eastern ladies. Octavian by contrast emphasized adherence to the traditional Roman values and folk symbols, camouflaging his assertion of dictatorship with a façade of republican titles. He made himself 'Chief Priest', 'Father of the Fatherland', 'Son of the divine Julius', and finally 'Augustus', the somewhat vague adjective with semi-religious overtones and a hint of monarchy without the hated connotations of kingship.

Augustus, as he now became known, adopted a detailed programme of cosmetic myth-making. His statue was put up in every city and each had subtle hints of divine origin and royal status. His coinage associated him with a series of successful projects, above all he chose as his main promotional platform the creation of peace in the Roman Empire. One of his master strokes was the closing of the Temple of Janus, an act traditionally symbolizing the end of war. Peace was to remain an important part of his agenda. At the same time he created what was virtually a new religion, emperor worship; it was particularly useful in the more distant and less cynical provinces which needed a concrete focus for their loyalties. Temples to Rome and Augustus were erected throughout the empire and this provided a useful hierarchy for local image projection as well as a subject for a new imperial style of architecture which in turn contributed to the overall image. The new cult was thus an important factor in the spread and penetration of Caesarism.

Meanwhile, the campaign to discredit Mark Antony had reached its climax. In his narrative of this period the historian Ronald Syme lays particular emphasis on the role of propaganda in enabling Augustus to force a war on Antony so that he would no longer have to split the empire with him. As he puts it: 'Created belief turned the scale of history.' The build-up to the Battle of Actium was contrived by Augustus using a programme of consistent denigration of Mark Antony and his supposed acceptance of Cleopatra's whim to move the capital from Rome to Alexandria.

Once the struggle with Antony was won Augustus was able to turn his attention to longer-term attitudinal change, a sphere where he showed unique flair. He began to harness the artistic and literary skills of a highly creative group to project the ideals of the Roman Empire in a new way. He was assisted in this by the wealthy Maecenas as his propaganda organizer and talent scout. Four major poets were recruited – Virgil, Horace, Tibullus and Propertius – and all were asked to devise a state-sponsored epic on the theme of the ideal Roman hero with a divine mission to found the Roman Empire. Only Virgil (70–19 BC) accepted this particular challenge and produced the *Aeneid* which ranks as one of the world's great epic poems and a masterpiece of literary propaganda. Aeneas, an exiled defender of Troy, sent by Venus to found Rome, sacrificing all in the long struggle to fulfil his mission, summed up the new imperial message and its ethos with 'Parcere subjectis et debellare superbos' [To spare the conquered and defeat the haughty]. The Troy/Rome ancestry myth was even later recycled to boost the medieval monarchy in both England and Scotland.

Roman mythology was both given new life and linked symbolically with the new dynasty. All Roman history was seen as a progression towards the climax of Augustan rule. Though Virgil was such a perfectionist that it was said he wanted to burn the *Aeneid* on completion yet was dissuaded, it is most unlikely that his self-doubt had anything to do with the propaganda content of his work. It had already been evident both in the apocalyptic passages of the *Eclogues*, with the idea of the new golden age, and the themes of good agriculture and conservation in his *Georgics*.

The contribution of Horace (65–8 BC) to propaganda poetry was shorter and more lyrical with, for example, his brilliant encapsulation of the ethic of militant patriotism: 'Dulce et decorum est pro patria mori' [It is sweet and honourable to die for the fatherland]. The phrase has often subsequently been reused as a motto for war memorials throughout the world.

It is probable that the propaganda patronage of Maecenas also inspired the historian Livy. His *History of Rome* ranks as one of the great artistic works of history in any age, accurate so far as his sources allowed and containing an overall concept of progress and destiny leading up to the Augustan mission which paralleled the *Aeneid*.

While the literary output of this period was necessarily restricted to a small readership by the huge expense of copying, the penetration of some of the graphic arts was much more widespread. Coinage continued to be significant and the standard mission statement of Augustus, known as the *Monumentum Ancyranum*, was inscribed on tablets in many key cities of the empire. Buildings such as the Altar of Peace at Rome added a superb symbolic visualization of the achievements of the empire, while sculpture and architecture generally were major components of the overall imperial message.

The combined propaganda skills of Julius Caesar and Augustus provided a sound foundation in image terms for a further 400 years of empire and for a residual image of Caesarism which could still be recalled to life in the twentieth century by Mussolini.

WESTERN EUROPE

As with many primitive peoples the propaganda of the Celtic nations is difficult to elucidate, but certainly within its own social boundaries it was strong. Any people who could produce something like the Uffington White Horse, carved in chalk on a hillside by the Belgae in the first century AD, must have a strong sense of image projection. The Gundestrup Cauldron and its like, the symbolism of the Druids and their rituals, the visual impressiveness of the dolmens, the totem boars, triple mothers, bulls and horses were all part of a now ill-understood but clearly then very potent message system.

In general the classical period witnessed a huge development in the technicalities of artistic and literary communication but their deployment was marginally less focused than in the previous period.

14

Christian Era

PALESTINE

To some it may seem sacrilegious to describe Jesus Christ (*c.* 4 BC–AD 30) as an exceptionally able propagandist. Others may dispute the claim on the grounds that major results were not achieved until after his death. The fact remains, however, that Christ by an extraordinary communications *tour de force* did achieve what was probably the single most effective example of image projection in human history. It was the more remarkable in that his access to media was virtually non-existent, yet by brilliant linking of many of those themes and symbols which can be most potent in reaching a human audience he turned his lack of media control into only a minor handicap.

It is clear from reading St Paul, the Acts of the Apostles and Eusebius's *History of the Church* that Christ's supreme act of sacrifice and similar acts of martyrdom by many of his followers were a significant factor in helping bring about the conversion of many adherents, although crucifixion was by no means unusual. The importance of this is evident in particular when we assess the competing effect of several other sects, especially Mithraism which in other respects stood almost as good a chance as Christianity at that time of achieving multinational recognition. There are, however, a number of other features of the spread of Christianity both before and after the crucifixion which contributed to its successful propagation.

Christ's message was aimed, to some extent, at the disadvantaged Jewish sub-group in Galilee but its attitudes happened to mirror those of the much larger similar sub-groups of slaves and near-slaves throughout the Roman Empire. As Professor Barclay pointed out there were 60 million slaves at that time in the Roman Empire and many other displaced minorities at a level only slightly above them. This provided a very substantial initial audience of spiritually disoriented people potentially receptive to an appropriate message.

Christ also had the benefit of a very useful propaganda infrastructure in the Judaistic system. Amateur preaching at synagogues was normal, so they were a promotional medium open to any parallel new sect. The habit of open-air preaching with demonstrations or visual gimmickry was also accepted. Isaiah had worn a yoke, Ezekiel broke models, Ahja tore his robe in twelve pieces. In addition there had been a widespread habit of apocalyptic prophecy, warnings of future Messiahs, astrological portents and dramatic events like Herod's slaughter of the innocents which Christ was able to adopt as part of his own build-up. Prophets were expected to speak with words direct from God and it was not unusual for them to have the rhythmic quality and assonance which could create crowd hysteria. Luke, probably exaggerating, in the Acts of the Apostles tells of the mass conversion of 3,000 people in one meeting. John the Baptist clearly had this same ability as did the evangelists of Mithraism, the new magi. Preachers of this period, including Christ, used the technique of extracting a member of the audience and asking him or her to make public confession, now an accepted means of assisting crowd control. Christ and the apostles also made very effective use of their ability to achieve public successes in faith healing, which became a major part of the publicizing of their mission.

Christ, at least as recorded in the Gospels, also demonstrated outstanding ability in terms of structuring his message. His superb use of metaphor – 'the house built on sand', 'the camel through the eye of the needle', 'the seeds on stony ground' and so on – gave huge power to his preaching. This was extended by his masterly use of parable like the story of 'the prodigal son' and his sense of the dramatic as with the scene in the temple. All this was given further credibility by his ability to quote Old Testament precedent, his use of readings in the tradition of the rabbis and his general development of existing scriptural themes.

Another important plank in the propaganda structure came from Christ's appreciation of the need for an organized mission. He selected the first twelve apostles with a further seventy who were primed to go out in pairs after the crucifixion. The preaching ability of these men like Timothy who went to Ephesus and Titus in Crete, to say nothing of the outstandingly energetic Paul, rapidly covered a wide geographical area and achieved remarkably high rates of conversion. Even if the traditional religions of Greece and Rome were much too weak to put up serious opposition, Christianity still had to compete with the almost equally energetic magi. Like Paul many of the missionaries kept some control over converted towns after they moved on by keeping in touch via regular correspondence. The sect began to produce its own new more elaborate legend system. The Gospels, with their fully developed biographical structure from virgin birth to resurrection, fitted in with the help of time the prophetic format laid down by the Old Testament and by the experience of numerous other ancient cultures. The massacre of the innocents, for example, was a legend of babies born to be kings who were all but murdered by the present incumbent, a legend which had been part of the image projection of Moses and several other heroes and gods – Apollo, Cyrus the Great of Persia, Romulus the founder of Rome and Augustus founder of the Roman imperial line. The new religion continued to produce new generations of highly effective missionaries like Ignatius, Quadratus or the brilliant Origen, many of whom enhanced their own credibility by fierce levels of asceticism, sometimes eventually martyrdom or severe self-mortification.

A further contribution from Christ himself was his sense of liturgy and event management. It is possible that he foresaw the re-enactment of the Last Supper as a significant part of the development of his followers' mission, while many of his other acts provided models for subsequent rituals. The events in his life and death provided Christianity with a calendar of participatory anniversaries which became of huge value in ongoing propaganda. The crucifixion was the climactic metaphor which underlined the credibility of every other aspect of his mission.

These techniques of evangelism achieved remarkable results for Christianity in its first half-century or so as a largely underground movement, see Acts 19. But by that time defeat had effectively been conceded in the religion's own country of origin. The Jews, already well accustomed to a monotheistic religion and well used to a number of derivative apocalyptic sects, found nothing in Christianity to retain their interest and were diverted into a destructive political confrontation with the Romans. The Christians now began to adopt new media techniques as they set about winning over the entire Roman Empire from below. Matthew, Mark and Luke gave literary form to the mythological versions of Christ's life, now with all the trimmings of symbolic hagiography: the virgin birth, the star of Bethlehem, the Magi and numerous other embellishments which helped both to project Christianity to a mass audience and legitimized it in the prophetic tradition of the Old Testament. In a world where belief in supernatural powers was quite commonplace, it was essential to credit apostles, as well as Jesus himself, with plenty of miraculous acts: healings, visions, purveying divine wrath, prophecies and triumphs over the natural order. The use of Paul's Letters and later the Gospels provided a literary tradition which was soon amplified by substantial numbers of popular tracts like *The Shepherd of Hermas*, *The Sayings of the Lord Explained by Papias*, short pamphlets like *The Rich Man who finds Salvation* or the new genre of martyrologies full of sadism, like Eusebius's *Collection of Martyrs*. A popular technique of the early Christian apologists was to write 'open letters' to the emperor or other prominent people, which added an element of challenge to otherwise apparently querulous tracts. Miltiades of Phrygia (fl. 170–90) was an example.

Even before printing it is clear that Christianity got its copying very well organized and that circulation of books was quite widespread. In this respect it took advantage of the experience which the Jews had acquired in spreading their religion in the Greek-speaking world over the previous three centuries. It also took advantage of the new technological improvement of the codex or primitive book which was much easier to use than the traditional scrolls. In the third century AD the apocalyptic style of writing very much revived in popularity, presenting the message in the form of dreams, visions or voices, a style also used by Mohammed for the Koran, pushing the idea of doom and destiny. As St Augustine (354–430) – in his early career he had a stint as panegyric writer for the

Frankish general Bauto – put it, 'there is no conversion without fear'. Often such works were given spurious credibility by being attributed to long-dead authors who were thus shown to be prophesying events after their own deaths with uncanny accuracy.

In addition, from an early stage Christianity was strong on fund-raising, emphasizing the widow's mite and tapping the guilt-ridden middle classes. This in effect enabled it to finance very large numbers of professional convertors, many of whom made use of impressive faith-healing skills, prophetic preaching, well-timed forecasts of natural disasters and above all displays of exorcism to achieve dramatic increases in their followings. The level of emotive preaching using these techniques led to 'speaking in tongues', as described by Paul, and to audiences being 'possessed', a state akin to mass hypnosis, and shamed into submerging their rational faculties. A classic example of this kind of preacher was Gregory the Miracle-worker from the Black Sea coast; when this style lost its novelty the next fashion was for extreme asceticism.

Christianity was slower to make use of the visual arts. The fish symbol and the chi-rho ☧ graphic were relatively early, followed in due course by the symbol of the cross which came to real prominence after the vision of Constantine. Little is known of the early use of sculpture but certainly there were monuments to Peter and Paul in Rome which have long since been lost and the use of multicoloured mosaic for religious pictures was adopted from the Romans. By the year 200 paintings of biblical scenes were being used as in the catacomb of St Calixtus in Rome. Church architecture, however, evolved fairly rapidly and Eusebius gives a fine description of the magnificent cathedral at Tyre with an indication of its promotional objectives clearly understood.

Music also came to some prominence in this secondary stage of Christian proselytization. From the first century AD onwards there is mention of new hymns and psalms as the Christians adapted to the idioms of the western Mediterranean. With the development of event management, the mass, Easter and other celebrations, Christianity had now the full range of media techniques.

There is no doubt that a number of early martyrs were conscious of the publicity value of their sufferings: as Tertullian put it 'the blood of martyrs is the seed of the church'. At an early stage the sites of particular martyrdoms were developed into key pilgrimage venues, as, for example, the Vatican hill itself and Tours. Above all as the Roman Empire remained politically oppressive and with an increasing divergence between extremes of wealth and poverty, the fundamental message of Christianity –'Blessed are the humble and meek for they shall inherit the earth'– remained attractive to increasing numbers. The Christians soon began to take advantage of the more sophisticated forms of media. Commodian was probably the first Christian poet. Cyprian (200–58) was an able propagandist writer, Ambrose the first major hymn writer (339–97). The Emperor Constantine himself was an able propagandist with his own useful vision of St Andrew's Cross before Mulvian Bridge and had able support from writers like Lampridius. When Constantine eventually decided to give Christianity his official protection, thus ending a long period of persecution, the Christians were still very much a minority in the empire, even in its eastern half, but they were a very significant and vociferous minority with a well-articulated and coherent policy of image projection.

ROME

By comparison the Roman emperors between Augustus and Constantine showed only minor innovations in propaganda techniques during the Christian period. Certainly in many reigns the image projection remained strong. Expenditure on sculpture, architecture and to a lesser extent literature remained considerable and the overall projection of the Caesars was strong enough to survive the eccentricities of some of the more unbalanced emperors. One of the ongoing techniques was the establishment of cults to worship each recently dead emperor as a god. There were some individually remarkable pieces of propaganda, including the Arch of Titus with its record of the defeat of the Jews, and Trajan's Column with its amazing spiral sculptured narrative of the campaign against the Dacians (see pl. 3). With each generation the image of Caesar became more and more elaborate. Severus probably introduced the regular wearing of purple as a symbol of power, then came the long sceptre as a sign of divinity, the orb with Caracalla, the diadem with Gallienus. The official throne, torch-bearers and cheerleaders accentuated the imperial dignity which reached perhaps the ultimate heights when Diocletian gave himself the names Jovius or Jove, introduced the halo in royal pictures and proskynesis or ritual prostration as a strict part of court etiquette. Alongside all this was a range of panegyric literature projecting the imperial image and his alliterative slogan of 'renovatio, reparatio' was well promoted to create confidence in his economic strategy.

Constantine (274–337) maintained the same theme, concentrating mainly on his role as a successful general, but he also added the Christian dimension. Firstly, he projected himself as 'Victor' on coins and buildings, then grafted on gradually the new Christian symbolism, much of which, like the *labarum* would also be interpreted in pagan terms. The abbreviated slogan IC XC NIKA – conquer in Jesus Christ – was carved on numerous monuments, on house doors and even used on bread stamps. He created a substantially built infrastructure for Christianity with the emphasis on 'martyria', halls to welcome large crowds of pilgrims visiting the relics of martyrs, and it was his mother Helena who essentially invented the fashion of pilgrimage, particularly to Jerusalem, so that this became a new facet of Christian propaganda. The manufacture of pilgrim

tokens and medallions supported this effort which was soon also
extended into the collection and cult of relics, a further technique for
mass manipulation and fund-raising. His lasting propaganda coup was
without question the publicity generated for his 'dreams', most especially
his vision of the cross at Mulvian Bridge. True or false this had the
capacity to grab the imagination for several generations, just as it did
when recycled in Scotland a few centuries later.

The ultimate public relations novelties for this period were the pillar
saints like Simeon Stylites (387–459) whose extreme asceticism attracted
huge attention to his preaching perch near Antioch. Outrageous acts of
self-torture were to be a key propaganda technique in many parts of the
world during the Middle Ages.

The last great propagandist of the Roman Empire was the poet
Claudian (fl. 395–408) who wrote on behalf of General Stilicho
(365–408) and the Emperor Honorius in the last few years before Rome
fell to Alaric the Goth. The Roman imperial propaganda machine kept
going even while the empire was attacked from all sides. Themistus
(prefect of Constantinople c. 384) for example, was an able propagandist
for the emperors Constantius II and Theodosius I. The remarkable
feature of this period was the way in which the image of the Roman
Empire survived the reality and was to be borrowed by new institutions,
both church and state, for a further 1,400 years.

INDIA

One other part of the world showed spectacular propaganda dynamism at
this time: India. In political terms the Gupta dynasty was not particularly
novel in its approach to propaganda, but it did revive many of the
techniques of Ashoka. Indeed Samudra Gupta who became king in
AD 335 actually reused Ashoka's stone pillars for his own eulogistic
inscriptions. The Gupta kings were all keen patrons of the arts,
encouraging poets, musicians, theatre and the visual arts, often to the
benefit of their dynasty. Even when the arts were not directly
propagandist they were expected to help emotional balance not merely
entertain. The popular play *Devi-Chandra-Guptam* was an example of the
use of theatre to develop dynastic heroes; poets like Kalidasa with his
Shakuntala graced the Gupta court, and as usual in empires of this period
coinage was taken seriously as a propaganda medium.

However, the Gupta period was even more remarkable for the energy
of its religious propaganda, with all three of India's mainstream religions
adopting a proactive approach. This was most physically obvious in the
remarkable development of sculpture as a propaganda medium. The
influence of Greek sculpture brought east during the conquests of
Alexander the Great had clearly been highly inspirational, particularly on
the Gandhara school of sculptors who developed images of Buddha, by

this period more a god than a prophet. The visual image of the carved, contented and relaxed Buddha became one of the most powerfully consistent examples of the use of sculpture as a propaganda medium in world history. Not all that different was the Mathura school which concentrated on statues of Mahavira and the Jain saints. In both cases a contented face and often massive size were features of the work, which was patronized by the Kushana kings and many wealthy merchants. The Buddhists were also substantial users of narrative sculpture including, for example, the second-century *Dream of Maya*, the sculptural record of Buddha defeating his rival Devadatta. Hinduism, not to be outdone, also evolved a new style of sculpture, with Vishnu being the most popular god in terms of visual imagery, and the use of the multiple-arm concept to concentrate a number of different symbolic messages in a single statue, an idea adopted from temple dance movements.

In literary terms this was also an active period for the three religions. The Hindu *Puranas* date from this period with their interpretation of history by the Hindu hierarchy of the Brahmins, and their rules for ritual event management. The Buddhists were also very active in the production of texts, many of which were shipped out to China and other neighbouring countries as missionaries pursued an energetic policy of conversion. In fact Buddhism became the state religion of China in 379. This despite the fact that the Chinese, making the first clumsy efforts at printing, had taken ink rubbings of the stone-carved classics of Confucius from around AD 200.

The travelling Buddhist monks of China were achieving remarkable results with a highly emotive technique of preaching full of moral anecdotes. Huei Yan in the fourth century AD caused tears and trembling among his large audiences when he spoke of the punishment of sin in the afterlife, inducing large crowds to repent and convert to Buddhism.

Already there were signs that Buddhism was becoming more isolated in its home nation by sectarian argument, by the building of elaborate, protective monasteries, and by excessive use of a dying language, Sanskrit. Nevertheless this was a period of remarkable expansion and outstanding propaganda success. In addition Buddhism had the resources to spread its own architectural style, the round stupa or later pagoda, which significantly contributed to its visual awareness throughout the state.

Dark Ages

Despite its reputation, the so-called Dark Age was a period of considerable propaganda innovation. There were a number of significant developments worthy of consideration, particularly in the Far East.

WESTERN EUROPE

The main propaganda technique of Attila the Hun (406–53) was without doubt intimidation, but even he organized the embellishment of his own legend long before his death. For example, it was put about that his special powers derived from an old magic sword which only he had been able to pluck from a rock, the theme soon afterwards adopted for King Arthur.

Theodoric the Great (455–526) the Ostrogoth conqueror was more sophisticated and showed a remarkable capacity to pick up the strands of image projection left behind by his Roman predecessors. He used a major building programme in Ravenna and other cities to extend his reputation, encouraged propaganda mosaics and had his chief minister Cassiodorus write a *History of the Goths* which was designed to boost the image of his race and dynasty. The Archbishop Agnellus also wrote pamphlets on his behalf and overall Theodoric's desire to incorporate Roman features in his propaganda was to be a tactic imitated by new north European dynasties for many centuries to come.

Meanwhile, further west Archbishop Isidore of Seville promoted the image of the Visigoths in Spain and their right to enslave the eternal city since they were descended from Japheth and Noah.

BYZANTINE EMPIRE

The virgin princess Pulcheria, sister of Theodosius II, played a major part in fostering the mass production of icons in the Byzantine Empire, adopting many artistic conventions from the paganism, such as the halo and royal garments as indications of divine rank and using a portrait of Mary supposedly created by the apostle Luke as the starting point for the visual cult of the Virgin. The Emperor Justinian (482–565) added little in terms of technique to the propaganda armoury of the old Roman Empire, but he was very conscious of its value and did allocate considerable resource to developing the image of the new Byzantine

SCULPTURES AS PROPAGANDA

Pl. 1 A ninth-century BC Assyrian relief sculpture showing King Ashurnasirpal thanking the gods for his victories, proof that they were on his side. (Mary Evans Picture Library)

Pl. 2 The propaganda effect of demolishing statues is as useful as that of putting them up. George III is symbolically toppled in New York, 1776. (Mary Evans Picture Library)

Pl. 3 Trajan's Column in Rome, a gigantic stone advertisement for the Emperor's victories in Dacia.(Ancient Art & Architecture Collection)

Pl. 4   Playing cards putting across French Revolutionary slogans. (Mary Evans Picture Library)

Pl. 5   A cigarette pack promoting US presidential candidate Michael Dukakis's election campaign, 1988. (Mary Evans Picture Library)

Pl. 6   Russian Communist propaganda cart with gramophone, Urals, 1917. (Mary Evans Picture Library)

Pl. 7   Conquered Ethiopians watch an Italian propaganda film, 1937. (Mary Evans Picture Library)

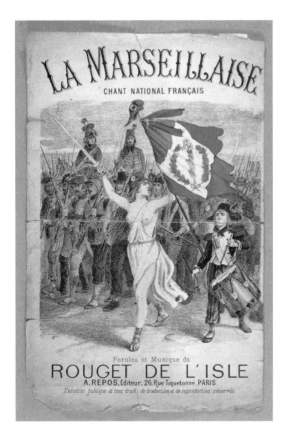

Pl. 8 The cover of sheet music for the 'Marseillaise' showing Marianne leading the French people, 1792. (Mary Evans Picture Library)

Pl. 9 La Muette de Portici, *the opera which partly precipitated the Belgian revolution of 1830. (Mary Evans Picture Library)*

Pl. 10   Section from the Bayeux Tapestry of 1082 showing King Harold's oath of allegiance to Duke William, the justification for the Norman conquest of 1066. (The Bayeux Tapestry – 11th Century. By special permission of the City of Bayeux)

Pl. 11   Benjamin Franklin's broken snake image and slogan symbolizing the eight disunited colonies, from the Pennsylvania Gazette, 1754.

Pl. 12   Pope Urban II preaching the First Crusade, a classic of event management, at Clermont, France, 1095. (Mary Evans Picture Library)

Pl. 13   Emperor Napoleon presents the eagles to his troops, engraving by Seberg & Oertel after and original by 'David', 1804. (Mary Evans Picture Library)

Pl. 14   Martin Luther nails the Ninety-Five Theses to the church door at Wittenberg, 1517. (Mary Evans Picture Library)

Pl. 15   *Typical Communist armaments parade in Tiananmen Square, Beijing.*

Pl. 16   *Suffragette procession, London, 17 June 1911. (Mary Evans Picture Library)*

Empire using the propaganda tools already established. He encouraged the cult of his predecessor Constantine as 'the equal of the apostles' and adopted his motto 'in this conquer' to give authority to the wars he waged in his attempt to reunite the Roman Empire from the new Eastern capital. He hired John Lydus to write panegyrics on his rule and a favourable history of the war. Even Procopius (499–565) wrote his initial history of the reign as a partisan piece until his bitterness against the Empress began to sour his work. The epic poem *Johannid* was intended to provide the Byzantine Empire with a national epic poem, immortalizing its heroic struggle against invaders as Virgil's *Aeneid* did for Rome. There can be little doubt that Justinian's encouragement of the vast work of codifying Roman Law was partially a propaganda exercise, particularly in so far as it projected the image of Roman justice. However, the propaganda medium which most appealed to Justinian's sense of the future was without question architecture. The Sancta Sophia designed by his architects Anthemius and Isidore was appropriate both to an imperial capital and the headquarters of a religion, the size of its dome alone underlining the image projection intentions. From the churches of Ravenna with their brilliant mosaic pictures of the Emperor to the buildings in the numerous other cities of the empire in Africa, Asia and Europe, Justinian devoted vast funds to construction projects which emphasized the power and stability of his reign, plus its links with Christianity. His style of architecture, mosaic decoration and use of sculpture, the first cruciform churches – explained in some detail by Procopius, who recorded all his building activity – dovetailed well with the imperial idea of ceremonial. Complex techniques of event management became a characteristic of the Byzantine Empire, emphasizing its mystic strength with elaborate coronation rituals, hymns, genuflexions and blessings. The contribution of Justinian to the establishment of the long-term Byzantine image was very considerable. The concept of 'one god, one Empire, one Church' became part of the imperial ideology. An extra means of adding credibility to this idea was the development of the icon as more than just a painting, letting it become a source of miracles in its own right, the focus of loyalty to local saints and annual events, eventually reflecting their credibility back on the divinely ruling emperors. The linking of icons of emperors with those of saints, the enhancement of both by candle displays and rituals, endorsed the quasi-divine status of the emperors. The extensive use of very expensive raw materials like porphyry for statues and gold for the background of icons created a special aura.

The other great development of Byzantine propaganda was the huge new industry of hagiography. The contrivance of cults for numerous ascetic saints became a standard technique for boosting the power and wealth of monasteries, shrines, cities and even rulers. Exaggerated accounts of their miracles and austerities were backed up by icons and processions generated in a variety of fund-raising drives which made possible major building programmes, in turn often the foundation for new power bases of church or state. Typical was the development of the image of St Theodore of Sykeon (*c.* 540–620) an ascetic who usefully foretold that Maurice would eventually become emperor and had his biography circulated by Georgios. Similarly St Demetrios of Thessaloniki was promoted as a valuable regional focus for loyalty.

A remarkable phase of propaganda was the surge of iconoclasm in Byzantium from AD 726. This technique of turning the destruction of artistic propaganda material into an act of counter-propaganda is similar to the idol-smashing of Moses or the British Puritans, more recently the widespread destruction of Communist statues during 1990/1. It was inaugurated by Leo III (680–741), a self-made emperor. Having repelled a heavy attack from the Saracens, he was concerned at the way Byzantine Christianity was open to the charge of idolatry by the Muslims, so he instigated a wave of revulsion against religious art. This was accompanied by a campaign of deliberate humiliation of monks and nuns, and the smear campaign against Stephen, Abbot of Auxentius. The chief propagandist on the difficult pro-icon stance was John of Damascus.

Other insecure imperial claimants used different ideas. The Empress Irene in 780 conveniently managed to discover a long-lost ancient prophecy stone which forecast the virgin birth and its own uncovering in the year 780. Similarly the Armenian claimant John I Tzim-iskes in 969 happily unearthed a stone in a garden which foretold his own elevation to the purple and he then made a triumphal entry to Constantinople with a horse-drawn icon of the Virgin.

The imagery of proskynesis, of birth to the purple, of association with saints, was all carefully exploited. Even the end of iconoclasm became a propaganda event from 894, when an extravagant annual feast, the Triumph of Orthodoxy, was inaugurated to celebrate the restoration of icons as a key component of Byzantine propaganda. By this time the criteria established for the sanctity of an icon were whether it reduced the onlooker to tears.

ARABIA

As a propagandist Mohammed (570–632) shared a number of char-acteristics with founders of the other great religions. And as with the others it is not easy to account for the propaganda success which led to the early spread of Islam. Nevertheless there are a few clear pointers. Firstly, Mohammed did, to some extent like Christ, target a specific audience; this group was largely young, poor and belonged to the Bedouin, nomadic communities with their tradition of military raiding, as opposed to the wealthy merchants of the caravan routes. What is more these peoples had an ascetic trait to be worked on and a level of literacy which allowed an essentially verbal appeal. Neither music nor the visual arts played any part until much later, but there was already an established tradition among these people of poetry writing with professional reciters to ensure a wide audience. The popular format was the qasida, a poem of 100 lines, all with the same rhyme.

Secondly, there was the strong clear message, both negative and positive. On the negative side there was the very realistic use of hell-fire images leading audiences to feel faint and shocked at the prospect of punishment. The attacks on infanticide, alcohol, usury and Jews were very specific. On the positive side there was the promise of instant access to paradise for all those who died in the holy war, the Jehad; there was a hint of democracy, as well as the acceptance of male-dominated marriage, and a very straightforward explanation of life and the universe which made for easy assimilation.

Mohammed had, like some of the ecstatic prophets or Kahin of his era, the personal charisma of a genuine visionary, emerging from trances with sweat showing on his brow, which helped reinforce the claim that his pronouncements came straight from Allah, that all his views were carved on tablets of stone in heaven. The first word which he said the angel had spoken to him was iqra – recite. He also took advantage of a number of mnemonic techniques. There was the use of rhyming phrases, constant recitation and repetition of particular ideas, like 'Allah, compassionate and merciful' and the effective acting out of visions. Islam had several mnemonic numbers: the five pillars of wisdom, five prayers, four prostrations, ninety-nine names of god. The rapid compilation of the Koran and the organization both to recite it by heart and to produce numerous manuscript copies was exceedingly important, and it was backed by the concept of silsila, the direct transmission of ideas through a chain of witnesses which started with the prophet himself. It is also significant that the copying of manuscripts extended into the development of decorative calligraphy incorporating texts from the Koran which became the main visual art form of Islam. It helped that the Koran was composed in Arabic; the book helped the spread of the language and the increased importance of the language helped the book, whereas the Bible stagnated for many centuries in a dead language which was not even its original. In the same way, because of the rejection of music as a vehicle for Islam, chanted, semi-musical recitation did play an important part. An understanding of the value of ritual and event management was also a key factor from early on. The four prostrations, the duties of ablutions and almsgiving, the facing of Mecca and the oath of loyalty were its foundation.

The concept of the muezzins like human alarm clocks summoning worshippers from the tops of their minarets, the yearly communal act of asceticism, Ramadan – comparable to Lent or the Passover – plus the idea of the once-in-a-lifetime pilgrimage to Mecca, the Haj, all at an early stage provided Islam with a repetitive life pattern, a substantial repertoire of stimulus and response which created a powerful message system making up for the absence of visual symbols and idols.

Despite the fact that initial recruitment to Islam was quite slow, with perhaps only about a thousand adherents by the time of the prophet's death, its roots had by that time gone deep and its imagery was set. The adaptation of the Bedouin war raid to the requirements of Islam, and war's adoption as an additional 'pillar' of wisdom was significant but even in warfare propaganda played a part, for instance the very biased reporting of the defeat at Mota by Ibn Ishaq. The creation of superb military self-confidence backed up by the promise of paradise for dead soldiers was as much a feat of propaganda as of military skill. In addition Mohammed from the beginning knew how to exploit control over water supplies on the trade routes of a dry country and how to manage proper fund-raising (the third pillar) to support his sect.

Since language was such a key part of Mohammedan propaganda, the quality of expression, particularly the use of poetry was paramount. The poetic qualities of the Koran were very considerable and the role of poets was seen as crucial. Both Asma bint Merwan and Abu Afek, the two major anti-Islamic poets were killed while Hassan ibn Thabit was projected vigorously as the leading Islamic poet. Popular biographies of the Prophet were produced by writers such as Mohammed Ibn Ishaq (d. 767) and Mohammed Ibn Sa'd (d. 845). When Islam acquired greater wealth some aspects of its propaganda became more sophisticated. Architecture took on a role as providing a visual image for the faith which had previously been lacking and tied in with the developing art of decorative calligraphy to provide mosques which were massive propaganda documents. The Dome of the Rock was built from 690 onwards and from 690 the official coinage carried a message from the Koran. Various ancillary items such as prayer rugs became unique Muslim media.

The Umayyad dynasty, based in Damascus for nearly a century from 661–750, began this development and asserted universal authority over the whole Muslim world with propaganda written by Abi Sufyan. Then the Abbasids, a substitute dynasty, developed a propaganda campaign similar in many respects to that of the papacy in the same period, basing a claim for temporal power on a hereditary connection with the Prophet. Based first in Kufa in Iraq, later in Khurasan, they masterminded a propaganda effort to depose the Umayyads, promoting tirelessly the message that only a descendant from Mohammed's family, in this case his uncle Abbas, could be a religiously acceptable ruler of the new and expanding Arab empire. In charge was Abu Salama and among the better known evangelists was Khidash who ran a campaign from 727 to 738. A network of travelling traders was used as cover for the operation, known as da'wa – one of the world's earliest words meaning propaganda; the propagandists were du'ats. The campaign culminated in the mass unfurling of black banners at the end of Ramadan in 747 which triggered the emergence of the new, imam-blessed dynasty and contrasted with the white corporate colour of the Umayyads. The very title Khalif was projected as religiously sanctified unlike the less popular title of king or malik. Poets like Khatib al Baghdadi (1002–71) produced short biographies of Islamic heroes and Al Mutanabbi (915–68) did panegyrics for the court of Aleppo.

In addition to such political objectives there also emerged new religious ones as rival sects sought to establish new images. The most important and strongest in propaganda terms were the Shi'ites, supporters of the other branch of Mohammed's family, the descendants of his son-in-law Ali and from 680 they built up the legend of the martyrdom of Husayn and a distinctive image for the power of the imams. As in the medieval West it was not unusual to forge documents proving some apocryphal relationship with the prophet. The Shi'a sect demonstrated the persistent use of a number of propaganda techniques somewhat different from those of orthodox or Sunni Islam. In particular there was the cult of the twelve imams, especially Husayn; his martyrdom was recited to groups in a highly emotive way by rawda khans or narrators, the audiences often weeping or beating their chests. The processions for the anniversary of his death were accompanied by rhythmic beating of chests, chants and self-flagellation, mosques draped in black. Banners depicted his life, paintings of his last battle adorned the entrance to Husayniyya and by his shrine at Karbala began to be performed the Islamic version of the Passion play, the ta'ziya or Tazies which played on Shi'ite hatred for Sunnis and was to be revived by Ayatollah Khomeini in the twentieth century. Overall Shi'ite propaganda demonstrated the power of a highly emotive atmosphere, obsession with martyrdom or flagellant masochism in response, and with the Messianic concept of the Mahdi's return.

The monastic arm of Islam, the Sufi, had a range of effective techniques centred on poetry, like the rubais of Sheikh Saadi. Their favourite symbol was light. The mystic rhyming poetry of al Hallaj (d. 922) was particularly popular and Jalal al Din Rumi (d. 1273), founder of the Mevlevi or whirling dervishes whose fame made them a major force in the Ottoman Empire, wrote the very effective Mathnawi or rhyming couplets. Yet another variant of Islamic propaganda technique was evident in North Africa where the Ismaili branch of the Shi'ites projected a popular message, suggesting as Rousseau did a thousand years later, that laws and conventions were man-made tools of exploitation. It was the use of this theme which helped the Fatimids win control of Egypt in 969, focusing on the millennial return of the Mahdi.

ROME

The propaganda coup which created the power of the papacy was not the work of any one man, but it was a remarkable example of a succession of propagandists working over several centuries with remarkable consistency of purpose. The papacy as an institution had all the hallmarks of a creation of propaganda: it achieved enormous power without the use of military force, or even initially vast wealth or political influence. It was given a useful propaganda basis by the translation of the Bible into Latin by St Jerome, 'the Vulgate'. This contained a large number of political nuances not in the original and achieved vast influence among educated classes in early Europe: in particular the passage from St Matthew about Peter, the rock of the church, receiving the keys of the kingdom of heaven, became ever more frequently quoted. Early in the fifth century this idea was extended by the publication of *The Letter of St Clement*, a kind of pseudo-will of St Peter, translated by the publicist Rufinus of Aquileia (345–410), who also translated Eusebius's biased *History of the Christian Church* into Latin. These various strands were pulled together if not actually masterminded by the first of three great propagandizing Popes, Leo I (390–461). He made his name standing up to Attila the Hun and Gaiseric the Vandal. Then, as Walter Ullman has shown, he coordinated all the real or manufactured evidence, historical and scriptural, for the idea that St Peter had intended the Bishop of Rome to be the unchallenged leader of the universal church, or as Leo more cleverly put it: 'the unworthy heir of St Peter'.

The powers of the Pope as defined were exceptional, because each one succeeded not his own immediate predecessor but St Peter himself directly. Thus he had what was called 'plenitude of power' with both a kind of divine authority and a form of imperial role modelled on the Roman emperors. Leo not only revived the metaphor of the keys of heaven which were to become the papacy's visual corporate identity, but developed others like the portrayal of St Peter as the source of a river from which all other rivers flowed or branched out. It is clear that from as early as the fourth century the visual depiction of St Peter was encouraged in Rome, long before there was any tendency to produce pictures of Christ himself. The image of the founder of the papacy was deliberately accentuated as, for example, when he was depicted striking a rock to bring forth a fountain, a miracle borrowed from Moses. He was frequently shown as the 'good shepherd' with a lamb on his shoulders, also being crucified, carrying the cross and 'enthroned in Majesty'. Many mosaics, medallions and sarcophagus reliefs were produced projecting his image in this way. Further highly influential tracts were produced by the propagandist known as Denys the Areopagite, who developed the image of the Pope as an exceptional church ruler above the law and above criticism.

The second of the three great propagandizing Popes was Gelasius I (fl. 492–6), himself a prolific writer of tracts who continued to assert the superiority and sovereignty of the Popes, including their superiority to temporal rulers. This concept of the papacy being above kings and emperors was the second stage of the extraordinary propaganda coup achieved by these early Popes. Two further propaganda publications of enormous influence contributed to the development of this image: first the popularly written and widely read *Legenda sancti Silvestri*, a highly effective piece of what was essentially make-believe, and model for the equally spurious but also highly influential Donation of Constantine probably forged in the late eighth century. According to this the Emperor Constantine had wanted to 'give the Roman Church imperial power and dignity of glory, vigour and honour'. So the Pope had been notionally given all the corporate symbols of empire: lance, sceptre, orb, imperial standards, purple mantle, and so on. In the tract the Emperor was depicted as leading the Pope's horse, symbolizing their relative positions. Thus with a succession of manipulated texts and clever reconstructions of history, the fifth-century Popes created the image of an extraordinary power base which many of their successors were to treat as a reality.

Gregory I (540–609), the third of the early group of propagandizing Popes, built on the work of his two predecessors to spread the image of the papacy to a very much wider area. Like his predecessors Gregory had the authority of great personal sanctity and asceticism, the essential credentials for propaganda effectiveness for the fathers of the church. His particular strength lay in his ability to communicate with and organize his vast international network of bishoprics, and bring them as much as possible into alignment both with orthodox Catholicism and with the new theme of papal sovereignty. He was a great organizer of missionary work, and perceived the need of the papal church to widen its attitude towards the use of new media. He wrote 'paintings can do for the illiterate what writing can do for those who read', and this was the beginning of a period of long and successful patronage of the visual arts by the Catholic Church, begun just about the time when the Byzantine Church was abandoning visual icons under the taint of graven images. There was a revival in the use of story-telling miniatures as, for instance, in the Utrecht Psalter of 833 in which there were 166 illustrations of the psalms, including many horrific images of hell. Another medium given encouragement by Gregory was the use of music; this was not a new idea, but was now given a substantially more significant role in church image projection.

Gregory's other remarkable achievement was the propaganda campaign which he himself conducted to promote the new order of St Benedict (486–547). He wrote a biography of the saint embellishing it with numerous miracles, like the story of him rolling naked in thorns to banish temptation and the thorns turned to roses. The Benedictine Order was encouraged to spread, to help provide Gregory with a strong international administrative network for the expanding papacy. The monastic movement generally was promoted by a number of talented hagiographers such as Gregory of Tours (538–93) who produced his influential *Liber Vitae Patrum* in 591 promoting twenty French saints. The extreme asceticism of the desert saints and their early Western imitators was in itself a means of attracting attention and thus a propaganda tool.

Specifically it played a major part in spreading the ideal of celibacy, one of the most remarkable achievements of early medieval propaganda, with by the same token a less favourable image for traditional marriage. These saints then in turn became a peg upon which kings as well as bishops could hang their legitimacy.

FRANCE

A review of early papal propaganda leads on quite naturally to the other great propaganda feat of Dark Age Europe, the work of Charlemagne (742–814). It would be exaggeration to suggest that this King of the Franks and Emperor of Rome was original in his propaganda. His father Pippin had already used the prestige of the papacy to give some legitimacy to his upstart dynasty in 757. This was helped by Pope Stephen II's invention of a daughter for St Peter, Petronella, who conveniently became a Frank. Charlemagne very successfully revived a number of the techniques developed by the Roman emperors which had not been used for centuries.

The centrepiece of his reign in public relations terms was the dramatic rescue of Pope Leo from the rebellious Romans in 800 followed by his own coronation as Emperor of Rome on Christmas Day. For a Frankish king, grandson of the illegitimate Charles Martel and therefore of suspect legitimacy himself, to revive the Roman Empire after such a very long lapse was in itself remarkable. He had at least his military record to back him up, but the sheer historical opportunism of his act and his understanding of its implications were masterly. His utilization of the networks of the Catholic Church to help control his enlarged kingdoms, particularly the network of the Benedictine Order, showed his understanding of the church as a channel for communication. His edict on Cultivating Letters was put out to the clergy to encourage them to teach reading skills and his General Admonition from Aachen in 789 projected Charlemagne as a modern version of the Old Testament King Joshua. The literary case for his imperial stature was put across by clerics; Alcuin of York (735–804) explained the concept of empire and Einhard (770–840) the abbot historian produced the *Annales Francorum* and his biography of Charlemagne in 820, the first written of a layman during the Middle Ages, included a damning smear on the previous dynasty, the Merovingians.

To assist the administration of church and state in his new territories Charlemagne encouraged the production both of Latin literature and vernacular textbooks even to the point of developing a more utilitarian alphabet, the Carolingian minuscule. His concern for the visual arts was also significant. He used his coinage to put across the imperial message. The art and architecture of his capital at Aachen imitated the imperial style of Ravenna and his cultivation of ceremonials showed the same appreciation. His encouragement of the use of painting to illustrate Christianity was enshrined in the *Libri Carolini* and the numerous pictures produced by the schools of Ada and the palace in Aachen. Like so many self-made rulers the Carolingian Franks invented a new genealogy in which they were descended from Adam and Hector of Troy. Charlemagne also understood the significance of good event management, encouraging Amalarius to develop dramatic variants of the Easter mass and the Palm Sunday procession, which became the foundation of medieval theatre.

The effectiveness of Charlemagne's image-making was demonstrated not only by the respect which he acquired during his own lifetime, but the way in which it was frequently revived during the rest of the Middle Ages. The deeds of Charlemagne's paladins, Roland and Oliver, were the largest source of military and knightly role models in Europe and the fact that he was known so universally as Charles the Great, that the three words became one, is symbolic of the strength of his image.

His successors were not quite so effective, but the Capet dynasty did show remarkable ability to boost its image by religious metaphor. The two propagandists Hilduin and Hincmar of Reims (806–82) devoted considerable effort to developing the new legend of St Denis, even identifying him with Dionysius the Areopagite so that a raft of pseudo-Greek documents and forgeries could be used to assist the aggrandizement of the Capet family, the city of Paris and its monastic establishment. The St Denis image machine, grounded on the saint's remarkable walk carrying his own head, was an important building platform for the self-perception of the French nation and the prestige of its monarchy. Hincmar's biography of Dagobert I and his *Miracula Sancti Dionysi* were the basis for the Capet dynastic chronicles.

ENGLAND, IRELAND, SCOTLAND AND SCANDINAVIA

One other Dark Age ruler stands out for his remarkable grasp of the techniques of propaganda, again probably forced into such concentration by military weakness and political difficulties; he was Alfred the Great (849–99), King of Wessex and of England. Starting from a position that was almost hopeless – the classic stimulus to work harder at crowd persuasion – Alfred had to learn to motivate his own subjects and assert himself against the Danes who had taken over his kingdom. To help this effort he made significant use of published texts, translating Boethius's works and Pope Gregory's *Pastoral Care* as well as Bede's *History of the English Church*, positioning himself in the prefaces as a modern-day Solomon. He produced a new English legal code and initiated the *Anglo-Saxon Chronicle* as a myth foundation for his own dynasty and ethnic justification of his nation's case for independence. Not only did he have the successes of his military efforts exaggerated as in 878 but introduced the fable that he had been made king by Pope Leo in 853 and was thus a predestined ruler. He developed his own personal image with tales of how he went around in disguise, and acts of role reversal, even the endearing absent-mindedness of burning the cakes. He worked against the Danes by presenting them as usurpers and oath-breakers, staged an elaborate coronation for himself and began to issue coins with a dynastic message. The strength of his image outlasted his death and is an excellent example of how even in a community which to start with was virtually illiterate and had very few communication media, an imaginative approach to self-projection could be effective.

The focus generally of Anglo-Saxon literature was on the supreme need for loyalty between subject and ruler as shown in the long poem *Beowulf* from around 700 and the homilies of men like Leofric of Mercia, now better known as the husband of Godiva. The obvious image-making failure of Anglo-Saxon England was Aethelred the Unready (968–1016) who was saddled with judgemental disasters by the unforgiving Archbishop Wulfstan. The great success was in the Benedictine revival imported from Cluny after 910 which brought new standards of poetry, calligraphy, illustration and ritual to the projection of both church and state.

Ireland was the source of a most energetic and creative missionary effort for Christianity during this period. Saints such as Patrick, Bride and Columba had a remarkable capacity to project their image and were backed up by competent hagiographers like Adamnan who added rich embellishments and permanence to the saintly propaganda. In addition a very high level of craftsmanship in calligraphy, illustration, carving and metalwork gave a unique style to the campaigns.

The Vikings had an immensely strong tradition of oral epic poetry which was used not merely to entertain but for moral tuition as in the *Havamal*, for their religion and for the boosting of their warrior kings. Examples of this were the great funeral ode for King Haakon the Good and the *Knutsdrapa* for King Cnut, by the Icelandic bard Ottar the Black.

CENTRAL AMERICA

Eighth-century Central America saw the development of a new strain in aggressive propaganda from the Maya. The image of the Toltec warriors of Chichen Itza was the jaguar; the theme of their society was the need for human sacrifice. The murals of Bonampak painted in 790 showed torture and a high level of event management in the ceremonials leading up to the annual sacrifice of living hearts. The bas-reliefs of 746, the dynastic stelae of Yaxchilan, showed the Maya kings with their corporate symbols such as two-headed serpents. The combination of threatening pyramid temple structures, sadistic sculpture, painting and ritual seem like the later Aztec culture to have been in the meso-American mould of terror propaganda to induce abject mass obedience. Perhaps the special trick developed by Maya leaders was their study of astronomy which enabled them, for example, to prophesy the appearance of Venus just before it was actually seen in the sky, thus lending credibility to their other prophecies on war or peace.

ASIA

Meanwhile, in China as early as AD 589 the new self-made Emperor Yang Chien – renamed Wen Ti – founder of the Sui (fl. 581–604) had organized the printing and distribution of 300,000 leaflets in favour of his regime and attacking the Southern Emperor, a piece of propaganda technology more than a thousand years in advance of its availability in the rest of the world. The use of clay stamps to print images on cloth or paper was noted from 673 and there were intaglio plates of Buddha dating from 750. The missionary I'Ching claimed that Buddhists in India were making use of woodcuts from the late seventh century. By 751 the technique of paper manufacturing had spread west from China to Samarkand. Even the kings of Korea had a type factory in 1390, eighty years before Caxton printed his first book in England. Meanwhile Wen Ti developed the image of his dynasty with his Palace of the Cosmic Ultimate in his new capital. He borrowed the corporate symbol of his Han predecessors – fire – and adopted a new corporate colour – red. He propounded a case for the legitimacy of his reign on a Buddhist formula and encouraged the publication of a mixture of Buddhist and Confucian texts as background to his strategy. There was extensive use of poetry, song and rhyming prose to project the imperial image and its state philosophy. Between 601 and 604 the Emperor Wen Ti put up over 100 stupas adding architectural propaganda to the Buddhist campaign, justifying his heavenly mandate. Just like his contemporaries in the West he organized the multiple enshrining of relics as foci for group loyalty. His chief publicity writer Sui Wei (540–621) projected the ethos of popular obedience as an extension of filial submission – hsiao – and the Five Teachings, a remarkable package to control 9 million taxpayers.

Perhaps even more remarkable was the propaganda of the Empress Wu (630–705), a humbly born dowager empress who got rid of her son and appointed herself the first female emperor of China in 690, then circulated copies of the *Great Cloud Sutra*, a text which very conveniently prophesied the reincarnation of Buddha as a female monarch.

In the East generally the mechanics of printing developed steadily. In 868 Wang Chich printed the Buddhist *Diamond Sutra* on rolls about 16 feet long, using single blocks and the spread of woodblock printing generally can be linked to the growth of Buddhism in China using illustrated prints. Eighty years later the Confucian classics were being printed by Feng Tao. It was still to be four centuries before such feats could be emulated in Europe. The Chinese were genuine pioneers also in the use of fables and anecdotes to promote Buddhism. The Pien Wen mixed prose and poetry in short propaganda novels like *Mu Lien rescues his Mother* or on the political front *The Stubborn Prime Minister*, an attack on the Sung chief minister Wang An Shih (d. 1086) or *The Debauchery of King Hai Ling of China* also in the eleventh century, part of the dynastic propaganda of the Sung.

Japan borrowed Buddhism, Confucianism and propaganda techniques from the Chinese. The Emperor Shomu (701–56) involved the whole population in contributing to the massive bronze Buddha (still 452 tons in its surviving reduced format) at Todaiji in 737, to celebrate his own link with the Buddha which had helped the people to survive a smallpox epidemic. He is also recorded as distributing substantial numbers of a pamphlet, *The Sutra of the Sovereign King of the Golden Light Ray*, popularizing his concept of the ideal emperor. Then in the 760s the scandal-ridden Empress Shotoku is reputed to have defended her Buddhist monk consort with a leaflet distribution of a million copies, surely an exaggeration, but probably still a massive exercise.

India showed less novelty in propaganda terms at this time but the Pallava Kings like Mahendra Varman I (*c.* 600–30) did show awareness of visual image. He adopted the lion as his corporate symbol, carved huge stone chariots and was a big temple builder in the truncated pyramid style which now became popular. Perhaps more remarkable was the introduction of Buddhist art to Tibet by King Songsten Gambo (fl. 627–49) who built new temples in Lhasa and inaugurated a spectacular tradition of Buddhist visual propaganda which was to be both long-lasting and remarkably effective.

Throughout the world these centuries were a period in which exhibitionistic abstinence was a vehicle for religious propaganda. Whether it was the desert anchorites or northern hermits, the charisma of asceticism proved very powerful at this time. In general closer examination reveals the Dark Ages were by no means lacking in skill from a propaganda point of view, though there was not unexpectedly an emphasis on intimidation, deception and ascetic exhibitionism. The obvious key virtue on which much propaganda dwelt at this time was loyalty, the necessary ingredient for holding together empires of whatever size.

Early Middle Ages

ROME

The Middle Ages produced a number of major if not totally novel initiatives in propaganda, and all the most spectacular were connected directly or indirectly with the Catholic Church. The papacy continued in this period to be a remarkable example of consistent propaganda effort, mainly because it at times achieved such massive influence from such a flimsy foundation. Leo IX (fl. 1048–54) recognized the value of two-way communication in his development of the use of synods or Lateran Councils. He also perceived the value of using holy relics as a centrepiece for event management leading to effective crowd manipulation and to the tighter control over groups of provincial clergy. He exploited the concept of public confession of sins in the cases of malpractice by bishops. As a vigorous organizer and tireless traveller Leo concentrated on tightening the discipline of the hierarchy, to which end he founded the College of Cardinals. He also began to pioneer new methods of direct appeal to the populace.

Hildebrand or Gregory VII (1020–85) was one of the most propaganda-conscious of all Popes. This preoccupation was mainly the result of his prolonged struggle with the Emperor Henry IV over whose authority was the higher, but it was also born out of the parallel pan-European quarrel between church and state over who had the right to appoint senior clergy. Gregory's own public relations campaign against the Emperor reached its pinnacle with the incident known as the Humiliation of Canossa, in which he succeeded in so isolating Henry from his own grandees that the Emperor had to beg for forgiveness on his knees in the snow outside the town of Canossa. Once in receipt of public forgiveness and in a position to regroup his forces Henry was never again to lose the initiative, so that in reality Gregory paid dearly for this high point of papal image projection. However, the incident had been so visually dramatic that even in a society virtually without major media it had achieved widespread awareness.

Gregory also presided over a considerable pamphlet war between the supporters of clerical supremacy and those of lay investiture. Manegold of Lautenbach wrote a typical pamphlet for Archbishop Gebhard of Salzburg depicting kings as swineherds. Peter Crassus was one of a group of lay writers from Ravenna who supported the papal case, while the pamphleteer known as Anonymous of York produced tracts in favour of the divine right of kings and Benzo of Alba produced pro-imperial poetry. While this propaganda war was aimed at a relatively small audience, senior European barons and clergymen, it was a significant development, one by-product of which was the development of the world's first university at Bologna.

Like Leo, Pope Gregory also sought means of wider, more direct publicity. He greatly encouraged wandering hermits with their capacity for rousing crowd enthusiasm, helped by their ascetic appearance and reputation. He sponsored an almost mystic zeal for improvement of priestly standards, attacking the lazy materialism of the clergy just as Leo IX had done by a contrasting idealization of young fanatics. However, by far the most influential propaganda concept conceived by Gregory was the idea of the crusade, one of the most dynamic pieces of image packaging in human history and in some respects one of the most damaging. Gregory's idea was to launch a crusade to bring the Greek Orthodox Church under the wing of Catholicism, one of the dearest ambitions of the universal church. That plan came to nothing, but the principle of a volunteer army with the church's blessing was to be brought to fruition less than fifty years after Gregory's death.

Meanwhile St Bernard (1090–1153) and later Innocent III (1160–1216) played a major part in extending the promotion of the cult of the Virgin Mary, which had been growing steadily but was now amplified with the creation of four major annual festivities, celebrations in music and the visual arts. The image of St Bernard himself was projected by a number of writers like Chrétien de Troyes (d. 1183) who presented him as a monkish version of Sir Galahad searching for the Holy Grail, a theme which Wolfram von Eschenbach (c. 1200) used in *Parzifal* to embellish the image of the Templars. This great revival of Arthurian and Carolingian romance, knights and the Holy Grail, fitted well with the objectives and desired imagery of the Crusades. The *Song of Roland* was full of anti-Muslim propaganda and the myth of Mahoud in popular literature presented Mohammed as a satanic pervert. The new *History of Charlemagne* of 1150 projected the Saracens as idolators and crusaders generally were encouraged to refer to them as filth. Bernard in fact was a remarkably able propagandist having been put in charge of Clairvaux Abbey in 1115 and produced his *Apologia ad Gulielmum* in 1124 with its heavy attack on the Cluniac brotherhood, following on the ingenious *Dialogue of Two Monks* of 1115 by Idung of Prüfening using the question and answer technique to great effect. Bernard, having initially condemned the artistic extravagance of other orders, recognized the importance of visual propaganda commenting, 'Bishops have a duty to make use of material ornamentation to rouse devotion in carnal people.' Early examples of this in practice were the huge display of narrative sculptures by Gislebertus at Autun Cathedral (c. 1130), the rose windows of Amiens promoting the cult of the Virgin Mary and the 153 painted panels of the life of Christ done by Lopicinus for the Church of St Martin at Zillis.

When Pope Urban II (1042–99) launched the recruitment drive for the First Crusade at Clermont it was to become one of the most ingeniously conceived and carefully planned propaganda exercises at any period of world history (see pl. 12). He chose France rather than Italy in order to create a more international appeal – Italy was not a nation at this time and French-speaking knights dominated Europe – and because there were larger military recruitment grounds than further south. To add to the tension he had already excommunicated Philip I, the somewhat uninspiring King of France, for his intransigence over the investiture problem. Thus to seize the military as well as the spiritual initiative in Philip's own country was a masterly challenge. Urban had also created some excitement beforehand by spreading rumours that he was about to make an announcement of great importance at Clermont, what in the twentieth-century came to be called media hype. He chose a large field at Clermont where a special platform was built for the occasion and employed Raymond of St Giles to look after the administration. When he at last made his speech he began with a long and harrowing description of the atrocities committed by the Saracens against the Christians in the Holy Land. He then produced a probably forged letter from the Byzantine emperor supporting his case. Then when he came to his climax and announced the Crusade, a number of key men, perhaps planted in the crowd, began to shout 'Deus vult, Deus vult' [God wills it], a good rhythmic chanting slogan. Then the Bishop of Puys, perhaps also briefed beforehand to get the momentum going, came forward as the first to volunteer and shouted 'I confess'. Fulcher of Chartres has left a description of the tears and convulsive weeping of the crowd as more volunteers stepped forward and the concept of delivering the Holy City had been launched.

Norman Cohn, who made a special study of the manipulation of the medieval mind, recognized this as a classic example of crowd control based on a highly charged approach to the emotions. Within weeks a task force of wandering preachers using much the same technique had spread the idea of the movement through France and beyond. Typical was Peter the Hermit (*c.* 1050–1115) riding his donkey and carrying a personal letter from God. He showed remarkable skill in crowd control, cultivating a highly ascetic image, and preaching apocalyptically about Saracen cruelties. The unofficial recruitment drive produced four armies of more than a quarter of a million men, which headed for Palestine. The first was slaughtered in Bulgaria, the second under Peter himself was defeated at Nicaea, long before it reached the Holy Land, and the other two were both exterminated in Hungary. A fifth army of 600,000 reached Antioch, but was ravaged by disease and produced relatively modest results.

During the later Crusades the recruitment propaganda became more sophisticated. Pope Alexander III (1159–81) introduced the methodical distribution of crusading Bills like the *Cor Nostrum*. Innocent III (1198–1216) improved the coordination of crusade preaching, hiring powerful speakers like Fulk of Neuilly (d. 1202) and from around 1220 the role was taken over by the official mendicant orders.

As an example of seizing the propaganda initiative, organizing mass motivation and highly skilled event management, the papal promotion of the Crusades has few parallels in human history. The packaging of the idea was also ingenious, with the crusader's cross as a corporate identity, the slogan/battle cry 'deus vult', the ritual of oath taking, the great battle hymns and the link-up with millennialist attitudes. With masochism as a response to sadism, and anti-Semitism as an outlet for pent-up frustrations, the great adventure carried the potential for wealth or conquest yet brought instant remission for all past sins. Many other highly effective recruiting preachers followed Peter the Hermit. Walter sans Devoir used banners and psalms as well as the same emotive preaching techniques. The cumulative effect of numbers of uncontrolled fanatics of this kind was the division of the original idea into a variety of deviant forms and several major physical disasters, such as the Children's Crusade, where mobs of children preached to by ten-year-old fanatics, marched thousands of miles without any organization or equipment, deaf to all rational warnings about their probable fate. There were also the wild outbreaks of Jew baiting, flagellation and other forms of hysteria. Nevertheless the basic event management of the Crusades was effective and by the time of St Louis there were textbooks on exactly how to organize a crusading recruitment rally, such was the remarkable understanding of mass manipulation which was developed at this time.

Peter of Blois was one of the semi-professional propagandists working on crusader recruitment in England in 1189: Richard Cœur de Lion, who became the hero of the Third Crusade, was his ideal subject. In 1216 came the recruitment textbook *Ordinatio de predicatione Sancti Crucis in Anglia*, a guide to emotive techniques by which preachers could reduce their audiences to a trance-like state. They used plenty of simple metaphors and built up to a climax by constant repetition at intervals of the punchline 'Arise therefore, take up my cross and follow me.' The Welsh preacher Giraldus Cambrensis (*c.* 1147–1223) used this technique and noted its effectiveness. Every disaster in the Holy Land was also exploited as when the Pope instructed preachers to use the fall of Ashdod and other towns. Atrocity stories were manufactured when no true ones were available, for example in the forged letter of Sultan Khalil which had an air of authenticity and was recycled by the chronicler Bartholomew Cotton. Many crusader books became extremely popular and contributed to the enhancement of the crusading image at least among the literate classes. The *Travels of Sir John Mandeville*, and Philip de Mézière's *Songe du vieil Pèlerin* were typical examples in the 1380s, as were histories like Prince Hayton's *Flowers of the History of the East* (1307). Equally there were anti-papal propagandists like the poet Ottokar of Steiermark who blamed the Popes for the disasters of the East and argued that crusades against Christians always led to judgemental failure.

Among the diversifications of crusader propaganda was the development of the new orders of celibate knights. The Templars, for example, founded in 1118 by Hugh de Payens rapidly acquired an international reputation. Their original corporate identity of two knights on one horse symbolized their lack of funds, a problem which was rapidly reversed. The idea of monkish knights defending helpless pilgrims in remote places had its own charisma, but it was given a substantial boost by St Bernard's pamphlet *De Laude Novae Militiae*, which with his usual skill linked the fight against the self, with the fight against the Saracens. The orders of knights each had their visual identities and artistic themes. For example, the Teutonic Knights had their Schreinmadonna, a fold-away Virgin Mary with an apple in her left hand, and their German crusading poets like Walter von Vogelweide.

One final strain in later crusader propaganda was the poetic, the spread in the twelfth century particularly of romantic tales of the Holy Grail or variations on the theme of the *Chansons de Geste*, the epic stories of the two proto-crusaders Roland and Oliver, recited in verse by the trouvers or troubadours and spread along the pilgrim routes of Europe. Huizinga, the great Dutch historian of ideas in the later Middle Ages commented that the concept of chivalry which the religious wars fostered was 'a source of tragic political errors'. The portrayal of Muslims as perverts, imposters and subhuman in their behaviour was encouraged in a substantial swathe of popular literature, which was to be influential for many centuries to follow. In Provence the poets produced *sirventes* to fit popular songs of the day, often critical of the papacy's official line on crusading policy. Many of the crusaders produced poems or songs themselves, for example Thibaut IV of Champagne. Folquet, Bishop of Toulouse helped adapt the crusading concept to give respectability to the suppression and massacre of the peace-loving Albigensian heretics in his own area of France. Some poets like Raimbaut of Vaqueiras were hired as propagandists, in his case by Boniface of Monferrat. Large numbers of song poems like the *Chanson d'Antioche* or the *Canso de la Crotzada* enjoyed widespread popularity. A new style of illumination, tomb sculpture and painting helped project the visual image of the crusading ideal. The stalls of Toledo Cathedral carried carvings of the Reconquista. In Sicily the Norman King Roger I (1031–1101) projected himself as a variant crusader for the conquest of the island in 1091 and filled the churches of Palermo with magnificent propaganda mosaics and frescoes to project his legitimacy.

Rudel of Johansdorf produced his epic on the Third Crusade and Bohemond of Antioch, one of numerous insecure new monarchs, not only sponsored the writing of the *Gesta Francorum* but actively promoted sales on a recruitment drive back in France before returning to battle with the Byzantine Emperor in 1106. Conrad of Montferrat in 1190 circulated a large picture of the Holy Sepulchre being defiled by Arab horses and later crusader propaganda became steadily cruder. Mohammed was portrayed in one popular cartoon as hitting Jesus and in another as practising child sacrifice. Street theatre, such as Jean Bodel's play *Jeu de Saint Nicolas* performed in Arras around 1199, encouraged anti-Islamic hysteria.

The evaluation of the balance of benefit and disaster accruing from the Crusades is fruitless, but as a propaganda concept it certainly gave new vitality to papal leadership; it gave a new political and moral focus to many Europeans and stimulated considerable mental realignment. In due course the favourable image of the Crusades was borrowed to give false legitimacy to other acts of violence such as the suppression of the Albigensians in 1208, France's attack on Flanders and the colonization of the Baltic states by the German knights.

The propaganda of the Muslim side against the Christians should not be forgotten – the image of Saladin was enhanced by Imad ad Din of Isfahan (1125–1201) and another example was the *Ornament of Chevaliers and Banners of Gallants* written by Ibn Hudayl in Granada around 1400 to encourage resistance against the infidel Spaniards. The Arabs had after all invented the concept of a holy war and indeed were to maintain it long after it lost credibilty in Europe.

GERMANY

The other outstanding propaganda coup of the high Middle Ages was without question the second revival of the Roman Empire by Otto the Great and the development of its image into the Holy Roman Empire by Frederick Barbarossa. The feat was remarkable because again the basis of the idea was so flimsy – the claim of succeeding dynasties of German kings to be rulers of the world. Otto I (912–73) was, like Charlemagne, an opportunist in his assumption of the empire and did so on the strength of his military prowess, but after a gap of effectively 150 years it was remarkable that the Roman Empire concept could be revived at all. The work that had been done on the image of Rome itself as the so-called 'eternal city' helped the situation and Otto's advisers, like his court historian Bishop Liutprand (*c.* 922–72) went so far as to prove the eternity of Rome by reference to the 72nd Psalm. The myth of the discovery of St Peter's staff on the banks of the Tiber, the whole long-term build-up of the mystique of Rome as a holy city, centre of the world, the jingle 'urbis et orbis' suited both the Popes and the emperors.

Otto emphasized his position with no fewer than four coronations, a number which was to become essential – at Rome, Aachen (the second Rome of Charlemagne), Monza for Italy and Arles for Burgundy. The concept of four crowns in four different metals was developed, with the Lombard iron crown made from nails of the true cross. In addition Otto encouraged new developments in religious fresco painting and illumination, in particular, for example, the work of artists like Ekkehard at St Gallen. The level of artistic propaganda of the Ottonian period is also demonstrated by the efforts of Bishop Bernward of Hildesheim who in 1015 commissioned a bronze column, like Trajan's in Rome, illustrating stories from the Bible, a remarkable technical achievement. He made Hildesheim a centre for manuscript illumination and bronze casting as a vehicle for church propaganda.

The level of propaganda effort or innovation from subsequent German Emperors of Rome varied considerably. The main issue driving the image machine was the ongoing struggle for moral supremacy with the Popes. Henry the Lion (1129–95), Duke of Saxony and a Guelf leader who never made it to the purple, is one example of a medieval princeling who had the ambition to devote special care to his image. His need coincided with the appearance of what was in effect almost a new medium, the corps of troubadours, professional singer/composers who hung round every European court, particularly that of Queen Eleanor, wife of Henry II of England. They composed heroic ballads for up-and-coming rulers, romanticizing their deeds by comparison with the age's favourite role models: Roland, Oliver, King Arthur, Tristan, Hannibal and so on. Henry also hired the historian Arnold of Lubeck to write a chronicle extolling him as a new Solomon. The monk Konrad was paid to translate the *Rolandslied* from the *Song of Roland*, particularly emphasizing that Charlemagne was an ancestor of Henry the Lion. The German *minnesingers* regularly performed Eilhart's *Tristan and Isolde*, while Henry's scholars also produced the massive *Lucidarius*, the first encyclopedia in German. At the same time Henry set about a substantial building programme to turn the Saxon capital into an imperial city. St Blaise's Church and Lubeck Cathedral were rebuilt in 1173 as repositories for important relics, a demonstration of Henry's power. The Brunswick citadel was rebuilt as a palace and a large symbolic iron lion was put up in front of Dankwarderode Castle. The book illuminators at Helmarshausen were encouraged to include Duke Henry in pictures beside appropriate poems about his prowess.

Even more impressive was the image campaign constructed by Henry's contemporary Frederick I (1123–90), major developer of the Hohenstaufen dynasty who cleverly added the word 'Holy' to the imperial title, thus giving it an even greater lustre. He organized the canonization of Charlemagne as patron saint of the Hohenstaufens, adopted the eagle as a corporate identity and cultivated his crusader image as the Kaiser Rotbart (Barbarossa). He hired the painter Rainald of Dassel (fl. 1157–67) to paint pro-German, anti-papal frescoes and the sculptor Magister Nicolaus to develop the imperial inconography. Frederick also appreciated the value of good event management and it is known that he organized the pageantry surrounding the capture of Milan in 1163 with trumpet serenades, prostration of conquered enemies and crowd manipulation. The poet Ligurinus was official court panegyricist and even theatre was deployed on Frederick's behalf when the play *Ludens de Antichristo* exalted the Emperor as a shield against the devil. It was with this combination of propaganda flare and political skill that Frederick made Austria a dukedom and Bohemia a kingdom, both under his control, with Poland, Hungary, Denmark and Burgundy also under his feudal superiority, at the same time also keeping the papacy in relative subservience.

Barbarossa's grandson Frederick II (1194–1250) also had the capacity to carve for himself an image that was larger than life. He patronized the great minnesinger Walter von der Vogelweide (c. 1170–1230). He exploited the confrontation which was now normal between Emperor and Pope to appeal over the head of Innocent IV to the poorest level of the monastic groups, and position himself publicly as 'the chastiser of the Church in the Last Days'. He was aided significantly in this by the highly popular writings of the hermit Joachim of Fiore (1145–1202) who in about 1190 had produced his prophecies of a new world order due to commence in seventy years' time. This most influential of millennialist tracts suggested that a new order of monks would preach a new Christianity and a great 'Emperor of the Last Days' would preside over the punishment of the corrupt old church as the world entered a new age of spiritual enlightenment. This thesis had great public appeal, suited quite well the aspirations of the more extreme wing of the Franciscan friars and suited particularly the combative posture of Frederick II who could pose as the reincarnation of his own crusader grandfather, a millennialist saviour who would prepare the way for the second coming.

Pope Innocent used the propaganda idioms of the Crusades to paint Frederick as no better than an infidel Turk. The fact that Frederick was excommunicated by the Pope did him little damage and his image was further enhanced by a new tract, in imitation of Joachim's style, the *Commentary on Jeremiah* which prophesied that he would actually overthrow the church in the year 1260. The papacy fought back by presenting Frederick as the 'Beast of the Apocalypse' and his Holy Roman Empire as Babylon, but most of the wandering preachers of Germany were on the Emperor's side and could paint him as perfect when compared with Innocent IV. Brother Arnold, a Dominican friar based in his Duchy of Swabia, produced tracts talking of the new 'Third Age' about to dawn and Frederick as the champion of the poor who would confiscate the wealth of the Catholic Church. It was revolutionary propaganda giving the Emperor a most unlikely base of popular support and the Hohenstaufen dynasty a somewhat exaggerated image as national champions.

Frederick II died in 1250, ten years before the expected new age, but his image lived on. It was useful to believe that he would return to the world 'vivit et non vivit' ['he lives and he does not live']. The fantasy that he was waiting to reappear from the bowels of Mount Etna or was the disguised Emperor of the Black Forest, was useful for those who needed a symbol for the fight against clerical corruption or political oppression. As Norman Cohn so eloquently described in his *Pursuit of the Millennium*, this is a classic use of the golden-age-around-the-corner theme of propaganda or the revival of a popular dead ruler or a prestigious dead empire which was used in France for Charlemagne, in England for Arthur or Edward the Confessor and in Germany for the three successive Reichs.

In addition to his Messianic posturing Frederick was a significant patron of the arts, encourager of sculptors and author himself of an illustrated book on falconry. His propaganda may have been of little long-term value to his dynasty – it did not long survive him – but corporately the Hohenstaufen had had a remarkable record.

ITALY

Only slightly older than Frederick II was one of the real geniuses of medieval propaganda, St Francis of Assisi (1181–1226). His career started in 1210 with the self-positioning legend of riches to rags, his own version of the road to Damascus and the populist emphasis on the vow of poverty. He then set about recruiting his initial eleven disciples yet by the time of his first General Assembly nine years later he had 5,000 members. In addition to this he displayed a grasp of literary and visual media which was quite exceptional. His own poetry and hymns were among the earliest works in metrical Italian and even his prose was of a high poetic quality – indeed it was from his love of the French poetry of the troubadours that he acquired the name 'Il Francesco' which he adopted for the rest of his life. His verbal image of the floating palace, his ingenious use of the word 'brothers' as a form of address to all living creatures or 'Lady' as the personification of poverty, were all highly effective. He was a brilliant preacher, making liberal use of gestures and movements, even appearing dancing in his patched and dirty tunic, once even naked to draw attention, begging in the streets, washing the feet of peasants, consorting with lepers. His own literary work was extended by that of followers such as the poet Jacopone da Todi (1230–1306) and 'The Canticle of Creatures' of 1223 was probably the first song in the Italian language. Raymond Lull (1232–1315), the Spanish propagandist theologian was involved in the adaptation of popular folk tunes for Franciscan lyrics. In due course the brotherhood made a common effort to recruit good singers and had its own composers like Henry of Pisa and Vita of Lucca. Highly effective were the simple repeated choruses like:

> Christe deus
> Christe meus

or

> Stabat mater dolorosa
> Iuxta crucem lacrimosa

and the new concept of the immaculate conception. He also displayed a keen understanding in his visual imagery for the Order of Poor Brothers with their grey and brown habits, the symbols of the cross and the lily, the skull and the three knots, all giving the Franciscans a corporate identity rich in meaning yet simple and memorable, to which in his final two years were added as his own ultimate personal symbol the marks or stigmata of the wounds of the Crucifixion. The paintings of Bonaventura Berlinghieri at Pescia, others at Pisa, Arezo, Siena and Venice, the development by Giunta Pisano of the new suffering image of Christ in 1236 provided a huge stimulus to production of crucifixes and of pictures of the Virgin Mary. These visual ideas were in turn extended by the group of painters who developed the Franciscan theme and were indeed main pioneers of medieval Italian art – Giotto di Bondone (1267–1337) who executed twenty-eight frescoes of the saint's life for the church at Assisi and later the Dominican Fra Angelico (1387–1455) who dedicated his art to projecting the monastic ideal, particularly the Franciscan ideal of suffering and the beatitude of the elect. John de Caulibus of Gimignano wrote his *Meditations on the Life of Christ* which fleshed out the Gospel stories with plenty of visual detail and was a substantial stimulus to the development of the new religious painting.

Francis also showed an awareness of the value of event management with the ritual stripping of new brothers, the three vows to 'Lady Poverty', and the re-enactment of the Last Supper and the forty days in the wilderness. It was the Franciscans who also developed the visual imagery and sense of occasion of Christmas, recreating the nativity scene, using model cribs as an aid to conversion. The life story of Francis was embellished by hagiographers such as Thomas de Celano in 1229 and St Bonaventura so that he was canonized by the Pope, Gregory IX, two years after his death in 1228. Both Francis himself and his supporters had the propaganda skill to package the new order most effectively, ensuring the rapid and successful spread of its ideas.

On the instructions of Francis's successor, Brother Elias, Assisi was developed as a major cult centre with a new basilica and convent complex and the commissioning of explanatory murals before the elaborately staged reburial of Francis in 1230, endorsing the papal canonization. Literary output remained at a high level with popular tracts like *The Golden Sayings of Brother Giles* and the *Little Flowers of St Francis* or the *Book for the Lover and the Beloved* with its 366 mottos, one for each day. The *Postilla Literalis* of 1322 still survives in 1,200 manuscript versions and was reprinted 100 times. The romantic quality of Franciscan propaganda, its affectionate diminutives, its frequent mentions of love, its veneration for human relationships and its anti-materialistic stance all contributed to its considerable popularity. The Franciscans also adopted from the start a very professional attitude to their main activity, the job of preaching. Their training standards for this work were high and their style, as with their writings, highly emotive. With exciting use of anecdote, metaphor and highly charged attacks on sin they had the ability to induce a trance-like ecstasy in their audiences. Many of them, like Oliver Maillard and

Antony of Padua, could attract massive crowds and reduce them to trembling penitents. Outbursts of self-flagellation were a common follow-up. Some like San Bernardino drew additional attention by carefully staged 'bonfires of vanities', one with 1,000 backgammon boards and 4,000 packs of cards. In due course the Franciscans developed a long-term international image, with their five-cross corporate identity and style of architecture associated with their projection of the Holy Land pilgrimage. In England Henry of Avranches wrote a metric life of Francis and John Pecham of Canterbury produced the poem 'Philomena', both contributing significantly to Franciscan propaganda. Julian of Speyer wrote his *Officium Rhythmicum* in 1231, extending the Franciscan use of music to Eastern Europe.

A remarkable example of contagious propaganda techniques was shown in the spread of the flagellant movement. It was a classic of event management in which the well-orchestrated spectacle included dramatic self-violence bringing spectators and participants alike to a climax of hysteria with the chanting of confessions. Emerging from Perugia around 1260 the movement soon acquired the packaging of a populist cult – the uniform for participators, the processions, the ritual of whipping and bloodletting, the marble tablets which shone with a spiritual light and sometimes the added excitement of bursts of anti-Semitism. The participants were roused to hysteria by the masochistic hymns of Hugo Panziera (*c.* 1330) and the sermons of Robert of Leece. It spread rapidly northwards and accentuated the causes with which it was associated: religious extremism, crusading and anti-Semitism.

The Dominican Order (St Dominic of Calaruega 1170–1221), established by Pope Gregory IX at the same time as the Franciscans, was less concerned with promoting its own image, more with the spread of orthodoxy. Nevertheless it was to play a major part in the building up of the mythology of heresy, first against the Albigensians, then the Templars, later when it ran out of semi-genuine heretics, against witches (see p. 163). And Dominic promoted the notion that it was easier to attack a poverty-admiring sect like the Albigensians if the propagandists themselves avoided appearing rich and comfortable. The order used the technique of extracting very lurid confessions of sexual malpractice which then provided excellent raw material for further publicization. It was probably also responsible for spreading the use of the rosary, an idea borrowed from the East, which was an aid to the counted repetition of personal prayers and an example of clever long-term indoctrination technique. The poetic St Catherine of Siena (1347–80) was also a charismatic promoter of the Dominican ideal, purportedly displaying the stigmata from 1375. The order increased rapidly from 60 houses in 1221 to 582 in 1303 with huge emphasis on the techniques of preaching and crowd control. Jacques de Vitry (1180–1240) produced collections of sermon stories and Humbert de Romans laid down techniques for preaching which included searching out the aspirations of the audience beforehand, the formula 'what, to whom, when, where and how', subsequently borrowed by the modern advertising industry, and little tricks such as the use of the five fingers to count out the five wicked luxuries.

ENGLAND

Most examples of early medieval propaganda success were either the promotion of new religious orders or the aggrandizement of dynasties. Typical of the latter was the effort of the Norman dynasty to establish its legitimacy in England. Duke William of Normandy (1027–87) known as 'the bastard', or the 'tanner's son' had the classic reason for needing propaganda help to achieve his objectives – a weak case. Even before 1066 he had begun to show his skill as a propagandist in a campaign of vilification against the Archbishop of Ronan, prior to his being in a position actually to replace him with a more amenable candidate. At the same time he cultivated an image of religious sincerity by parading the bones of St Edmund at St Valery. Then he commenced his smear campaign against King Harold of England. This was based around Harold's shipwreck on the coast of Normandy and subsequent oath of loyalty to William taken on the relics of Bayeux, punishable by God if broken. William was aided in his smear tactics by Lanfranc the Prior of Caen, his tame ecclesiastical advocate, who embellished the case against Harold to help justify William in seizing his throne. Then came the war of 1066 in which William was accompanied by his court bard Taillefer, who developed the anti-Harold theme, followed by William's emblematic coronation at Westminster on Christmas Day. Because William was king by conquest he had to continue the propaganda against the dead legitimate predecessor, Harold. Bishop Guy of Amiens was employed to write a poem about the Battle of Hastings, denigrating Harold's performance. William of Jumieges' *Gesta Normanorum Ducum* of 1071 and William of Poitiers' *Gesta Guilielmi* of 1072 continued the theme with the exaltation of the Norman dynasty and the vituperation of Harold, as did the poem 'Carmen de Hastinga Proelio' in which Harold appeared as Cain. The *Anglo-Saxon Chronicle* which up to 1066 had been the native English interpretation of history, was resumed from 1067 to 1086 as a pro-Norman account of events.

In visual terms William left behind a propaganda masterpiece; the Bayeux Tapestry of 1082 is a running account of the conquest showing scenes including Harold breaking his oath and suffering the subsequent punishment (pl. 10). On a much more massive scale was William's huge building programme which imprinted the Norman image on the English countryside – large numbers of imposing mottes at every population centre and seven new cathedrals.

William's son William Rufus (d. 1100) was most noticeable in the propaganda context as a victim. He allowed his image to be successfully blackened by his enemies in the church, particularly by the Cistercian monks and Ordericus Vitalis who projected him as corrupt, homosexual and depraved. His younger brother Henry I (1068–1135), having a more difficult path to the throne, had greater need of image building, specifically to discredit their eldest brother, Robert Curthose. He cultivated the image of prophecies, including ones that he, Henry, would one day rule England and Wales. He also adopted the mantle of Edward the Confessor, the last totally legitimate ruler, and married a Saxon bride, going on, with the help of Archbishop Anselm, to project his own legitimacy.

During the civil war which followed Henry's death the most notable public relations event was the burgeoning of the Welsh national image, as Geoffrey of Monmouth (1100–54) produced his pro-Welsh *History of the Kings of Britain*, aiming at the concept of a Celtic anti-Norman confederacy and using an imaginary source-book to boost his credibility. Merlin was projected as the national bard and ancestor of all Welsh bards with King Arthur as the heroic role model for a new regime and the Red Dragon as its visual emblem. Politically there were no real results but the idea acquired lasting influence and helped make the ethnic identity of a tribal grouping at least semi-permanent. To all this the young Henry II (1133–89), originally sarcastically known as Henry Fitzempress, had to respond by asserting his own right to the crown of England. He used the visual image of the Planta Genesta – yellow broom – that responded to the prophecies of Merlin and attacked the image of his predecessor King Stephen as a usurper who had caused anarchy. Rather cleverly he made sure that Edward the Confessor was canonized in 1161 as the Saxon saint-hero who had passed on the crown to the Normans. He justified his taxation policy with his *Dialogue of the Exchequer*. In 1171 with the Pope's help he began a propaganda campaign against the Irish who were painted as a brutal and barbarous people to justify his invasion of the island. Similarly Jordan Fantosme contributed a verse history of the Scots war, depicting Henry II as the greatest king who ever lived and the Scots as deserving of defeat. To combat the popular image of the martyred Thomas à Becket, he organized Bishop Gilbert Foliot of London to put across the royal case. Ultimately it had little effect and Henry had to make his public act of penance at Canterbury. Roger of Howden and Walter Map did their best to project the Plantagenet image in their biased histories, but there was also a significant propaganda flow from Henry's numerous opponents. Girald Cambrensis (1146–1223) put the Welsh point of view and depicted Henry as coming from the devil and due to go back to him, though later in 1189 he wrote propaganda defending Henry in his conquest of Ireland. The French compared him to Nero and Judas, descended from the 'demon countess of Anjou' while Alain de Lille compared the decadence of the Angevins under Henry with the upright King Philip Augustus of France. The propaganda onslaught on Henry was abetted by his rebellious sons Richard and John, who were supported by the troubadour Bertran de Born in a verbal tirade during 1182. Henry's response – describing his sons' behaviour as like Absalom attacking his father David – was a readily understood biblical parallel which was to be used again in British history in the reign of Charles II.

The last three Plantagenet kings all had different reasons for needing propaganda help. Richard I (1157–99) needed it because of his obsessive desire to wage war abroad. His coronation was exceptionally elaborate and he even repeated it in 1194 after his release from prison. He was the first king to use the royal 'we' and to adopt a coat of arms. He deliberately built up his dashing 'cœur de lion' image as the ideal crusader, and was helped by hired bardic jongleurs to spread it. In Roger of Howden's words Richard I 'enticed with gifts singers and minstrels from France that might sing of [him] in the streets and then it was said everywhere there was not such another man in the world'. He used his Chancellor William Longchamp both to help project his image and to ease the task of raising money. The minstrel Ambroise was taken on the Third Crusade to enhance the image of Richard's clash with Saladin. In due course when Longchamp lost favour for being too pro-French he turned to the Bishop of Coventry to attack Longchamp in turn. But in many senses Richard was not so much a propagandist himself as a pawn in the propaganda scheme of Pope Alexander III who had begun the promotion of the Third Crusade in England in 1165.

Richard's successor, King John (1167–1216) had an image of usurpation and later incompetence and needed to overcome the rumour that he had cheated on his brother and murdered his nephew Arthur. The efforts of his main publicist Savaric were in vain. His propaganda was outmatched abroad by that of Philip Augustus on the question of legitimacy in Normandy, by the barons at home, by Peter des Roches, Bishop of Winchester, by the efforts of William the Marshall, and by the *Histoires des duces de Normandie* by the French troubadour Bertran de Born who had also attacked his father. Thereafter the black legend of John was developed fairly or unfairly by Matthew Paris and William the Briton. 'Hell is defiled' said the *Historia Major* compiled for Roger of Wendover, and as the ultimate symbol of John's propaganda failure there appeared the alternative role model in the fast spreading legend of Robin Hood.

This blackening of King John continued during the minority of his son Henry III (1207–72) with the works of Thomas Wylie and Roger of Wendover. Henry had to suffer the reissuing of Magna Carta in 1225 and made desperate efforts to reverse its intentions, but his techniques were not particularly successful. He increased the chanting of 'laudes regiae' at Westminster Abbey, further developed the cult of Edward the Confessor even to the extent of building his own tomb alongside the Saxon saint-king's. There were also new wall paintings in the abbey of royal exploits, placed deliberately beside some of Alexander the Great.

Henry even tried to cultivate the image of a crusader like his uncle and organized a campaign to try to acquire the Holy Roman Empire for the English crown with his son Edward as King of Sicily. The propaganda odds were against him, however, and there was a build-up of opposition material. There was the popular song 'King of Alemaigne' of 1252 attacking his foreign pretensions and the 'Song of the Barons' in 1263, a poem in the style of the *Chansons de Geste* with Sir Roger de Clifford opposing King Henry. By contrast the opposition leader Sir Simon de Montfort enjoyed a rapid improvement in image, proclaimed as 'the flower of knighthood' or as the *sirventes* poem of 1265 put it:

> Il aime droit et het la tort
> Si avera la maîtrise Montfort.*

Montfort's image climaxed with his victory over the King at Lewes and the poem of 1264 *The Song of Lewes* which described it, the first major piece of propaganda in England since 1066 to be written in English rather than French or Latin. Significantly this reign marked not only the beginning of parliamentary history in England but the first concerted effort at popular opposition propaganda.

Meanwhile, England was the object of yet another wave of papal propaganda as Ottobuono organized further recruitment to save the Holy Land from the Mongol hordes. The Knights Templar contributed to the international public relations effort with their system of newsletters to embassies, some actually written in blood to emphasize the extremity of danger. The Templars were also very able fund-raisers, while the Cistercian order provided an international network of monk preachers to recruit for the holy war and numerous scribes to produce multiple copies of important papal bulls. At the same time the clerics of Canterbury demonstrated significant ability to develop a cult, as the martyr Thomas à Becket became a focus for pilgrimage. The visual imagery of the cult was extended to the sculptures and stained-glass windows of the cathedral.

FRANCE

Early French propaganda had without question peaked with Charlemagne and for several subsequent centuries there were little more than limited attempts to recapture that brilliance. Gradually, however, the Capet dynasty began to show some initiative of its own. Philip Augustus (1165–1223) was certainly adept in exploiting the opportunities presented by the quarrels of Henry II of England and his sons and his adoption of the old imperial title 'Augustus' showed just how ambitious he was.

---

* 'He loves the right and hates the wrong, so Montfort will have the power.'

Propaganda skills played a key role in his ultimate defeat of King John and recovery of vast tracts of lands from the Plantagenets, more or less restoring the natural ethnic frontiers of France. Philip Augustus was also responsible for the building of one of the world's great examples of propaganda architecture, Notre Dame in Paris, a focus both for French Catholicism and his enhanced capital city. The development of the flying buttress made possible the concept of the soaring Gothic cathedrals, not only propaganda in their own right but packaging for propaganda relief sculptures, paintings and ultimately stained glass to provide a multi-media experience. The pioneering patron of such work was undoubtedly Abbot Suger of St Denis (fl. 1122–51) who had served under Louis VII and the amazing Queen Eleanor. One special feature of Capetian monarchy was the importance attached to royal ceremonial, particularly coronations, the symbolism of the royal ceremonial sword called 'Joyeuse', attributed to Charlemagne. The combined images of the sword of justice and the lilies of mercy were widely displayed and the dynasty had a custom of showing off its gold and silver plate to impress visitors with its power.

Philip's grandson Louis IX or St Louis (1215–70) was utterly sincere in the image which he built up for himself, that of a crusading martyr. By this time the propaganda system for mounting crusades was a sophisticated and well-practised exercise. One of Louis's counsellors was Humbert de Romans, Master General of the Dominicans, who wrote one of the standard treatises on crusader recruitment, *On Preaching the Cross*. The evangelistic crowd manipulation and impressive event management were by this time quite slick. Standard parables, such as that of overhearing the devil in a wood reading out lists of the souls of barons which he had lost because they had taken crusading vows, were circulated for use by preachers. Poets like the Parisian Rutebeuf (1230–86) wrote works specially for mass crusader recruitment. Louis was able to take advantage of all this without having to devise anything new. He did, however, go to great lengths in 1238 to acquire the Crown of Thorns, a supposedly genuine relic, from the Latin barons of Constantinople and this treasure was brought to Paris in a silver box, delivered to the King who accepted it for his people barefoot and wearing only a tunic. This was symbolic of Louis's image, a king who wore sackcloth, spent long hours at prayer and devoted his life to the crusading ideal. He gave patronage to Thomas Aquinas's campaign against the Manichaeans and to the Franciscans. He had the magnificent Sainte Chapelle built to house further important relics, which on special occasions went in procession to Notre Dame, allowing further opportunities for crowd management. Louis's image was spread visually in the illuminated editions of the Bible and his statues appeared at Mainneville, St Germain-en-Laye and elsewhere. His life story, which was a biographer's dream, was recorded by a number of writers before and after his death, including Geoffrey of Beaulieu, John of Joinville, William of St Pathus, William of Chartres and later William of Tyre. With such a career and such a range of hagiographers it was little surprise that soon after

Louis's martyrdom in Tunis, Cardinal Simon of Brie was checking out the miracles in preparation for his canonization. The resultant image was one which added a new dimension to French monarchy.

Louis's grandson Philip IV the Fair (1268–1314) also had his pressing reasons to make a special effort in his propaganda, mainly a desperate need for money to build up an essentially weak crown. Thus the main theme of his reign was creating an aura of almost supernatural omnipotence for the Capet dynasty. Philip was anointed with oil from heaven, he could heal the sick and his successes in curing scrofula or the king's evil were well publicized. He positioned himself as the heir of Charlemagne and St Louis, the two ideal role models for French monarchy. He presented himself as an emperor with no earthly superior and defined the borders of France in a new nationalist way, giving France also the aura of being a nation with a special place in the Christian world. All French people were told they had to obey the king and had a religious duty to die for their country if required. This mystical theme of nation and monarchy was spread assiduously by Philip as part of a continuous effort to build up royal power.

More specifically Philip used public relations techniques to pick off a number of groups which stood in his way. Most famously with the help of Guillaume Nogaret and Pierre du Bois (1250–1321) he orchestrated a convincing smear campaign in 1307 against the Order of Knights Templar, whose considerable gold reserves he coveted. Well-spread allegations of homosexual and other deviant behaviour were followed by the elimination of the order and confiscation of its wealth. The technique of extracting absurd, potentially pornographic confessions from people by torture and then using them as negative publicity was further developed. Attacks on the Jews were mounted for the same reason and in nearly as disreputable a manner. Philip's toughest adversary was, however, the papacy, and here his pamphleteers such as Pierre du Bois who used the clever technique of pretending that his material came from ordinary members of the public and Pierre Flote, carried on the traditional verbal battle against clerical power. This was supported by independent writers such as Pierre Jame de Montpellier and the philosopher Henri de Gand, plus to some extent satirical poets like Geoffroi de Paris. All this was part of the struggle to defend royal power against clerical encroachment. Philip even resorted to the expedient of appealing direct to his subjects at specially summoned assemblies. Overall his campaigns did little to win him popularity but they did help somewhat in his difficult task of drastically improving the royal finances. Philip had the sense of showmanship to burn a papal bull in public, and the more detailed appreciation of symbolism which led him to stipulate that from this time onwards French kings should carry two sceptres, one for power and one for justice. In his foreign excursions Philip used the common medieval expedient of dressing up his attack on Flanders in 1302 as a crusade, the best available cover-up for any war.

HUNGARY AND SERBIA

A remarkable extension of French propaganda expertise at this time was the assumption of the Hungarian throne by the Angevins. Charles Robert (1288–1342) had some royal Hungarian blood through his mother, but made the most of a thin case for the crown by playing up the saints among his ancestors: Ladislaus, Stephen and the blessed Margaret. The latter was a Hungarian princess put into a nunnery at the age of four, whose main achievement was to refuse marriage to a highly eligible prince, then resort to self-flagellation and sackcloth when Humbert de Romans groomed her as a Dominican role model and icon for the royal dynasty. Charles Robert used Simone Martini to paint Ladislaus as part of his pre-propaganda for installing his younger son as King of Naples and for various other dynasty-boosting paintings.

At this time also the Nemanjic dynasty created a deep-rooted image for Serbia, portrayed as the new Israel on the frescoes of Pec. Cunningly they persuaded Rome to legitimize them as a kingdom and Byzantium to legitimize their independent church. Then with a galaxy of royal saints and martyrs and a tsar of their own, Dusan (1307–55), they built a nationalism which was to survive the long Turkish occupation after the defeat at Kosovo.

THE MIDDLE EAST

Meanwhile, with the rehabilitation of the visual arts Byzantium adapted its propaganda techniques to new situations. New self-made dynasties needed to establish their respectability by lavish and carefully publicized patronage of the church. Constantine IX Monomachus (982–1055), who acquired the purple by marriage, made the new monastery of St George of Mangana his showpiece. John II Comnenus (1090–1143) founded the Pantocrator monastery as a focal point for his dynasty.

On the Islamic side the most interesting propaganda development of this period was in Egypt. An élite fighting force of transported slaves trained to be fearless warriors became the basis of the Mamluk regime, where Sultans were chosen on merit and had to project a strong image for themselves and their army. Sultan Baybars (*c.* 1220–80) was not untypical, using a mixture of intimidation and romanticized chivalry. This was the period of great mosque building in Cairo, of the role models embodied in the *Arabian Nights Entertainments*, of hagiographies like those of al Nuwayri, of pomp and circumstance and the symbolism of the golden saddle, the *Universal History* of Ibn Khaldun in 1382. The Mamluks also paid considerable attention to the development of heraldry as a means of corporate promotion for national and regional dynasties.

CHINA

As ever in this period the Chinese ruling groups showed remarkable ingenuity in coping with the substantial size of their empire. While the Sung dynasty struggled for control, one of its less legitimate emperors, Sung Kao-tsung (1107–87) conducted a clever propaganda campaign based on Confucian values. He had texts carved in stone and rubbings taken to circulate to his supporters. He made use of a large number of painters and calligraphers to enhance his image and his chief propagandist writer was Tsao Hsun (1098–1174) who produced *Auspicious Ones of the Dynastic Record*, twelve well-embroidered stories illustrating the imperial destiny of Kao-tsung, including classic themes such as four sages being present at his birth and his having an awesome vision the night before his final victory.

The career of Kublai Khan (1214–94) demonstrated how a self-made ruler could use propaganda to consolidate power. As the Mongol conqueror of north China he moved the centre of his massive empire to what was to be Beijing. Having done so he wanted to acquire the image of a Chinese emperor, not a barbarian, which was how his newer subjects regarded him. To this end he devoted substantial effort to simplifying the Chinese alphabet and making colloquial Chinese a literary language. He founded a special printing department in 1269, long before this tool was acquired in the West, and organized the publication of useful texts. Like many predecessors he used the technique of inscriptions carved on stones in public meeting places. Having adopted Buddhism he encouraged its further propagation. So far as other art forms were concerned he contented himself with acquiring the kudos of sponsorship rather than attempting to press them into overt propaganda. Thus the Yuan Theatre was given great encouragement to expand as was painting and poetry. Some painters like Liu Kuan Tao did project the visual image of the Khan of Khans, his tame poet Chao Meng Fu (1254–1322) did so verbally. Even opposition poets were allowed some freedom, and the painter Cheng Ssu-hsiao (1241–1318) with the typical Chinese eye for an elegant metaphor compared his country to an orchid with no earth – the barbarians had stolen the earth. From this period was to spring the opposition literary tradition of the Water Margins. China was to remain an area where the use of images to achieve attitudinal change was always important.

JAPAN, CAMBODIA AND INDONESIA

In Japan too this was an interesting period in which the arts began to be used considerably to help shape attitudes in a changing society. The priest Jien (1155–1225) had written the history *Gukansho* to justify the Heian dynasty, as the country sank into civil war and Buddhism was on the decline.

This developed the idea of a warrior tradition, extended in the epic *Heike Monogatari* which further explored the samurai ethic. Various strands began to come together: a revival of the traditional religion Shinto; the adding of the new concept of Zen Buddhism promoted by the reformer Honen (1133–1212) who after thirty years on Mount Hiei wrote his popular *Senjakushu* as well as diaries, fables and poems. Zen spread rapidly, helped like so many monastic movements by the deliberate allocation of manpower to calligraphy, book printing, ink painting and poetry. The poetry was particularly effective with works such as those by woodcutter-poet Hui-neng, and the visual imagery was skilful as in the one-stroke Bodhidarma, the Buddha cartoon achieved with a single brush stroke. In addition to this came the development of the theme of the divinity of emperors, with *Jinno Shotoki* in 1339, the descent of the emperors from the gods by Chikafusa (1293–1354). Meanwhile, also, the resources of the Noh tradition of theatre were developed and plays on samurai themes were written by Zeami (1363–1443). Even event management became important with elaborate rituals from the tea ceremonies, to ritual suicide, to shogun processions and imperial protocol. All this combined to make the long-term Japanese mentality, at least among the upper castes, one of the most deeply manipulated by propaganda in world history.

In almost all parts of the East different versions of the visual image of Buddha were used to impose politico-religious attitudes. The 120 stone reliefs of the massive three-terrace temple of Borobodur in Java with its seventy stupas projected the entire life story of Buddha. In the similarly massive temple at Angkor in Cambodia Buddha was portrayed on fifty-four towers as Lokeshvare, Lord of the World, to the advantage of the Khmer ruler King Jayavarman VII who could thus be projected as a major ruler, while his princesses were shown as Buddhist disciples. In Japan the massive bronze 30-foot Buddha, Prajna paravita, Mother of all Buddhas, was as always portrayed with the lotus, book of enlightenment and miraculous jewel.

INDIA

In India by 1025 the attention paid to visual propaganda was already at a high level. King Rajenda I built a new Tamil city to commemorate his conquests, including elaborately decorated temples. Two centuries later the remarkable Sun Temple of Konarak in Orissa, with its extended narrative sculptures elaborating the highly permissive tantra, was built by King Narasimha (fl. 1238–64). There was steady development throughout the period in the technique of Hindu image making, for example the multiple image of the god Shiva with four arms cast in a circle of bronze or the image of Ganesha as a humanoid elephant with a contentedly protruding stomach. The total deployment of the arts in Indian religious propaganda remained remarkably high quality for a substantial period.

Overall the early Middle Ages were a period in which exaggerated posturing and extravagant symbolism were required to overcome the limited range of available media. Intimidation and deception remained significant ingredients in the propaganda mix and the exploitation of mass hysteria was expanded considerably. One isolated but particularly remarkable piece of propaganda was *Zohar*, a treatise written in the form of a novel by Moses de Leon which laid the foundations of the Kabbalah, a revival of Judaism which was still to be potent 800 years later.

Loyalty remained the key value extolled in the early Middle Ages, but this had now been embellished by the addition of honour, chivalry and the defence of Christendom. At the same time there were ingenious and conflicting attempts to enhance the image of the two main multinational organizations of the West, the papacy and the Holy Roman Empire. There were also hints that the black image of women was lifting as the Virgin Mary was brought into fashion but there also began the long-term and bitter mutual slandering of the two great monotheistic religions, with a third caught in the crossfire. The anti-Semitic and anti-Muslim elements were only two examples of a general trend to fan obsessions. Flagellation and millennialism were indicative of the techniques involved. Finally, it may be noted that this age of beautiful monkish manuscripts was also one of the main periods for the production of forged documents and fake relics.

Later Middle Ages

In the late thirteenth and fourteenth centuries the papacy and the Holy Roman Empire remained the two massive monuments in Europe erected by the power of propaganda, but both were in frequent need of repair and neither evinced any substantial new initiatives in this period. The accession of Rudolph of Habsburg in 1273 was a landmark in that it began the ascendancy of that dynasty, but Rudolf displayed none of the expertise in propaganda which was to be a hallmark of his Renaissance successors. Ludwig IV (1283–1347) used the Franciscan friars to damn Pope John XXII, just as the Hohenstaufen had done before. A priest from Cologne, Alexander of Roes, produced his *Memoriale* in 1282 which stressed that the Germans were the rightful rulers of the world and should retain that role. By contrast Dante in producing his brilliant idealization of a world empire, *Monarchia*, written about 1310, argued that 'The Roman people was ordained by nature to command . . . nature has ordained in the world a place and a people for universal command' yet he preferred to advocate a Roman empire based in Germany to the petty politics of the native Italians. Similarly Engelbert of Admont in his *On the Origin and Purpose of the Roman Empire* upheld the case for the superstate. Yet in spite of all these treatises, a further flurry of similar works justifying the papacy, and Arnold of Brescia's promotion of the divine right of kings, both organizations were struggling. Much greater propaganda confidence was to be seen among the nation states of the north and in due course the city states of Italy.

ENGLAND

English history in this period provided numerous examples of the utilization of propaganda to assist in the development of a nation-based monarchy. Medieval kings needed military success to keep their baronial subjects in harness and to maintain this power they needed money. Propaganda was therefore designed to project the heroic image of the king as a successful leader to his barons and to project the benefits of war to a wider group of people including townsfolk and clergy whose backing would be required to sustain the war effort. Not surprisingly, therefore, Edward I (1239–1307) was a significant royal exploiter of public relations techniques because his conquest of Wales required substantial baronial effort followed by heavy investment in the huge stone castles needed to make the conquest permanent. Edward began the practice of sending back regular newsletters to London and other major towns from the front, justifying the war in Wales. This included a deliberate blackening of the Welsh character to endow the conquest with some of the aura of a crusade. If the Welsh were painted as wild, depraved and pagan then the backing of the church could be more easily achieved for the conquest. In particular after the defeat of Madog in 1295 Edward extended his propaganda to the English taxpayers as he had to pay the masons of Conway and Harlech Castles, themselves majestic stone pieces of propaganda.

Another factor in Edward's Welsh campaign was his obvious awareness that the Welsh themselves were inspiring their own resistance efforts with a vigorous grass-roots public relations effort. This took the form of scurrilous anti-English ballads which were sufficiently effective and provocative to goad the would-be conquerors into an act of censorship. Edward revived the cult of King Arthur and twisted his Welsh heritage and the prophecies of Merlin to suit his own propaganda. Above all he took the imaginative step of declaring his son Prince of Wales.

Edward also directed propaganda against his other enemies. The poem 'Pers of Bermingham', based on an incident in 1305 was an early example of anti-Irish propaganda, encouraging them to be hunted 'like hares'. In the same way the court-inspired poem 'Song of the Flemish Insurrection' of 1302 was rabidly anti-French and the 'Song of the Execution of Sir Simon Fraser' of 1306 was rabidly anti-Scottish, though his main effort against the Scots consisted of sheer intimidation.

Edward II (1284–1327) showed little aptitude for propaganda. He had to face the challenge of maintaining the war effort begun by his father and not allowing a further drift towards bankruptcy threatened by its huge cost; without exceptional military charisma his chances on both counts were poor. Edward made this already difficult situation worse by being deliberately insensitive to public opinion and persisting in the employment of unpopular favourites. The Despensers and Gavestons made themselves targets for jealousy and intense hatred, so that the propaganda successes of this reign belonged to the opposition. The popular 'Song of the Times' in 1300, 'The Song of the Retinues of Great People' and the hymn on Gaveston's death in 1312 were good examples of populist resistance compositions.

The other area where Edward paid for inadequate propaganda was Scotland which produced its first great nationalist image projection during his reign. The 'Declaration of Arbroath' was the brilliant climax of a rehabilitation and image-building campaign by Robert Bruce. He had added to his growing reputation as a guerrilla leader by making the classic medieval public relations master stroke – offering single combat at Bannockburn and then killing de Bohun in spectacular fashion. This was the material of legend which the poets Blind Harry and John Barbour were later able to develop into an effective national myth system. In addition, after Bannockburn Bruce captured one of Edward II's main propagandist poets the Carmelite friar Baston. The unfortunate Baston had in his possession an epic to celebrate an English victory, so he was made to change it to a Scottish epic in return for his release.

Edward III (1312–77) had a grasp of propaganda skills even better than his grandfather's. From his victory over the Scots at Halidon Hill onwards he made sure that every military success was projected by a patriotic poem, using poets like Lawrence Minot and his chronicler Geoffrey le Baker. In that same year, 1333, he deliberately cultivated the xenophobic myth that the French intended to invade England and abolish the English language. Minot's battle epics all had a drumming chauvinist beat and Robert Manning's verse history *The Chronicle* preached the idea of a united Britain as prophesied by Merlin and called after the founder of the dynasty, Brutus of Rome, with whose arrival in Britain the story began. By a stroke of fortune or forgery in 1346 Edward obtained some secret French invasion plans from Caen and with help from John Stratford had them widely publicized in England, starting with a public reading at St Paul's to stir up nationalist feelings. Edward also resorted to the standard medieval propaganda technique of branding the French King Philip VI as an anti-crusader in 1339. Franciscan and Augustinian friars were hired to go round the country to 'fire the hearts of faithful subjects' with tales of French atrocities even using a false rumour that the French had Turkish sailors ready to pillage the south coast. Most insidious of all was the poem 'The Vows of a Heron' circulated widely in north France and Flanders at the behest of the dispossessed Robert of Artois. This suggested that Philip might not be the legitimate ruler of France and that it was Robert of Artois who had stirred up the reluctant Edward III to stand against him. The Bridlington prophecies, written by the cleric John Ergholme also fall into the category of unofficial pro-war propaganda.

In 1352 a major public relations effort was required to whip up patriotic feeling against the French and the victory of Crécy was used to inspire donations for a further military campaign. Bartholomew Burghard was employed to send two open newsletters to the Archbishop of Canterbury for onward dissemination. Edward III made sure that there was plenty of publicity for his offers of single combat with French leaders, particularly in the period after the French had put out a smear story about him raping the Countess of Salisbury. The diplomat John of Hainault was used to project stories of Edward's chivalrous behaviour to counteract such ideas. A massive tournament was staged at Winchester with Edward posturing as the new King Arthur, and a Round Table actually built in the cathedral's St George's Chapel symbolized the new image of dragon-slaying and knightly virtue. St George was used as the symbol of the new Order of the Garter. The Queen employed the court poet Jean Froissart (1333–1405) both to produce poems and his *Chronicle* on the knightly deeds of the day while the King hired thirty painters to decorate his new buildings with chivalrous motifs. At the same time he expanded the music of the Chapel Royal to cope with a greater level of pomp and ceremony – five trumpets were now used to punctuate proceedings. From 1340 Edward also made deliberate use of heraldry as part of his propaganda, quartering the arms of France and England. All his state seals and armorials were redesigned incorporating the fleur-de-lis to help project Edward as the rightful King of France, touches which would have had significant impact on opinion formers on both sides of the channel. Throughout Europe this was a period when greater attention began to be applied to the corporate identities of royal or aristocratic houses and image became more important as a form of power display. The combined glorification of the war against France and the revival of chivalry reached its apogee with the high profile and military image of the Black Prince. The propaganda efforts of Edward I and III had made a major contribution to England's self-image as an imperialistic nation.

Richard II (1367–1400), as so often with a king who succeeds a brilliant military leader, suffered from anticlimax and budgetary problems and inevitably became tarred with a pacifist and indecisive image by comparison with his father, the Black Prince. Richard was actually more concerned with the exhibitionistic trimmings of court propaganda than the tough realities. His coronation was elaborate and he took the title Emperor, casting ambitious eyes on the Holy Roman Empire itself. He paid serious attention to his corporate identity, adopting the white hart as his symbol and applying it to paintings, statues, shields and the liveries of his officers. While his father and grandfather had cultivated the Arthurian image, Richard chose to go back to the more peaceful role model of Edward the Confessor, new statues of whom he put up beside his own and whose Hall of Westminster he had rebuilt. He encouraged literary and artistic talent, giving Chaucer a pension, employing court poets like Thomas Hoccleve (1368–1450) and painters like Scheeve, and heroic tapestries became a new propaganda medium of the period; but overall he was out of touch with reality and this was once more a period when new propaganda initiatives were to be found among the opposition, rather than government.

In political terms this was a time of peasant protest and spontaneous rustic propaganda, the era of John Ball and Wat Tyler, *The Vision of William concerning Piers Plowman*, probably by William Langland, *Richard the Redeless*, an overt attack on the King, Gower's* *Vox Clamantis* and the popularization of Robin Hood stories as part of the anti-feudal protest. The *Chronica Tripertita* included such interesting hexameter rhymes as 'R[ichard] plebem taxat, taxas pius H[enry] relaxat' [Richard taxes the people, the pious Henry untaxes them]. Overall, therefore, there was evidence of significant anti-government propaganda and to this should be added the literary attack on the other half of the establishment, the Catholic Church. John Wycliffe (1329–84) was by any standards a major figure in the history of English propaganda for his ability as a speaker, as an organizer of itinerant preachers attacking the papacy and as the first prolific producer of religious tracts in his own native language.

---

* John Gower was a salaried poet supporting the Lancastrian cause from 1393.

In the two reigns that followed, the propaganda of the new Lancastrian dynasty bore all the hallmarks of initial insecurity of tenure combined with substantial ambition. Henry IV (1367–1413) was concerned to justify his coup against Richard and utilized a forged *Chronicle* organized by his father John of Gaunt to assert some legitimacy. He distributed a circular to the towns accusing Richard of plotting to introduce higher taxes – a familiar tactic in modern party politics – and posed himself as a righter of wrongs, showing how he too had suffered when Richard had deprived him of two estates. He also ensured that notes on his own record were distributed to the chroniclers, the author of the *Evesham Chronicle*, Adam of Usk and Thomas Walsingham (d. *c.* 1422), making particularly sure to give them his version of the trial of Arundel. After Richard's death Henry was assailed by propaganda suggesting that Richard was still alive and the thirty-seven copies of *Traison et Mort* which survive suggest that it must have been in wide circulation putting across Richard as a just and chivalrous king who had favoured peace with France. The *Créton Chronicle* with a similar message was also widely distributed to embarrass the Lancastrian dynasty. Ironically Richard II's propaganda had improved considerably after his death.

Henry V (1387–1422) was a king of vast ambition who used propaganda as a technique to motivate his own followers at home, encourage allies abroad and demoralize his enemies. Even more than the two Edwards he worked to create a super-hero image with the help of event management, poetry, music and proclamations. His coronation was impressive: John Lydgate (*c.* 1370–1451) was court poet and event manager for twenty years. Thomas of Elmham was Henry's propagandist poet employed to eulogize his wars and write his verse biography, *Liber Metricus* and other panegyric histories included *Gesta Henrici Quinti* of 1417 and the *Vita Henrici V* of Titus Livius. Henry was adept at circulating diplomatic documents to other European rulers, putting across the idea that he was forced into the war by French duplicity. (The famous tennis balls story was probably a quite fictitious public relations stunt, borrowed from Alexander the Great). Once at war he took every propaganda advantage: he sent a newsletter to London the day before he captured Harfleur, then managed the pageantry of its surrender with panache, entering the town himself barefoot at the climactic moment. Before Agincourt he offered single combat to the dauphin; afterwards he announced that he shared the victory with God and celebrated a Roman style triumph in London with tableaux of St George; the 'Song of Agincourt' became a popular nationalist song. Like his predecessors he emphasized the role of Westminster Abbey as an image focal point for his dynasty, rebuilding the tomb of Richard II beside that of Edward the Confessor plus a huge one for himself. Lydgate made effective use of heralds and trumpeters to enhance the mystique of the invincible monarch. The Treaty of Troyes was also well publicized and the only hint of opposition propaganda at this time was from the Lollards who sold illuminated tracts from little shops and used cryptograms in verses to put across such subversive ideas as that Richard II was still alive. As Margaret Labarge put it 'Henry was conscious of the value of planned propaganda' and remarkably successful at it.

After the death of the super-king the Duke of Bedford (1389–1435) inherited the difficult task of keeping hold of his new French empire. He employed writers and illuminators to try to convince the French of the legitimacy of young Henry VI's rule over them. Laurence Calot's *Book of Hours for Notre Dame* elaborated the young king's French ancestry. Coinage was issued with the leopard and the lily side by side. The English propagandists resorted to smear tactics to counteract the remarkable publicity and response achieved by Joan of Arc in 1431. Her image was promoted by a number of major writers, notably the poet Christiane de Pisane (1365–1430), who saw her as a symbol of female self-assertion. Under the Duke of Gloucester the English sought to revive the image of Henry V by using Titus Livius's 'Vita', with more poems from John Lydgate such as the 'Libel of English Policies' to encourage a naval build-up and from John Hardyng (*c.* 1378–1465) who organized the tableaux for Henry VI's entry to Paris, while Lydgate both wrote poems and arranged the pageantry for the elaborate coronation of Margaret of Anjou. This sustained propaganda effort to counteract French nationalism ended in failure but it did demonstrate considerable thought beyond the application of pure force.

As Henry VI's reign lost direction the civil War of the Roses which followed provoked the development of propaganda skills on both sides. In 1450 the *Manifesto for Rebellion against Henry VI* was well promoted in Kent and Essex. The famous Jak Napes series of verses drove the King's minister Suffolk to his death in 1450 and there are mentions of a number of scurrilous verses posted in public places including John Holton's attack on Henry VI and William Collingsbourne's:

> The Cat, the Rat and Lovel the Dog
> Rule all England under the Hog

which was posted on St Paul's. The correspondence between the King and his rival the Duke of York was publicized as was York's *Manifesto* of 1460 offering to lay down his arms if legitimate grievances were met. York also ruthlessly exploited the foreignness of the queen and he persuaded two Lancastrian writers, Sir John Fortescue (1394–1476) and John Hardyng to change to his side. He employed two historians, John Basset and John Herryson, to project the Yorkist theme. On the strength of his rising image York made himself Edward IV (1442–83), fought off a revival of Lancastrian propaganda by the Earl of Warwick and had his rule bolstered by two major publications, Fortescue's *De Laudibus Legum Angliae* and Malory's *Morte d'Arthur* in 1469. He also imitated the court ceremonial of Burgundy, employing Olivier de la Marche to provide written instructions. Notably the *History of Edward IV's Arrival*, his come-back in 1471, was translated and circulated in Bruges within three days of the event, as he wanted a good image in Burgundy. He also had prepared by Peter of Poitiers a most elaborate genealogy for himself and had the prophecies of Merlin as usual recycled to prove it.

Given Richard III's (reigned 1483–5) ultimate reputation it is hard to think of him as having worked hard on his image during his lifetime, but in fact, as is the way with self-made kings, he tried his best. He used the popular preacher Ralph Straw to denigrate his dead brother Edward IV. The Duke of Buckingham was bribed to speak for Richard at the Guildhall. A petition for Richard to become king was carefully organized and presented at Baynard's Castle. Richard then arranged the events of his coronation to perfection with royal spurs and a ceremonial reburial of Henry VI at Westminster Abbey. Poets such as John Rous were encouraged to publish work on his behalf. But all this was of no avail when he began to turn on his own supporters and in the summer of 1483 his enemies old and new began to circulate the rumours that he had murdered the princes in the Tower. The image of the Yorkists began to go into terminal decline.

FRANCE AND BURGUNDY

Meanwhile in France Charles V (1337–80) organized more aggressive anti-English propaganda and revived the image of the fading Capet dynasty with epics like *Florent et Octavien* and *Theseus de Cologne*. On the whole French propaganda in this period was less exciting. The Valois dynasty started ruling in a state of weakness in 1328; Philip VI (1293–1350) portrayed Edward III of England as a disobedient vassal, the guilty party in the opening of the Hundred Years War, just as Edward attempted to do the reverse and prove Philip a usurper.

In her amazing but short-lived campaign Joan of Arc had the exceptional qualities which make ideal propaganda raw material – meteoric rise from humble origins, air of mysticism, apocalyptic mission, unusual appearance, paradoxical role and ultimately martyrdom. Her projection was brilliant with white streamers, a special version of the arms of France and the slogan 'Jhesus Marie'. She was helped by Juvenal des Ursin's pro-Orleanist *Histoire de Charles VI* and the earlier Valois *Coronation Book of Charles* which set down the highly elaborate rules for the coronation followed by well-managed city tours, public appearances, use of costumes, insignia, with the King becoming a priest-like figure directly descended from Charlemagne. Christiane de Pisane's *Livres des faits et moeurs de Charles V* made a real effort to project the Valois King as a peaceful, non-aggressive king, appealing direct to the people over the feudal barrier and patronizing the arts and it was Charles VI (1368–1422) whose efforts re-established the harp as an accepted musical instrument.

Massive dynastic tapestries were used as portable Valois propaganda when the court moved from town to town and Girart d'Orléans (fl. 1356–64) became the first official court painter recorded in French history. Meanwhile, the political content of mystery plays was enhanced to bolster the struggling monarchy.

In northern Europe this was the period of active propaganda to promote the concept of chivalry, so well described by Huizinga in his study. Tournaments were managed with elaborate ritual, just as the orders of knighthood were embellished with layers of vows and ceremonial, with new, more deliberate corporate identities such as the Order of the Golden Fleece, the golden 'S' of Lusignan. Many families chose mottos which were marked in golden letters on all their accoutrements, thus becoming a form of dynastic propaganda. The Burgundian court in particular devoted considerable attention to the image building of chivalry, as Huizinga put it – 'a source of tragic political errors' as damaging as nationalism was to be for subsequent eras. Georges Chastellain was the propagandist court historian. The dukes cultivated self-advertising nicknames like 'Sans Peur' or 'Hardi'. Offers of single combat from one head of state to another became in Huizinga's words 'peculiar forms of advertisement'. The challenge by the Duke of Burgundy to Humphrey, Duke of Gloucester to prevent Christian bloodshed was a calculated boost to internal and diplomatic public relations. The careful preparations – pavilions, standards, banners, armorial tabards for heralds, the whole graphic pomp of two conflicting corporate identities, organized for the occasion by de la Borde – showed the high level of event management skills in the Burgundian court.

The idea of chivalry elaborated in the *Chansons de Geste* and other similar literary output, was paralleled now in the visual arts, as Van Eyck (1390–1461), pioneer of the oil medium, produced works like the *Knights of Christ* for the Duke of Burgundy. The brothers Limburg combined the roles of painters and pageant organizers for the Duc de Berry (d. 1416), Philip the Good made the Condenberg Palace in Brussels a centre for artistic effort and commissioned works like Giles of Rome's *Rule of Princes*. Similarly the tapestries of courtly love at Regensburg matched the image projected by the German minnesinger. The propaganda cliché developed for the original Crusades was still invoked as image camouflage for wars which were not remotely crusades: the attack of the Teutonic Knights on the Poles, even of Edward III on France or France on Flanders in 1302.

Christian propaganda in the West had also developed new trimmings. The most successful of the monastic orders in the later Middle Ages were the Carthusians whose major objective was the production and distribution of devotional books. Richard Rolle, Nicholas Love and Denis the Carthusian, with his *Twelve Follies*, were highly successful propagandizing authors. Thomas à Kempis (1379–1471) the German friar from the Augustinian order was a prolific producer of pious biographies and ascetic treatises which had a large following. Penitential

books like the *Livre des Seyntz Medecins* by Henry, Duke of Lancaster sold
well as did the *Fifteen O's* of St Bridget and the religious poetry of Jean le
Fevre. The Community of Brethren and Sisters of the Common Life
founded in 1380 by Gerhard Groote was another grouping with a high
output of propaganda literature from its base at Zwolle. Morality plays
were an increasingly popular medium presenting biblical themes to mass
audiences. Van Eyck's altar piece for Bruges in 1436 brought a new
realism to Christian visual propaganda, the woodcuts of Guyot Marchant
for the *Danse Macabre*, the frescoes of Campo Santo in Pisa, the new
fashion in miniatures, the sculptures of the churchyard of the Innocents
in Paris, all put across the consciousness of death and the expanding cult
of the Virgin Mary could also draw strength from the developments in
the visual arts. Soaring Gothic cathedrals projected by their sheer
immensity if nothing else the huge authority of the church and signified
a massive investment in religious image projection.

The objectives of Western European propaganda in the later Middle
Ages were very specific: to extend the mystic majesty and inviolability of
national kingship, to project the self-sacrificial ascetic lifestyle conducive
to protecting the Catholic Church and to motivate the military castes to
sustain acquisitive wars for their masters. The media utilized had grown
steadily more sophisticated with didactic poetry, the use of symbols and
corporate identities, a new realistic and allegorical approach to
representational art and a huge investment in architecture both lay and
ecclesiastical.

ITALY

A pioneering example of city state propaganda was that of Siena under its
independent republican regime in the early fourteenth century. It
provided the second major impetus for Italian painting after the almost
contemporary second wave of artistic campaigns by the mendicant friars.
The Sienese oligarchy projected their image of good government to keep
the loyalty of their own region and maintain it against the encroachments
of Florence. The poems of Bindo Bonichi, the city chronicle of Agnolo di
Tura, the architecture of the Palazzo Publico and cathedral, the flag-
waving festivals for the Virgin Mary and local horse races, all contributed,
but the new miracle of Renaissance painting had a special place. In
particular the *Maesta* of Duccio de Buoninsegna (1255–1318) provided
the city with a focal icon. The two other great Sienese painters of this
period, Simone Martini (1284–1344) and Ambrogio Lorenzetti
(1300–48) also added special lustre to the city's projection, the latter for
instance with his *City of Siena under the Good Government of the Nine*.
Ultimately, however, Sienese propaganda against 'the Florentine curs' was
ineffective; one of the Florentine writers contributing to anti-Siena
propaganda was Dante himself.

Rome also produced a remarkable propagandist at this time. Cola di Rienzi (1313–54) the self-appointed Tribune of the city, who, though not part of the Vatican establishment, sought to bring back the Popes from their captivity in Avignon. As a self-made ruler who retained power in Rome for seven years he had a remarkable understanding of propaganda techniques and on one occasion managed to cover Rome with a mural poster campaign produced overnight. The techniques of graffiti and cartelli (wall and paper posters) were developed in Rome with the special nuance of the pasquinade, scurrilous verses appended to the statue of Pasquino in the city. Meanwhile, primitive printing had at last made its appearance in the West. Woodcut propaganda prints were in evidence in 1418 and the printing of indulgences which was to cause much resentment was begun by the Catholic Church in 1454, a year before the first printing of the Bible.

Florence acquired an able propagandist in Coluccio Salutati (fl. 1375–1406) who worked in Florence's defence against the power of Milan and whose writings were said to be 'worth a thousand horsemen'.

CENTRAL EUROPE

One of the most malicious propaganda campaigns of the late Middle Ages was that aimed at creating and punishing the crime of witchcraft. It can be traced back to publications like *Malleus Maleficarum* in 1486 by the Dominican monks Heinrich Kramer and Jakob Sprenger (it went to eight editions by 1500), *Formicarius* by John Nider written in 1435, printed in 1470, or *Flagellum Haereticorum Fascinorum* written in 1458 by Nicholas Jacquier and printed in 1591. The early development of the printing industry, leading to the production of these relatively cheap Teufelsbucher, turned witch-hunting into a fashion. They built up the image of witchcraft as a form of heresy with detailed, apparently true confessions of ritual murders of children, cannibalism, sex orgies, sex with the devil. All became part of one of history's most far-fetched yet also credible, and therefore highly damaging, propaganda campaigns geared essentially to maintain employment prospects for the Dominican Order and the Inquisition, backed by Pope Innocent VII, as they saw a decline in the number of conventional heretics and Jews available for them to pursue. The campaign was also to some extent a by-product of the struggle for propaganda initiative between two rival Popes, Eugenius IV in Rome and Felix IV, the anti-pope in Avignon.

Not dissimilar was the campaign waged against the Jews throughout Europe. As Hsia has shown the myth of ritual murder by the Jews was fostered by a series of show trials and extorted confessions orchestrated by the municipal establishments of towns like Endingen and Nuremberg. These were further propagated in the media of the day. In 1390 the Francisan St Bernardino of Siena preached against the usurers who had crucified Christ, as did St Vincente Ferrer in Spain and Pierre de l'Ancre in France. The *Judenspiel* of 1470 was an anti-Semitic variant of the traditional mystery play, presenting the Jews as ritual killers, while the poem 'Von Heligen Simon' by Matthaus Kunig helped spread awareness of one of the more notorious show trials. The theme was extended in a number of biased chronicles aimed at a wide market, including Matthias von Kemnat's *Chronicle of Count Friedrich* and Hartman Schedel's *Nuremberg Chronicle* of 1493, an anti-Semitic history book illustrated with numerous woodcuts of ritual murder scenes and torture. At an even cheaper and more popular level there was a significant trade in broadsheets on anti-Semitic themes, specifically child murder (see pl. 22); the Passau broadsheet of 1480 with twelve woodcuts of ritual murder and short, lurid commentaries was a typical example. There was even a large anti-Semitic mural on the city walls of Frankfurt and a further anti-Semitic play by Hans Folz in Nuremberg. One of the most vicious smear campaigns in the history of the world, this was no more than a by-product of the Catholic establishment in the Holy Roman Empire attempting to distract its restless subjects by creating an alternative focus for their resentment.

A foretaste of the propaganda battles of the Reformation was embodied in the struggle of the Bohemians. John Zizka (1370–1424), supporter of King Wenceslas and the Taborites, certainly achieved a sharp image with their distinctive religious and anti-German stance. The corporate emblems of the chalice and the goose were consistently promoted as was Zizka's personal symbol, a dagger in a fist. Significantly the main Catholic establishment pamphlet written to discredit the Bohemians, the *Historia Bohemica*, was written by the future Pope Pius II. Another remarkable propagandist from the same era of Europe was Hans Bohm, the Drummer of Niklashaussen, who claimed to have seen the Virgin in 1476 and then began a campaign of revolutionary, anti-clerical preaching using highly emotive techniques which pulled in massive crowds. This preaching was backed up by special banners, new songs and demonstrations of healing.

TURKEY

The fall of Constantinople in 1453 did have a number of implications for propaganda history. In many respects the Ottomans simply took over the event management techniques, the pomp and ceremonial of their Greek predecessors. However, the Sultan Mehmet II (1430–81) mixed these techniques with a corporate identity of three globes, symbolizing conquest – an idea borrowed from Tamerlane – and an aggressive use of tiger stripes. The janissaries cultivated a very extrovert image with liberal use of martial music, exotic uniforms, a red and yellow flag, a two-bladed sword symbol and a mythology of utter ruthlessness to predispose their enemies to defeat.

The Sultans of Turkey projected their images with considerable skill. Mehmet II maintained the Byzantine/Islamic tradition of architecture as a major vehicle for dynastic propaganda, with Topkapi and numerous mosques, a revival of the use of ceramic tiles, of Persian-style calligraphy and miniature painting. Ahmed Pasha was the chief dynastic poet with his *Book of the Conquests of Sultan Mehmed* in 1485. In due course their dynamic history was embellished by writers like Mustafa Naima Effendi (1665–1716).

Despite a later reputation for corruption, the Ottoman Empire was one of the most efficient and long lasting in history, maintaining for several centuries the impetus of the holy war for expansion.

CHINA

The Ming dynasty established itself in China in 1368 when Hung Wu made himself emperor. He cleverly feigned reluctance to accept the job and initially emphasized his humble origins, using Buddhist and Tao images to disguise his monarchical powers. Then he adapted traditionally strong Chinese propaganda skills of myth development and dissemination to enhance his image, producing the *Ta Kao* text as his trade mark and hiring 190,000 civil servants to proclaim it throughout the country, blaming all problems on corrupt officials, a technique later used by Chairman Mao. His chief propaganda organizer was Tao K'ai.

The propaganda of the later Middle Ages had attained new levels of sophistication but began to lean towards levels of grandiosity which made it uncomfortably remote from its audience. If anything it involved an unhealthy concentration on hysterical defence of the establishment with the early signs of the development of nationalist propaganda, but the rulers still often looking beyond the nation to grander multinational empires based on family ties and their own magnificence.

Renaissance

In terms of propaganda history the Renaissance covers the brief interlude between the visually quite primitive image projection of the late Middle Ages and the huge quantitative surge in the penetration of propaganda made possible by the development of book printing in the sixteenth century. It was also helped by the promotion of the classical virtues of glory and honour which were given the sanction of ancient approval. Its protagonists were the Italian city states, the Habsburgs, the early Tudors, the late Valois, and the late fifteenth-century Popes. The first tsars also come into this remarkable period in which the visual arts reached new heights and the art of intimidation new depths.

ITALY

There was a major urban renewal programme in Rome under Pope Nicholas V (1397–1455) and the Vatican was rebuilt on a massive scale, an architectural renaissance of the eternal city which paralleled the revived interest in classical models. Pope Julius II (1443–1513) identified with Julius Caesar, just as did the victim of his conquests, Cesare Borgia. When he took over Bologna he posed as the new Roman conqueror and was borne through thirteen specially built triumphal arches by four white horses, the sign of a Caesar, followed by a float with a model globe surmounted by an oak with golden acorns, symbol of his family the della Rovere. The Arch of Constantine was decorated with pictures of his military victories and medals were minted with his effigy. He employed Michelangelo (1475–1564) to sculpt a grandiose tomb which was never completed and of course to paint the Sistine Chapel where already the papal theme was projected with paintings of emperors bowing their knees to priests. Raphael (1483–1520) was brought to Rome to decorate the Pope's personal apartments and all but made a cardinal; Bramante (1444–1514) was hired to rebuild St Peter's in 1506. The successor of Julius, Pope Leo X, the Medici, was if anything even more extravagant and it could be argued that the combined efforts of these two Popes simply enhanced the financial strains on the Catholic Church which did so much to provoke the Reformation. His publicity in Florence itself was managed by Andrea del Sarto and an unfortunate young boy painted in gold for Pontormo's pageant died soon afterwards. Leo's chief propagandist writer Pietro Bembo (1470–1541) was made a cardinal and even Machiavelli wrote a song for his election. The other Medici Pope

Clement VII (reigned 1523–34) used Raphael, Michelangelo, Sebastian del Piombo (1485–1547) for painting, Bembo as literary agent and Cellini for coin design. In the short term the propaganda results were indeed negative, yet overall this campaign was also part of the continued build-up of a massive image infrastructure which was to ensure the long-term survival of the papacy as an institution.

Florence with its small Tuscan empire under the Medici and for a period as a republic was also very image conscious. Much of its massive artistic talent was devoted to religious topics and much of the propaganda effect achieved by the sheer quality of output rather than any direct message. But the city was deeply concerned with its vulnerable position in time of war. Paintings of rebels and traitors were painted on prominent walls, like posters, to warn the citizens; they included a series of 'cowardly captains' by Andrea del Sarto. Enemies of the Medici were given deliberately ugly portraits by artists like Andrea del Castagno (1409–80), whose wall paintings were subsidized by Cosimo de Medici in 1434. As bankers the Medici had already shown some flare for image with the visual theme for their Milan branch, a falcon with a diamond and the legend 'semper'. The relatively subtle means by which Cosimo (1389–1464) achieved virtual dictatorship in a republic included the heavy patronage of architects and scholars, the sponsorship of Donatello and the encouragement of a Platonic school which would position him as Plato's idea of the philosopher king. Lorenzo the Magnificent (1449–92) employed Verrocchio to do the family monuments and Botticelli as his manager of imperialistic events. Michelangelo painted frescoes of the *Battles of Anghiari* and *Cascina* while the poet Jacopo Nardi composed an epic, the *Volterrais* to commemorate the sacking of rebel Volterra. The statues of David by both Donatello and Michelangelo are believed to have been associated with the projection of Florence as a David under attack by Goliaths like Naples and the Holy Roman Empire. The Florentines too were conscious of their corporate identity, a lion with a fleur-de-lis, symbol of republicanism, which was applied prominently in all the towns under its rule. The astute Florentine diplomat, Niccolò Machiavelli (1469–1527) noted the same trait in the Venetians: 'In all the places the Venetians make themselves the master they cause the image of St Mark to be painted, but with a sword in hand instead of a book.' In fact the lion identity of Venice was also prominent in every town of the new Venetian empire from Spoleto to Famagusta.

Both Florence and Venice made sure they had appropriately biased histories of their cities – Florence's by Machiavelli, written for the Medici, and Venice's by Marcantonio Sabellico. Venice too had its superb displays of military triumphs, paintings and murals by Gentile da Fabriano (1370–1427), Giovanni Bellini (*c.* 1430–1516) and Titian (*c.* 1490–1576), later also Tintoretto (1518–94), to impress voters, visiting diplomats and any other visitors to the doge's palace. In particular the propaganda projecting Venice's role in the victory of Lepanto was developed by both Tintoretto and Veronese.

The Medici had by 1552 finally turned Florence into their personal duchy and Duke Cosimo I (1519–74) devoted substantial efforts to the projection of his dynastic image. His chief propaganda organizer was Georgio Vasari (1517–74) who painted a massive series of forty-two panel murals for the Palazzo Vecchio, extolling the rise of the Medici and the achievements of Cosimo himself. There was a grand *Cosimo I being crowned by Fiorenza* and a *Siege of Siena* to celebrate their greatest military success. To this was added a substantial output of portraiture, by Bronzino (1502–72) and Bandinelli (1493–1560), a huge collection of pictorial tapestries and the equestrian statues of Giambologna, a huge Victory, the fountains of Benvenuto Cellini (1500–71), ceremonial, medals and engravings. In the process some of the earlier propaganda paintings of Michelangelo and Leonardo were covered over by probably inferior work simply because the political reality had moved on. Specifically important was Cosimo's aggressive propaganda in Pisa, the newest part of his little empire. The new techniques of bronze monumental sculptures allowed for more dramatic equestrian statues and ornamental fountains or tombs. The work of Leone Leoni (1509–90) for Ferrare Gonzaga, of Vincenzo Danti for Pope Julius III fell into this category as did Pietro Torrigiano's (1472–1522) for the Tudors of England and Jacques Jonghelinck's for Charles the Bold in Bruges.

Numerous other petty rulers made use of the great talents of the Renaissance artists in their personal propaganda. Ludovico Sforza of Milan (1451–1508) employed both Bramante (1444–1514) and Leonardo da Vinci (1452–1519) who not only produced portraits for the dynasty but decorated his Sala delle asse in the Castello Sforzesco, worked on an equestrian monument of the Duke's father, designed court uniforms and helped stage court pageants – an all round multimedia projection of the Sforza image. Meanwhile, the poet Francesco Filelfo had written a celebratory epic, the *Sforziad*, to complete the family's glorification. Similarly Assore Baglione of Perugia hired Raphael (1483–1520) to paint him as a heavenly horseman and the poet Matarazzo to sing his glories. Ludovico Gonzaga had Mantegna (1431–1506) as his court painter in Mantua while the Montefeltros of Urbino had their epic *Feltria* by Porcellio and Genoa had its *Liguriad*. The attention to the visual image of political greatness, the elaboration of protocol and corporate identity reached new heights of extravagance.

In Naples the alien Spanish regime of Alfonso the Great (d. 1458) arranged a triumphal entry on the theme of Julius Caesar, an image based on King Arthur and the Round Table and had Bartolomes Fazio as literary propagandist. With a range of eagle motifs, mosaics, medals and statues Alfonso worked at his projection and his greatest success was to prove that the *Donation of Constantine* was a forgery.

To some extent the great Renaissance artists contributed to the growing respectability of homosexuality in Florence and elsewhere with their idealized portraits of Ganymede and other hermaphrodite heroes.

Similarly they projected affluence as a virtue, and took the visual image of Christianity further away from its roots.

AUSTRIA

During much the same period the Habsburgs were also devoting a unique level of resource to the development of their image. The Emperor Maximilian (1459–1519) had significant difficulties in securing the support of the German princes against both France and the papacy and in this context gave patronage to a major group of artists and writers. As historian Hugh Trevor Roper put it 'to Maximilian all the arts were propaganda'. Looking for an image which blended latter-day medieval chivalry with Renaissance statesmanship he commissioned the verse epic *Theuerdank* by Melchior Pfinzing with its 118 pictures, design by Vincenz Rickner the court calligrapher and woodcuts by Schaufelein. It, like the prose epic *Weiss Kunig* was an idealized, thinly disguised biography of himself. He was portrayed as the enlightened crusader and jouster; Dürer (1471–1528) and Holbein (1497–1543) provided the visual identity. The poet Trithemius developed the legend of Maximilian as a new Alexander the Great while Sebastian Brant developed an apocalyptic theme to give him almost Messianic status. Joseph Grunpeck was employed to ghost Maximilian's autobiography and Max Treitzsauerwein to plan a whole series of publications with woodcuts by Dürer and Celtis. To help him rule a multi-ethnic empire Maximilian was shown as a master of seven languages. The poet Konrad Celtis projected the Battle of Regensburg with woodcuts by Hans Burgkmair. In 1518 came the set of 200 copies of the *Triumphal Arch*, a massive exercise in Habsburg dynastic propaganda complete with family trees, battle successes and the Knights of St George. Maximilian had organized widespread public relations to justify his war against Venice in 1509. The event management of military triumphs was extended to new heights as an art form to which the greatest artists of the time such as Leonardo, Dürer and Holbein contributed. The ingenious mnemonic AEIOU (Austria Est Imperare Orbi Universo – It is for Austria to rule the entire world) neatly encapsulated the Habsburg aspiration towards world empire as evolved by Maximilian's father. Court composers were hired to produce ever more elaborate dynastic music.

Renaissance propaganda, however, probably reached its pinnacle with the career of another Habsburg, Charles V (1500–58) grandson of both Maximilian and Ferdinand of Aragon, inheritor of two massive empires spanning the Atlantic. He developed further the image of the Habsburgs, working along the same lines as his grandfather, using some of the finest talent in Europe. The Italian poet Ariosto (1474–1533) presented Charles as the new Charlemagne, the epitome of Christian chivalry, in his *Orlando Furioso*. The scholar Erasmus rewrote Dante to produce a treatise on the duties of empire. Titian painted Charles as the new Marcus Aurelius and likened him to Hannibal crossing the Alps in the popular equestrian picture *Charles V at Muhlberg*. The latter showed the Emperor ready for his spectacular entry into Milan and engravings of it by Enea Vico were circulated widely. At the procession into Florence there were globes, arches, gods, the castles and rivers of Europe, classical motifs, a massive mobile funfair of dynastic symbolism, which in different ways was recreated for entries to major cities throughout the empire. He created the Halls of Princely Virtue in all the cities of his empire by commissioning two massive sets of tapestries – eight covering his victorious campaign at Pavia and twelve his conquest of Tunis – which were rolled up and transported with his entourage. Designed by Bernert van Orley and Jan Vermeyen and manufactured by Willem Pannemaker, this series was echoed in a set of prints engraved by Martin van Heemskerck and wider exposure for this rare victory over Islam was to be used thereafter as a regular prop for the Habsburg image. The decorations at Charles' imperial coronations in both Aix and Bologna were similarly massive and music too received considerable attention. At least one musical instrument, the trombone, possibly a second, the cornet, were heard for the first time as the Pope presided over the Bologna coronation.

The long-term effect of this direct and massively extravagant form of propaganda is hard to judge. Perhaps, as partially intended, it had more effect on historical image than on political reality. Perhaps even in the short term it was counter-productive because of its overt extravagance. In addition to some great works of art, however, one element of Charles V's image projection did survive: his identification with Hercules as a symbol of princely virtue and his use of the graphic symbol of the Pillars of Hercules on his coins lives on as the dollar sign. One other aspect of Habsburg propaganda of this time is worthy of note. Because the Turks were their main enemies in the East, the Austrians made a determined effort to blacken their reputation and to motivate all their subjects with a crusading zeal against the Muslim conquerors. Anti-Muslim woodcuts such as the *Massacre of the Innocents* were widely circulated as were numerous tales, true and false, of Turkish atrocities, Turks as racial oppressors, impalers and devil worshippers. This type of propaganda was not without long-term effects (pl. 25).

SPAIN

Roughly contemporary with Maximilian were the Catholic monarchs of Spain, Ferdinand and Isabella (1452–1516/1504), whose dynasty was shortly to merge with the Habsburgs. Their propaganda usage was limited, but they did make special use of the tool of language. Each represented a different subkingdom, Aragon and Castille respectively; collectively they had the idea of uniting their country's written language and produced the first dictionary in Europe. As Bishop Aida put it 'language is the perfect instrument of empire'. They patronized the arrival of the first printers in Spain in 1473 and the writing of Spanish knightly epics, which cultivated the image of the hidalgo later satirized by Cervantes. A highly popular example was *Amadis the Gaul*, published in 1508.

FRANCE

Italy was the area where kings could turn themselves into emperors and Louis XII (1462–1515) of France revived this idea with his conquest of Milan in 1513, where his ceremonial entry was stage-managed by Leonardo da Vinci. Francis I (1494–1547) also nursed imperial aspirations after his conquest of Milan in 1515. He advertised himself as Roman Emperor and put himself forward for the position in 1519. Rouen erected a superb equestrian statue of him to celebrate his joyous entry into the city and Francis provided a home and salary for Leonardo da Vinci during the last three years of the great artist's life. His court poet was Clement Marot (1496–1544) who composed an epic on the French victory at Ceresole in 1544, though he later became a Huguenot psalm writer. The main propaganda painter was Francesco Primaticcio (1504–70) who produced a series of murals for Fontainebleau between 1534 and 1538 glorifying Francis.

ENGLAND

Perhaps on the fringes of mainstream Renaissance propaganda, but nevertheless in the same basic mould, was the early projection of the Tudors in England. Henry VII (1457–1509) was a self-made king founding a new dynasty and therefore had particular need of strong image making. The lead-up to his seizure of power was marked by his use of the Welsh prophecies of Dafydd Lloyd that a new Owen Glendower (i.e. Henry) would return to save the English and the Welsh peoples. Then there was the carefully staged public declaration of Henry's candidacy for the throne at Rennes in 1483. The next move was the use of force – the victory at Bosworth in 1485 – but thereafter propaganda was again a key weapon. Every technique was used to blacken the reputation of the dead Richard III. Henry's coronation, with hundreds of dragon and rose emblems, was planned deliberately to outdo Richard's. The pathetic state of the dead king's body after the battle was deliberately projected and John Rous in 1486 produced a new *History of the Kings of England* in which Richard was depicted as the evil hunchback. This theme was developed in a poem by Pietro Carmeliano on the murder of the young princes in the Tower, in Thomas More's *History of Richard III*, which scurrilously expanded the hunchback image, and in Polydore Vergil's *Angliae Historia*, commissioned by Henry but not finished until 1533.

On the positive side Henry sent out circular letters and heralds with offers of pardon to all Yorkist supporters. He displayed his attitude symbolically on his marriage to Elizabeth of York when he joined the identities of red rose of Lancaster, white rose of York and gold portcullis on the walls of Windsor Chapel and St John's College, Cambridge. After 1504 Henry became the first English king to make extensive use of printing in his propaganda: William Caxton had set up his presses in 1476 and now the crown used print for broadsides and proclamations. William Facques was made royal printer. Dynastic poetry came from John Skelton and Bernard André who was also Henry's main event organizer. He wrote the odes for Henry's marriage, the investiture of Arthur as Prince of Wales and in 1497 he completed *Les Douzes Triomphes de Henry VII* in which Henry was portrayed as Hercules completing his twelve labours. André worked on the new Arthurian Camelot image with a Round Table, a new Prince Arthur, and in this he was assisted by the court's other main pageant organizer and composer Robert Fayrfax, who led the substantially expanded court orchestra. Both English court painters, like John Serle, and Flemish immigrants like the librarian Quentin Poulet, as well as tapestry-makers, contributed to the development of Henry's visual image. In death he was commemorated with a monumental bronze effigy by Pietro Torrigiano (1471–1522).

Henry VIII (1491–1547) had less need of propaganda than his father but nevertheless at least in the first half of his reign was keen to acquire a high-profile image. The theme of Camelot was retained, with young Henry as the ideal crusading knight, romanticized in Stephen Hawes's (1475–1525) poem to mark his coronation. The royal painter John Brown made sure he looked like a crusader – the publication of a new biography of Henry V was used to draw comparisons. Henry's appearance dressed as Robin Hood at a May Day parade, the elaborate dressing with cloth of gold, red hats and feathers, horses with gold and silver bells and music redolent of chivalry from Old More, all combined to present him as a heroic, popular young king. However,signs soon appeared that Henry had even higher aspirations. Like his contemporaries Francis I and Charles V he wanted the status of an emperor, not a mere king. The flagship of his fleet was named the *Great Harry Imperial* and in 1535 he assumed the imperial crown.

With the end of his marriage to Catharine of Aragon a new approach was needed. Nationalistic ardour was cultivated with a new style of publication such as Richard Moryson's *An Exhortation to styre all Englishe Men to the defence of theyr Countreye* produced at Thomas Cromwell's behest in 1539 to generate anti-Catholic feeling. Moryson suggested the sponsorship of plays to focus on the abominations of the papacy and the promotion of other events like bonfires and anniversary processions to increase awareness of the changes and deepen the unpopularity of the monasteries.

The sculptures of Torrigiano, the paintings of Lucas Hornebolte, appointed King's Painter in 1535, of Joos van Cleve and Holbein, the extravagant pageantry of the Field of Cloth of Gold and Anne Boleyn's coronation were the climax of Henry's image projection of himself as more than just a king. Anne herself was identified publicly with St Anne, the mother of Mary, and stunning pageantry was organized by Nicholas Udall and John Leland to mark her crowning. New translations of the Bible and Foxe's *Actes and Monumentes* were illustrated with Holbein woodcuts of the new imperial Henry. Catholicism was exploited as a useful scapegoat and mock water battles were staged on the Thames in which the highlight was the dunking of a mock Pope or cardinals. Holbein painted Henry as a Solomon and a Caesar, producing also a mural for Hampton Court Palace which observers said 'made men tremble'. The greyhound image of the Tudors was spread wide. There were developments both in the composition of court music and from 1530 the printing of musical scores. The effort was substantial and the long-term image creation was effective, but in the short term the extravagance and oppression were to some extent counter-productive as they were in other Renaissance kingdoms. The upsurge of grass-roots Protestantism led by Tyndale, Coverdale and Cranmer on the one hand and peasant reaction embodied in the Pilgrimage of Grace on the other, coincided with a loss of royal propaganda credibility. By this time King Henry was too obsessed with his marital problems to be bothered with his wider image. Latterly he acquired an almost ogre-like reputation with nicknames such as Mouldwarp: by that time he hardly cared.

NORTHERN AND EASTERN EUROPE

The absurdity of Renaissance propaganda was at its most extravagant in the Tournament Book of Duke Johann Friedrich the Magnanimous of Saxony with its colour prints by Lucas Cranach (1472–1553), portrait by Jorg Pencz (1500–50) and fourteen escutcheons. The book projected the swaggering image of petty German landlords and that of the struggling Burgundians. Meanwhile, Flemish artists like Cornil Anthonisz of Amsterdam (1499–1535) worked on the images of Henry VIII, Charles V and Francis I. Further east, such a minor Balkan ruler as Prince Vlad of Wallachia was given a lastingly odious image by German propagandists in the 1490s with woodcuts of his activities as an impaler of innocent Transylvanian peasants.

A more remote part of Europe began to create its own imperial propaganda at this time. Russian monks like Nestor had adopted the Byzantine style of elaborate hagiography and had begun to use fairy and dragon fables to bolster the ducal authority of Moscow. Dynastic saints, like Boris and Gleb, were iconized and paraded as martyrs. For some time the Grand Dukes of Moscow and their ambitious Orthodox bishops had been watching the Byzantine Empire totter to its fall. They saw in this an opportunity for Moscow to seize the mantle and become 'the Third

Rome' winning psychological legitimacy for a new power structure in rather the same way as the Holy Roman Empire in the West had done from the ruins of the old. Thus Grand Duke Ivan III borrowed the corporate image of Byzantium – the two-headed eagle – then married a Greek princess and styled himself Ruler of all the Russias. Dimitri Gerasimov helped lift the image of the grand dukes by forging *The Tale of the White Cowl*, pretending it was a document found in Rome, to justify the transfer of empire from there via Constantinople to Novgorod, then Moscow.

Ivan's son Ivan IV the Terrible (1530–84) went one step further and called himself Caesar or Tsar. In the spectacular new cathedral built by the Kremlin to celebrate his crusade against the Tartars Ivan followed Byzantine rituals and justified his rule with Byzantine texts. The revised *Book of Degrees and Imperial Genealogy* showed how the tsar was descended from saints and emperors, bringing together every genetic strand the new regime required and his 27,000-page church encyclopedia endorsed every detail of the more exclusively Russian Orthodox Church. Ivan flirted briefly with the introduction of printing, but distrusted the new medium and fanned the xenophobic, anti-Semitic mood which suited him better. Ivan's public image was coordinated by Bishop Makarii, blending the idea of the Third Rome with Muscovite legend and the tradition of the Orthodox Church to forge a new destiny for the Muscovite empire. He was deliberately promoted as 'Terrible' (not an insult for a Russian ruler until Ivan himself grew erratic) by Ivan Peresvetov in his *History of Kazan* of 1564 and elsewhere to help strike fear into the minds of his enemies. In the end his personal image was to be severely damaged by his own paranoia but the image of tsardom was to last three and a half centuries.

The anti-Ivan propaganda campaign was begun by Andrei Kurbsky (1528–83) to prevent Ivan's election to the throne of Poland. Significantly in 'the time of troubles' (1598–1613) it was noted that Russia was deluged with 'alluring pamphlets' on behalf of various pretender tsars including Boris Godunov who was himself brought down by accusations of murder spread by Semyon Shakhorsky.

Throughout European intimidation, the sharp image of torture was an extremely vivid threat to place alongside the pomp of pageantry and huge elaboration of artistic effort.

MEXICO AND PERU

The opening of the sixteenth century saw the Aztec empire in Mexico at its greatest height and its propaganda in an uncanny way resembled the image-broking of contemporary Europe. The Aztecs were driven by a particularly demanding religion in which large quantities of human hearts needed to be sacrificed to the sun and war god Huitzilopochtli. This in turn meant that they needed regular wars to maintain an adequate supply of sacrificial victims and so religion was used to justify imperialist aggression. Thus their propaganda system needed to motivate the upper military caste and to terrify everyone else into abject submission. No literature has survived but it is known that ballads were composed celebrating the deeds of Aztec knights and kings: both the scribes who 'work in red and black ink' and the minstrels were given significant social precedence. The two orders of knights, Jaguars and Eagles, each had their corporate identities, their codes, traditions and motivation systems. There were complex collections of emblems to distinguish the ranks from the king with his 'Golden Star' downwards. The overwhelming Aztec propaganda medium was, however, the combination of architecture and event management. The elaborately staged rituals of human sacrifice, awesome enough in their own right, were made even more intimidating by the backdrop of massive pyramids, terrifyingly grotesque statues and specially composed music. The ceremonies at Tenochtitlan, often involving substantial numbers of victims and huge audiences, must count as history's most comprehensive acts of mass manipulation. As Leopoldo Castedo put it: 'Aztec art was imbued with the dread, awe and grandeur necessary to dazzle the subject peoples and carve the image of an omnipotent and implacable state.' The stone sculpted version of the tzompantli, or rack of skewered human heads, ranks as one of the most obscenely effective pieces of propaganda sculpture in human history, comparable perhaps only with the bas-reliefs of the Assyrians in its undisguised threat. The substantial output of Aztec carving was all directed towards religious and political ends.

Similarly in Peru the Inca Pachakuti (fl. 1438–71) showed a firm grasp of propaganda skills as his regime subverted the previous Andean oligarchy. A state religion of worshipping all dead Incas became the focus for national motivation. Their statues stood in Cuzco and elsewhere. Their mummies were paraded in a number of carefully staged events often linked with the new seasons. Young nobles were indoctrinated at an early age to strive for the empire and go to a very inviting heaven when they died. As Cobo put it: 'The Incas made the people listen to this sort of nonsense every day so the people thought the Incas were much like Gods and full of more than human wisdom.' The Incas also constantly adjusted their own oral chronicles to suit each new regime, using fake history without scruple to justify their destiny as conquerors and to create a false record of achievement.

In general the propaganda of the Renaissance period in most parts of the world demonstrated a new skill and extravagance in visual display accompanied by an unhealthy reliance on intimidation. And the European version of intimidation was extended into both western Africa and the Americas.

Reformation

The Reformation is particularly remarkable in the history of propaganda because of a special coincidence: the first major European development in printing with movable type happened at the same time as the climax of a long period of restlessness within the Catholic Church. It produced one propagandist of outstanding skill in Martin Luther and a number of others of the highest calibre, such as Calvin and Loyola. As A.G. Dickens describes it, this was 'the first mass movement of religious change backed by a new technology'. The invention of printing was in Luther's words 'God's extremest act of grace'.

GERMANY

The Reformation and the printing industry helped each other, the movement supplying texts that were potential best-sellers, vastly assisting the budding industry with the resultant cash flow, while the printers gave the reformers a more effective medium than had ever been available before. At least half of all books published at this time were religious and the number of titles produced in Germany rose from 90 in 1513 to 944 in 1523; so propaganda was good business. Thanks to the resultant investment, printing speeds in the sixteenth century increased from about 20 sheets per hour to 200 and average editions rose to about 1,000 copies. Martin Luther(1483–1546) himself produced thirty major pamphlets between 1517 and 1520, some in as many as twenty-four editions and it has been estimated that there were 300,000 Luther works in circulation before the Diet of Worms. Only Christopher Columbus, whose four-page description of his voyages reached twelve editions, had come anywhere near this level of publishing success.

Luther's propaganda pamphlets were in the relatively new tradition of Fliegender Blatter of about fourteen to forty pages with woodcut frontispieces, which had begun to be produced in large quantities at the beginning of the century. Koberger, the Nuremberg printer had twenty-four presses and a sales force throughout Europe with catalogues of his publications. Luther's printers in the small town of Wittenberg must have had similar capacity, for his *Sermon of Indulgence and Grace* sold 14,000 copies in 1518 and 9,000 more by 1520; his New Testament in German sold 6,000 copies in its first year. The lack of effective censorship in the divided German states made this success easier, but it is significant that the Catholic printers did not do so well. One of their most popular pamphlets, Werner's *Great Lutheran Fool* was still a little too academic for widespread commercial success.

Given the help of printing technology, the willingness of the industry to sell his works and the absence of effective suppression, Luther made good use of his opportunities. His output was enormous, his style vigorous. He used plain German language laced with the common idioms of northern Germany and Austria. He used woodcut cartoons by brilliant artists such as Lucas Cranach who had previously worked for the Emperors Maximilian and Charles V as well as the Elector Frederick at Wittenberg, to caricature the papacy and Catholicism generally. His mixture of biblical quotations in the vernacular, folk wisdom and homespun metaphor gave his sermons and his writing the vigour for effective communication on a wide scale. There was also the relative novelty of his dialogue-type sermons, which put both sides, and his dialogue pamphlets, which made for the more effective demolition of his adversaries. Wittenberg with its tiny population of around 2,000 became not only the publishing centre of Europe but a training centre of great importance for the techniques of the pulpit.

Three other major propaganda writers aided Luther: Johan Eberlin von Gunzburg (d. 1553) published his pamphlet series *The Fifteen Confederates* in 1521 projecting a Protestant Utopia; Pamphilus Gengenbach (d. 1525), the Basel publisher and an early German language dramatic poet, wrote his *Novella* of 1525, a strong pro-Lutheran satire, and Niclas Manuel (d. 1530), also the painter of *The Dance of Death* and other subjects, wrote a number of pro-Reformation plays including *Die Totentresser*. Yet it was an unknown author who created what was perhaps the most powerful role model of the age, Karsthans, the evangelical peasant, one of those rare fictional characters like John Bull, Uncle Tom or Chauvin who became symbolic for a whole era.

Luther's message combined the negative and positive in equal measure. He attacked papal corruption, the buying and selling of church offices, the complacency of the monasteries and the humbug of clerical celibacy, all enshrined in the metaphor of the Babylonian captivity. These were all popular subjects guaranteed to please a wide audience. On the constructive side he offered a new native articulacy to the half-literate urban populations, with budding consciousness of having minds of their own, a nationality and a literary language. For virtually the first time in history a significant reading public was able to consider revolutionary ideas presented in a mass medium which combined both the literary and visual skills.

Beyond the use of sermon and pamphlet Luther had other propaganda techniques in his repertoire. His legendary nailing of the *Ninety-five Theses* to the church door in Wittenberg showed the panache of a great public relations man (pl. 14). Thereafter, the *Theses* were printed in three editions simultaneously in three cities. He also encouraged the use of theatrical performances – morality play derivatives – to contrast papal depravity with the purity of the primitive church. There was his superb contribution of the propaganda use of music. As he put it: 'I wish after the example of the prophets to make German psalms for the people so that the word of God may swell among the people by means of song also.' In addition the poet Hans Sachs (1494–1576) put Lutheran propaganda into verse form while Cranach developed the black and white woodcut illustrations which could for the first time be mass produced. Effective woodcuts contributing to the campaign included Peter Flotner's *The Poor Common Ass* of 1525 attacking Catholic usury, Mathias Gerung's *Shipwreck of Catholic Clergy* of 1545 and Hans Brosamer's portraits of Luther himself. Colour was also introduced to woodcuts, for instance with Leonard Beck's *Monk and the Donkey* followed by Cranach's depiction of the Pope as a donkey. Luther's stature was further enhanced by a copyist who used Dürer's *St Jerome* as the basis for a new Luther woodcut. David Joris brought his talent for glass painting to the Protestant cause, yet another tool in his graphic armoury.

The most extreme example of Protestant propaganda in Germany was in Munster where the Anabaptists in 1534 set up a populist dictatorship with remarkably modern features. Their leader John Bockelson appointed himself a king and called himself John of Leyden, having previously created a reputation for himself by running naked through the town and falling down in a three-day trance which was followed by a revelation from God that all property should be transferred to the poor. Women in particular were reduced to a state of hysteria by his rantings and he used intimidation on those who resisted his will, so that he achieved a brief, fanatical rule, introduced compulsory polygamy and some elements of primitive Communism before succumbing to suppression and massacre.

GENEVA

John Calvin (1509–64) was much less of an extrovert, much less of a mass communicator than Luther, but in his own way he created almost as wide a swathe of influence. Certainly his *Christianae Religionis Institutio* published in 1536 was a highly influential treatise particularly when he produced the French version in 1541. A pioneering example of French prose writing as well as a brilliant religious exposition, it was reprinted with considerable frequency and played a large part in the conversion of the French middle class. It helped and was helped by the Geneva printing industry. Laurent de Normandie, Calvin's leading printer, had 200 paid distributors and at one time a stock of 10,000 pages of type set up to print Calvin's writing. Calvin not only sent out teams of travelling pastors but also provided in Geneva a haven for exiled protesters from other countries, a number of English priests who went back to be key leaders of the church under Elizabeth, Huguenots and the energetic John Knox who was to capture Scotland for Calvinism. Within twenty years there were 2,000 Huguenot churches in France; Calvinism had established deep roots in a number of north European countries and gathered the momentum which was to enable it to dominate the North American colonies. Not only was it addressed in the first place to an essentially bourgeois audience, but it in turn fostered bourgeois values – resistance to aristocracies and tyrants, admiration for thrift and the work ethic. Calvin wrote vast numbers of pamphlets and sermons, but he deliberately set himself against some of the obvious available tools of propaganda. He suppressed the use of instrumental music as unnecessary, but he did allow the use of rhyming psalms and his later followers, particularly the French Huguenots soon became avid producers of great hymn tunes such as 'The Old Hundred'. Equally the Calvinists reacted violently against Catholicism's use of the visual arts, so that painting and sculpture were regarded as idolatry. What led to the rapid spread of Calvinism was probably its clear-cut image of uncompromising moral severity combined with genuine asceticism. Its very lack of visual trimmings or literary artifice were its most obvious propaganda attractions. The short haircuts, plain black clothes and sabbatarian self-discipline of the puritan sects became their own self-propelling propaganda machine. One classic of Calvinist propaganda was Guillaume Farel's *Summary and brief description of anything that is true for every Christian to have confirmed in God and help his neighbour*, published five times between 1539 and 1552. Calvinism did produce at least one other communicator of genius, John Knox (1513–72), an immensely gifted preacher and writer of tracts, whose best known publication was *The First Blast of the Trumpet against the Monstrous Regiment of Women*.

SPAIN, ITALY AND BEYOND

On the side of the Counter-Reformation the greatest figure in propaganda terms was without question Inigo Lopez de Recalde or St Ignatius Loyola (1491–1556), founder in 1534 of the Society of Jesus or Jesuits. In the tradition of the great medieval ascetics he imposed upon himself a punishing regime of service and renunciation which gave him high initial credibility in a corrupt age. From this he developed an ability to achieve deep conversion of proselytes using techniques akin to brainwashing – the thirty days meditation, the long fast in a cold darkened chapel before taking solemn vows for perpetual self-dedication. He followed this with integration into a closely-knit cellular system, insistence on absolute obedience and the superbly administered Jesuit educational machine, which was to become the prime propaganda organization for Catholicism for some years to come. The Jesuits' attention to the inculcation of their ideas to the young was one of their most remarkable facets, particularly as they concentrated this effort on the élitist minority of decision-makers, working from the top downwards.

By the time of Ignatius's death there were 1,000 monks, fifty years later the numbers were up tenfold. Their calibre was extremely high, partly because of the rigorous training to which they were subjected, partly the very strict level of discipline. Their sheer efficiency and commitment were such that they could mount a massive propaganda drive which turned the tide against Protestantism in Poland, stemmed it in many other parts of Europe and pioneered the conversion to Christianity of areas as far afield as Goa, Japan, China and South America.

In terms of mass media the work of the Jesuits was less obvious, but still significant. They made use of theatre with propagandist plays such as *The Sacrifice of Isaac, Pietas Victrix* and Luis Belmont's *El Diablo Predicator*, making substantial use of clever effects. The poet Robert Southwell (1561–95) produced a number of Jesuit poems before his martyrdom. The Jesuits also had a strong sense of visual imagery with the development of symbols such as the sacred heart and they went on to become substantial patrons of religious art. Hermann Hugo produced a compendium of Jesuit emblems in 1624, explaining the use of symbols like the sacred heart. The new sentimental melodramatic style of religious painting typified by the *Transfiguration* of Giovanni Girolamo Savoldo (1480–1548) or the *Madonna and Child with Saints* of Lorenzo Lotto (1480–1556) set a new fashion of illustrative propaganda which Loyola believed to be vital. These themes were to be even further developed by the most innovative of the Counter-Reformation painters El Greco (1541–1614) and Caravaggio (1573–1610). Both Loyola and Xavier were painted by Rubens in 1617 before they officially became saints. There were numerous pictures of victories of saints over sin, and orthodoxy over heresy, including examples by Rubens, Bernini and Carlo Dolci. Equally the Jesuits laid great store by architectural innovation and were pioneering patrons of the new baroque style, which they saw as yet another tool to divorce their image from older more corrupt periods of Catholicism and as a means of provoking interest from those who might otherwise drift away to Luther. The building of Il Gesu in Rome in 1575 was the beginning of a baroque/Jesuit fashion which swept Europe. Rubens worked with the architect Pieter Huyssens on the new Jesuit churches in Flanders. Pope Urban VIII (reigned 1623–44) was a major developer of propaganda art and of the creation of relic cults, particularly St Peter's. Overall the visual communication techniques, the categorization of meaningful symbols was enshrined in Cesare Ripa's *Iconologia* in 1593. Giovanni Baglione's painting of the dreadful death suffered by a Byzantine iconoclast helped underline the new respectability of religious art. Last but by no means least the Jesuits paid close attention to the use of music, so that coming together with their use of the visual arts and their sense of event management, the effect was substantial. Even at a local level they were great developers of the fiesta as a means of communicating and motivating, with elaborate processions, moving statues, theatrical sermons and a well-orchestrated calendar of events.

The Jesuits were not as energetic publishers of popular tracts as the Lutherans but they did have massive output of educational literature and research. Loyola's own *Spiritual Exercises* was a profoundly important training manual and works such as Edmond Auger's *Catechism* sold 38,000 copies in Paris alone, while Peter Canius's *Catechism* was compulsory reading throughout the Habsburg empire.

The flow of creative talent for the Counter-Reformation was almost inexhaustible. The composer Giovanni Palestrina (1525–94) was given a number of major commissions by the Council of Trent, Bernini (1598–1680) developed the full theatricality of St Peter's both inside and out, his last commission significantly being the small Jesuit church of St Andrea al Quirinale. Andrea Pozzo (1642–1709) painted the *Apotheosis of St Ignatius* and the *Allegory of the Jesuit Mission* of 1691, developing the typically baroque *trompe l'œil* dome paintings, almost literally adding a new dimension to the persuasion of the faithful. In Domenico Zipoli the Jesuits had a tunesmith who created exciting new church music which even worked well on the flutes of the Guarani Indian converts in Paraguay.

One unsavoury by-product of Counter-Reformation propaganda was the outburst of papal anti-Semitism typified by Pope Paul III's bull *Cum omnis absurdum* of 1553 which blamed the Jews for the death of Christ; this was, of course, not the first version of this concept, but it was now extended as a form of scapegoat propaganda which had the immediate effect of prompting the creation of ghettos in Italian cities in the following two years. Meanwhile, Paul III commissioned Michelangelo to paint *The Last Judgement* and Titian to record Paul's own image.

The main propaganda successes of the Jesuits were the total restoration of the Austrian empire to Catholicism, and the amazing conversion of the Polish peasantry from Orthodoxy in the face of strong Lutheran and Calvinist competition. Thereafter they achieved notable propaganda successes in South America. The career of St Francis Xavier (1506–52) in Goa, Ceylon, China and Japan was by any standards extraordinary, and longer-term success in the conversion of China might well have been achieved if the papacy had allowed the modification of the Christian message to suit a Chinese audience. Yet in some respects the very intensity of Jesuit propaganda was to provoke an especially bitter strain of counter-propaganda 130 years later, when even the austere corporate black of the Society was to be turned into a symbol of its wickedness.

ENGLAND, HOLLAND AND SPAIN

One of the lasting features of Reformation propaganda on both sides was the deep and damaging rift of prejudice which it left for subsequent generations. Much of this was due to the addition of political conflicts to the religious struggles of the century after Luther. One example of this was England where the Tudor dynasty was itself divided. For the brief reign of Edward VI (1537–53) propaganda was managed ineptly by the Seymours and his successor Queen Mary was too convinced of her own religious infallibility to bother about the niceties of mass persuasion. The great communicators of her reign were all on the other side: Thomas Cranmer (1489–1556), author of the *Prayer Book*, Thomas Wyatt (1503–42), the poet, John Foxe (1516–87), the recorder of martyrdoms, and they were supported by very heavy pamphlet activity. It was also the period of the rise of anti-Spanish xenophobia, particularly inspired by Mary's unpopular marriage to Philip of Spain. There was an international campaign of vilification against Philip led by his Dutch subjects and Italians, accusing him of incest and the murder of his son; the 'legenda negra' was projected in five languages and even the writings of the Spanish bishop Las Casas (1474–1566) went into over 100 editions in English because of their account of Spanish atrocities in South America.

The Dutch were good at propaganda perhaps because, as unwilling subjects of Spain, they had to be. In particular they pioneered techniques of political engraving. Philip complained about the large number of leaflets and placards arguing against him which were put up in the towns. Hendrik Goltzius produced his *Punitio Tyrannorum* in 1578. Their campaign against Philip was masterminded by William the Silent of Orange (1533–84) leader of the Dutch revolt against Spain. His military position was so weak that he needed the help of propaganda skills to keep his armies motivated. He encouraged the 'legenda negra', attacked Philip in his own *Apology* written in 1580, attacked Philip also for his ill-treatment of the Spanish Jews and for atrocities in Antwerp in 1576. His chief propagandist was Philip Marnix de Sainte Aldegonde who wrote the song 'Wilhelmus van Nassouwe' in 1567, a rhymed catalogue of his leader's deeds linking his cause with that of the Netherlands. This, together with William's *Apology*, which was authorized by the Estates General, and Duplessis Mornay's *Vindiciae contra Tyrannos* stimulated the new Dutch nationalism with lines like: 'Let us together embrace the defence of this good people' and Nassau's motto: 'Je maintiendray Nassau'. The *Apology* was published in four languages at Delft and Leyden with a number of editions circulated to a wide European audience. William's image building ranged from his use of the Orange tricolour and his active publishing enterprise, to his encouragement of artists like Peter Brueghel (1520–69) who produced the *Massacre of the Innocents*. The Duke of Alva was smeared as 'an effeminate Sardanapalus'. In addition the Chambers of Rhetoric organized plays, poetry and processions in the Dutch cities, with a new national strain of poetry from Heinsius and history from Pieter Schryver. The secret signs and the charisma of the Sea Beggars all contributed to the ultimate success of his campaign and the failure of the less politically aware Spanish Duke of Alva.

The Low Countries saw a pictorial war between the two sides. Matthieu Merian and others produced a series of prints of Catholic atrocities, including the Massacre of St Bartholomew, while the Antwerp Catholics responded with their versions of Protestants disembowelling Catholics and similar activities. A medal was issued in some quantity showing the King of Spain offering an olive branch to the Belgian lion, but hiding a collar and chain behind his back.

Philip II himself worked hard on his own image as a dogged defender against heresy. Titian was commissioned to produce his *Spain Coming to the Aid of Religion* after the victory at Lepanto over the Muslims in 1571. Philip hired Niccola Granello and Lazzaro Tavarone to paint battle scenes in the long gallery of the Escorial, seeing in Lepanto and the siege of Antwerp his own positioning as the new Charles V/Hercules Hispanicus. Leoni sculpted him as a Roman emperor. The massive tomb built for him at Seville had eight statues of the Virtues, pictures of sixteen of his victories, eight altars and an arch on the Hercules/Gibraltar theme.

El Greco (1544–1614), meanwhile, began his career as a propagandist painter working for relatively minor clients, for example Don Diego de Castilla, Dean of Toledo, on whose behalf he worked on a series of frescoes projecting his ancestry and defending the liberal Archbishop Carrenza against the Inquisition. He was also involved in the projection of the blessed Alonso de Orozeo (1500–91) an Augustinian prior and potential candidate for sainthood in Madrid, but he was rejected as a court painter by Philip II.

The other important topic for Spanish propaganda was South America where a number of writers contributed to the notion of Spain's mission to civilize. Jose de Accosta with his *Historia Natural y Moral de las Indias* (1590) was the great Jesuit advocate of Catholic imperialism, while the Dominican Gregorio Garcia developed the myth that the South American aboriginals were the degenerate survivors of the Ten Lost Tribes of Israel and Bernardo de Balbuena produced an epic poem on New Spain. All this material classified the native Americans as barbarian heathens who needed to be forced to learn European habits from the benevolent Spaniards.

When Queen Elizabeth (1533–1603) succeeded her Catholic half-sister Mary in England in 1558 her position was far from secure, so she had need of good image building. As J.S. Neale put it 'no sovereign could have been more sensitive about her popularity'. The event management of her first journey from Hatfield to London and subsequent coronation were well handled with a mixture of pageantry and informality, gun salutes and young children reading speeches, which spread her image in a matter of weeks. During the remainder of Elizabeth's long reign the two main strands of her propaganda effort were the undermining of any claims to the throne by Mary, Queen of Scots and the denigration of Spain. In the first campaign John Aylmer (1521–94) wrote the response to Knox's famous *First Blast of the Trumpet against the Monstrous Regiment of Women*. Thomas North (1535–1601) wrote an anti-Mary play *Gorbodin* in

1571; Wentworth attacked 'the most notorious whore'. After Mary's implication in the Babington Plot of 1585 a campaign of rhymes, ballads, pamphlets and bonfires was organized to help build up the pressure for her execution. Among the techniques used against her was the printing of fake letters from Elizabeth's subjects purporting to demand strong action against Mary. This went alongside a consistent promotional campaign for the merits of the new Church of England organized by Bishop John Jewel (1522–71) and others.

Meanwhile, Elizabethan propaganda's other great topic, the denigration of Spain, was also under way. Richard Hakluyt (1552–1616), the geography teacher, argued that the Elizabethans deserved a transatlantic empire on the grounds of the conquests of Arthur and Madoc. His *Principal Navigations, Voyages and Discoveries of the English Nation* assisted in raising the profile of the merchant adventurers and funds for the navigational and colonizing projects of Drake and Raleigh. Raleigh himself produced his strongly anti-Spanish tract on the *Revenge* in 1591 as well as other pro-expansionist material. Elizabeth's visit to Tilbury, the chauvinist ballads which followed, the Armada medals with their motto – 'the wind blew and the Armada was scattered' – and the many Armada prints, all combined to put across the government's mission to defeat the Spaniards with God on the side of the English. Francis Walsingham organized groups of travelling speakers and troupes of actors to visit the English cities, almost as an extension of his espionage responsibilities. Delaney's ballet, which appeared in the year of the Armada referred to: 'The strange and most cruel use of whippes which the Spaniard had prepared to whippe and torment English men and women.' This was a xenophobic basis for imperialistic thinking which was to be resurrected many times in British history. It was duly extended to Ireland where the vilification of the native population was becoming a regular feature of English propaganda – 'They never leave a man for dead until they have slit open his belly to remove his heart' (anonymous pamphlet) – and Edmund Spenser in his *View of the State of Ireland* compared the Irish to 'foul moss to be cleansed and scraped away' before any fruitful crops could be planted. This anti-Irish propaganda, which from the Reformation onwards had the added bite of religious difference, was used over several centuries to justify the colonization of land by English settlers, was later carried on by Cromwell and was to do lasting damage, more serious than any similar trend in Scotland and Wales.

In her later years Elizabeth was attacked from two sides, by Jesuit propaganda as an 'incestuous bastard and Jezebel' and by the Puritans in populist pamphlets like the *Marprelate Tracts* whose printer John Penry (1559–93) was executed. Against both Elizabeth was now protected by the development of a quasi-divine image, symbolized by the extravagant celebrations for her birthday each November, the cult of her as Astraea, and the idolization in Edmund Spenser's (1552–99) *Faerie Queene*.

Christopher Marlowe's play *The Massacre of Paris* of 1597 concentrated on a defence of legitimate monarchy as well as the obvious anti-Catholic stance. Shakespeare's *Henry V* in 1599 was a rather two-edged paean to the Tudor dynasty and the ideals of aggressive patriotism. Miniatures, medals and woodcuts of an idealized young Virgin Queen were given wide circulation from 1586 onwards. John Sharrock's *Valiant Acts and Victorious Ballads of the English Nation* and the music of court composers such as Thomas Morley (1557–1603) with his *Triumph of Gloriana* in 1601 added to the effect. Her established church hired the playwrights Robert Greene (1558–92) and Thomas Nashe (1567–1601) to defend itself. The other campaign in Elizabeth's declining years was that against the Earl of Essex who himself had inspired some populist public relations efforts. Even illustrated playing cards were among the media used to undermine his popularity. Thus overall Elizabethan propaganda had achieved a remarkable unity between an even more elevated concept of monarchy and xenophobic imperialist ambitions for the English nation set against judgemental disaster for Catholic Spain.

FRANCE

In France too religious and political propaganda were mixed up in the post-Reformation period. Paris was stunned in 1534 by an overnight posting of Protestant placards in numerous public places, attacking 'the insufferable abuses' of the mass and starting rumours of an impending massacre. Writers like Bernard du Haillan (1555–1610) produced pamphlets on the glory and destiny of France in the 1570s. The last three Valois kings maintained the tradition of elaborate coronations and well-staged tours round the country, culminating in the Grande Voyage of Charles IX (1550–74), but he was guilty – in public relations as well as other terms – of a massive blunder in the Massacre of St Bartholomew. R. Kingdon has shown how this was cleverly exploited by Calvinist propagandists, particularly in the dialogue tract *Le Réveille-matin des françois* first published in Basel in 1573 but then reissued in different forms in France, Scotland, England, Germany and Poland, to project the anti-Catholic message. Even the papacy was involved in the smear tactics accusing the French King of complicity in the massacre through a pamphlet of Camilo Capiluppi, while Antoine Caron developed a new genre of massacre painting to spread the idea of a Protestant backlash. Zagorin claims that the French civil war was one of the first in which 'political propaganda played a vital role' and there was massive output of pamphlets. The propaganda battle reached new depths when King Henry III was depicted as a witch by the Catholic League and his murderer, Clement, was put forward as a saint by the writer Jean Boucher. The Huguenots did also produce some fine propagandist writers: Agrippa D'Aubigné (1515–89) was the major Protestant poet with his *Tragiques*,

Theodore de Beze (1519–1605) provided the Calvinist interpretation of history and La Primaudaye was another effective Calvinist writer.

French political and religious propaganda, however, reverted very much to the norm when the last of the Valois, Henry III, was murdered and succeeded by the former Protestant leader Henry IV (1553–1610), first of the Bourbons. He chose the traditional route to dynastic image projection by relying on spectacular event management and grandiose architectural schemes. He set about a massive construction programme in Paris, including the Pont Neuf, the Luxembourg, Fontainebleau and other palaces, using Salomon de Brosse as his main architect. He commissioned an equestrian statue of his predecessor Henry III, the first royal statue in Paris, by Giovanni da Bologna. Rubens was among the artists employed at the Luxembourg and Dubreuil and Fréminet did the *Surrender of Amiens to Henry IV* for Fontainebleau, featuring Henry as the god Mars. Frans Pourbus did the royal portraits and the court sculptor Pierre Bearet produced a likeness of Henry as *Jupiter scattering the Catholic League*, plus a bas-relief on the *Battle of Ivry* for Fontainebleau, while Guillaume Dupré did his coin portraits. The publishing of engravings demonstrating the validity of the Bourbon succession was greatly encouraged as was the poetry of François de Malherbe (1555–1628) who produced the *Prière pour le Roi Henri le Grand allant en Limousin* in 1605. Finally, of the many spectacles organized to boost the new dynasty, the most lavish was the series of three-day festivals for the marriage of Henry's son and heir, Louis, to Anne of Austria. In propaganda terms the Bourbons were to be one of the great exhibitionistic dynasties of world history.

INDIA, CHINA AND JAPAN

Coincidentally with the European Reformation, India at this time produced some of its great reforming propagandists. The guru Nanak (1469–1538), the effective founder of Sikhism, demonstrated a remarkable ability for the neat packaging and propagation of his ideas, which was ultimately proven by their lasting strength. The use from 1669 of the five Ks – kesh [hair], kangha [comb], kara [wrist band], kirpan [sword], and kachch [trousers], themselves the visual corporate identity of the sect – linked mnemonically with another five Ks – the Khalsa or realms of the five Sikh virtues – overall created a very ingenious example of religious packaging. Nanak left a number of writings, particularly the chant 'Japji', whose words were so important that it was never set to any specific tune. This and his other hymns were collected in the *Adi Granth* and his life was embellished by the hagiographic janam-sakhis. The poetic style of both Nanak and later Arjan was developed from that of the Persian Sufis, strong on rhyme, alliteration and homely metaphor. The Sikhs even made use of acrostic poems starting each line with the same letter. The sect was given its first architectural focus at Amritsar by the Guru Arjan (1581–1606) and further major literary embellishment by the heroic ballads of Bhai Gurdas. In propaganda terms Sikhism had all the classic qualities which make for expansion and continuity except that it never really got beyond its own ethnic infrastructure.

Also remarkable was the propaganda of the Hindu mystic Chaitanya whose preaching could reduce his audiences to a trance-like state. The use of choral singing and endless repetition of texts was used to build up huge intensity of feeling with rolling on the ground and hugging, all parts of a highly emotive conversion technique.

In China this was a period of Buddhist propaganda dressed up in the form of popular novelettes like the *Story of San Tsang's Search for Buddhist Sutras*, romantic fiction with a message being one of the characteristic propaganda tools of the Ming period.

In Japan Toyotomi Hideyoshi (1536–98) had pacified the country by 1585 but needed the help of propaganda to legitimize his self-made power. Particularly he made use of Noh theatre to convey the link between the shogun and the emperor in Momoyama society. The concept of Bushido, 'way of the warrior', was a packaged set of values based on filial piety and truthfulness developed as motivational propaganda for the élite of the Tokugawa shogunate by Yamaga Soko (1622–85).

The foremost propagandist of the shoguns was the samurai monk Suzuki Shosan (1579–1655) who projected the samurai ethic of glorification in death through a chain of temples. This campaign was developed over the next century with works like *Hagakure* in 1716, 'The way of the Samurai is found in death' and Fujiwara Seika (1561–1619) projecting the imperial image along Confucian lines.

Overall the Reformation period showed a new capacity for propaganda to reach an extended audience through print, to build increased fanaticisms and to contribute to new divisions. Particularly great was the permanent bitterness engendered by propaganda between the two main branches of Christendom.

Civil Wars

GERMANY AND AUSTRIA

The German civil war known as the Thirty Years' War was ostensibly between Protestantism and Catholicism, but the Habsburgs used the spilt to try to boost their powerbase. Both sides were at times ill defined and other European countries entered periodically. It was a conflict in which propaganda played a particularly large part. This has been well documented by E.A. Beller, who described the vast proliferation of pamphlets and prints sold in large quantities through the shops – 400 different pamphlets appeared between 1618 and 1621 alone. The war coincided with the first development of copper printing plates which were marketed through the Leipzig fair by Paul Furst in the 1630s; this made possible images both better in quality and larger in quantity than the woodcuts produced in the previous two centuries. In a war notorious for its brutality the detail of the copper plate was ideal for projecting the atrocities of the other side. Scaremongering posters with appropriate rhymes or music dealt with topics like 'Croates eat children' (see pl. 26) and 'noses and ears cut off to make hat bands!'

Such propaganda probably contributed to the bitterness of the war and the escalation of violence. It was sufficient in its volume and simplicity to reach even the poorest classes: as Beller put it, 'in spite of a low rate of literacy all classes of the population were reached by propaganda in the Thirty Years' War'. On the Protestant side – though for dynastic reasons – the French subsidized a propaganda effort, hiring Father Joseph and Johann Stella to write on their behalf. The Swedes – also roped in on the Protestant side – made an effort to promote their ideal role model, King Gustavus Adolphus, who had the perfect visual charisma for a Protestant champion and a huge cult of Gustavus was built up with the sale of numerous kinds of artefacts showing his image. They even borrowed the Austrian technique of wordplay to show the word Sued (i.e. Swede) spelt backwards as Deus or God. Both the Old Testament and Greek mythology were quarried for comparisons with modern heroes of the war. One new epic portrayed the current struggle in the guise of the Trojan War with the Austrian general Tilly as Hector and Gustavus as Achilles, the Protestants as the Greeks and the Catholics as the Trojans. Poets like Martin Opitz (1597–1639), who was given patronage by Prince Ludwig of Weimar Kothen, produced the first glimmerings of literary German nationalism with a xenophobic attack on the world ambitions of the

Habsburgs. Tilly was a popular butt of satire, nicknamed Crokotill and taunted with his fondness for sweets.

For the Catholics the enemy leader who offered the most scope for ridicule was the Elector Frederick, ex-King of Bohemia, who was portrayed as the 'Winter King', the king who had lost his throne and had nowhere to go, victim of the defenestration of Prague. In addition, responding to the crisis in their 'Holy' empire, the Habsburgs under Ferdinand III (1608–57) encouraged propaganda to focus on the cult of their dynasty as defenders of Catholicism and Peter Lambecius was employed as a librarian/propagandist. The most active of the Catholic poets were Angelus Silesius (1624–77) and Friedrich von Spee (1591–1635). The war also stimulated a number of anti-war novels, not so much belonging to the partisan propaganda of the war itself as the flickering long-term image of pacifism; most notable were *The Adventures of Simplicismus* by Hans von Grimmelhausen and *The most wondrous and veritable Adventures of Philander of Sittewald* by Johann Moscherosch of 1642, both works emphasizing the atrocities of total war. To this must be added the remarkable series of engravings done by Jacques Callot (1593–1633) which showed in graphic detail the miseries of war and prevalence of atrocities. Thus overall the Thirty Years War was important in the development of propaganda both because the blurring of the line between the two sides meant that there were floating supporters to appeal to and because its very cruelty stimulated an artistic response which spelt out a message, however weak, to future generations.

SPAIN AND FRANCE

Outside Germany two remarkable chief ministers, Olivares in Spain and Richelieu in France, both exploited the civil war and used propaganda skills heavily to justify their role in it. The Count of Olivares (1587–1645) revived the theme of Hercules for his master Philip IV to boost his own ambitious plans for the dynasty. The image of Hercules as sun or virtue, symbol and ancestor of the Habsburgs, with his twelve labours, was often subtly linked with the twelve victories of the Spaniards and the twelve signs of the zodiac. Similarly Hercules's connection with Gibraltar and his funeral pyre with its connotations of immortality were invoked in the funeral monuments of Charles V and the Capella Ardente of Brussels, while his killing of monsters was used to illustrate the extermination of heresy as in Rubens's picture *Hercules Triumphant over Discord*. The theme was developed in Titian's *Spain coming to the aid of Religion* and Francisco Zurbaran's series of Hercules paintings. The coordinator of this new Hall of Princely Virtue was Diego de Velasquez (1599–1660) who himself contributed five equestrian portraits of Spanish kings and queens in 1633 plus one of Olivares himself. Velasquez also had the role of overall coordinator of the visual impact of Olivares's campaign. In addition a group of literary figures supported him, the poets Francisco de Rioja and Antonio de Mendoza (1503–75), and the historians La Roca and Francisco Quevedo (1580–1645), who helped explain away the disaster of Cadiz and projected the rescues of Genoa and Brazil. Rapidly produced court plays, such as Lope de Vega's *El Brasil restituido* in 1625, followed each Spanish victory. Such was the substantial pool of talent utilized to support Olivares's grandiose but ultimately futile campaign to expand and glorify the empire of the Spanish Habsburgs.

In France the art of propaganda continued to flourish, even if at times at a modest level. The two cardinals Richelieu (1585–1642) and Mazarin (1602–61) were driven by their ambition to appreciate the need for image projection. Richelieu licensed *The Gazette* in 1631 so that he could manipulate public opinion, although its owner Théophraste Renaudot pioneered the concept of press advertising to make the whole business profitable. Both Richelieu and Louis XIII provided articles on government policy and Renaudot scattered the streets of Paris with pro-regency leaflets. Richelieu subsidized a substantial output of pamphlets supporting his foreign policy and employed François Langlois de Fancan both as a writer and organizer of other writers such as Jean de Silhon with his *Le miroir du temps passé*. Richelieu opened his own theatre as ballet and drama were not only his passions but his special method of image projection. In 1641 he staged the *Ballet de la Prosperité des Armes de la France* with music, dance and elaborate scenery to celebrate the seven victories won over Spain by Louis XIII. Philippe de Champaigne (1602–74) was employed as the court's propagandist painter – he painted *Louis XIII at the siege of La Rochelle*, vast numbers of portraits of Richelieu himself and the Galerie des Hommes Illustres at the Palais Cardinal. Richelieu's favoured sculptor was Berthelot who produced a number of idealized likenesses of Louis XIII. Pierre Corneille (1606–84) was one of five poets hired by Richelieu and his *Cinna* of 1639 projected the idea of absolute monarchy and world conquest. Most significant was the all-round propagandist writer Desmarets de Saint-Sorlen (1596–1676) who wrote, produced and performed in a number of Richelieu's theatrical productions.

Mazarin emulated Richelieu's use of the theatre for propaganda. His staging of the spectacular opera *La Finta Pazza* by Strozzi was pure exhibitionism without any specific propaganda message, but he followed this in 1660 with Cavalli's (1600–76) *Xerxes* which quite overtly celebrated the victories over Spain. In the same year he organized a massive ceremonial royal entry with triumphal arches, some of them designed by Charles le Brun (1619–90). Like Richelieu, Mazarin regarded architecture as a useful tool to project his image so he employed Le Vau to build the College Mazarin, his main monument. The opposition, specifically the Fronde, used the cruder tools of broadsheet and song, including the Mazarinades of which it is estimated around 5,000 appeared between 1649 and 1652.

BRITAIN

The other notable civil war of this period was British. It too arose partly from the religious controversies of the age and it too was remarkable for the heavy emphasis on propaganda by both sides. The Stuarts were still a relatively new dynasty in British terms and James I (VI of Scotland 1566–1625) had not been particularly sensitive in working on his image. Admittedly he had William Shakespeare as a writer on his side with the famous ghost scene in *Macbeth* celebrating the origins of his family and the *Tempest* for his daughter's wedding. Much of the propaganda effort in his reign had been outside his control: for example, the efforts of men like John Rolfe to whip up enthusiasm for the new colony of Virginia in 1616 and Walter Raleigh's *History of the World* with its strong anti-Spanish theme and encouragement for British empire building. Thomas Mun put across the ethic of the merchant adventurers for whom trade was noble and pleasure contrary to the law of God. James's one real public relations success was his exploitation of the Gunpowder Plot to provide a long-term focus for anti-Catholic feeling with its annual celebration an example of self-perpetuating pro-establishment event management of the most effective kind.

His son Charles I (1600–49) was self-evidently a failure in terms of overall image projection, but as Joyce Malcolm put it he did 'keenly appreciate the importance of propaganda despite his insensitivity to popular prejudice'. If the employment of Van Dyck (1599–1641) as one of the greatest of all royal image makers, of Inigo Jones (1573–1652) to be royal architect and with Ben Jonson (1572–1637) to organize court masques still resulted in failure to project the right image, it simply shows once more that great art is very often not automatically effective propaganda. The failure was not for the want of trying. A huge range of measures included the masque *Britannia Triumphans*; written by William Davenant and produced by Inigo Jones in 1638, it was an elaborate and impressive attempt to boost the role of the Navy in fighting Spain and to justify King Charles's heavy Ship Money taxes.

Typical of the anti-Stuart propagandists was the Puritan William Wynne (1600–69) who produced a succession of pamphlets against the Anglican hierarchy and the monarchy, one of 1633 under the title *Histrio-Mastrix; the Players' Scourge*. The focus for parliamentary propaganda was men like John Hampden (1594–1643) and John Pym (1584–1643), figureheads for the battle against royal tyranny.

Once King Charles had been ejected from his capital and understood at last that he had failed to put across to his people the ideology of the divine right of kings, he paid far more practical attention to the propaganda needs of his now much more difficult position. He had a new print works set up in York which in 1642 produced 74 different tracts, while a further 95 were put out by the royalist print works at Shrewsbury. Print runs were increased to 10,000. Charles used church pulpits and universities to project his image and when he lost control of the postal services network he set up a new service of special messengers or Mercury men and women often dressed as beggars. Printed copies of the King's speeches were distributed to crowds. The mechanics of propaganda were well enough thought out, but the writing tended to be too extreme, pedantic and too remote from reality to salvage the drifting situation. One of the few real propaganda successes was the work of John Cleveland as a poet and ballad producer, particularly his very popular *When the King enjoys his own again* which was even enjoyed on the parliamentary side. 'The Commoners' Ballad' of 1645 by Alexander Bone spread rapidly with:

> And the scum of the land
> Are the men in command
> Our slaves are become our masters

as did 'Rupert's March'. The use of the royal motto 'Give Caesar his due', the colourful corporate scarlet and generally extrovert, dashing image of the Cavaliers did at least something to boost a losing cause. Another unusual feature of the Civil War was both sides' use of popular almanacs as a propaganda tool. Astrological predictions were used to lend credibility to forecasts of victories by both Royalists and Parliamentarians.

Oliver Cromwell (1599–1658) and the Roundheads, however, paid even greater attention to their corporate promotion than Charles did and were undoubtedly more tuned in to the popular mood. At first Cromwell concentrated on his military image, developing an aura of invincibility for his ingeniously named 'Ironsides', displaying his black flag with the five gold baubles and his mottos 'God with us' and 'Truth and Peace'. Once in power he was an insecure dynast, still open to attack from the defeated Royalists but also from the other end of the political spectrum, the extreme Puritans and Levellers. He had some formidable talent on his side. John Milton (1608–74) was his foremost propaganda writer. His *Areopagitica* in 1644 was a major attack on royal censorship; his *Eikonoklastes* a remarkable examination of the principles of hereditary monarchy, a justification for the execution of King Charles and a masterly defence of the new Commonwealth. This theme was continued in his *First Defence of the People of England* of 1651 and in his *Second Defence* of 1654 he justified Cromwell's war against Spain using the usual 'legenda negra', updated with the tale of Spanish atrocities like Amboyna in India. Cromwell also justified his harsh treatment of the Irish with a range of anti-Irish myths, including roasted Protestants eaten alive, papist massacres and murdering of parsons, all of which was subtly associated with the Stuart cause. This fomenting of public opinion plus the massacres at Drogheda and Londonderry was to do lasting damage to the Irish communal psyche for the sake of a short-term propaganda advantage. John Milton had contributed to the theme in his *First Defence* which alleged that 200,000 English had been killed by the Irish, calling the latter 'part papists, part savages . . . justly made our vassals', all of which was partially derived from John Temple's influential *History of the Horrid Rebellion in Ireland* of 1646. All this in turn provided raw material for retaliatory Irish nationalist propaganda which embroidered on Cromwell's satanic career significantly and made him the figure of hate.

One other poet of stature, Andrew Marvell (1622–78), though he much later became a firm anti-monarchist, was in Cromwell's lifetime more attuned than Milton to the idea of presenting the Protector as a quasi-regal figure; his *First Anniversary of the Government under His Highness the Lord Protector* falls into that category and he too contributed to anti-Irish propaganda in his *Perfect Diurnall*. In addition the playwright William Davenant (1606–68), a renegade royalist, produced the first operas in Britain which had a pro-Cromwellian, anti-Spanish aura, while the active pro-Commonwealth press, *Mercurius Britannicus*, under Thomas Audley, and *Mercurius Politicus*, under Marchamont Needham (1620–78), initially dominated the circulation battle. Needham organized the pamphleteers Francis Rous and Anthony Ascham to work on the theme of divine providence for the Commonwealth.

By the late 1640s Royalist propaganda had begun to revive and Cromwell – the establishment – was more open to attack. The Royalist newspaper *Mercurius Aulicus* had been remarkably successful with a circulation up to 5,000 under Sir John Berkenhead (1617–79) and Peter Heylyin, a literate vein of satire on current events and a good line in London gossip, but it was certainly aimed no lower than the squirearchy. The *Mercurius Civicus* of 1643–6 had been the first newspaper to use woodcut illustrations but was too Presbyterian to have a major effect. Aimed at a lower socio-economic group was the *Mercurius Rusticus*, edited by Bruno Ryves, which used anti-Cromwell atrocity stories. Meanwhile, as his end approached, Cromwell's image making became everyday less republican. A broadsheet showed him wearing the crown and the new issue of his coins had him with the imperial laurel and a crown on the reverse side. All this meant that the Royalists could now attack his delusions of grandeur with names like 'Ruby Nose', 'Copper Nose' and 'Nose Almighty'. Satire was rampant and the Levellers added their bit with pamphlets like *England's New Chains Discovered*.

The collapse of the image of the Commonwealth so soon after Cromwell's death in 1658 was some proof of the deeply inculcated long-term credibility of monarchy in Britain. The event management of the Restoration was impeccable with well-orchestrated pomp and public exposure for the restored Charles II (1630–85). Henry Muddiman ensured some favourable press cover with the *Mercurius Publicus*. John Dryden (1631–1700), one of the wittiest of propagandist poets in British history produced many works in Charles's favour. His *Astraea Redux* of 1660 welcomed the Restoration, his *Annus Mirabilis* of 1667 glossed over the difficult year of the Great Fire of London and the Dutch Wars, then a trinity of satires, starting with *Absalom and Achitophel* in 1681, did a reasonable job of debunking the Whigs. The other great figure was Henry Purcell (1659–95), one of the most effective of all composers of emotive patriotic music, his works included 'Britons Strike Home' from the opera *Arthur* which he wrote with Dryden and which was to be a highly popular nationalist anthem for the next century together with 'The Prince of Denmark's March' from the next reign. However, royal efforts failed to stem the effective Whig propaganda of the exclusionists, Shaftesbury and the Green Ribbon Club, opponents of a long-term Stuart succession, who encouraged pamphlet writers like Booth and Blount, poets like Shadwell and Aycliff, producers of political ballads and playing cards, the rabidly anti-Catholic plays of Elkanah Settle and above all the spectacular Pope-burning processions of the 1678 to 1680 period which attracted crowds of around 200,000.

Among major religious innovators at this time was George Fox (1624–91) who had many of the qualities of the earlier missionaries. His credibility had been enhanced by nine periods of imprisonment and unbounding energy as an itinerant preacher. He had the emotive ability to make his congregations shake and he produced a prolific output of mystical writings. The image of the Society of Friends was to be remarkably clear-cut and well communicated with teams of apostles, the 'valiant sixty', going out from his base at Swarthmore Hall. Although his movement never achieved massive numbers of converts it had at least 100,000 members by 1700. Fox's use of language buzzed with originality – his constant references to churches as 'steeple houses', to priests as 'hirelings', the attention-grabbing call 'to join the lambs' war'. In addition the Quakers had a good understanding of the value of controlled silence and audience participation with their revival of the concept of 'tongues'. Other able Quaker propagandists included John Woolman (1720–72) whose *Journal* was a best-seller and who campaigned effectively against slavery and William Penn (1644–1718) of Philadelphia, an extremely able pamphleteer whose works included *Sandy Foundations Shaken*.

RUSSIA

Not dissimilar to George Fox was Danilo Filipov (fl. 1690), the Volga hermit and founder of the Doukhobors or Russian 'Quakers'. They too practised pacifism, universal love, a hard work ethic and ascetic outlook. Filipov created an image by claiming birth from a woman aged 100 and there was a legend that he was crucified in the Kremlin. The Doukhobors whirled around in a hypnotic circle and some of their sub-sects drifted into the more extreme areas of hysteria, flagellation and self-castration. As one of history's more extreme examples of emotive crowd control it left a lasting mark and the sect still survived in Canada in the 1930s when members were arrested for public indecency.

HOLLAND

The other remarkable stage for propaganda effort during this period was Holland where the skills honed by years of building up national morale against invaders were adapted to domestic issues like the projection of a strong work ethic. Writers and artists combined to develop the image of the virtuous housewife, as Simon Schama has brilliantly shown. Jacob Cats was a prolific producer in the 1650s of illustrated moral rhymes on the house-proud super hygienic *Christelyke Huyswijf*:

> A wife that by all virtue goes
> But of her virtue little knows

while Jan Luiken produced his emblem book of the godly household and Jan Steen his admonitory painting of *The Dissolute Household*. At the same time the Dutch continued to develop their skills in political and religious propaganda with artists like Van de Venne (1589–1624) who worked for Prince Maurice and Gerard ter Borch (1617–81) who did the event management to publicize the peace of 1648.

The most obvious general trend in propaganda in the first half of the seventeenth century was its continued role in exacerbating confrontation, both religious and political. In addition there was a move away from the visual and towards the literary with a proliferation into different genres. Specifically it remained a period in which the image of women was still damaged and this formed part of the background to the final widespread bouts of witch persecution.

Age of Absolutism

The age of the so-called enlightened despots almost by definition was a period when propaganda was superficial rather than real. Rulers who inherited power from established dynasties had limited motivation to work on their image making, except to project the trappings of absolute power, propaganda for the sake of exhibitionism rather than specific political objectives.

PRUSSIA

Frederick II of Prussia (1712–86), who proved with his pamphlet *Antimachiavel* of 1744 and his *Political Testament* of 1769, both written in French, that he was a potentially able self-publicist, nevertheless made remarkably little effort to enhance his image. Like his father, the first Hohenzollern king, he cut back on coronation expenses, and despite the fact that the Prussian monarchy was so new, avoided elaborate tours round his kingdom, refused gun salutes and other marks of respect, thus gaining for himself a somewhat Spartan image which was to do no harm to his popularity when his country was ravaged by the effects of war. Equally Frederick made very little appeal to German national sentiments, himself much preferring French culture to anything in his native Prussia. In fact it was his friend Voltaire, not a Prussian, who suggested that he should be referred to as 'the Great'. It was Frederick's sheer military stamina in the face of adversity that won him a populist image abroad – wax models of him were displayed in other parts of Europe – and which left him as a role model for future German leaders. The one area in which he was obsessive about event management, like his father, was in military drill; it was Frederick I who had first introduced from Sicily the idea of marching in step, with the knees straight and a deliberate banging of the foot to make a noise. This proto-goose-step was almost a propaganda tool both for those who practised it and those who watched. It went well with the new fashion of indoctrination of young potential officers, pioneered by August Francke (1663–1727), which indoctrinated them from an early age to put loyalty to state ahead of personal comfort.

Beyond the military, Frederick's main concession to the idea of propaganda was the encouragement of a new Prussian interpretation of history which was to justify and chronicle Prussia's expansion from backward East European electorate to major West European state – and very tight control of the news in the Berlin press. For the rest Frederick certainly surrounded himself with talented poets, philosophers and musicians. His encouragement of music was particularly significant, with his court composer J.J. Quantz (1697–1773) at the centre and J.S. Bach (1685–1750) as a major figure in the wings; specifically Frederick was by his patronage mainly responsible for the development of the keyboard instrument, the pianoforte. His new palace, Sans Souci, at Potsdam, was busy with the arts but as the very name he had chosen for the building suggested, the atmosphere was French, not Prussian, the culture for private not public enjoyment.

AUSTRIA

The most remarkable propagandist of this period in Vienna was the Augustinian/Jesuit monk Abraham a Sancta (fl. 1677) whose sermons and publications focused hard on his three main hates: Muslims, Jews and Protestants. The Habsburgs were on the whole too secure to be over concerned with their image. Certainly Charles VI (1685–1740) was extravagant to the point of self-damage. With the architect Fischer von Erlach (1656–1723) he rebuilt Vienna as a noble capital; the Karlkirche celebrated the defeat of the Turks, Prince Eugene's Belvedere Palace symbolized the victories over the French. The dome of the saloon at Klosternenburg was decorated with *The Glory of the House of Austria* by Daniel Gran and the Habsburgs still used the image of Hercules as they had in the days of Charles V.

Charles's daughter the redoubtable Empress Maria Theresa (1717–80) saw little requirement for image projection, except perhaps for the desperate cultivation of her own Hungarian subjects when she needed their help in the war against Prussia. Her court at the superb new Schonbrun Palace frequently housed great artistic talent. Its own theatre staged spectacular baroque operas, masques, and displays by the Spanish Riding School. Gluck (1714–87) was employed as her court composer and the young Mozart (1756–91) performed there, but the idolization of French and Italian styles negated any nationalist culture. The dynasty was unassailable so the need for propaganda was almost non-existent. Maria Theresa's son and successor Joseph II (1741–90) was in much the same position, though he, like Frederick the Great, chose the route of active reform without self-promotion. To some extent he did contribute to the nurturing of the talents of Mozart and Haydn (1732–1809). The one with the first German language opera and the second with his national anthem incorporated in the 'Emperor Quartet', created a remarkable musical infrastructure for the Austro-Hungarian empire. Some of the music was actually propagandist, such as Mozart's operas *Idomeneo* glorifying benevolent despotism and even *La Clemenza di Tito* for Leopold II. Joseph did relax censorship on the basis that adverse propaganda could do him no real damage, even *The Forty-Two Year Old Ape* which was a virulent personal attack. The 'Broschurenflut' [flood of leaflets] released pent-up opposition without leading to any real activity.

RUSSIA

In Russia there was growing scope for propaganda. The two reforming Romanovs, Peter the Great and Catherine, tended to seek achievement by action rather than persuasion, but nevertheless Peter (1672–1725) did make significant propaganda efforts with the help of his court poet Feofan Prokopovich (1681–1736), who made his name with a poem (*Epinikion*) on the victory of Poltava in 1709 produced in three languages. He also wrote a *Panegyric Discourse on the Russian Fleet* in 1720, and a play *Vladimir* in praise of Peter. He established a team known as the 'Learned Guard' to project Peter's ideas as opposed to those of the conservative 'Big beards'. Peter's own *An Honest Mirror of Youth* was published to project Western values while Prokopovich's plays, pamphlets and poems developed Russian nationalism and the historian Tatishchev worked on the Russian myth. Even Peter's sister Natalya wrote a play – *Peter at the Golden Keep* – to promote the theme of modernization. Like other absolute monarchs Peter saw architecture as the perfect medium through which to project his mission statement, at least to his own aristocracy, the massive project of constructing St Petersburg being a symbol of reorientation. Catherine II (1729–96) encouraged a process of middle-class political education and her most remarkable propagandist in this context was Nikolay Novikov (1722–1818) who helped produce material for her *St Petersburg News* and then published a series of weekly essay magazines such as *Truten* [The Drone] rather on the *Spectator* model. In addition the poet Gavriil Derzhavin (1747–1810) produced the 'Ode to Felitsa' in praise of the Empress herself.

FRANCE

Following the regimes of the two cardinals Richelieu and Mazarin, Louis XIV (1638–1715) took over direct power in 1661 and had no real need, any more than the other absolute monarchs of the century, to work on his image. However, perhaps inspired by the talent nurtured in France by the cardinals, perhaps out of sheer vanity, he did devote substantial resources to the glorification of his image, mainly through the somewhat minority media of art, architecture and music; as Colbert put it, 'It is by the size of their monuments that kings are remembered.' The Louvre was extended by Bernini (1598–1680) and huge equestrian statues were introduced. It was Bernini's bust of Louis XIV as *Apollo* which developed the image of 'the Sun King'. The massive development at Versailles employed some 30,000 people over a five-year period to create one of the most spectacular dynastic advertisements since the pyramids. The painter Charles Le Brun (1619–90) was hired to decorate the Galerie des Glaces with murals of Louis's victories over the Dutch and also to depict Louis as *Alexander the Great* at the Louvre. For Versailles he produced *The Capture of Ghent in Six Days* in 1678 and *The Franche Comté Conquered a Second Time* in 1674, the titles indicating the arrogance of the pictures themselves. The work of Jules Mansard (1645–1708) on Les Invalides and Jacques Soufflot (1709–80) on the Pantheon and St Sulpice, the victory obelisks, more *arcs de triomphe* like the Porte St Denis, all added to the environmental propaganda. The numerous paintings and sculptures of flowers and fruit to symbolize prosperity, the huge output of the Gobelin tapestry factory run by Le Brun to produce dynastic decoration, the striking of commemorative medals, all amounted to a massive visual onslaught on at least the upper end of French society.

Giovanni Lully (1632–87) became the highly influential court composer and shared with Le Brun the responsibility for event management and ceremonial for le Roi Soleil. Lully's patriotic opera *Armide* was performed at Versailles and in 1693 François Couperin (1688–1733) was also added to the musical team. Meanwhile, Louis's chief minister Colbert organized the literary patronage through Jean Chapelain, with more basic state propaganda in mind. This included the journalist Donneau de Vise on the *Mercure Galante*, the pro-Bourbon historian Mézeray, and to a lesser extent the tragedian Racine (1639–99) who staged his *Phèdre* for Colbert in 1677 after he had produced a number of congratulatory odes for the King. The danger of Bourbon propaganda, in its sheer extravagance and emphasis on 'la gloire', was that it could cause as much resentment as admiration, but Louis did at times show a remarkable ability to remember the motivation of his people. During the peace talks with the Duke of Marlborough he managed, despite the facts, to present France to his own people as the injured party, starving yet unbowed, so that he stirred patriotic feeling to fight back, even though the wars had in fact been caused solely by his own dynastic ambitions. His successors were not to be so effective.

BRITAIN

In Britain the age of absolutism was not quite so much in evidence and propaganda played a much more significant role in the fortunes of dynasties and ministries. After the Restoration Charles II kept reasonable media control, subsidizing Henry Muddiman, founder of the *Parliamentary Intelligencer* and circulator of political newsletters, while the government also controlled the *London Gazette* which had a monopoly on foreign news. Roger L'Estrange ran the pro-government *Observator*, was a prolific Tory pamphleteer and as chief of Stationers' Hall organized the

censorship of opposition material. This alongside the imperial rebuilding programme of Christopher Wren (1632–1723), the masques and
voluntaries of Purcell, the poetry of John Dryden (1631–1700) with his
attacks on Shaftesbury, gave the penultimate Stuart king an image at least
as a survivor and helped fend off his biggest threat, the Exclusion crisis,
when Shaftesbury tried to exclude James, Duke of York, from the
succession.

One of Charles's other main propaganda requirements was to achieve
public backing for war against Holland and to combat insidious Dutch
propaganda which was smuggled into Britain to undermine this policy. In
this he was helped by Andrew Marvell whose *The Character of Holland*
referred to the country as 'This undigested vomit of the sea', by George
Downing, the xenophobic Owen Felltham and by Henry Stubbes who
expounded on 'the outrages of the Dutch'. The Dutch meanwhile had an
extremely proficient printing industry and excellent illustrators such as
Romeyn de Hooghe (1645–1708), whose Blauwboeckje of atrocities such
as the French attack on Utrecht, were sold into Britain and France as well
as in his own country. All this was good practice for the subsequent
undermining of the Stuart dynasty by Dutch propagandists.

Charles's brother James II (1633–1701) had little concept of
propaganda and was ultimately its victim. Insensitive to his own image
and that of his religion which was highly unpopular in Britain, he
blundered on regardless though Henry Care and the Marquess of Halifax
did their best to advise him. The late birth of his son and heir was
greeted with incredulity and rumours of cheating symbolized by the
warming-pan (the means by which a baby not sired by James was allegedly
smuggled into the queen's chamber), a classic smear, which thereafter
became a standard prop for anti-Stuart rallies and scurrilous prints. Populist
disgruntlement was focused by one of history's most effective political
melodies, *Lilliburlero*, with its anti-Catholic lyrics by the Duke of Wharton.
As Winston Churchill later put it the tune 'cost James II three thrones'.

William III (1650–1702), 'Dutch Billy', achieved a major new
propaganda coup when he and Mary assumed the British throne in 1688.
The Dutch had needed strong propaganda to help defend the House of
Orange and had pioneered a new quality of etched battle pictures which
was soon copied by the British. Romeyn de Hooghe etched prints
deriding James II and later became propagandist chronicler for
Marlborough during his victorious campaigns. In 1688 in advance of
Willam's invasion his European public relations were masterminded by
Hans Wilhelm Bentinck helped by the writer Ericus Watten. William's
most important propaganda exercise was the *Declaration*, edited by
Gilbert Burnett, of which 60,000 copies were produced in secrecy using
printers in three different Dutch cities, a massive print run for that
period. It was written in English to please wavering loyalists rather than
committed Whigs, and cleverly played down the role of William and the
Dutch, emphasizing more the return of Mary, his Stuart wife, to replace

her wayward father. In addition, there was a special version of the *Declaration* for Scotland and a *Letter to the Army* distributed to all officers. Two printers, John Dunton and Richard Baldwin were major coordinators of Whig propaganda including a rapid succession of anti-Jacobite plays, projecting the 'Dutch Deliverer and the glorious revolution'. William brought his own printing presses over from Holland and substantially raised the level of military illustration, a useful tool for rousing national sentiment, by importing Dutch engravers. Thus Theodor Maas immortalized the Battle of the Boyne, Schonbek the *Siege of Londonderry* and Van Diest the *Battle of Cape la Hogue*. In addition William used broadsides, playing cards, tracts and medals, as well as having James Johnstone to look after his relationship with the newspapers.

One of the most remarkable achievements of propaganda was the dressing up of the Dutch conquest of Britain as a 'glorious revolution'. Thereafter William's propaganda effort switched back to Holland where his return was celebrated with a classical triumph: tableaux, obelisks, triumphal arches and epic poems in both Dutch and Italian.

The most accomplished government propagandist of the reign was without question the multi-talented Daniel Defoe (1660–1731) whose poem *Trueborn Englishman* of 1700 was a major tribute to the Dutch King William. As journalist, pamphleteer, novelist and essayist Defoe's substantial output over a thirty-year period served not only Whig partisan objectives, but also the general development of the British mercantile ethos. Also in government pay was William Congreve (1670–1729) most of whose work was non-political, but who did produce *The Mourning Muse of Alexis* on the death of Queen Mary. The tradition of Whig panegyric nationalist verse was kept moving by Thomas Shadwell (1642–92), the new poet laureate, and there was steady expansion of the tri-weekly *Post* newspapers, which as their names suggest coincided with the tri-weekly postal service out of London. Despite the short-term successes of his propaganda machine, William left two negative long-lasting images: the scandal of Glencoe, an event mismanaged, and the Battle of the Boyne, one of the most damaging millstones in political folklore.

The image of Queen Anne (1665–1714), 'Brandy Nan', is not of any great historical significance but her reign did see a new intensification of party political propaganda. The Duke of Marlborough created a succession of dazzling military victories, which were glorified by spectacles at St Paul's, bonfires, processions, gun salutes, the poem 'Campaign' by Joseph Addison (1672–1719), the engravings of Thomas Brodick and Hugo Allard, the battle tapestries of Blenheim Palace. It was all the more remarkable, therefore, that at the climax of his victories a Tory propaganda nexus effectively swung public opinion away from the successes. The attack was inspired by Henry St John, later Viscount Bolingbroke (1678–1751), probably the most gifted propagandist in British history. His newspaper *The Examiner* had nearly 5,000 subscribers and a high readership, with an able writing team which included

Jonathan Swift (1667–1745). Swift was responsible for the brilliantly written pamphlet *The Conduct of the Allies* which sold 1,000 copies in three days. In a few pages of biting sarcasm, in which Marlborough and his Duchess were shown purloining 'the dupes and baubles of Europe' and Britain was 'fighting for an alliance of merchants whose perpetual harvest is war', Swift succeeded in totally undermining the 'Grand Vizier's' prestige and making peace with France respectable. Taking into account Swift's earlier successful religious satire *A Tale of a Tub*, the brilliance of *Gulliver's Travels* as a political satire, and his later *Drapiers' Letters*, he must rank as one of the greatest literary propagandists of history. His assistant on *The Examiner*, Mary de la Rivière Manley (1672–1724), contributed hugely to the destabilization of the Marlboroughs with two highly successful and scurrilous novels, *New Atlantis* (1709) and *Queen Zarah and the Zarasians* (1711). She was the mistress of the Tory printer John Barber who, with Swift, Matthew Prior, John Arbuthnot and Alexander Pope, made up the Brothers' or Scriblerus Club under Bolingbroke, a remarkable pool of literary talent available on request to produce anti-Whig propaganda. Pope's (1688–1744) contribution at this time was his *Windsor Forest* with its patriotic plea for maritime empire and Arbuthnot (1667–1735) added his *History of John Bull* which provided an archetypal long-term role model for British chauvinism. Bolingbroke, as the orchestrator of this remarkable vein of high quality propaganda enjoyed four brief years of power and then threw it all away with his indecisive behaviour over the Hanoverian succession when Queen Anne died.

The new dynasty of Hanover took over without great difficulty in 1714 and without any obvious burning desire to attain a popular image among its new subjects. The two supreme literary propagandists of the new reign were Joseph Addison and Richard Steele (1672–1729). Steele produced the brilliant pamphlet *The Crisis* in 1714 and his periodical *The Englishman* was devoted to the same cause, while Addison, already famous for his patriotic play *Cato*, wrote the pro-Hanoverian *Freeholder*. The two had a steadying effect, just as Defoe had done for 'Dutch Billy'. The sponsorship of Laurence Eckhart's anti-Jacobite *History of England* contributed and prints appeared emphasizing George I's role at the Battle of Blenheim. By contrast a poem possibly by Swift contrasted George's behaviour at Oudenarde with that of the Old Pretender: 'Not so did behave Young Hanover brave.' The first Hanoverian coronation was well managed with actors playing the parts of the Dukes of Picardy and Normandy as George was crowned King of France, England and Ireland. The white horse of Hanover was emblazoned on medals and the history painter James Thornhill (1675–1734) began a series of pictures at Greenwich illustrating the Protestant succession. He also continued his huge output of nationalist allegory for the dome of St Paul's, Hampton Court and Blenheim Palace.

However, George's inability to speak English and his overt preference for Hanover over Britain made him a difficult subject for effective propaganda and the ingenious publicity of the Jacobites began to make some headway. They exploited the Königsmark scandal, nicknamed the king 'George the Sultan' and in etchings showed the unicorn being trampled by the white horse. They also circulated xenophobic rhymes about the court such as:

> Two Turks, three whores and half a dozen nurses
> Five hundred Germans with empty purses.

Robert Walpole (1676–1745) had already been leading the government for six years when George I was succeeded by his son George II (1683–1760). Walpole was not particularly innovative or proactive in his image projection, but with his usual conscientiousness and determination to keep power, treated it as a necessary evil. Just as he bribed numerous potential opponents with government places, so he bribed newspapers to support him by means of heavy subsidies. John Peele, part proprietor of the *London Journal* was subsidized by the government and also became a major publisher of government pamphlets. Samuel Buckley at the *Daily Courant* was in the same position and Thomas Gordon, the able owner of the anti-government *British Journal*, was bribed to change sides in 1727. The government's distribution network grew in efficiency and copies of government newspapers were mainly delivered to the Clerks of Roads by way of the comptroller Joseph Bell, so that nationwide circulation was ensured and free copies were supplied to all coffee houses where at this time most of the politically literate population met regularly. In addition Walpole had access to a number of able essay writers such as Benjamin Hoadly who contributed as 'Britannia' to the *London Journal* and John Hervey who produced pamphlets such as *The Conduct of the Opposition*. By 1735 Walpole felt able to reduce his press subsidies and amalgamate the pro-government newspapers under the new *Daily Gazeteer*.

At the same time, although of less political importance, the image of the King was worked on in most art forms. George Friederich Handel (1685–1759) who had produced his *Te Deum* for the Treaty of Utrecht, his *Water Music* for George I's procession, his *Zadok the Priest* for the coronation of George II, went on to *Atalanta* for the Prince of Wales's wedding, *Judas Maccabeus* for the 'conquering hero', the Duke of Cumberland, and the 'Fireworks' for the end of the war in 1749, a superlative musical infrastructure for any dynasty. A host of panegyric poets and adequate artists paid tribute to the monarch and Hawksmoor refurbished Westminster Abbey as a revived cult focus for the British corporate ego.

Meanwhile, the very indestructibility of Walpole's administration provoked a long-term opposition propaganda campaign which was to deploy more talent over a long period than almost any other in history. Behind it for many years was Viscount Bolingbroke who had already shown his remarkable understanding of propaganda techniques in the Tory administration of 1710–14 and who now had the added motivation that as a pardoned but disfranchised traitor he had no other way of exercising his still huge political ambitions. Bolingbroke wrote to his friend Swift:

> This monstrous beast [the public] has passions to be moved, but not reason to be appealed to . . . the plain truth will influence half a score of men at the most in a nation, while mysteries will lead millions by the nose.

This understanding of propaganda technique, worthy of a twentieth-century dictator, was to be demonstrated in the highly innovative style of journalism which he harnessed for his new paper *The Craftsman* from 1722. Its combination of biting satire, classical allusions and probing wit achieved high sales and high readership. Various of his own pieces were collected and published as *A Dissertation on Parties* and *Letters on the Study of History* while his output inspired a number of other able writers to join in the campaign. Both William Pulteney and Philip Stanhope, Earl of Chesterfield, politicians displaced by Walpole, proved brilliant journalists with an added talent for rhyming ballad, Chesterfield in due course going on to found another highly influential opposition newspaper *Common Sense*.

At the same time other media were being utilized to develop the opposition campaign. John Gay (1685–1732) provided the libretto for the *Beggar's Opera* which offered not only a very entertaining attack on Walpole but virtually introduced a new art form, the ballad opera, which was to be used regularly and successfully by opposition writers for the next ten years. Others in Bolingbroke's circle of the 'Brothers' joined in: Swift with his *Gulliver's Travels* of 1726 which like Gay's work succeeded in being highly entertaining at the same time as damning Walpole. In the same year Alexander Pope began to renew his attack with the first version of the *Dunciad* and he followed with a series of *Satires* and *Epistles of Horace Imitated*, an idea apparently inspired by Bolingbroke. Cumulatively they were a *tour de force* of poetical satire directed against the 'Robinocracy'.

To the group of 'Brothers' was now added a new generation of highly talented writers brought in by Bolingbroke himself, the Prince of Wales, Chesterfield and the talent-spotting Viscount Cobham. Henry Fielding (1717–54) contributed two years of devastating theatrical satire at the Little Theatre in the Haymarket culminating in the *Historical Register* of 1736 which helped provoke the Licensing Act and a long period of theatre censorship; Fielding turned to opposition journalism for the next couple of years. James Thomson (1700–48) produced a series of romantically patriotic poems, including the provocative 'Liberty' of 1729, as well as a group of plays with an underlying anti-Walpole message which culminated in the masque *Alfred*. Here, in collaboration with his friend David Mallet and the composer Richard Arne, he introduced 'Rule Britannia', the emotive distillation of the nationalist theme developed by the anti-Walpole patriot party. Other literary contributors included Samuel Johnson with his *London*, Glover with his *Leonidas*, Whitehead with his scurrilous *Manners*, Akenside with his *Philippic*, Mallet with his *Mustapha* and many more.

Apart from literary propaganda the two main campaigns against Walpole, one on the Excise Bill, the other on his appeasement policy with Spain, were supported by virtually every other art form. Hogarth may only have been on the fringes but many other engravers joined in the fray. Music was provided by Henry Carey, Arne and Johann Pepusch. Output of popular ballads increased dramatically. Sculpture of patriotic heroes became highly fashionable as did pictures of the Navy at sea. The public relations campaign which brought the contempt for Walpole's peace policy and the desire for war against Spain to a head was brilliantly orchestrated round the focal point of Captain Jenkin's Ear, a classic publicity stunt where the sailor's severed ear was displayed in Parliament. On balance it is reasonable to assert that this is one of the very few occasions in history when a government has been happy to make peace but an opposition created such mass hysteria that war became unavoidable. Not only that but the cumulative effect of ten years of patriotic slogan-mongering laid the foundations for an imperialist fashion which was to make the conquest of foreign colonies the done thing for centuries thereafter. It may in some respects have been a revival of the 'legenda negra' attitude toward Spain fostered by the Elizabethans, but the impregnation was even deeper, the foundations of the concept of imperial destiny exploited by Pitt the Elder, and dislike of the French was linked by writers such as John Brown (1715–66) with contagious effeminacy, a French plot to undermine the British nation.

In this atmosphere the story of the Black Hole of Calcutta could be built up by the governor Zephaniah Holwell to become a new 'legenda negra' of the East and justify a new empire and his own vast fortune. The Muslims were played off against the 'inferior' Hindus with disastrous long-term results. The hero status of Robert Clive was built up by Robert Orme and Calcutta furnished somewhat incongruously with a new Roman imperial temple. Robert Orme also used the argument that Hindus were effeminate by nature so that this contributed to their unreliability.

This racist language, positioning the Indians as heathen barbarians, echoed the similar statements about the native Americans in the North American colonies as published by the Puritan preacher Increase Mather (1639–1723) and his witch-hating son Cotton, an attitude which could also be traced back to the original Catholic denigration of the Caribbean natives as cannibals and heathen savages, with the black Africans even further down the ethnic scale and so-called half-breeds lower still. Thus in Africa, India and the Americas what might now seem reasonable resistance by the aboriginal populations against white invasion was portrayed as murder and treachery, so that genocidal retribution by white settlers was quite justified. This demonization of coloured peoples was to have serious consequences over a 300-year period. With the parallel demonization of the French, Benjamin West's painting of the *Death of Wolfe* would become an icon of the new imperialism and was sold in substantial numbers.

The audience for patriotic paintings was greatly increased by Jonathan Tyers's decision to exhibit them as focal points in his popular Vauxhall Gardens: examples included Hayman's dramatic *Surrender of Montreal* of 1762 and *The Triumph of Britannia*. Similarly Farquhar's *Recruiting Officer* and Samuel Foote's *Englishman in Paris* won xenophobic ovations in the London theatre. The slogan 'Hang Byng and take care of your king' was apt for an admiral who lost a battle and failed to live up to the new role models. William Pitt the Elder (1708–78) was an able advocate of the new imperialism. An epitaph on his monument reads: 'Commerce when united and made to flourish by war' and as the historian J.H. Plumb put it, he was the first politician 'whose power rested on a magic symbolism of his own personality and beliefs'. The groundwork for this had been done by Bolingbroke and the Brothers, then continued by the pro-Pitt *Monitor* subsidized by William Beckford and the City of London.

The enthusiasm for nation and empire which had come to a head in the War of Jenkin's Ear in 1739 was matched in the same year by a new religious enthusiasm in Britain. This was inaugurated by John Wesley (1703–91) who found a new talent in himself for creating high emotional tension in his audiences by vigorous use of fire and brimstone. As he wrote in his journal: 'While I was speaking one before me dropped down as dead and presently a second and third in violent agonies.' Preaching something like fifteen sermons a week over a period of nearly fifty years Wesley developed his technique, regularly inducing forms of hysteria among his congregation. Accusations of sin, threats of everlasting damnation, disrupting the attitude-patterns of his audience, bewildering them and shattering them, he would then offer them an escape, a rescue from the hell-fire, salvation in return for repentance. It was the type of emotive conversion achieved by St Paul and many of the great medieval preachers of Christianity.

Wesley recognized, however, that this type of road to Damascus conversion in an emotion-packed few hours was not enough: it had to be followed by regular reinforcement. Methodist classes limited in numbers to twelve were held once a week under class leaders. Discussions were secret. Members were encouraged to confess and discuss their deviations. Often the class leader would follow up with a home visit to the members between classes and those who did not keep up with the course were expelled. In fact the whole cellular system built up by Wesley had much of the neatness and dedication achieved previously by Loyola and later by Lenin.

The other great propaganda asset of Methodism was its use of music. Both John and his brother Charles produced superb hymns, from 'Before Jehovah's awful throne' by John to 'Gentle Jesus meek and mild' by Charles, and music remained a major adjunct to emotive preaching in the steady spread of the new church. In addition Wesley was able to take advantage of the development of new, cheaper printing techniques and economies of scale to achieve a large increase in distribution for religious literature.

A different example of the use of emotional propaganda techniques was the remarkable personal image-building campaign orchestrated by the Young Pretender, Bonnie Prince Charlie in 1744–6. Mainly concentrating on visual imagery such as the Jacobite rose and versions of his own portrait by Le Brun, Baudouin and others, Charles's supporters promoted sales of ephemeral media such as glasses, medals and fans through a network of pedlars in Britain, a remarkably effective underground campaign, which despite political and military mismanagement was later revived by his apotheosis in song.

Another of many manifestations of the increased accessibility to printing in eighteenth century England was the propaganda battle over the Jew Bill of 1753. This has been well researched by T.W. Perry and is of special interest because of the use of emotive language and exploitation of prejudices. It began with the proposal by the Whigs to let their Jewish supporters in London have the full privileges of London trading. The London merchants, almost entirely Tory, responded with sixty pamphlets opposing the plan in a single year, many of them using crude and emotive language. *The Modest Apology for the Citizen Merchants of London* which went to three editions contained examples such as: 'You know a Jew at first sight, his dirty skin, the malignant blackness of his eyes which bespeaks guilt and murder.' The *Oxfordshire Journal* kept up an attack every week for six months, mostly in the form of letters to the editor, referring to the Oxford Whigs as 'favourers of infidelity and circumcision', mentioning the killing of a baby in circumcision by a Northumbrian curate. There were also numerous anti-Semitic articles of varying subtlety in the *London Evening Post* and other papers, even accusing the Jews of hoarding art treasures and Whigs of being bribed by Jews to support the Bill. Satirical prints on the subject multiplied and the Tories employed their tame clergymen to condemn the Bill from their pulpits. This was an early example of a pressure group which made use of fund-raising dinners, rallies, banners saying 'NO JEWS', the women wearing ribbons or crosses with effigies of Jews. It thus became a social stigma not to wear some form of anti-Bill identification such was the level of emotional mass manipulation. Significantly the Whig writers Philip Carteret Webb and Josiah Tucker had an almost impossible task in trying to offset such rampant prejudice by rational means and the government withdrew the Bill.

EUROPE AND SOUTH AMERICA

Elsewhere in the world major examples of able publicists included Jean Baptiste La Salle who in 1684 founded the Christian Brothers and whose *Rules of Propriety and Christian Civility* went to 126 editions. The new Jewish prophet Israel Baal Shem Tod (1700–60) projected the pacific ideals of Hassidism successfully in Poland and the Ukraine. The remarkable propagandist Nicolaus Count von Zinzendorf (1700–60) was inspired by the sight of Fetti's *Ecce Homo* to found a new colony for the persecuted Moravians at Herrenhut in Saxony. He was to write over 100 tracts and a number of popular hymns.

As if in rehearsal for the great outburst of anti-establishment propaganda in the last quarter of the eighteenth century many potential revolutionaries cut their teeth on destroying the image of the Jesuits. On the one hand the Guarani Republic set up by the Jesuits in Paraguay had been a remarkable success, given wide publicity by writers such as Montesquieu, Voltaire and Muratori, but on the other the Society's multinational tentacles made it unpopular with most of the new breed of despots and its fanaticism was disliked by many of their subjects. Blaise Pascal's *Letters Provinciales* of 1656 was a devastating attack. Two ingenious forgeries did massive damage: Etienne Pasquier's *La Catechisme des Jesuites* from 1594 was translated into seven languages and used the format of a pretend Jesuit textbook to draw cutting attention to Jesuit ambitions, while the even more mischievous *Monita Secreta*, produced by Zahorosky, a drop-out Jesuit in Poland in 1661, created the idea of a kind of world domination plot which was later to be used in the similarly forged *Protocols of the Elders of Zion*. From this point a sustained propaganda campaign was mounted throughout Catholic Europe, which made the Jesuits as unpopular there as they had always been among Protestants. In the 1760s they were expelled from Paraguay, the Spanish, French and Portuguese empires, then the order was dissolved in 1773 by the papacy, an ignominious if only temporary end for one of those few institutions in world history which had been genuinely multinational and had many other worthy qualities.

Except in Britain the first seven decades of the eighteenth century were a period in which propaganda lost touch with much of its target audience. The techniques developed by Bolingbroke and Wesley were, however, to have real importance for the future. The Orange dynasty's virtual conquest of Britain and its disguising of this conquest as a quasi-democratic revolution together undoubtedly formed one of the most ingenious propaganda achievements of all time and it is not entirely surprising that its imagery is still fresh in Northern Ireland 400 years later.

Revolutions

The rapid expansion in print output together with the dynastic intransigence of two kings, George III and Louis XVI, and their ministers were together mainly responsible for the two great revolutions at the end of the eighteenth century. The role of propaganda was significant in both of them.

BRITAIN

While it escaped revolution, Britain itself continued to hone the skills of propaganda both for and against the establishment. A number of propagandists trained in the anti-Walpole school, such as David Mallet and James Ralph, later moved over to the government side to work for Prime Ministers the Duke of Newcastle and the Earl of Bute. But the pioneering Opposition journalist of the new generation was without question John Wilkes (1727–97) who with the famous issue No. 45 of his paper the *North Briton* achieved a circulation of 60,000, six times that of *The Craftsman* at its peak. With some support from more orthodox politicians like Pitt and Grenville he had launched a merciless attack on Bute, George III's first prime minister. Despite the support of able writers like Samuel Johnson, Tobias Smollett, the historian William Robertson and the artist Hogarth, Bute was vulnerable to the scurrilous, barely rational style of Wilkes, who even accused the Prime Minister of having an affair with the queen mother. Almon, publisher of the anti-Bute *Political Register* joined in with an attack on 'the blast of Scotch tyranny' and 'Jack Boot' cartoons were carried in front of numerous protest marches.

The Grenville ministry of the next two years was supported by the *Political Register* and by a well-controlled press release programme directed by Thomas Whately and Charles Lloyd. Then after the Rockingham interlude the new Chatham Grafton ministry of 1766 came under attack from Almon and most notably the anonymous *Letters of Junius*, the most vitriolic of which appeared in the *Morning Advertiser* in December 1769. Later the warmongering tone of *Junius* was to goad Lord North's ministry towards war over the Falklands with the same kind of emotive hectoring: 'Britain is an injured, insulted, undone country.'

In Britain there were a number of other strands of revolutionary propaganda which formed the foundation for future pressure groups. In 1792 Mary Wollstonecraft (later Godwin, 1759–97) wrote her pioneering *A Vindication of the Rights of Woman* and her husband William Godwin (1756–1836) followed with his novel *The Adventures of Caleb Williams*, a fine example of the use of the novel as propaganda and a vigorous attack on 'the modes of domestic and unrecorded despotism'. The other great propagandist for freedom was William Wilberforce (1759–1833) who founded an Association for the Reformation of Manners in 1787 and began his campaign for the abolition of the slave trade a year later. In addition to tireless lobbying he wrote his own *Practical View of Christianity* which went to fifteen editions in 1797 and edited the *Christian Observer* from 1801. He produced well-researched statistics for release to the press in general, emphasizing the evils of the slave trade and conducted a wide-ranging propaganda campaign which involved the poets Samuel Taylor Coleridge (1772–1834) and William Cowper (1731–1800) together with his hymn writing friend John Newton (1725–1807) who produced 'How sweet the name of Jesus Sounds' ('Amazing Grace'). Also involved were the Wedgwood family who produced cameos for the movement and a number of woodcut artists who drew atrocity pictures for cheap reproduction in pamphlets like Cowper's poem 'The Negro's Complaint set to music'. There is little doubt that Wilberforce's sheer persistence and publicity skills contributed to the abolition of the slave trade and also to the general development of the Victorian middle-class conscience. With the organization of public meetings, petitions, the distribution of sloganized snuff-boxes and other ephemera, the boycott of sugar – all early examples of the mobilization of public opinion – the movement was highly effective.

Henry Mackenzie (1745–1831) was remarkable for writing a successful novel attacking slavery, and pamphlets defending it while his *Man of Feeling* in 1771 attacked the tactics of the East India Company. Parallel were the efforts of the writer Hannah More (1745–1833) who having achieved reasonable success as a novelist moved to Cowslip Green and wrote a series of staggeringly successful propaganda tracts and moral tales which, aided by the new developments in cheap printing, could sell in very large quantities at a low price.

AMERICA

Meanwhile, on the other side of the Atlantic in the American colonies there had been a similar steady development in the press since 1740. Some of the publishers were local postmasters who therefore had good access to news, others dissident printers like the Franklin family. The burden of the halfpenny tax on all publications and legal documents in the colonies imposed by the London Stamp Act often meant that it was better for them to take risks on content to gain a profitable circulation. Samuel Adams (1722–1803) wrote under twenty-five pseudonyms in various publications, especially the *Independent Advertiser* from 1748, then the *Boston Gazette* which reached a circulation of 3,600. His cousin John Adams (1735–1826), later president, was also a writer and helper of the 'Sons of Liberty'. A number of the colonial journalists had strong emotive styles: for example, Josiah

Quincy with 'Shall we, dare we pusillanimously surrender our birthright?' and Joseph Warren with 'Your feet slide on the stones bespattered with your fathers' brains'. James Otis (1725–83) kept hammering away with his alliterative 'cabal against this country'. Stephen Hopkins was an active campaigner against the Stamp Act for his *Providence Gazette.*

Other notable writers included John Dickinson who produced *Letters from a farmer in Pennsylvania* in 1767, the *Patriot's Appeal* with its 'United we stand, divided we fall', and the following year wrote the *American Liberty Song.* Also there was Alexander McDougall, 'the John Wilkes of New York' who spent some time in prison for his handbills *To the betrayed Inhabitants of New York* in 1770. Benjamin Franklin (1706–90) himself had pushed many previous causes in his long journalistic career from *Mr Dogood's Letters* in 1722 to *Poor Richard's Almanac* (1733–58) which sold about 10,000 copies a year. One of his most direct contributions to revolutionary propaganda was to employ Thomas Paine (1737–1809) as editor of the *Pennsylvania Magazine* in 1774 but during and after the Wars of Independence he was to become a major propagandist for the revolution in his own right. Alexander Hamilton (1757–1804), later George Washington's Secretary of the Treasury, was a notable author of pamphlets before and after the revolution. The colonies also produced the first black anti-slavery writer of note, Olaudah Equiano, who worked in Philadelphia in the 1760s, producing his *The Interesting Narrative of Olaudah Equiano or Gustavus Vasa,* but it was to be a century before it had any real effect.

Initially the prime organizer of anti-British agitation was Samuel Adams. It was in the offices of the *Boston Gazette* that the clever public relations exercise known as the Boston Tea Party was planned in 1773. Anti-Stamp Act demonstrations had been common since 1765 with effigy burning and the planting of 'Liberty Trees'. Adams was also a regular organizer of parades, firework displays, bonfires and celebratory dinners. He exploited the incident of the Boston Massacre to the full with broadsheets and illustrations by his assistant Paul Revere. He used heavy black borders, coffin motifs and a masthead featuring a mutilated Britannia. Ezekiel Russell of the *Salem Gazette* produced a highly popular broadside with forty coffins and the legend 'Bloody Butchery'. Isaiah Thomas of the *Massachusetts Spy* cunningly moved his press into hiding two days before Lexington and pushed the slogan 'Americans – Liberty or Death – Join or Die'. The first revolutionary flag was a coiled rattlesnake with thirteen rattles and the motto 'Don't tread on me'. Other visual ideas were the use of the symbolic '45' to commemorate John Wilkes's *North Briton*, statues of Pitt as he was an opponent of the Stamp Act, the Franklin concept of a broken snake with the slogan 'Join or die' (pl. 11) and artefacts such as teapots with the slogan 'No Stamp Act'. Committees of Correspondence were formed which became the organizational basis for the Revolution, with James Otis, author of the slogan 'Taxation without Representation is Tyranny' in 1765, providing considerable inspiration. There was the remarkable opera *The Disappointed* by Barton in 1767 which included

'Yankie Doodle' as one of its tunes. As the tension built up Paul Revere was again part of a publicity stunt with his stagecoach dash to the capital and Patrick Henry's (1736–99) slogan 'Liberty or Death' was printed on shirts. Effigy hanging or burning was a common technique as were fake funerals.

The War of Independence began almost accidentally with the tiny skirmish at Lexington. Within a few days the artist Ralph Earle had produced four pictures of the incident and these were engraved for bulk printing by Amos Dolittle; the image of the colonists as sharp-shooters was eagerly fostered at a time when their military organization was very poor, while the British were always blamed for firing first, for burning and raping. By using a fast ship the colonists sent their version of the Lexington campaign to the London press two weeks ahead of official news from General Gage. Casualty figures in the War of Independence were grossly misstated in the British press. Sensitive to the need for sound propaganda Washington appointed the brilliant Tom Paine as his aide. Paine in 1776 produced the incisive *Crisis* pamphlet which he was asked to read aloud to the troops: 'The summer soldier, the sunshine patriot will in this crisis shrink from the service of his country. . . .' The press in the freed areas flourished: the pro-independence *Connecticut Journal* reached a circulation of 8,000, massive for this period. A corporate identity was designed in 1776 – thirteen stripes alternately red and white plus crosses of Sts George and Andrew. Thomas Jefferson (1743–1826) meanwhile masterminded not only the drafting of the *Declaration of Independence* with its cleverly repeated attacks on George III, but also its effective distribution through the network of Committees of Correspondence. Paine and Washington concentrated on special appeals to the French Canadians, the Indian tribes and German soldiers in the British army. This segmented kind of approach was also followed by Franklin who had been posted to organize the pro-American campaign in France. He was helped there by the French government-subsidized *Affaire* and little hindered by the British subsidized French language newspaper *Courier de l'Europe* printed in Holland. Franklin became a cult figure, pictured on medallions, snuff-boxes and handkerchiefs; he published *The Sale of Hessians* on the British press-gangs in Germany and *To the good People of Ireland* as well as a fake issue of the *Boston Independent* in which the British boasted of scalp hunting. This was one of the most thorough campaigns of diplomatic isolation by propaganda ever mounted.

Once the War of Independence was won the new American government did not need to maintain such a high profile. The constitution itself was potentially a very fine propaganda document but the overall tone of government now became relatively conservative. Washington himself was cultivating almost a Hanoverian image as head of state, insisting on outriders in his presidential procession, allowing no one to sit in his presence and no one to shake his hand. He almost reluctantly maintained his efforts with the press, wooing the public through David Stuart's newspapers like *The Federalist Gazette of the United States*. Early US Presidents including Washington all tended to be heavily attacked in their own press and took active steps to deflect it. Jefferson, the first politician to use the phrase 'public opinion' which came from Gibbon's *Decline and Fall*, founded the *National Intelligencer* and employed professional writer Philip Freneau to work on his image and attack Washington. James Madison (1751–1836) wrote for the *Federalist* and *National Gazette* and was a major polemicist for Jefferson before his own presidency.

A substantial propaganda war did develop between the pro- and anti-Jacobins in the United States as the new nation slowly felt its way towards an image of its own. But the centre of creative propaganda moved to France and it was the French who were in due course to present the Americans with one of their most permanent visual images – the Statue of Liberty.

FRANCE

The French Revolution involved a whole succession of political movements each with a remarkably sophisticated propaganda repertoire. In fact the French revolutionary period offers more examples of mass manipulation skill than almost any period between the Reformation and Hitler. Perhaps this is a reflection on the French attempt to establish a totally new form of government, a new religion and a new way of life; the greater the attitude change required the greater the need for propaganda skills. Russia and China in the twentieth century are parallel examples.

With a total population of around 26 million, 600,000 of them in Paris, France in 1789 had reasonably well-developed media at least for the upper classes. In spite of fairly severe censorship there was even some opposition press activity – from 1677 the anti-establishment *Gazette de Leyde* was published bi-weekly from Holland by the Huguenot de la Touts. His successor Etienne Luzac helped to translate Adams's American propaganda into French as well as assisting the Polish and Dutch nationalists. A network of travelling salesmen ensured wide distribution of cheaply produced booklets, particularly the popular almanacs, songs and broadsheets. The tradition of the mazarinades developed into the 'gazettes en vers' like the *Mercure galant*. Denis Diderot (1713–84) in his *Cyclopaedia* of 1737 had produced a highly influential compendium of contemporary thought which was in itself a work of propaganda for new ideas and significantly included a realization of the need for propaganda to achieve any change in society. The sepulchral etchings of dungeons by the Italian architect Giambattista Piranesi (1720–78) created an image of frustrated liberty and oppression. Jean Jacques Rousseau (1712–78) produced his obscure if highly influential *Contrat Social* in 1762 with its 'Man is born free and everywhere he is in chains' as well as the beginnings of the slogan 'Liberté, égalité, fraternité', while in the same year Voltaire (1694–1778) wrote a series of anti-clerical pamphlets which proved extremely popular. Helped by this intellectual infrastructure the French aristocracy in their 'parlements' were concerned to reduce the

King's despotic power and inefficiency. Popular novels like those of Restif de Bretonne entertainingly undermined the image of the Ancien Regime and attacked corruption. A pamphlet, the *Grand Remonstrance* of 1753, sold 20,000 copies in three weeks. In the theatre Beaumarchais's *Marriage of Figaro* of 1784, with its barely concealed anti-establishment innuendo, had both great theatrical success and propaganda influence. It was hugely popular with the aristocracy and even the queen Marie Antoinette, demonstrating how much revolutionary propaganda was encouraged and initiated by the frustrated upper layers of society who later came to regret dearly the Pandora's box which they had opened.

Government censorship was highly inefficient which resulted in the increasingly open circulation of revolutionary material. *Le Gazetier Cuirasse* of 1771 attacked the court vigorously and the most prolific printer of the time Charles-Joseph Panckoucke, who had twenty-seven presses, was commercially dominant before, during and after the revolution. In the context of increasing mass propaganda the travelling salesmen of the countryside were of huge importance with their distribution of works like the *Almanac Mathieu Laensberg* which sold 150,000 copies annually to the lower bourgeoisie and adjusted its message to fit the popular political trends of the day. The production of pamphlets was financed by businessmen such as the banker Kornmann. In addition the problem of reaching the illiterate section of the population was solved by the organized public reading of newspapers during the eighteenth century for 6 sous per person. The cult of Franklin was spread on glasses, snuff-boxes, textiles, inkwells and in almanacs including the translated version of his own *Poor Richard*. By 1788 with a further influx of new ideas from the United States, revolutionary pamphlets were appearing at the rate of twenty-five per week, steadily getting more radical. One of the most influential of these was Sieyes's *Qu'est-ce que le Tiers Etat?* with its neat use of the question and answer technique. The new hunger for reading matter reached its climax in 1789, a year when sixty new newspapers were started in France; a German visitor, Storch, commented that the French at all levels seemed to spend every spare moment reading. A major propaganda campaign orchestrated by the Society of Thirty including Abbé Sieyes (1748–1836), Mirabeau (1749–91) with his daring *Essai sur le despotisme* and Condorcet (1743–94), all of them part-time writers, bombarded a people suffering from acute economic crisis and governmental chaos. Antoine Rivarol (1753–1801) produced his highly effective satire *Petit Almanac de nos grands hommes* in 1788. Jacques Pierre Brissot (1754–93), the Chartres lawyer and later a pioneering newspaper editor, was already writing revolutionary pamphlets throughout the 1780s. Brissot had experience of the new American propaganda style from a visit in 1787 and like Mirabeau had been a hack propagandist for the government before 1789: Other publicists included the priest Gabriel Mably (1709–85), Simon Linguet, Mallet du Pan and Elysée Loustallot, who wrote *Les Révolutions de Paris*. Two able propagandists who later founded newspapers were certainly agitating before 1789: Camille Desmoulins (1760–94) a lawyer and pamphleteer who urged on the crowds to the Bastille and the doctor Jean Paul Marat (1743–93), who in 1788 was reading aloud, explaining the *Contrat Social* on street corners and was one of the revolutionaries who paid particular attention to the development of reading clubs so that his message also reached the illiterate. By May 1789 pamphlets were appearing at the rate of 100 a month, by June 300. There was a very substantial group of practised if not professional writers, many of them certainly earning money out of it, helped by the patronage of wealthy aristocrats, even the Duc d'Orléans who regarded himself as a liberal candidate for the throne who should show himself to be on the side of revolution by helping men like Desmoulins. Their common themes were the principles of the *Contrat Social* and the proper recognition of the Tiers Etat. Many of them frequently resorted to the emotive threat of 'La Grande Peur', the idea, sometimes not without foundation, that the King was secretly gathering together an army to smash all insurgents; this notion was to remain a useful tool for revolutionary propagandists for the next ten years.

The other medium important in the propaganda immediately preceding the Revolution itself was the poster. As Louis Sebastien Menic observed in 1789: 'In the storm of revolution the placard is the tocsin . . . a course in morals, politics and literature.' Another observer commented that in Paris in 1789 there were 'innumerable paper sheets of every shape and colour'. When the combination of such saturation in revolutionary ideas, desperate economic crisis and deep fear of reprisals had enabled Desmoulins and others to raise crowds to fever pitch, the actual Revolution began.

The period after 14 July saw two crucial developments in the propaganda nexus of the Revolution: its visual identity and its organizational infrastructure. On the visual side it is highly significant that within three days of the storming of the Bastille King Louis was presented with a tricolour hat cockade by the Marquis de Lafayette (1757–1834) in front of Bailly the new mayor of Paris and leader of the Tiers Etat. As a soldier who had seen service under Washington Lafayette perhaps had a special appreciation of the value of uniform and corporate identity, but the speed with which the tricolour was introduced and spread was still remarkable. The visual symbolism of the Revolution was rapidly extended with the addition of the Phrygian cap which was used on flagpoles, church towers, posters, fans, watches, crockery, buttons, rings and earrings. The tricolour sash was almost as common. It became part of a complete uniform known as the Carmagnole. Then came additional symbols such as the oak tree or a female figure for liberty, the spirit level for equality and the rods or fasces – borrowed from Rome – for fraternity. The extension of propaganda to ephemeral media such as playing cards with 'Liberty' instead of the King and Queen (see pl. 4), board games and fans was remarkable. This was one of the most thorough and rapid spreads of a new corporate identity system by spontaneous adoption in any period of human history. It helps to explain the early quality of crowd control. Rudé has described the rapid development of techniques of crowd manipulation: sounding the tocsin, fireworks, burning of effigies and hostile tracts, processions and chanting of slogans such as 'Vive le Tiers Etat'. The sense of identity was soon afterwards extended also to terms of address, with the use of the title 'Citoyen' a fairly natural choice, but the extension of 'tu', the *tutoiement* was a more imaginative change. The environment of the coffee house acting as a club was crucial to networking, the *gazetiers de la bouche*.

The next development combined visual symbols with crowd control into event management. Mirabeau, a major organizer of spectacles, wrote to Jacques Louis David (1748–1825) the painter who was to take over the role: 'Speak to the senses, speak to them incessantly, at every moment place before their eyes the desolating image of slavery, the ravishing image of the day of independence.' He had both a real understanding of the emotive effect of well-managed events and of the way in which those who saw them would pass on the message to the rest of the population. In 1790 he organized a celebration for the anniversary of the Tennis Court Oath. There were bronze tablets, busts of Rousseau and Franklin, waitresses dressed as patriotic nymphs, speeches by Danton and Robespierre, deputies crowned with oak leaves and a model of the Bastille which was ceremonially smashed to pieces by members of the National Guard. The idea of planting liberty trees was adopted from the Americans, perhaps through Lafayette again, for he had borrowed some of Jefferson's phrases in his own plea for human rights. David, some of whose earlier paintings of Roman republican subjects had been regarded as moral propaganda, now began to produce major works for the Revolution itself: his *Tennis Court Oath* in 1792 and his *Death of Marat* in 1793. The visual image of the capture of the Bastille was perpetuated in numerous etchings and prints, even extended into a board game. Augustin Dupré became the official chief engraver of revolutionary images. Pierre Palloy invented a whole new industry of Bastille propaganda souvenirs.

On the organizational side the Société des Amis de la Constitution, known shortly as the Jacobin Club, was founded in November 1789 and soon had a tight network of branches throughout France. In the Constituent Assembly there was wide divergence of views – the terms left and right in politics first emerged from the two-sided Salle de la Manège. The deputies were perhaps overeducated by the wealth of propaganda material to the point where there was too big a choice for them to settle on simple decisions. The proliferation of media exposure for variations on the revolutionary idea continued since virtually every significant or ambitious deputy had his own newspaper. Marat took over a royalist press and founded *L'Ami du Peuple* in which he developed an aggressive style of journalism reminiscent of Bolingbroke or Wilkes in Britain. A particular feature of the paper was its use of correspondence columns to allow the inclusion of very extreme views. Marat also helped in the development of the Popular and Fraternal Societies which disseminated ideas to the artisans and sub-literate sections of Paris society. Marat's style was highly emotive with regular use of epithets like 'blood-sucking'. Loustalot had not only a very racy reporting style but was the first journalist to include line drawings of current events in his paper, often of violent scenes. Mirabeau secured the contract for publishing the reports of the Estates General in his *Journal* which must have ensured it a profitable circulation. As a pamphleteer he had a liking for the use of obscenity to shock his readers. Danton was backed by the emotive poet-journalist Camille Desmoulins and the entrepreneurial printer Momoro. Desmoulins published his *Révolutions de France et de Brabant* bringing in the Austrian Netherlands which had rebelled against Joseph II and he commented: 'Today in France it is the journalist who holds the tablets, who inspects the senate, the consuls and the dictator.' Brissot's *Le Patriote-Français* tended to the left but became less so when it came to symbolize the stand of the Girondins, the pro-war party, 'the war of the peoples against the kings'. Brissot was a great exploiter of the 'grande peur' theme, creating plot scares, international conspiracies and acute xenophobia. Marat in *L'Ami du Peuple* described him as 'apprenticed to chicanery, a would-be wit, scandal-sheet writer, apprentice philosopher, speculator, criminal, prince's valet, clerk, police spy, publicist, municipal inquisitor etc.'. But Brissot was also concerned to make sure that propaganda skills were made use of to help the French army. He wrote to General Dumouriez on the north-eastern front: 'Carry pamphlets in German on your bayonets'.

Brissot's greatest political rival was Robespierre who also had his own newspaper, *Le Défenseur de la Constitution.* When his Committee of Public Safety took over the government in July 1793 it not only had to tackle a radical reorganization of French resources to defend the country against invasion, but had moved so far from traditional points of reference that very substantial propaganda was required to fill the void. This took the form mainly of massive processional pageants organized by David with victory parades for the army. Large funds were allocated to the anniversary fête of 10 August 1793 with people from all over France brought to the Place de la Bastille to see a succession of elaborate floats representing the new republican virtues, a huge procession lasting sixteen hours moving along the boulevards through triumphal arches, past large temporary statues to the national altar in the Champs de Mars. Similar was Robespierre's Fête of the Supreme Being at which he ceremonially put a torch to a huge figure of Atheism hiding a figure of Wisdom. This and similar events throughout the provinces were masterminded by David and assisted by the Jacobin network. Robespierre's own style of oratory was highly emotive with frequent offers to die if his views were not accepted and many repetitions of his visionary 'I see'. The new regime had altered the calendar, even the length of the week; it had its own fashions for hair and clothes, its own religion and rituals from 1791, its own new red flag as well as the tricolour, its own regulatory system of spying, public confession and show trials.

Not surprisingly French revolutionary propaganda had become an effective export. Initially it was in the interests of the Girondin party to encourage republicanism among neighbouring countries so that their military attacks on France would be blunted. There was rapid contagion of ideas through masonic lodges, reading clubs for joint purchase of French newspapers and a remarkable growth in the printing of revolutionary texts in almost every European language. In Belgium Tom Paine was published in Flemish and Walloon and *Le Cosmopolite* was the new revolutionary paper. In Holland it was *La Batave* and the Dutch were using 'Liberty, Equality, Fraternity' as their slogan as early as 1795. In fact there had been an earlier remarkable period of anti-monarchical propaganda in Holland in 1787 with William V of Orange being attacked by a radical press and on numerous artefacts such as teapots, breadboards, beer tankards and textiles with slogans such as 'Liberty or Death'.

In Poland there was a Jacobin club where they wore Phrygian caps, sang French songs and in Kosciuszko (see p. 228) produced a charismatic national leader. In Hungary, Romania, Serbia and other parts of the Austrian empire again there were French-inspired newspapers, translated songs, pamphlets and even Jacobin haircuts. In England there was the London Corresponding Society, an organization for the distribution of Jacobin propaganda collecting 1*d* per week from each member; it succeeded in selling 200,000 copies of the *Rights of Man* in 1793. In Ireland the *Belfast Northern Star*, published twice weekly at under 2*d* per copy, has been described as 'one of the most significant democratic papers in English', encouraging the development of the Orange Lodges. On the Catholic side the revolutionary Irish writings of Wolfe Tone (1763–98) were encouraged.

Some credit for this pan-European spread may be due to Brissot and his foreign secretary Lebrun who like him was an ex-journalist, but some of the spread was spontaneous. This would certainly be true of the many newspapers set up in imitation of the ultra-left *Le Père Duchesne* founded by Jacques René Hébert (1755–94). Written in the most basic language and laced with obscenity this publication seems to have peaked at an exceptionally high circulation, into the hundreds of thousands, vastly greater than any previous journal in France and at a time when the biggest selling newspaper in Britain, *The Times*, had a circulation of 4,000. This boost in circulation was helped by government subsidies which ensured that 1 million copies of *Le Père Duchesne* were sent free to the army during nine months of 1793/4. Similarly obscene were the numerous pamphlets issued to project Marie Antoinette as a nymphomaniac. In 1790 *The Amorous Evening of General Mottier and the Fair Antoinette* described her affair with a dog in some detail.

The propaganda of this period was characterized by extreme emotive language, obscenity and vituperation. Titles became more sensationalist – *Le Vomissement Aristocratique* [Aristocratic Vomit]. As with other aspiring utopias, the removal of traditional values and benchmarks and the attempt to replace these rapidly by the use of propaganda techniques tended to be dictated by the learning curve of the slowest in a society. Around 5,000 copies of the *Journal des hommes libres* were distributed free to the army, which received up to 30,000 free newspapers every day from the Convention.

The Jacobins also appreciated the value of getting at their audience young and their youth propaganda section was a forerunner of the Hitler Youth and the Komosol. Two other media played a part in the French Revolution: music and theatre. At the popular level the most successful song, 'Ça ira', dominated many rallies and was translated into almost every European language; 'The Carmagnole' – 'Dansons la Carmagnole, vive le son, vive le son' – was both chant and dance. Different in function but equally popular was the great war anthem the 'Marseillaise' (see pl. 8) which met the need of the moment for the army of the Rhine in 1792. Even the leaders of Thermidor had their own theme tune 'Le Reveil du Peuple' and at the more serious level composers like Gossec and Étienne Méhul were sponsored by the Revolution's National Conservatory of Music. It was Gossec who wrote the special music for the Voltaire festival of 1791 with chariot floats designed by David. Few of the plays performed in the theatres from 1789 to 1799 had any lasting appeal, but Marie Joseph Chenier's *Charles X* had been the great success of theatrical propaganda in 1789. Particularly under Robespierre theatres were encouraged to follow the revolutionary theme and fitted in with the general fashion for open-air political spectacle.

Despite its ultimate plunge into dictatorship and aggressive war the French Revolution does supply a remarkable illustration of both the strengths and weaknesses of well-managed propaganda. Overall the French Revolution turned into a classic example of the way in which uncontrolled, highly emotional propaganda using panic phobia, obscenity, and bloodlust can quite quickly create a level of mass hysteria far greater than was originally intended and easily twisted into self-destructive violence. It also showed that traditional attitudes in the end have great powers to withstand heavy onslaught from radical propaganda.

In general the last quarter of the eighteenth century was a period of vital innovation in the history of propaganda, enhanced by rapid advances in the technology of printing. It was a key period for the development of certain crucial ideas in the minds at least of the middle classes, including the notion that people have rights and are entitled to air grievances, even aspire to liberty and equality.

Empire and Nationalism

FRANCE

Napoleon ranks with several other of the great tyrants as among the most able self-propagandists of history. Brilliant though he was as a soldier and political opportunist it was by deliberately creating an image that he gained the power to dominate Europe for fifteen years and to enable Bonapartism to survive long after his death. As Robert Holtman put it 'he was the first to use the machinery of government in a systematic fashion to control public opinion and he was utterly unscrupulous in doing so'. At the same time it must be acknowledged that the propaganda tools which he used had nearly all been developed or used successfully under the Revolution.

Bonaparte's awareness of the value of propaganda came early in his career. As a Jacobin army officer he obtained the help of a Corsican colleague, Saliceti, to write a pamphlet called *Souper de Beaucaire* which put across the case for the people of Marseilles to surrender to the Jacobin army without a fight in 1793. From 1797 *Le Courier de l'Armée d'Italie* was used to boost military morale and even Napoleon's first coup, Brumaire, was based on a false impression of his modest victory at Lodi, the invasion of Egypt, false rumours of plots and a lie by his brother Lucien who suggested that Bonaparte was about to be killed. Thereafter he made sure that the good news about his battles outweighed the bad. Captured flags were ceremoniously sent back to Paris. He sent in an account of Marengo which gave him sole credit for a brilliant victory, and secured good press coverage, whereas the greater victory by Moreau at Hohenlinden received poor press coverage. He published his *Bulletin of the Army of the Reserve*, his equivalent of Caesar's *Gallic War*. He always cultivated the 'whiff of grapeshot' image, but played down his defeats. Copenhagen he distorted; Trafalgar he kept out of the French press for two months, then blamed on Villeneuve; Waterloo he of course blamed on Marshall Ney. Numbers on both sides in his battles were always twisted to his benefit, and overall, though it was based on a strong element of truth, his reputation as a dashing, invincible commander was exaggerated in order to retain domestic loyalty.

At the same time he exploited the old revolutionary tack of plot and panic. He had used it for Brumaire, spreading rumours of royalist invasions, and he did it again when organizing the change of title from First Consul to Emperor, this time grossly exaggerating the Cadoudal conspiracy to enhance his role as a saviour.

At an early stage Bonaparte also paid close attention to his visual image, encouraging the creation of a romantic, Byronic profile by painters such as David, 'Painter of the Government'. David went on to produce the major set pieces of the reign including *The Proclamation of the Life Consulship*, *The Coronation* and imaginative settings like the image of Napoleon crossing the St Bernard Pass reading Livy's account of Hannibal as he negotiated the frozen torrents. Antoine-Jean Gros (1771–1835) romanticized the military with his *Napoleon at Arcola*, *Bonaparte among the plague-stricken at Jaffa*, and *Napoleon at Eylau*. Theodore Géricault (1791–1824) contributed his absurd *Ossian receiving the generals of the Republic in Walhalla*, and idealized military figures like *Officer of the Chasseurs* and the *Wounded Cuirassier*. There was an entire mythology of glorified militarism, the concept of 'mon aigle', or 'soldats, il vous suffira de dire "J'etais à la battaile de l'Austerlitz" pour que l'on respond "Voilà un brave"'.* For mass circulation there were the engravings of Pellegrin. This idolization of 'la gloire' was the climax to a campaign that went back to Jacques Pierre Brissot where the rights of man were less important than the willingness of man to sacrifice his life for his country. Napoleon had said that history was a 'myth which people choose to believe', and he exploited this ruthlessly for his own dynastic ends. Emotive words like 'hero', 'genius', 'liberation', 'saviour' and 'noble' were used to lard every narrative and he referred to himself as the second Charlemagne. The obverse side of the visualization of 'la gloire' was the series of caricatures of Napoleon's enemies, in particular William Pitt, commissioned by the politician Fouché.

Other visual arts were harnessed to the same objective. The Venetian sculptor Canova (1757–1822) was called to Paris to model a colossal statue of the Emperor and did produce an image of Bonaparte as Apollo with Josephine as Venus. Chaudet carved a likeness of him as a Roman to surmount the Column of Vendôme which had a spiralling bas-relief of the battles of 1805–7 while François Rudé carved the powerful 'La Marseillaise' group for the Arc de Triomphe. This grandiosity went with the new Empire style of architecture, redolent of all the great empires of the past, big in everything. Napoleon's architects were men like Chalgrin who designed the massive Arc de Triomphe and the Odéon, and Vignon who created the Madeleine and the Pont d'Austerlitz, but there were also plans for lesser war memorials in every French town. At the same time many details of imperial life were also impregnated with the Napoleonic identity. Medals proliferated, as did maps and engravings of famous battles, the icons of the Napoleonic era. In 1809 the legend 'Napoleon Empereur' replaced 'Republique Française' on the coinage. The Napoleonic house bee was

---

* 'Soldiers, it will be enough to say "I was at the Battle of Austerlitz" for people to say "There's a brave man".'

everywhere. The Emperor was obsessive too about uniforms, for civil servants as well as soldiers, for men and women. This was the period of epaulettes, crossed belts, tailcoats and extravagant hats. Medals and badges were also treated as matters of great importance; Napoleon devoted a lot of attention to obtaining maximum benefit and show from his honours system. This in turn linked in with his love of spectacle. Under the direction of the painter Pierre Prudhon (1758–1823) event management reached new heights (pl. 13). Firework displays, massive parades, balls, free meals on the Emperor's birthday and annual celebrations of his coronation were just some of the many. The anniversaries of Jena and Austerlitz were similarly treated and Napoleon was a regular exploiter of flag ceremonies, for example the handing over of 400 Prussian flags together with Frederick the Great's sword was an ideal way of demonstrating French superiority. The use of civic fêtes, chantings of 'Vive Napoleon', horse races and numerous other forms of display all contributed to glorifying the empire.

The use of theatre was no more than an extension of the display that went on outside and actors were often used to read out Napoleon's orders of the day or news of victories from the stage. Theatres directed by Napoleon's Superintendent of Spectacles, Auguste de Rémusat and Joseph Esménard, editor of *Mercure de France*, put on patriotic plays such as *Le Pont de Lodi* and *William the Conqueror* or faced closure. A heroic opera on *Cortès* by Paisiello glorified Napoleon in 1809 as did Esménard's *Le Triomphe de Trajan*. Poetry was harnessed with obvious titles such as 'Austerlitz' by Charles Millevoye and 'Marengo' by Viguerie. There were specifically anti-English history books like *Le cri d'honneur* and school prizes were awarded for patriotism. The history of France was rewritten by Napoleonic hagiographers to emphasize the decadence of the Bourbons and contrasting brilliance of the Emperor. Unquestioning admiration of Napoleon was symbolized by the role model soldier Nicolas Chauvin in songs and *Les Aides de Camp* by Bayard and Dumanoir, further popularized in Charet's *Conscritt Chauvin* and Coignard's *La Cocarde tricolore*. Rouget de L'Isle, writer of 'Marseillaise', and Pierre Lebrun were commissioned to produce more new patriotic music and propaganda songs, some of which were quite successful though ironically the most popular, 'La Lyonnaise', did not come until the more defensive period of 1814. Court music was supervised by Paisiello and Jean LeSueur.

As soon as he had achieved supreme power Napoleon also took complete control of the French press and used it to his advantage. As he said himself: 'Three hostile newspapers are more to be feared than a thousand bayonets. . . . If I had a free press I would not last more than three months.' Thus in 1800 he closed down sixty out of seventy-three French newspapers and within a year removed another four. The *Bulletin de la Grande Armée* was regularly used as a means of fostering morale and was read aloud by actors in theatres, schools and churches, with bells or drums to announce the event beforehand just as the *Couriers* from the various armies had been used for home public relations. The *Moniteur* became the official government paper and was circulated free to the army while censorship was intensified. In 1810 the Direction Générale de l'Imprimerie et de la Librairie was set up to take responsibility for all aspects of cultural life. By this time there were only four newspapers left. The *Mercure de France* had been suppressed because of an offending article by the poet Chateaubriand, while the *Journal des Curés* had appeared to help spread Napoleon's religious policy. Alexandre Hauterive managed the press relations of the French foreign office. Government press hand-outs went only to the favoured titles and pro-Napoleonic writers were given the incentive of prizes and pensions. Even a number of foreign language titles were printed in Paris, to encourage Bonapartist thinking in conquered territories or enemy countries. *Il Corriere d'Italia* was an example, fostering a level of Italian nationalism at the expense of the Austrians and there were *Monitors* in Westphalia and Ionia, as well as a *Gazette de Madrid*. Talleyrand produced an English language paper, the *Argus* edited by Lewis Goldsmith and distributed in the West Indies or to British prisoners of war at places like Verdun. Later Goldsmith edited the *British Monitor* before finally changing sides and writing French propaganda on behalf of the British. The overall control of Napoleon's large foreign language propaganda campaign was in the hands of Marshal Berthier, who had been with Lafayette in America, and Henri Clarke, with newspapers being produced in almost every European language. The deliberately misleading *Bulletin* in German was particularly effective. Wherever possible Napoleon employed natives in each foreign country to produce the propaganda for that area so that it seemed more authentic. He also used the standard ploy of encouraging semi-genuine or forged letters and testimonials from 'members of the public' to boost authenticity.

Other major contributors were Talleyrand who masterminded the anti-Austrian campaign of 1800 and Murat who saturated Sicily and Naples with Napoleonic propaganda. Language differences were always taken seriously; and an example was the anti-Russian pamphlet *An old Ottoman and his brothers* which was produced in both Arabic and Turkish for use in Bosnia, a classic example of an area of prejudice which was to be kept alive by propagandists over several centuries. Berthier organized propaganda in Polish urging desertion from the Russian army. The two main outside targets which were the subject of sustained Napoleonic propaganda at home were Russia, where the atrocity story and barbarous horde image were the standard weapons, and Britain, the nation of shopkeepers, perfidious Albion, where treaty-breaking, killing of prisoners of war, murder plots and starvation tactics were the regularly repeated accusations. One of the more devious anti-Russian ploys was the publishing of the fictitious 'Will and Testament of Peter I' in which the tsar purportedly committed his successors to a mission of world conquest, a good excuse for Napoleon to strike first. This world conquest plot phobia was later imitated by the Russian secret police under Nicholas II when they produced the *Protocols of the Elders of Zion* in 1903 to justify a similar pre-emptive strike against the Russian Jews (see p. 247).

Overall, therefore, propaganda played a significant role in both establishing and maintaining Napoleon's remarkable hold over the French people. It was also of major significance in the effort to reduce resistance to his rule throughout the empire and to undermine the credibility of his opponents elsewhere. Much of it was also dedicated to the establishment of a long-term dynastic image which was to be thwarted by Napoleon's own overambition and was to have only some residual influence on the career of his nephew Napoleon III. In historical terms the French revolutionary period had been a major turning-point because of the introduction by Carnot of the idea of mass conscription, the possibility of massive armies. Napoleon extended this by the development of new ideas in mass motivation. For fifteen years Napoleon as the new Charlemagne, peacemaker and saviour, created a highly effective image for his regime and though it began to lose credibility after 1813 – the new slogan of 'Emperor, country and honour' was ringing hollow – it was capable of revival once the horrors of 1815 were forgotten. In order to achieve the level of support and motivation necessary for the massive tasks of conquest and settlement which he set himself, he had devoted massive resources to propaganda and been totally unscrupulous both in distortion of the truth and manipulation of every available emotion.

The propaganda of the July Revolution of 1830 in Paris was masterminded by Louis Adolphe Thiers (1797–1877) who made his name as a literary historian with the *History of the Revolution* (1827). He was editor of the newspaper *National* founded with the help of Talleyrand and the Duc d'Orléans. This was a revolution created very much by press activity with an emotional stimulus from the production of Victor Hugo's play *Hernani*. Thiers also wrote the manifesto and had Paris deluged with posters. Within three days, 'les trois glorieuses', the Revolution had been accomplished and Orléans was in power. Honore Daumier (1808–79) attacked the Bourbon restoration in his acerbic cartoons, particularly the pear-shaped caricature of Louis Philippe. Delacroix's superb *Liberty guiding the People* resurrected the female goddess symbol for the 1830 Revolution.

The February Revolution in France in 1848, like its predecessor of 1830 owed a lot to newspaper encouragement. The provisional government of the Second Republic was made up almost entirely of the editorial boards of *La Reforme* and *National* though they had a combined circulation of no more than 3,000, whereas *La Presse*, which was shortly to help bring down the republic, had seven times that number. Alexandre Ledru-Rollin (1807–74), editor of *La Reforme*, was a leading figure in the government, as was the poet Alphonse Lamartine (1790–1869) whose *History of the Girondins* and the play based on it, *Le Chevalier de la Maison Rouge*, played a major part in stirring up the Parisian middle classes against Louis Philippe. But the objectives of the short-lived republic were confused, as were the groups who supported it. What was remarkable was the speed with which the news of the February Revolution swept through Europe and set off a chain of mimetic movements. In terms of the press this was probably at least partly due to the foundation of the Havas news agency in Paris in 1840, connecting major cities by a pigeon-post service, followed by Reuters founded in Aachen seven years later.

BRITAIN

The most obvious result of and reaction to Napoleon's conquests was a wave of nationalist propaganda which affected almost every area threatened by his power. This was perhaps at its least natural in Britain where William Pitt's government deliberately encouraged such activity to goad an often demotivated populace into supporting the war effort. British opposition press was censored from 1789 and new government newspapers such as the *True Briton* were launched, while both William Cobbett's *Porcupine* and *The Times* were subsidized to uphold the patriotic line. Joseph Doane was specifically appointed by Pitt to limit the public relations damage to the monarchy which arose from the 'madness' of King George III. On the stage Charles Dibdin (1745–1814) projected the jolly Jack tar image with numerous songs and light operas. Naval dramas were highly popular with Sheridan's *Glorious First of June*, the *Defeat of the Dutch Fleet* at Covent Garden and a realistic *Trafalgar* at Sadler's Wells, complete with 'Rule Britannia', flags, guns and singing sailors. Nelson was the great role model of the era with paintings by Lemuel Abbott, heroic battlescapes by Clarkson Stanfield and Felix Philippoteaux, poems like 'Nelson' and 'Ode of 1814' and biography from Robert Southey (1774–1843). Later, Prime Minister George Canning was to hire James Gillray (1757–1815) to continue the development of Nelson's image which was extended by Haydn and boosted quite considerably in the short term by the exhibitionist skills of Lady Hamilton.

This was also a period in which improved printing technology made possible the production of cheap popular tracts or stories designed to improve the behaviour of the working classes. From the *History of Little Goody Twoshoes* (1765) to Hannah More's tracts, print was used to project the work and thrift ethic.

ITALY AND BELGIUM

The new nationalism in Italy also owed its inspiration to Napoleon and in turn had links of style with the Romantic movement in the arts. Poets like Alessandro Manzoni who produced 'Il Trionfo della Liberta' in 1801 and

'Marzo' twenty years later were followed by a succession of brilliant writers. Guiseppe Mazzini (1805–72) was one of the greatest inflammatory writers of the century, founding his Young Italy in 1831, issuing a stream of nationalist pamphlets and publishing his newspaper *Young Italy* from a base in Switzerland. Using the slogan 'Dio e Popolo' and introducing new ideas such as the concept of 'the Third Rome', he worked hard at the distribution as well as writing of his publications in a way that could best be compared with Lenin. A succession of nationalist papers came from his stable, including *Il dovere*, and the *Popolo d'Italia*, all suffering from the handicap of narrow circulations due to censorship and the numerous frontiers in post-Napoleonic Italy. Eventually *Il Diritto* and *L'emancipatore Catolico* began to achieve some national impact.

Meanwhile, a new medium was added to the repertoire of those working for Italian unification when Rossini (1792–1868) produced his opera *Guillaume Tell* in Paris in 1829, immediately recognized as a plea for Italian freedom. Thirteen years later came Verdi's (1813–1901) *Nabucco* with its 'Chorus of the Hebrew Slaves' which was adopted as a nationalist hymn and which continued the heightening of emotions. His *Lombardi* of 1843 was in the same mould and Verdi's popularity was only increased when he was exiled. Ironically it was an opera, *La Muette* by Auber which had a rebellion in Naples as its subject, that caused a semi-spontaneous outbreak of nationalist hysteria in Brussels, leading to the successful liberation of Belgium from Holland in 1830. This revolution, which produced another famous piece of revolutionary music, 'La Brabanconne', took a day longer than the one in Paris so it was known as 'The Four Days of Brussels'.

Significantly the man who ultimately proved most effective architect of Italian liberty began his political career as a journalist. Camillo Cavour (1810–61) founded the newspaper *Il Risorgimento* in 1847, advocating constitutional government in Piedmont. It was a paper subsidized by the Sardinian government, appealing to the upper and middle classes to inspire patriotic feelings against the interference of Austria in Italian affairs. Cavour was notable for his skilful use of the technique of the plebiscite and well-organized canvassing in regions like Tuscany in order to achieve the public prestige of a big majority. The local landowners were encouraged to rally the peasants to the polls with flags, bands and free wine. Other media used in the general drive for Italian freedom included the patriotic novels of Guerrazzi and Nievo, the plays of Tallinucci and Vincenzo Gioberti's (1801–52) superbly argued case for the Italian identity – *Del primato morale & civile degli Italiani* of 1843.

The last major figure in the propaganda for Italian reunification was Giuseppe Garibaldi (1807–82), the charismatic man of action who led a life of such picaresque brilliance that his image was almost self-combusting, but he did have a natural flair for its development. His army of 'a thousand heroes', the red shirts, the slogans, songs and dramatic actions all contributed to make him the ideal hero figure of a reviving nation.

GERMANY AND AUSTRIA

The build-up of German nationalism sprang from Napoleon's humiliation of Prussia and of the many other tiny states of German-speaking peoples. The dead poet Johann Schiller became a cult figure because of his 'William Tell' and 'Maid of Orléans'. The new poets included Ernst Arndt (1769–1860) who attacked Napoleon in his 'Geist der Zeit' of 1807 and produced a succession of nationalist lyrics including 'Was ist der Deutschen Vaterland?' Ludwig Uhland's (1787–1862) 'Gute Camerad' and Friedrich Schlegel's 'An die Deutschen' of 1800 and 'Am Rheine' added fire. Among prominent pamphleteers were Ludwig von Arnim (1781–1831) editor of the *Zeitung für Einsiedler* and Frans Bernard von Buchold. The work of the brothers Grimm (Jacob 1785–1863 and Wilhelm 1786–1859) was also significant: their huge collection of German folklore provided yet another essential part of the foundations of the new ethnic awareness and motivation.

Important too, if less easy to define precisely, was the role of music led in 1803 by Beethoven's (1770–1827) Eroica, his famous act of revulsion against Napoleon. His 'Battle Symphony' of 1813 for Wellington was highly popular with contemporaries and his incorporation of Schiller's 'Ode to Joy' in the Ninth Symphony of 1823 was to some extent a move in the nationalist direction. Similar was the position of Johann Wolfgang Von Goethe (1749–1832) who had admired Napoleon but refused to transfer his allegiance to the German nationalists, and projected, as it turned out vainly, the idea of a humane Germany in his 'Iphigenia', making himself thus the figurehead for German liberalism. Symbolically Haydn's 'Habsburg Anthem' was adopted by the Germans in 1841 with new words by Hoffman von Fallersleben (1798–1844), eventually recycled as 'Deutschland über Alles'. The Germans also introduced a whole new dimension to event management. Friedrich Jahn (1778–1852) founded the gymnasts and their displays, combined with the contribution of the fast growing singing societies and shooting festivals, provided a range of occasions for emotive crowd manipulation with displays of flags, bonfires, singing of Arndt's 'Vaterland' and so on. Many of these tools were later reused by Adolf Hitler.

Even the Habsburgs made some effort to generate populist Austrian propaganda to defend their ethnic dominance over so many minorities. Metternich encouraged patriotic papers like the *Wienerisher Diarium*, but generally the dynasty maintained rigid censorship and saw little need to project their image. Franz Schuselka and Matthias Koch produced quite effective anti-Habsburg literature but made little real headway. There was a vast output of propaganda poetry, songs and pamphlets with the lull in censorship in Vienna in 1848, but its effect was superficial and short-lived.

The Swiss started an aggressive assertion of their nationhood during this period with a revival of their history, the adulation of the nationalist role model William Tell, the Lion of Lucerne, and two great new newspapers the *Neue Zurcher Zeitung*, founded in 1821, and *Appenzeller Zeitung*, first published seven years later.

In the long term the most influential of the journalists working in the 1840s was to be Karl Marx (1818–83) who in 1842 was editor of the liberal *Rheinische Zeitung*. He was an exciting writer who managed to raise the circulation from 400 to 3,400 by 1843 but he was regarded as too aggressive by the Prussian government and the paper was banned. He was to revive it briefly in 1848 only to be closed down again by the Prussians when they had recovered from the shock of the 1848 revolutions. Significantly soon afterwards they set up the Berlin Literary Bureau which was to manage Prussian government propaganda for the rest of the century. Meanwhile, Marx had developed his career as a propagandist. He launched a trial issue of the *Kommunistische Zeitschrift* in 1847 with the new slogan 'Proletarien aller Lander vereinigt euch' – 'workers of the world unite'. In 1848 he produced, with the help of a draft from Engels, the brilliantly written pamphlet the *Communist Manifesto*, published in German in London but soon translated into most European languages. With its remarkable depth and its apocalyptic style it was eventually to become one of the most influential single pieces of propaganda in the history of mankind. His *Das Kapital* published in 1864 was initially promoted in vain by Engels with reviews planted all over Europe: after a slow start it built up to become a regular best-seller.

GREECE, EASTERN EUROPE AND TURKEY

The liberation movement in Greece was first inspired by French propaganda and particularly stirred the imagination because of the respect for the classical heritage and dislike of the Turks as conquerors. Lord Byron (1788–1824) supported it with poetry and deeds and the work of the Hetairia Philike which spearheaded the movement was supported by a revival in Greek literature by Adamantios Koraes (1748–1833), author of *War Trumpet*, who published 'an exhortation which could be heard as far away as 300 leagues'.

Throughout north-eastern Europe each racial grouping developed some kind of propaganda structure at this time. Poland was particularly inspired by its oppression and the interference of Napoleon. Their last king Stanislav Augustus had left at least a level of residual imagery – the palace at Lazienki, the coronation portraits of Bacciarelli, the special *History of the Polish Nation* by Adam Naruszewicz and the exotic winged cavalry uniforms of the Hussaria. The new hero Tadeus Kosciuszko (1746–1817) had the charisma to create a new romantic image for Polish nationality. This was given a solid propaganda infrastructure by poets like Karpinski with his 'Sarmatians Lament' of 1802 which epitomized the Polish aspiration for liberation. Visually the battles of Kosciuszko were iconicized by the paintings of Aleksandr Orlowski, the heroic prints of Piotr Michalowski and the engravings of Bellenger. Polish journalism was extended by Niemcewicz and the rebels of 1830 had at least some ability to agitate and sloganize with their 'For our freedom and yours'. Friedrich Chopin (1810–49) undoubtedly contributed to the international appreciation of the Poles' situation as he was perhaps better known to the outside world than any other Polish national – his Polonaises kept the image of the country alive even after its defeat. The survival of the Polish instinct for nationhood in the face of so many setbacks is an example of the way in which even in a conquered country the arts can maintain national consciousness over very long periods. After the débâcle of 1830 the Polish patriotic propaganda continued with the poetry of Adam Mickiewicz (1798–1855) and novels like *The Memoirs of Soplica* (1839) by Henryk Rzewuski.

The situation in Hungary was not dissimilar: unlike Italy it failed to free itself from the Habsburgs until 1918. Yet the heroic career of Louis Kossuth (1809–94) who was the successful editor of the newspaper *Pesti Hirlap* before becoming the national leader, the general revival of Magyar literature at this time, the nationalist poetry of Sandor Petofi (1823–49) and the plays of Katona, helped keep the ethnic Magyar will for nationhood aggressively alive. Budapest was built into an extravagantly spectacular ethnic advertisement as minorities were marginalized at the expense of idealized Magyar folk heroes.

Bedrich Smetana (1824–84) working in Prague provided a similar musical focus for Czech nationalism with his *Ma Vlast* and other works, matching the revival of ethnic consciousness created by the historian Frantisek Palacky (1798–1876) with his *History of Bohemia* looking back to the age of Wenceslas. Rukopis Kraloredvorsky created a fake mythology to add warmth to Czech feeling.

Russia too developed a new awareness of the role of literary and musical propaganda at least in terms of influencing the middle classes and above in this period. Up to this point it had been simply the knout and the icon. The poet-historian Nikolai Karamzin now preached Russia's imperial destiny, though rather erratically. Vissarion Grigorievitch Belinsky (1810–48) created the new concept of literature as ideology. The early response from the poets Aleksandr Pushkin (1799–1837) and Mikhail Lermontov (1814–41) was frustrated romanticism, but with at least the beginnings of a national identity. Pushkin contributed to the romantic notion of Russia civilizing the barbarian Caucasus, a theme which was twisted by avid imperialist writers like Radozhitsky and even more by Rotislav Fadeev who described 'Holy Russia's triumph over the Muslim filth' in 1860, a strain of vicious anti-Muslim propaganda which was to be revived under the Soviets and leave an unpleasant legacy when Russia began to break up again in the 1990s.

The main Russian anti-establishment propagandist was Alexsandr Herzen (1812–70), novelist and pamphlet writer, whose newspaper

Kolokol was smuggled into the country from Prague. Ivan Turgenev (1818–83) advanced the propaganda novel considerably with his *Sportsman's Sketches* of 1852 and its influential attack on serfdom, while Gleb Uspensky's (1840–1902) *Power of the Soil* in 1882 pursued the idea of peasant deprivation. The poet Mikhailov with his *Proclamation to the Young*, the pamphlet series *Great Russia* and *Young Russia*, then the work of more radical revolutionaries like Mikhail Bakunin (1814–76), all began to show Russia as a place where the written word was beginning to have influence in both a nationalist and liberal direction. In addition music enjoyed an exceptional flowering, to some extent stimulated by the desire for national identity. Mikhail Glinka (1803–57) with his *Life of the Tsar* in 1836 led the way, appearing within nine years of Pushkin's *Boris Godunov*, but to varying degrees Borodin, Mussorgsky and even Tchaikovsky all contributed to the expression of a Russian nationalism based on ethnic roots. Tsar Nicholas I encouraged this musical embellishment of the nationalist ideal and commissioned Bruillov to paint patriotic frescoes for the Winter Palace. He patronized plays like *The Hand of the Almighty saved the Fatherland* in 1848. Despite censorship and repression Russia, at least at the middle-class level, was becoming rapidly aware of itself.

Meanwhile, the Ottoman Empire made spasmodic efforts to improve its image. The Sultan Mahmoud II organized the first Turkish newspaper in 1831 to improve his credibility as the empire began to contract. To offset Russian nationalism in the south the Turks had set up the *Tercuman* in 1883 to unite their own ethnic minority in the Crimea.

SOUTH AMERICA

One of the most spectacular imitators of the techniques of Napoleon was Simon Bolivar (1783–1830) who was in Paris in the 1790s. He helped found the Venezuelan Patriotic Society which began the revolution of 1810, but this middle-class group failed to persuade the mulatto majority who preferred old style Spanish rule to Creole *nouveaux riches*. From his next base in Colombia Bolivar began to rectify his failure, first with a spectacular act of military disobedience which enabled him to claim hero status after his self-publicized mini-victory on the Magdalena River, then with a series of proclamations. His slogans all referred to a war of extermination: 'Spaniards you will receive death at our hands, Americans life', captured the right note and his victorious return to Venezuela was ensured. The event management of his ceremonial entry to Caracas in a coach drawn by beautiful maidens, his emotional funeral speech for his General Girardot's heart carried from Valencia with flowers, his image as 'the Liberator', all gave him substantial charisma even if the new Latin American regimes were rarely to achieve long-term credibility.

IRELAND

Another example of an ethnic identity which might have subsided, merged, accepted its lot and avoided a century and a half of perhaps unnecessary violence, was the Irish. There were, of course, a number of social and religious factors which helped cause resentment among the Irish more bitter than that, say, among the Welsh, the Bretons, the Bavarians or many other groups which have accepted sub-ethnic status gracefully. Unless such resentment finds a propaganda focus and a medium it is unlikely to grow to the point of mass motivation to action. The medium which essentially kept Irish nationalism alive, as in a number of semi-literate sub-nations, was the wandering minstrel. The oral tradition of the rape of Ireland by the English and Protestants was largely fed in the 1690–1790 period by a class of itinerant teacher-poets who preserved and expanded on it. The mixture of song and epic like 'A Roisìn Dubh' made for a continuous mythology, the 700 years of slavery, and also lent itself to that other specially Irish idiom, the prophecy of future change. Scaremongering tales of impending Catholic clearances were balanced by prophecies of doom for the Protestants offered by writers like Bishop Pastorini in 1771. The Irish also relished the notion of the secret society, so that their political movements often tended to be small and reclusive. The Ribbon movements, like the Orange Lodges, had a quasi-Masonic structure and many had a short life cycle. Ireland did, however, also produce a number of very able mass propagandists; Father Matthew (1750–1856) the great temperance crowd puller and 'the Liberator' Daniel O'Connell (see p. 233) were both communicators of the highest calibre. Antony Rafferty was a propaganda poet of the same period and the Young Ireland newspaper *Nation* was for some time after its foundation in 1842 a significant medium for bringing together most of the strands of Irish protest. From 1858 the ITB or Fenians took the initiative and the 1890s saw a major revival of Irish home-built culture. Significantly it was a journalist, Arthur Griffith (1872–1922), who in 1905 founded Sinn Fein, while Eamon de Valera (1882–1975) encapsulated the Irish dream, the warriors of destiny, in Fianna Fáil.

AFRICA

Aggressive nationalism was not confined to the white or oriental races. One remarkable proponent of African propaganda was Seko Amadu who made himself Commander of the Faithful in the western Sudan in 1820, and made his new capital at Handullahi. He organized the careful forging of a fifteenth-century prophecy which forecast that a man called Amadu would be the final caliph and imam. In 1825 he captured Timbuktu, achieving a significant cross-Sahara empire.

The hallmark of propaganda in the Napoleonic and post-Napoleonic eras was the promotion of a new style of emotive nationalism by a new type of poet-journalist and musical composer, highly motivated on ethnic lines, and nourished by the romantic movement. But Napoleon had also revived the image of Caesarism, of Alexander the Great, the idea that one nation might master the rest of the world.

Pressure Groups and Party Politics

BRITAIN

In Britain anti-slave trade campaigner William Wilberforce had pioneered many of the skills of the one-issue pressure group, using the press, tracts, harrowing illustrations and music. Others like social reformers Lord Shaftesbury and Samuel Plimsoll were to follow. Two larger pressure groups in the 1840s showed how the techniques of propaganda could be developed to exploit the spread of working-class literacy: the Chartists and the Anti-Corn Law League. Although ultimately a failure Chartism had significant success initially. Feargus O'Connor (1794–1855) was an able newspaper propagandist, using his *Northern Star and Leeds and General Advertiser* to spread the Chartists' reforming message, but he failed to achieve much circulation growth outside Yorkshire. He did, however, organize the mass signing of the Charter petition which eventually grew to three miles long and was taken to Westminster on a decorated cart to be presented to the government. There were other good examples of event management skills during the period, including the Chartist Grand Demonstration in Glasgow of 1839 which was supported by 43 bands, 300 banners, 70 unions and 200,000 people. There were vigorous slogans, like 'Equal representation or death', torchlight processions, Chartist hymns, slop-shop propaganda, a field force of well-briefed missionaries and studied use of the Mechanics' Institutes to spread ideas to the illiterate.

Irishman Daniel O'Connell (1775–1847) known as 'the Liberator', a good nickname in propaganda terms, also showed talent in event management. He organized passive resistance in Ireland after the potato crop failure of 1830. Having founded his Repeal Association in 1840 he brought it to life with his own paper *Nation* in 1842, a succession of mass meetings throughout Ireland, fund-raising banquets and the implicit threat of armed rebellion. Ultimately he was thwarted by internal divisions, but, like O'Connor, he had successfully demonstrated the capacity to initiate a mass movement, based on mass-produced print. Other able journalistic agitators included Wooler with his *Black Dwarf*, Hengist Horne (1803–84) with his *Reformist Register* and the hugely successful William Cobbett (1762–1835) whose *Register* on occasions between 1802 and 1835 reached a circulation of 60,000, helped by its brilliant writing, low price of 2*d* and a superb distribution network of pyramid letters.

During this period the man most successful in combining journalistic and organizational skills was Richard Cobden (1804–65), founder member of the Anti-Corn Law League. Cobden showed himself an able pamphleteer with his *England, Ireland and America* of 1835, which preached the liberal idea of free trade, and *Russia* of 1836 which attacked the prevalent war fever against the Russians. He had a fund-raising target for the League of £160,000, much of it obtained with highly emotional crowd manipulation. He was able to hire six full-time travelling lecturers to cover the country which was divided into twelve organizational districts. The League built numerous Free Trade Halls, which could hold up to 8,000 people, or hired theatres like Drury Lane. The League's newspaper campaigns were well orchestrated with a threefold approach: they founded their own papers, the *Economist* in 1843 and the *Manchester Examiner* when the *Guardian* failed to give them full support. Secondly, they often bought large numbers of copies of particular titles such as the *Manchester Courier* for eight successive weeks, then gave away the copies containing apparently independent editorials in favour of the League's policy. Both Cobden himself and his ally John Bright (1811–89) were assiduous in their third technique, the issuing of press releases or sometimes paid-for advertisements to the rest of the press. Their pamphlets were well distributed: one with a print run of 15,000 was read by 200,000 people. From 1839 their tracts were sold at cost price to distributors and they achieved virtually saturation coverage of Britain by 1842. In 1843 alone 9 million tracts were despatched from Manchester. They even had gummed slips with their slogan for sticking on envelopes. With poetry from Ebenezer Elliot and emotional woodcuts showing starving workers, with banners and badges, their careful canvassing based on study of the voters' roll, and their lobbying of Parliament, they formed one of the best organized pressure groups of the century, achieving a remarkable about-turn in government policy when Prime Minister Robert Peel at last repealed the Corn Laws and allowed cheaper food into the country.

As newspaper circulation grew and the franchise in certain countries was extended political leaders became more sensitive to their public images. The British Prime Minister Lord Aberdeen (1784–1860) worked on his public relations to the extent of obtaining support from the *Morning Post* and feeding both information and other help to John Delane (1817–79) of *The Times*. Edward Everett helped with the publicity for the American Civil War question as did Nassau Senior (1790–1864) particularly on the Oregon dispatch. Aberdeen even made efforts with the French press, but by 1853 his press manipulation efforts were failing. He was being attacked as 'a wet blanket who turned the national fire into smoke' by the *Morning Herald* and in due course Delane began to find too many faults with the management of the Crimean War, one of the earliest major successes for investigative journalism.

Using the press in the same way Lord Palmerston (1784–1865) cultivated a firebrand image with episodes such as the Greek maltreatment of the Gibraltan Jew Don Pacifico, exploited in his 'Civis Romanus sum' speech. Thereafter he cultivated John Easthope of the *Morning Chronicle*, the circulation of which benefited in return with a rise from 800 to 9,000. The *Morning Herald* echoed 'Lord Palmerston's very name is a war cry over the whole continent' and the *Morning Post* hero-worshipped him as the 'staunchest conservative'. Gradually he even won over *The Times.*

William Gladstone (1809–98) never courted personal publicity in the same deliberate way as his great rival Benjamin Disraeli (1804–81), relying instead on his principles and his domination of the House of Commons until the last decades of his career. However, he did use Thornton Hunt of the *Daily Telegraph* as his effective public relations adviser, and Hunt helped him cultivate an avuncular image as 'the people's William'. To encourage the image he even gave journalists breakfast at Downing Street. The *Telegraph* remained the mainstay of his image creation until the *Daily News* thrust its way forward to give him its backing over the Bulgarian atrocities in 1876. William Stead (1849–1912) of the *Northern Echo* also gave unwavering support. Gladstone's pamphlet *The Bulgarian Horror* sold 40,000 copies in a few days: his 'bag and baggage' alliteration, not superficially a very memorable phrase, somehow grabbed the public's attention. In 1880 he bypassed the traditional media and orthodox speech venues to launch his remarkable Midlothian campaign against Disraeli, achieving so much press coverage that it took him to a further election victory, acquiring by this time his 'Grand Old Man' image. This campaign was an early example of mass electioneering. Significantly Gladstone gave out six knighthoods to members of the press. In addition he had a major literary supporter in the shape of John Morley (1828–1923), an able propagandist for the concept of Irish home rule.

Benjamin Disraeli was of all British politicians one of the most natural and skilled propagandists. At the age of twenty he had already conducted public relations for the financier J.D. Powles and in 1825 he helped found a new Tory newspaper, *The Representative.* The following year he engineered publicity for the publication of his novel *Vivian Grey*, orchestrated a high-profile confrontation between himself and the Chartist O'Connor and won excellent press coverage for the subsequent challenge to a duel. In 1836 he assisted Robert Peel's propaganda effort with the *Runnymede Letters* and as an MP from 1837 cultivated a distinctive public image by his dandyesque fashions. Having founded Young England in 1842 in opposition to Robert Peel he won attention for it and himself with his novels *Coningsby* in 1844 and *Sybil* the year after with its strong image of 'the two nations'. His command of ironic oratory was helped by his use of memorable images like 'I caught the Whigs bathing and walked away with their trousers' or 'Whigs . . . like flies in amber', alliterations like 'dethroning this dynasty of deception', 'political pedlars', 'revolutions are not made with rosewater', the rhythm of 'conservative government is organized hypocrisy', the sarcastic irony of calling Stanley 'the Prince Rupert of debate', describing Lord John Russell as Jack Straw or Aberdeen's cabinet as a 'ministry of mandarins' and 'antiquated imbecility'. He had cultivated Delane of

The Times, won over the imperialist-minded *Morning Post*, launching another new paper of his own in 1853. As Prime Minister he orchestrated the translation of Queen Victoria into Empress of India in 1874 after his dramatic purchase of the Suez Canal. His belligerence was further projected at the Congress of Berlin, the occasion for George McDermott's 'By Jingo' song against the Russians which added a new word to the English language. Having spent his early career developing a remarkable image for himself out of unpromising material, given his name and background, and having done the same for his party, he devoted his later years to the steady build-up of the imperial image, the architecture and showmanship of empire, including the Albert Memorial and 'the Thin Red line' and the slogan 'Empire and Liberty'. Lady Elizabeth Butler (1850–1933) painted her *Roll Call* in 1874 and her *Inkermann* three years later, the epitome of Disraeli's desired image for the empire.

UNITED STATES

Andrew 'Old Hickory' Jackson (1767–1845) brought a new intensity to the use of propaganda when he stood for the presidency of the United States in 1824 and 1828. Having had a somewhat controversial military career and marriage he was attacked on both by the pro-Quincy Adams press led by Charles Hammond of the *Cincinnati Gazette*. Coffin pamphlets were used to draw attention to his alleged war crimes. He brought in Duff Green to organize his defence. Green invented a marital scandal for President Adams as the best form of retaliation and bought the *United States Telegraph* to make it in due course virtually a government propaganda organ. Green moved on and was succeeded as Jackson's chief press organizer by Francis P. Blair, with the *Washington Globe* now becoming the main vehicle for government propaganda. Amos Kendall of the *Argus of West America* and Isaac Hill of the *Hampshire Patriot* joined Blair in the Jackson team along with some fifty other journalists. The wheels of this system were oiled by the administration's allocation of lucrative printing contracts to the editors who helped, a practice which lasted until 1860. Venomous cartoons became a feature of the press war on both sides and Jackson made continual strong use of a captive, well-organized press not only to secure his re-election in 1832 but also to bolster his economic policy, specifically his argument with the supporters of the Bank of the United States. Overall this presidency demonstrated the value of devoting resources to cultivating a favourable press.

The mid-nineteenth-century contribution to the history of propaganda lay in a steady increase in newspaper print runs with consequential fall in costs, allied to signs of better ability to use crowd manipulation based on cheaper public transport for the ordinary citizen in many parts of the world.

More Empire Builders

FRANCE

Napoleon III (1808–73) has one claim at least to originality in the history of propaganda – he coined the word communiqué. In other respects he very much traded on the late 1840s' revival of his uncle Bonaparte's image. This was bolstered by Victor Hugo (1802–85) in his 'Ode à la Colonne' and other pro-Napoleonic pieces, though he later changed sides to write the vitriolic 'Napoleon le petit' of 1852 and the brilliant 'Les Châtiments', one of the cleverest propaganda poems of all time. Pierre Jean de Béranger (1780–1857) was also an effective Bonapartist poet of this period. The whole cult began to spread with prints of 'the great Martyr of St Helena', medals, brooches, *image d'epinal* cut-outs, miniature Arcs de Triomphe and other artefacts. Louis Thiers (1797–1877), the very able publicist whose newspaper *Le National* had contributed to the July Revolution of 1830, also fanned the Napoleonic resurgence with his *Memorial de St Helena* and the would-be new emperor himself produced a number of quite effective pamphlets. His *Les Idées Napoléoniennes* of 1839 was bound in green with an eagle on the cover. This was followed up by his development of an image as a 'plebeian emperor' and his adoption of his uncle's technique of calling for popular referenda or plebiscites as stages towards power. His *L'Extinction du Pauperisme* went further in promising some hint of revenge for Waterloo, reviving the empire and again copying his uncle by probing at the neurotic fear of leftist revolution – *le spectre rouge*.

As his campaign for leadership came to its climax in 1848 he produced slogans such as 'L'empire c'est la paix' and engineered crowds chanting rhythmically 'Nous l'aurons, nous l'aurons Napoleon'. His bid for power was backed up by heavy poster campaigns, including small bills produced for cafés and tobacconists, with print images of broken chains, lions harnessed to chariots, Phrygian caps and the Bonapartist bee. As the hysteria was built up by event management, brass medals and eagle hat badges were given out in the Champs de Mars. Louis-Napoleon was given significant help by Emile de Girardin (1806–81) whose newspaper *Presse* had a circulation of 22,000. The total romanticization of the First Napoleonic Empire had been achieved and a new period of French machismo ushered in on the strength of a well-promoted but second-hand image. The hollowness was to become evident all too soon and before his military downfall Napoleon was being heavily attacked by Henri Rochefort's flame-coloured *Lanterne* which sold up to 500,000 copies from 1860. The remarkable book *Dialogue aux Enfers entre Montesquieu et Machiavel* produced by Maurice Joly (1821–78) in 1864 was another precursor of the plot phobia used later by the *Protocols of the Elders of Zion* though it in turn was modelled on the Abbé Barruel's *Memoire* which attributed the French Revolution to a plot by the Templars.

France did its best to resuscitate an imperial ethos in the aftermath of Napoleon III's ignominious defeats. The development of French machismo consisted of propaganda designed to obliterate the memory of the defeat of Sedan, to romanticize victories in North Africa and to pick on the Jews as the source of weakness at home. The Grande Armée was revived, there was a vogue for kepis and pantaloons, the Foreign Legion look (pl. 17). The Legion was idealized and Marianne, the female personification of France, was now always shown armed; there was even a resurrection of 'the last cartridges of Sedan'. Count Joseph Gobineau (1816–82) had written *The Inequality of Human Races* creating the theory of racial superiority borrowed by Nietzsche. The pamphlet *La France Juive* which alleged a diabolical plot by the Jews to ruin France was a best-seller and was serialized in the anti-Semitic *Le Petit Journal* which had a circulation of 800,000. Free copies of a similar journal, *La Croix*, were given out at mass. Anti-Semitic posters based on the theme of *exposition des horreurs* – the freak show – were circulated and a bustling trade in racist ephemera, including a working model toy gallows with its noose round a midget Dreyfus, sold in 1898 with the slogan 'Extricate yourself from the beast's infected claws'. There was also a model of novelist Emile Zola (1840–1902) with removable trousers to amuse the population of the world's most sophisticated city. Chocolate wrappers featured prominent Catholic leaders; song sheets, board games, toys and kaleidoscopes were produced all attacking the Jews and idolizing 'la patrie' or 'le drapeau'. Zola, with his *J'accuse* which sold 300,000 copies, made a splendid effort to turn the tide over the Dreyfus Affair in 1894. Georges Clemenceau (1841–1929), who had been a journalist covering the American Civil War and now wrote more than 100 articles attacking French anti-Semitism, was another journalist *en route* to national leadership. But the establishment had the capacity to manage events and outpace the scandal. Mobs were organized to chant anti-Jewish slogans and wear the blue cornflower of anti-Semitism. Even umbrellas were produced with anti-Jewish slogans. General Georges Boulanger (1837–91) was helped by popular song and a touch of charisma to create significant mass hysteria for the reclaiming of Alsace from the Germans. This thwarted belligerence was to remain the overriding French attitude up to 1914. In addition the French were programmed to fight for more than their share of Africa by politician journalists like Eugene Etienne (1844–1921), the Algiers-born founder of *La Depêche Coloniale* while novelists like Julien Viaud (Pierre Loti) produced imperialist romances such as *Le Roman d'un Spahi* to create a populist fantasy of empire.

GERMANY

The ultimate cause of Napoleon III's downfall was Otto von Bismarck (1815–98), himself an exceptionally able propagandist. He had the two classic characteristics of a strong political propagandist, a very vulnerable platform for his own career to provide the motivation, and an interest in journalism to make him effective. In 1848 he founded his organizational springboard, the Association for the Protection of the Interests of Landed Property, an attempt to unite the junkers and the peasants of Prussia against the new liberal ideas of the revolution. Soon afterwards he helped launch the *Neue Preussiche Zeitung*, which became the *Kreuzzeitung*, symbolized by the iron cross of liberation as its corporate identity. Its editor Hermann Wagener used a combination of humour and irony to create a considerable public following and Bismarck himself was a regular contributor as was political writer Ludwig von Gerlach. The Patriotic Society and Association for King and Country were set up to boost Prussian nationalism at the expense of liberal ideas. At the same time Bismarck used his journalistic contacts to lift his own political career.

Once he had achieved government in 1862 Bismarck was able to reapply the public relations skills used in the acquisition of power to its deployment throughout Europe. His objectives for the expansion of Prussia to take over a united Germany required an aggressive attitude at home and the wrong-footing of opposing nations abroad. To assist in this Hermann Wagener was encouraged to found the *Preussiche Verein* which later became the *National Verein*. A network of favourable journalists was set up inside the German states and throughout Europe with subsidies to encourage them to write favourable pieces about Prussian foreign policy. Bismarck founded yet another newspaper, the *Neue Allgemeine Zeitung*, in 1863, himself writing key articles on major aspects of policy. The *Preussiche Jahrbucher* contributed to the same task of bolstering the regime and German academics were encouraged to project the German imperial destiny. Leopold von Ranke (1795–1886) rewrote German history to show it as a progression from First to Second Reich; Theodor Mommsen wrote about the Romans with a very obvious Caesar/Kaiser comparison; Droysen with his *Geschichte der Preussiche Politik* undertook the very pertinent attack on Austria in the period immediately before Bismarck provoked a war with her; and Heinrich von Treitschke (1834–96) hammered home again the Prussian interpretation of history and the value of war in promoting the new empire. Particularly ominous was Bismarck's effort to promote annexation of Alsace.

Bismarck willingly exposed his own private life to help his image, encouraged hero-worshipping biographies such as that by Hans Blum and publication of his own speeches which ran to sixty volumes. When he had no direct control over particular newspapers he took pains to infiltrate them either by subsidizing individual journalists such as the liberal August Brass or by saving money for the whole paper by providing it with a free supply of foreign news, or a free stock-market service using the government-controlled Wolff Telegraph Company, bought with the help of the banker Gerson von Bleichröder who was also a friend of both Bismarck and Reuter.

Significant figures helping Bismarck to manipulate the press were Lothar Bucher of Wolff Telegraph Company from 1864 to 1878, Dr L. Metzler and Moritz Busch, a specialist in the smear. In addition to the twelve full-time writers in the Literary Bureau, there were numerous subsidized freelancers, so that the annual expenditure on propaganda was quite substantial. Respectability was lent to the campaign by employing academics, such as Professor Aegidi who assisted on the anti-Austrian smear campaign. Typical of the new breed of long-term government public relations assistants was Theodor Fontane (1819–98) who was in service on and off from 1849 to 1884 including eight years spent in England organizing Bismarck's press coverage there, helped by Max Schlesinger. Both at home and abroad Bismarck's approach was always manipulative, whether it was encouraging press campaigns against his own ministers as a prelude to dismissing them or stirring up war rumours as a softening-up before his diplomatic manoeuvres.

Meanwhile, a new fashion in massive idealized monuments began with von Klenze's *Walhalla* near Regensburg in 1842 followed by the highly popular *Hermansdenkmal* in the Black Forest in 1875. Anton von Werner and others painted the image of the new imperial Germany. Nationalistic music also persisted as part of the new German motivational formula and Bismarck himself encouraged the composition of new victory songs after 1871 as well as providing less overt musical support for the Second Reich with his patronage of friendly composers like Brahms and Joachim. Coincidentally came new strains in anti-Semitic propaganda such as the remarkable *Die Eroberung der Welt durch die Juden* written in 1875 by the Bosnian Osman Bey (Millinger), alleging strange international conspiracies along the lines later encouraged by Hitler. Herman Goedsche, a journalist with the *Preussiche Kreutzeitung* wrote his violently anti-Semitic novel *Biarritz* in 1868 with its echoes of Maurice Joly. He described a conspiratorial meeting of world Jews in a Czech churchyard in such graphic detail that it could later be treated as fact.

The Germans advanced to a new level of the cult of empire in 1890 when Kaiser Wilhelm II (1859–1941) dismissed Bismarck. The rituals of the gymnasts, the singing societies and the shooting festivals had deepened, spread and fitted in well with the Prussian military academy ethos which the Kaiser sought to project. He himself adopted a swash-buckling public image and his speeches tended to be inflammatory. At the time of the Boxer rebellion in China he was talking of the 'Huns standing together against the common foe . . . the yellow peril' ['Gelbe Gefahr']. A commentator on seeing his newly painted portrait said 'That is not a portrait, but a declaration of war.' Treitschke and his fellow historians had meanwhile been preaching the value of war linked with the expansion of Germany. Wagner's 'Kaisermarsch', the superman theory which had been projected by Friedrich Nietzsche (1844–1900) in his *Also Sprach Zarathustra* in 1885, the paintings of Anton von Werner, the sculptures of the Sieges Allee, the unveiling of the *Hermansdenkmal* and a succession of other massive memorials to the German ego, all combined to create a franchise for aggression similar to that in France, Britain and the other empires. The new memorial opened in 1913 to commemorate the Battle of Leipzig bore the inscription 'Let us fight, bleed and die for German unity and power.' German youngsters read patriotic adventure stories like *Karl May*, George Heym wrote his poem 'War', expressing his longing for violence and the *Berliner Tageblatt* warned the rest of Europe not to 'wake up the Great Pan', the German sleeping giant, during the Morocco crisis of 1911. One of the main instigators of imperialist propaganda was the Pan-German League which put out its own weekly paper the *All deutscher Blätter* under Erst Hasse promoting the idea of the Greater Germany from 1894 and the Kaiser echoed the expansionist theme in his own speech for the twenty-fifth anniversary of the new empire in 1895.

One of the German leaders most active in the promotion of propaganda likely to create a climate for war was Bernhard von Bülow (1849–1929) who was chancellor from 1900 to 1909. He greatly expanded Bismarck's foreign office press department and made it responsible for all German government propaganda under the control of Dr Otto Hammann. He had himself worked on Bismarck's propaganda team in which one of his specialities had been the concocting of fake letters from the provinces supporting various policies which suited Bismarck's drive against Austria. Von Bülow ensured heavy coverage of German activities in both the domestic and foreign press, intimidating the domestic press into a patriotic stance, and ensuring good coverage abroad of Germany's aggressive posturing over the Boer War and Morocco. Typical was his action in the Russo-Japanese crisis of 1902 in sending the Japanese press material likely to stir them up against the Russians, and the Russians material to stir them against the Japanese.

There were two specific sub-currents in German propaganda of this time. One was to create an image for the new German navy, which had no tradition to fall back on but had a formidable publicist in Alfred von Tirpitz (1849–1930) with his Information Bureau. It was he who organized the first German documentary film *Life in the German Navy* as part of this effort in 1902. The high profile enjoyed by the competition in naval ship building between Germany and Britain was a significant factor in the war neuroses of 1914. As Tirpitz put it 'I considered it my duty to bring home to the broader masses of the public the interests that were at stake' and it was his magazine *Die Flotte* which put across the emotive idea of the possibility of 'a place in the sun' and 'the war of survival'. Copies of his annual illustrated *Naval Album* were given away by the Kaiser as school prizes and the Kaiser credited Tirpitz with winning over a recalcitrant German nation within a mere eight months. The subsidized Navy League led by August Keim held leaflet distributions and rallies and Tirpitz had August von Heeringen managing the Information Bureau. Herman Rassau used new ideas such as travelling slide shows about the navy and postcards were put up in railway stations. There was even a specially produced novel *Meister Theser* to back up the naval theme. The fanatical soldier-turned-journalist Keim then moved on to found the Army League which produced massive quantities of propaganda leaflets, song sheets, postcards and memorabilia with its emblem, a medieval knight. Keim regularly quoted Prussian General Moltke's saying that the Germans would become decadent unless they had a war. He even resorted to suggesting that the French would use their black colonial troops to invade Germany, a new variant on the Schwarze Gefahr. The Christian Book League was also a massive producer of patriotic papers, pamphlets and calendars promoting right-wing policies.

The other special facet of German nationalist propaganda in the 1890s was the resurgence of anti-Semitism. Otto Boeckel the anti-Semitic peasant leader of Hess from 1885 to 1894 was a regular user of crowd manipulation techniques to exploit this tendency. The gutter anti-Semitism (*Raddau antisemitismus*) of Bruno Wagener produced 20-pfennig pamphlets describing Jews as 'enemies of the Reich'. In 1887 was founded the *Munchener Beobachter*, an anti-Semitic newspaper which thirty-six years later was one of the first to assist Adolf Hitler.

AUSTRIA

The propaganda of the Austrian Habsburg dynasty in its final century was fairly lethargic but during the Napoleonic Wars there had been an effort to build up loyalty to 'Österreich über Alles' by a number of musicians and writers, particularly Josef von Hormayr with his patristic papers. Generally the Habsburg empire was unique for the century in hardly fostering nationalism in its own leading race, but rather in trying to stress a supranational mission. This was to some extent the work of Friedrich Funder, editor of *Reichpost*; it was also the theme of Hugo von Hofmannsthal's lyrics for *Der Rosenkavalier* and of the highly popular, unaggressive character Papa Biedermeier invented by Ludwig Eichrocht. One example of relevant sub-strains in the Austro-Hungarian Empire shows that it too was cultivating the same kind of aggressive stance as Germany. Dr Karl Lueger, Mayor of Vienna from 1897 to 1910 was a pioneer of propaganda techniques much admired later by Hitler. A tireless event manager he constantly staged festivals and processions at which he could appear, to the accompaniment of the special 'Lueger March', his followers always wearing a white carnation, his flag red with a white cross. He had medals struck, he made use of photography, he ruthlessly exploited anti-Semitic feeling and equally unscrupulously professed himself a supporter of Catholicism.

Thanks to the Strauss family the Austrian army had more than its fair share of superb military marches. Both the opera and theatre in Vienna were heavily subsidized to encourage patriotic performances, but the Habsburgs continued to lack imagination in creating a propaganda focus for their empire.

BRITAIN

Meanwhile, the British imperialistic ethic moved from strength to strength fed by a constant supply of populist propaganda. Alfred Tennyson (1809–92) was not overtly political as a poet but he always projected the patriotic virtues and his 'Charge of the Light Brigade' of 1854 encapsulated the British version of Bushido. The tradition was carried on by Rudyard Kipling (1865–1936) whose 'Recessional' from the *Five Nations* was published in *The Times* in 1903, and was the apex of imperialist poetry. Robert Southey with his 'Poet's Pilgrimage to Waterloo' had preached Britain's imperial destiny and Kipling wrote of 'the white man's burden'. A variety of novelists at various levels projected the imperial ideal; Rider Haggard (1856–1925) did for the British Cape Colonists what Kipling did for British India and significantly the film of his novel *She* was the first to be shown in Ceylon in 1897. The younger age groups were also well supplied with patriotic literature: the 'pluck and piety' of Thomas Hughes's *Tom Brown's Schooldays*, G.A. Henty (1832–1902) with his *By Sheer Pluck* and Angela Brazil (1868–1947) with her *A Patriotic Schoolgirl* were typical of the attitude-forming writers for the young. Edward Elgar (1857–1934) was the prime musical exponent of patriotic propaganda with his *Caractacus* and 'Pomp and Circumstance'. Periodicals such as the *Union Jack Magazine* and the *Illustrated London News* projected a consistent imperial line.

The new Victorian Gothic architecture by men like George Gilbert Scott (1811–76), who designed the India Office, the Colonial Office and the Albert Memorial, spread across the empire, so that there were Gothic cathedrals in Sydney and Calcutta, the Gothic palace of the White Rajahs of Sarawak or the Gothic parliament buildings in Ottowa. Edwin Landseer's lions were moved into Trafalgar Square and statues of Queen Victoria were set in prominent positions throughout the empire. Lady Elizabeth Butler's *Rorke's Drift* and Robert Gibb's *The Thin Red Line* were the models for countless paintings of military glory or death in battle. From about 1880 onwards 200 companies produced cigarette cards encouraging hero-worship of soldiers, sailors and empire builders. James Froude (1818–94) orchestrated a strain of racist pro-imperial propaganda and in 1871 a pamphlet called *The Battle of Dorking* was widely circulated, describing in detail a German invasion of England. Such invasion scaremongering was to become quite regular in the 1880s.

From 1867 onwards most British males had the vote, so even the lowest of the electorate had to be portrayed as superior to the heathen aboriginals of the colonies. Outlandish habits like widow suicide (sati), thug ritual murder and the violence of the Indian Mutiny were publicized as a sound justification for treating the Indians as inferior, just as in the same way violent acts by American native peoples were presented in the USA as excusing their virtual genocide. In 1829 a pamphlet by George de Lacy Evans entitled *On the Practicability of an Invasion of British India* inaugurated a long period of British paranoia about Russian plots to invade through the Khyber Pass, a style of heroic myth-making which significantly became known as 'The Great Game' and was developed by writers like Kipling and Henty. The invention of conspiracy theories became the standard form of window-dressing for British attacks on native Indian rulers which led to the eventual conquest of the whole sub-continent. The 1868 novel *First Love and Last Love* by James Grant presented an hysterically exaggerated picture of maltreatment of British women by the mutineers as did a large number of contemporary paintings.

Similarly it suited the European settlers in Africa to present the local tribesmen as cannibals, pygmies, idle and stupid. Muhammed Ahmed al Mahdi (1840–85) was always the villain in the epic tales recounting the exploits of Gordon of Khartoum and many able African resistance leaders were portrayed either as dervishes or witch doctors. For example, the Tanganyikan prophet Kinjikitile Ngwale united some twenty tribes to resist brutal conquest by the Germans, but was pilloried as a witch doctor and brutally suppressed in 1907. This continued demonization led to the whites eliminating rather than building on native traditions, so that when decolonization began in earnest the Africans were even more poorly equipped for self-rule than might otherwise have been the case.

British boy's magazines like *Chums* or *Young England* as well as newspapers like the *Daily Trident* were hysterically nationalistic. Large lithographs of 'the Great White Queen' hung not only in every British home but in most Indian and Ceylonese middle-class houses. The Queen's jubilee in 1897 called forth an even bigger output of propaganda artefacts from mugs to scrapbooks, flags and plates, board games with toy soldiers, military songs, vast numbers of brass bands. The *A.B.C. for Baby Patriots* of 1849 had its 'C is for Colonies'. Even Bovril advertisements extolled Field Marshal Roberts and the imagery of cigarette smoking was inextricably entwined with the virtues of naval expansion. At the Crystal Palace in 1898 a pageant of the Afghan campaign was staged with British soldiers dressed as Pathans.

The ethos of empire probably reached its zenith with the Boer War which demonstrated both its strengths and weaknesses. This was a war which the British government as such did not really want but was manoeuvred into by a small imperialist minority which used its money and press connections to make the professional politicians look pusillanimous. Cecil Rhodes (1853–1902) began the process with the Jameson raid, though even his excellent public relations campaign could not hide the raid's disorganization. More subtle was Alfred Milner (1854–1925) who had been part of the jingoist newspaper set with Stead on the *Pall Mall Gazette* and used these contacts when he moved on to become governor of Cape Colony. With his friends at the *Morning Post* and *The Times*, helped by the gold reserves of Alfred Beit, and his hired publicist Percy Fitzpatrick he was able to manipulate his own superior Joseph Chamberlain and the Prime Minister Salisbury into a position from which they could not avoid war in 1899, despite the fact that they had no real desire to annexe the Transvaal. As early as 1868 the Boers had in fact started to develop their own propaganda of pioneering martyrdom with the slogan 'Think of Slagsternak' and a play developing this theme was performed in Cape Town. S.J. du Toit published the first Afrikaner interpretation of history in 1877 and this inaugurated over a century of Boer self-mesmerization.

In the 1901 parliamentary election the blackmail of patriotism was used to help achieve a Unionist victory against the Liberals with 2.4 million votes against 2.1. Joseph Chamberlain (1836–1914) sporting a daily fresh orchid and preaching the ideals of Anglo-Saxon manhood, accused the Liberals of being unpatriotic with slogans like 'A seat lost is a seat sold to the Boers' or 'A vote for the Liberals is a vote for the Boers'. George Cadbury bought the *Daily News* in 1901 in a vain effort to project an anti-war message but the tide was too strong. Henty produced his *With Buller in Natal* giving a very one-sided view. Lord Roberts controlled the press coverage of the war itself quite astutely by organizing the programmes of the war correspondents. Film, the medium which entered the history of propaganda at this point, was used without scruple. *The Setting to between John Bull and Paul Kruger* was shown while blank cartridges were fired in the cinema for realism and emotive impact. Out-of-context or faked documentary footage was used to show the apparent bombing of Red Cross tents by the Boers. Baden Powell was made a hero and there was even a board game of the Siege of Ladysmith.

Thereafter, the focus returned to Germany. Horatio Bottomley (1860–1933) founded the patriotic magazine *John Bull* in 1906, supported aggressive policies and by 1914 was writing 'This is more than a war'. Lord Northcliffe boosted the sales of the *Daily Mail* by serializing a novel describing a German invasion of England, Quex's *The Invasion of 1910*, like Erskine Childer's *Riddle of the Sands* (1902), and supported the belligerent stance of the National Service League. By 1909 even a socialist editor like Robert Blatchford (1851–1943) of the *Clarion* was calling for war against Germany and mass conscription. Admiral John Fisher (1841–1920), obsessed with his lust to build Dreadnought class battleships, was pursuing a devious policy of deliberate leaks to his favoured journalists to help make the British public more nautically paranoid, feeding secret statistics to writers like Thursfield of *The Times*, then feigning horror at the belligerent tone of the results. His substantial use of public relations to heighten pressure for building up the navy was paralleled by a similar campaign by Tirpitz in Germany.

THE FRINGES OF EUROPE

Alongside the general fertilization of imperial images in Europe there were also a number of examples of the engineered revival of almost forgotten nationalisms, some of which were to cause future problems. Zionism reappeared in 1880 and the Hebrew language was brought back from the dead. In the 1890s the Basques, the Bretons and the Welsh all began new nationalist movements in areas where independence had been lost centuries previously. Most dangerous of all at this time were febrile ethnic overlapping groups in Bosnia and Serbia where the secret group Ujedinjenije ili Smrt – Union or Death, subsequently nicknamed the Black Hand – was founded in 1911. The poet-singer Filip Visnjic of Bosnia in 1804 revived the traditions of their nationalist epic accompanied by a one-string gusla (Radovan Karadžić did the same 180 years later) which again became hugely popular. The Black Hand promoted the idea of Greater Serbia using its newspaper *Pijemont*, modelled significantly on the Piedmont *Risorgimento*, and set out on the path which was to climax at Sarajevo in 1914. It also legitimated the tradition of sacred murder, sanctified tyrannicide in the Greek tradition. The Serb Garasanin had published a nationalist programme, *Nacertanije*, and the revival was given poetic backing by Vuk Karadžić (1787–1864) creator of a new national mythology. Meanwhile, Tchaikovsky composed the 'Marche Serbe' to honour the Russians serving in the Serb army against the Turks.

Propaganda skills in tsarist Russia were modestly effective: the massive coronation display for Nicholas II in 1894 with a vast procession and specially constructed triumphal gates, the huge statue of Alexander III, the icon-laden imperial sarcophagi in the Fortress of Sts Peter and Paul, the deep mumblings of the Orthodox clergy and the dread of the Cossack charge – in a country so huge with a population still largely illiterate superstition could still be exploited as a tool of propaganda. As it fought to retain the initiative the Russian government resorted to a whole new range of ethnic themes. As it suited these could vary between the pure Russian and the wider Slav. They could be anti-Western, anti-Eastern or when all else failed anti-Semitic. Greater Russian nationalism* offset liberalism after the Polish uprising of 1863, but pan-Slavism soon proved more useful. The government-sponsored paper *Russkiy Invalid* was violently anti-Polish and anti-Catholic.

* In different ways Pushkin in his *Evgeni Onegin* and Tolstoy in *War and Peace* had worked to build up the Russian sense of identity.

More extreme, warmongering propaganda was orchestrated by Aksakov and Mikhail Katkov of the *Moscow News*, the two pillars of the semi-official right-wing yellow press. Katkov's *Epistle to the Serbs* of 1860 was too patronizing to be very successful, but Russia and the Russian Orthodox Church did play a significant part in the stirring up of Serbian nationalism which was to have such disastrous consequences in 1914 and 1990, and there was an anti-Muslim strain, backed even by Feodor Dostoevsky (1821–81), which was to reappear several times in the twentieth century. General Mikhail Chernaiev exploited the Russian press's graphic descriptions of the Bulgarian atrocities to justify accepting command of the Serb rebel army against the Ottomans, employing a journalist on his staff to ensure continued good coverage and turn himself into a hero figure, while Dostoevsky promoted his lofty soul. The poems of Feodor Tyutchev used apocalyptic prophecy to justify a new pan-Slav empire with seven seas and seven rivers. Katkov's pro-tsarist xenophobia attacked liberals and Western Europeans as the enemies of the Slavs but also Hungarians, Asian interlopers and the Japanese. This was backed up by writers like Nicholas Danilevsky Fadeev and the novelist Shatov. It also fitted in well with the increasing output of chauvinist music. Nicholas II who refused his Prime Minister Witte's request to spend 10,000 roubles on sensible government propaganda in 1906, loved Glinka's work and once attended sixteen opera performances within a single month – there were over sixty opera companies in Russia to choose from. That very year the Russian Foreign Office formed its first press office to dampen down the belligerent pan-Slavism which threatened to push the establishment into war.

The reactionary lawyer Pobedonotsev was probably the minister most responsible for the deliberate fostering of anti-Semitism to distract attention from the injustices of the tsarist system. Particularly after the murder of Alexander III the Jews were identified with the liberals and anarchists by the right, yet could be presented as wealthy parasites to the extreme poor. The secret police produced the classic *Protocols of the Elders of Zion*, a fake plan for world domination modelled on Joly's *Dialogue* and a pamphlet produced by Napoleon to make the same smear against the Russians themselves. In 1903 it was published in the St Petersburg paper *Znamya* possibly as part of Pyotr Rachkovsky's attempts to undermine Witte. Given its subsequent reuse by Hitler this must rank as one of the most viciously effective propaganda publications of all time. The myth of ritual murder by Jews was also revived to stir up peasant hatred and a wave of pogroms was encouraged or condoned by the government not just in Russia itself but specifically in some of its ethnically volatile satellites such as Romania, Lithuania, White Russia and the Ukraine. The Baltic states were becoming nearly as ethnically fraught as the Balkans with Russian papers like *Novoye Vremya* leading a campaign against the German minority. The main strain of the new Latvian nationalism of 1868 and its first paper *Balss* [The Voice] was anti-German, while Finnish nationalism focused on dislike of the Swedes. Estonian nationalism also grew rapidly with its remarkable pseudo-epic poem of 1854 the *Kalevipoeg* by Kreutzwald and Latvia similarly had its *The Bear Slayer* by Andrejs Pumpurs in 1888. Overall, the vast, crumbling Russian empire could only bolster its self-confidence by pushing an image of martial omnipotence which meant showing no sign of hesitation if there was the least chance of war.

UNITED STATES

The Americans began to forge a more aggressive corporate identity during this period. The Mexican War of 1847 provided a whole new mythology of heroes such as the soldier Samuel Ringgold who fell at Palo Alto and was eulogized in poetry, song and prints. Writers like George Lippard produced a romanticized version of American history which focused on hero-worship of Washington as the founder of a new empire – 'the sword of Washington blazed over Mexico'. Charles Fenno Hoffman referred to 'a divine mission' to conquer Mexico. Operas like the *Maid of Saxony*, the *Rio Grande Quick March*, songs by George Pope Morris, the dedication of the massive Washington Monument with a live eagle perched on the foundation stone during the ceremony, and massive sales of battle pictures, all contributed. A deluge of sentimental war poetry filled the newspapers and 'Old Zack' Taylor was projected as a popular war president.

Superficially Abraham Lincoln (1809–65) might seem very different from Bismarck, but while the Prussians wanted to unite Germany under their king's regime, Lincoln wanted to keep the United States united under an anti-slavery regime. As was to be expected of a politician who was very much a self-made man Lincoln also had a strong appreciation of public relations techniques and was to become the archetypal role model for the log-cabin-to-White-House image so popular in the later nineteenth century. As early as 1837 he was conducting his own local election campaign in the *Sangamo Herald*. He followed this up by running the campaign for the Whig candidate Henry against Desmond Adams in the *Sangamo Journal*, using a series of anonymous letters, then circulating anonymous handbills accusing Adams of fraud two days before the election. Adams still won, but Lincoln was gaining excellent experience of press campaigns.

Some twenty years later it was his oratory which helped Lincoln make the final breakthrough to national political prominence. His 'House divided' metaphor was one of the most powerful images of the decade and his campaign for the senate in 1858 while unsuccessful did raise his public profile considerably. In 1859 after the martyrdom of John Brown, he allowed his curriculum vitae to be circulated to the press by Jesse Fell of Bloomington and he was supported as a presidential nominee by the

Pl. 17   Self-sacrifice: a gallant Arab soldier lays down his life for his adopted fatherland, France. (Mary Evans Picture Library)

Pl. 18   Population control: a 1970 Hong Kong poster encouraging Chinese men to practise birth control.

Pl. 19   Temperance and thrift: a nineteenth-century advertisement promoting temperance and selling a savings plan. (Mary Evans Picture Library)

Pl. 20   Japanese primary school children learn the parts of a battleship, 1907. (Mary Evans Picture Library)

Pl. 21   The Chinese Emperor Wu-Ti (c. 100 BC) reads a Buddhist text to his court. Note mural propaganda in the background. (Mary Evans Picture Library)

Pl. 22   Saint Dominique of Val on a crucifix. Typical anti-Semitic smear, the myth of child murder by Jews in Spain, Zaragoza, thirteenth century. (Mary Evans Picture Library)

Pl. 23 The terrors of hell from sixteenth-century Troyes. (Mary Evans Picture Library)

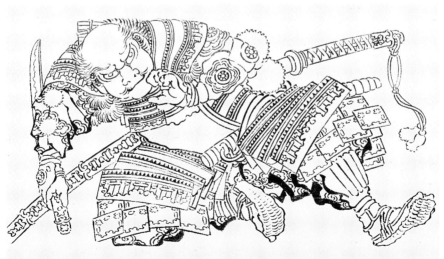

Pl. 24 Projecting aggression: typical image of a Samurai warrior, Japan, by Katsushika Hokusai (1760–1849), (V&A Picture Library)

Pl. 25   Anti-Muslim propaganda: a Christian prisoner is tortured by a Turkish soldier, produced in Munster, 1553. (Mary Evans Picture Library)

Pl. 26   Anti-Catholic and racist propaganda from the Thirty Years' War from Lamentations of Germany, *1638. Note the legend: 'Croats eate children'.*

Pl. 27   Joseph Smith receiving the Golden Plates in 1827, from a Mormon textbook. (Mary Evans Picture Library)

Pl. 28   *The sentimentalization of martyrdom used in rival Irish posters, 1923. (Mary Evans Picture Library)*

Chicago Press and Tribune. He made a major speech in New York on the key topic of the Union and slavery, then exploited his new 'railsplitter' image with businessmen using the nickname given by his cousin. As his campaign developed he showed his versatility of technique with a number of ideas: trying his own local German-language newspaper to go for the ethnic vote, exploiting cheap rail fares to increase convention attendance by likely supporters. Jesse Fell even printed bogus convention entrance tickets to keep out supporters of the rival candidate, Seward. The ultimate presidential campaign of 1860 was based on the 'Honest Abe', railsplitter, backwoods image, backed up by barbecues, pole raisings and railsplitting re-enactments. Once Lincoln was in office it was John Locke Scripps of the *Chicago Tribune* who organized the new, more mature presidential image. Abe became 'the Great Emancipator', 'Father Abraham', 'Saviour of the Union' and ultimately martyr. The combination of his humble beginnings, although this was turned from a disadvantage to an asset, and the enormity of the task which he undertook in waging a civil war against his fellow countrymen, meant that image projection was more vital to him than to any previous president.

Another less personal propaganda war climaxed as Lincoln entered the White House. This battle begun thirty years before was based on the two opposite and equally entrenched viewpoints on slavery. William Lloyd Garrison (1805–79), a printer and journalist edited the *National Philanthropist* from 1828 and founded the influential *Liberator* in 1831, making it a prime focus for anti-slavery propaganda. For many years it had carried the masthead slogan 'No union with slave holders'. Theodore Weld contributed the successful pamphlet *American Slavery As It Is* in 1839 and in 1852 came the hugely popular *Uncle Tom's Cabin* by Harriet Beecher Stowe (1811–96) which sold 300,000 copies, one of history's most effective propaganda novels, followed up by another anti-slavery novel *Dred* in 1856. At an even more populist level there was doggerel like John Ramsdell's:

> What bend the knee to Southern rule
> What cringe and crawl to Southern clay
> And be the base, the simple tool
> of hell-begotten slavery?

This protracted, highly emotive attack on the slave owners of the south was echoed by the extravagant figure of John Brown who gave the movement its main martyr, blessed by Ralph Waldo Emerson and sanctified by Louisa May Alcott as 'St John the Just'. It was also given a more practical infrastructure by the foundation of the official Republican Party in 1854 to support the anti-slavery movement, backed by the journalistic force of Horace Greeley at the *New York Tribune*.

The spectre of 'the Black Terror' had by this time evoked an equally substantial response from the South. George Fitzhugh of Virginia was typical of the more aggressive and emotive end of the Southern propaganda campaign with his *Sociology of Slavery* in 1854 followed two years later by his *Cannibals All*. The economic argument was presented most successfully in David Christy's *Cotton is King* of 1860. The propaganda by both sides was so prolonged and so emotively prejudiced that it created a climate in which war was preferable to recantation by either. Horace Greeley's *New York Tribune* ran aggressive headlines like 'On to Richmond' and the 'Prayers of Twenty Millions'. In the visual arts, Thomas Nast was the major Union cartoonist who attacked first the Confederates and later corruption in New York, developing the emblematic Uncle Sam in the process. Not surprisingly once the war had started the most noticeable propaganda medium was the most emotive of all media – music. This was the period of Julia Ward Howe's (1819–1910) 'Battle Hymn of the Republic' 1861, and Dan Emmet's 'Dixie' of 1859, copied by the North which created its own version by Fanny Cosby.

Whereas Lincoln constructed a reasonably solid foundation for Union propaganda during the Civil War, the Confederate states paid little attention to it. Certainly they put their case very effectively to the European media, but at home they neglected the basic techniques of fostering a nationalist spirit for the Confederates or of using their media properly to sustain civilian morale when the news from the front was bad. Jefferson Davies briefly promoted himself quite well in 1864/5 and put across effectively the difficult case for using black soldiers in their army, but there was no prolonged effort at corporate motivation and some historians have blamed the loss of the war on this failure. One particular feature of propagandist ideas on both sides in the Civil War was its religious fervour, often millennialist in its overtones, with suggestions of a deserved Armageddon from the North and hints of 'God wears grey' complacency in the South.

Significantly when General Ulysses S. Grant (1822–85) had won the war and was elected President in 1868, ostensibly the typical case of military renown being converted into political success, he attributed his victory to 'Republican gold and the pencil of Thomas Nast'. Nast, the acerbic cartoonist of *Harper's Weekly* also helped Grant's re-election four years later and was perhaps one of the most politically influential cartoonists in history.

With the Union saved, the United States also began to develop imperialist ambitions. In 1885 John Fiske produced his influential article on the 'Manifest Destiny' of the US to promote the idea of a new, White-led empire. Ten years later William Randolph Hearst (1863–1951) took over the *New York Journal* and using techniques of sensational headlines, large pictures and aggressive promotion trebled its circulation. Four years later it was Hearst's entire chain of newspapers which grossly misrepresented the Cuban crisis and fanned anti-Spanish feeling with atrocity stories. Joseph Pulitzer (1847–1911), owner of the *New York World* and other titles, followed the same policy. Spaniards always cut off the ears of the dead, killed babies, raped women and fed prisoners to the sharks. President McKinley (1843–1901), elected on the slogan 'The Advance Agent of Prosperity', was now the president 'with a spine like a chocolate eclair'. Attacked by Hearst as a 'pygmy slave' he was pushed reluctantly into war with Spain, by slogans like 'Remember the Maine'; Pulitzer's headline was 'Stop the Nonsense'. Admiral Mahan wrote his highly effective *Influence of Sea power in History* in 1892 which persuaded the Americans that they needed foreign bases for their navy and justified the annexation of the Philippines, while Theodore Roosevelt (1858–1919) made himself a hero commanding his 'roughriders', an aggressive image which was to give him eight years in the White House.

JAPAN

The other great national act of consolidation based on a propaganda concept at this period took place in Japan. The shoguns had been discredited by their condoning of the arrival of Western traders on Japanese soil and the xenophobic reaction was channelled into a structured campaign by the supporters of the restored Meiji dynasty with the slogan 'San No Jo I' [Revere the Emperor, expel the foreigner]. Though the samurai as a class were officially disbanded, their ethic was resuscitated for the benefit of the replacement caste of military officers. In 1872 the new regime founded the Bureau of Rites which was given the task of motivating the new middle class, particularly to encourage a less pacific attitude. The *Taikyo* or Great Teaching projected the ideas of patriotism, loyalty to emperor and duty which were to be both a fundamental and extreme part of Japanese attitudes for the next seventy years. The *Rescripts* of 1885 and 1890 emphasized this. Buddhist monasteries were destroyed in large numbers, while the cults of Shinto were revived. New national newspapers like the Tokyo *Nichi Nichi* and *Asahi* of 1879 followed the state's lead. Fukuchi Gen'ichiro (1841–1906), the talented editor of *Nichi Nichi*, and long-term imperial propagandist helped to write the *Imperial Rescripts* with its neatly packaged ethos of five military virtues: duty, for example, 'Is weightier than a moth while death is lighter than a feather'. The prints of artists like Migita Toshide with his *Splendid Deed of the Brave Soldier Shirakami* of 1895 and *Attack and Massacre* of 1894 translated the image of the samurai into the new age of total warfare. Treatises like Dr Nitobe Inazo's (1862–1933) *Bushido* in 1899 and Hibino Yutaka's *On the Way of the Subject of Japan* in 1904 put across the unique self-sacrificial role of the Japanese military caste to devote their lives to state and emperor. The perfect role model was the story of the forty-seven Ronin who had devoted their lives to a suicidal plan to avenge their master in 1702; this tale, the *Chushingura* [Treasury of Loyal Heart], became immensely popular in almost every available medium: prints, novels, plays, puppet theatre and eventually film. Significantly one of the earliest Japanese films was *The Actual Scene of the Kobe Naval Review* of 1903 and the war with Russia both thrived on and encouraged the newly born Japanese film industry.

This cultivation of a revived military and expansionist ethic, which soon bore fruit with the conquest of Korea in 1894, was one of the most remarkable and deliberate examples of planned propaganda within a relatively short time scale and was taken to a very deep level (pl. 20). This was the creation of a mass ethic which was to produce the extraordinary burst of imperialist activity between 1902 and 1945 and to some extent leave the residual motivation for the economic imperialism which followed. The kamikaze of 1945 were in the direct tradition fostered by *Chushingura.*

TURKEY

One of the most complex variants on the nationalist theme was in the Ottoman Empire where the Young Turks to some extent posed as liberals in opposition to the Sultan but were at the same time asserting a strong new Turkish identity and a mission to save the Turkish empire from its own disaffected sub-nations, the Armenians in particular, the Macedonians and the Asian Greeks. Patriotism, an idea foreign to the Ottoman Empire, was imported from France and started to emerge in Turkey after the Crimean War when the first newspaper appeared, *Mirror of the Fatherland,* and in Egypt with the poems of Sheik Rifaa. A conscious revival of Turkish literature followed as well as new nationalist journals such as *Hurriyet* [Liberty] and the popular patriotic plays of Namik Kemal (1840–88) such as *Fatherland or Silistria* of 1873. The Sultan Abdul Hamid II (1842–1918) tried to restore the image of the Ottomans by creating a fake graveyard of medieval Turks in Istanbul and associating himself with the heritage of the caliphs. Like the other great empires. Turkey dare not be seen to flinch from war.

CHINA

Though China had been one of the cradles of propaganda skill it had subsequently lost the knack under successive dynasties. However, there was some use of the technique and in 1850 Hung Xiuquan positioned himself as the young brother of Jesus Christ and launched a peasant revolt against the Ching dynasty in the guise of a millennial cult. His use of voices and dreams made the propaganda of the Taiping, or Heavenly Kingdom, remarkably effective and but for Western intervention his regime might well have survived even longer. Three influences brought about a new style of Chinese propaganda towards the close of the nineteenth century: the introduction of Western printing technology in Shanghai, the example and stimulus of the highly active Christian missionaries and a Chinese reaction to the competitive, sometimes helpful, interference of the Japanese. The initial result was a substantial expansion in Chinese media. Papers like the *Shanghai Shen-pao*, founded by an Englishman in the 1880s even had woodcut illustrations of the news and its circulation rose to 50,000. The new anti-Manchu, republican theme was put across by the journalist Liang Qui Chiao in his *Self-strengthening News* (1895–8), then his *Political Commentary* produced during his exile to Japan in 1898. Huang Chich's *Yellow History* of 1904 was typical of the new approach to a Chinese nationalist tradition and papers like Chang Ping-Lin's revolutionary *People's Journal* projected the image of warrior heroes rebelling against decadent dynasties.

As the Manchu empire tottered towards extinction, the aspirations of the new breed of Chinese middle-class intellectuals, gentry and business people were encapsulated in the lectures of Dr Sun Yat Sen (1866–1925), the 'Three Peoples' Principles – nationalism, democracy and socialism – which in 1911 became the slogan of the new republic. The articulation of nationalism continued, especially after the successful student demonstrations in Tiananmen Square in 1919 against concessions to the Japanese. This was known neatly as *Wus ssu* or 5–4, the Chinese habit of having numerical mnemonics for great events occurring on particular days – 4 May. The new slogan of nationalist essence (*kuo ts'ui*) was accompanied by a reform of the alphabet which made media usage more practicable. The xenophobic trend accelerated under the leadership of Chiang kai Chek (1887–1974) who with Russian help evolved the Kuomintang and set about unifying the Chinese states. Significantly one of the young propaganda assistants working for the Kuomintang in 1925–6 and editing its *Political Weekly* was Mao Zedong who at this point concentrated on a nationalist not a party message. Chiang went off to do battle with the warlords with an army driven by patriotic fervour and singing a nationalist song to the unlikely tune of 'Frère Jacques'.

INDIA

India was slower to develop national consciousness, mainly because of its size and diversity, particularly because of the deep divide between its two great religions. The Indian Mutiny of 1857 was both an example of reaction to the insensitive public relations of the imperial British and of the deep divisions of the two main nationalist groups. India now developed its nationalist literature with writers like Muhamed Iqubal, the patriot poet (1877–1938), promoting the Muslim or Pakistani stance. Calcutta had its first Indian language newspaper from 1820 and the revived cult of Rama Krishna provided new respectability for the Hindu cause. One of the most aggressively anti-British campaigning journalists was Bal Gangadhai Tilak, editor of the *Kesari*, who in the 1870s revived the Hindu Maratha tradition of resistance to foreign invaders.

The First World War is conventionally attributed to a combination of the Balkan crisis, naval rivalry and governmental posturings. To this must be added the general mass attitude of admiration for war which had been inculcated by forty years of intensive propaganda from the leaders in the main participating powers. In addition there had been the unscrupulous stirring up of ethnic minorities as a means to imperial ends.

One of the least savoury causes espoused by philosophical missionaries in the nineteenth century was that of racial inequality. Nietzsche, Gobineau and Houston Stewart Chamberlain had given racism a thin veneer of respectability in Europe. General Nathan Forest founded the Ku Klux Klan in 1865 with its alliteratively mnemonic name, its preposterous but deadly rituals, its distinctive corporate identity – the fiery cross – its exotic uniform and its appeal to the basest instincts of the Southern states of the USA.

Overall, the second half of the nineteenth century had seen the tools of propaganda taken over and exploited with dangerous intensity by leaders who saw them as a useful companion to guns and battleships in the race towards larger and larger empires. The ethos of competitive nationalism taught to competitive youngsters was at its height and alongside it survived the ethos of the duel and of corporate insults which could only be avenged by war.

Age of Missionaries

The nineteenth century produced a significant number of individuals and groups who developed ideas which they felt impelled to spread and who in different ways showed remarkable levels of propaganda skill. Karl Marx, like so many of the really great propagandists, did not live to see the success of his efforts and is best remembered as a theorist. He did, however, have good practical experience in projecting political ideas (see p. 228) and the effort to spread his ideas continued throughout the forty years after his death. During the same period Henri Dunant (1828–1910) evolved what was to become one of the most lastingly effective corporate identities in the modern world when he founded the Red Cross in Geneva and the Geneva Convention, which was to be extended by the League of Nations, though the projection of peace has remained one of the big failures of propagandists worldwide.

BRITAIN

William Booth (1829–1912) achieved one of those highly imaginative pieces of ideological packaging when he founded the Salvation Army in 1865. The idea of calling his group of missionaries an army, of giving them a uniform and a corporate identity – the letter 'S' – the adoption of army drill and the military style of music were all highly effective. In addition the Army had its own newspaper the *War Cry* which reached a circulation at times of up to 2 million and carried the military metaphor of the war against disease, poverty and paganism even further. His motto 'Blood and Fire', his crimson flag, the skilled event management with rituals of public confessions, witnessing and emotive preaching worked well. Booth's main message 'Joy' was simple and effective and he himself was a very able publicist who used metaphor, trick effects and said that 'he would beat a drum standing on his head if it meant an extra convert'. Apart from its considerable success in the Western world its straightforward appeal achieved remarkable results in Third World areas like the Congo.

UNITED STATES AND BEYOND

Mary Baker Eddy (1821–1910) founded the Church of Christ Scientist at Boston in 1879 four years after publishing her principles in *Science and*

Health with Key to the Scriptures. From its inception this sect was fully conscious of the power of print, founding its own major newspaper the *Christian Science Monitor* with a target of middle class, mainly middle-aged and female readers. Its slogan was 'God is Mind' and it developed a substantial publishing and book-lending operation with networks of reading rooms in countries where it had a foothold.

Charles Taze Russell (1852–1916) launched the International Bible Students Association in 1874 in Pittsburgh. This sect too had a strong publishing infrastructure, with a vast output of cheap newspapers like *Zion's Watchtower Tract*, delivered door-to-door by volunteers from his own large print works in Pittsburgh. It revived the apocalyptic theme of Armageddon with a heavy emphasis on the end of the world and the rhythmic slogan 'Millions now living will never die'. Again, it achieved considerable worldwide penetration, achieving a high level of resistance to Nazi persecution and significant success in some African countries such as Zambia.

Joseph Smith (1805–44) was in some respects the most creative of all the American sect founders when he first preached his thirteen articles at Fayette, Seneca County in 1830. A natural publicist he adapted the techniques of Moses and Joan of Arc to an Illinois audience, seeing an angel, finding his golden plates and the decoding stones, publishing the *Book of Mormon* (pl. 27). Before his death he had converted 20,000 to his cause; his imprisonment and subsequent martyrdom made it easier for his successor, Brigham Young (1801–77), to lead his followers away to the promised land of Utah. The Mormon expansion abroad was based very much on a well-financed network, well-trained, well-supported missionaries and once it had given up some of its more eccentric ideas like polygamy, a strong, clear message.

There were numerous other well-publicized Christian off-shoots including the Seventh-Day Adventists and the cult of St Bernadette at Lourdes (1844–79). In the Middle East the most able religious publicist was without question Mirza Hussein Ali or Baha Ullah (1817–92) – his new name meaning 'Splendour of God' – who developed the new Islamic off-shoot founded by the martyred Bab-ed-din in 1843. Among able African practitioners was Zulu Isaiah Shembe who used his own poetry and adapted tribal dance and music to help project his church. Further east the most effective reformer and reviver was Rama Krishna (1836–86), 'the Hindu Wesley'.

TEMPERANCE

One of the most dynamic pressure groups in terms of propaganda in the nineteenth century was the Temperance movement. Timothy Shay Arthur (1809–84), a newspaper editor, wrote the melodramatic novel *Ten Nights in a Bar Room and What I Saw There* in 1858, a massive seller which when it was adapted to the stage or tent show was second in popularity in the United States only to *Uncle Tom's Cabin* for about twenty years. It included the song 'Father dear Father come home with me now', in its own right one of the major successes of temperance propaganda. Father Matthew in Ireland conducted a remarkable personal propaganda campaign from 1839 to 1842 which gathered some 4 million abstainers. The Anti-Saloon League in the United States, the British Temperance Society, the Women's Christian Temperance Society, all had a extraordinary determination to achieve their ends. The American Society for the Promotion of Temperance used massive pamphlet campaigns, professional organizers, camp meetings, songs, stories and 'Cold Water Parades'. The international propaganda effort involved plays, novels, illustrated pamphlets, songs, sampler designs and other artefacts (pl. 19).

FEMALE SUFFRAGE

Propaganda for women's suffrage was harder to achieve. Mrs Emmeline Pankhurst (1857–1928) had to resort to extreme methods to attract media attention. The Pankhurst ladies, mother and two daughters, had been working for some years on the fringes of the Independent Labour Party with some encouragement from Keir Hardie, when in 1905 they founded the Women's Social and Political Union (WSPU). Initially response to straightforward propaganda was poor, though there had been good sales of tracts like Olive Schreiner's *The Story of an African Farm*, but then Christabel Pankhurst saw the way to achieve instant notoriety and awareness by her intervention at a Liberal rally in Manchester where she hit a policeman to earn a gaol sentence. From that moment membership leapt up. The WSPU's pamphlet *Votes for Women* was sold on street corners by a large army of female recruits and from 1907 the *Women's Franchise* was published weekly, followed later by the *Suffragette* newspaper which in 1915 was to rename itself more patriotically *Britannia*. The movement's ability to organize rallies with good banners ensured coverage in the new era of photo-journalism (pl. 16), and sometimes this could be enhanced by stories of police brutality, ladies chained to railings, forced feeding and hunger strikes in prison. The suffragettes produced a good range of ancillary media, their white flower symbol, button badges, china figures, postcards of Christabel, the ingenious Suffragette Alphabet in which 'H' stood for Holloway Prison, the Suffragette Salvation Army and a number of good songs including the 'March of the Women' composed by Elly Smith.

The major propagandist for feminism in France was Léon Richer (1824–1911) who founded *Le Droit des Femmes* in 1869, backed by Victor Hugo. Significantly in Germany the Federation of German Women's Associations under Gertrud Baumer from 1908 backed August Keim's Army League propaganda by projecting the domestic role of women as breeders of good soldiery with their slogan 'Kinder, Küche, Kirche' [Children, Kitchen, Church]. In the United States Lucy Stone (1818–93) conducted a long personal campaign.

LABOUR

Propaganda for the Labour movement was developing. In the USA the socialist paper *Appeal to Reason* was selling 750,000 copies while in Germany *Vorwarts* was Europe's most successful labour journal. In Britain the tendency was towards local free sheets which were limited in their scope by cost. The *Leeds Forward* and *Gloucester Progress* were among the more successful. James Keir Hardie (1865–1915) began his political career as a journalist and was founder editor of *The Labour Leader* and for a period the Independent Labour Party was distributing up to 30 million free newspapers a year at considerable cost. It was to be some time before Labour achieved any real share of the national press and the main means of obtaining coverage remained the strike with its event management add-ons such as the picket, marches and demonstrations.

First World War and Revolution

While scholars argue endlessly over the complex causes of the First World War, it is undeniable that the basic motivation behind it was an ethos of competitive imperialism which had been fostered by at least two centuries of propaganda for the concept of national glory and military prowess. In August 1914 all the participating nations in the war protested their innocence and the guilt of the other side. Chancellor Bethmann Hollweg (1856–1921), for instance, blamed Russia and France, the German *White Book* explaining 'How Russia and her Rulers betrayed Germany's confidence'. Propaganda played an important part in winning the secondary nations over to one side or the other. The Germans made a major effort to dominate the Turkish press and to good effect while the British, French and Russians worked hard on the Italian press, the French going so far as to pay the youthful journalist Benito Mussolini to give up his pacifist stance and become a pro-war columnist with *Popolo d'Italia*.

The German army had an existing small propaganda section at the start of the war in the OHL (Oberste Heeresleitung) run by three of von Moltke's majors, one of whom, Hans von Haeften, encouraged the rapid spread of atrocity stories and other material likely to encourage war hysteria among the populace. As the war went on and conditions became more difficult Ludendorff called for greater efforts at 'patriotic schooling' with a vast deluge of propaganda material to help stiffen resistance among both the troops and those at home, but this became increasingly difficult as the situation deteriorated. The one exception was the Eastern Front in 1917 where the Germans could drop leaflets in Russia suggesting that the troops should go home quickly before the Provisional Government finished distributing their land.

The emotive propaganda throughout Europe, the United States and Japan which had helped cause the war by breeding aggressive attitudes, was also used to motivate the menfolk of these nations to volunteer to fight. In Britain 1914 was the year of the white feather and significantly the first film version of *The Four Feathers* was shown in that year. Kitchener's accusing finger in the Alfred Leete poster campaign 'Your country needs you', anticipated the even more insidious blackmail of Savile Lumley's poster 'Daddy what did you do in the Great War?' Massive armies were recruited in every participating nation by similar messages, in due course backed up by conscription, and prepared for mass sacrifice in a way which suggests comparison with lemmings. Perhaps the most successful of all the recruiting messages was the subtle playback of the Kaiser's supposed comment about 'the contemptibles'. In Germany the posters were by Ludwig Hohlwein and the films *Call of the Fatherland* and *Watch on the Rhein*. In Russia there were poster designs reincarnating the knights and dragons of medieval Muscovy, but they ran out of glue in 1917. The main films were *Down with the German Yoke* and *The Holy War*. Generally this somewhat absurd war was supported by the media throughout at least its first year with the blackmailing emphasis in each country on the moral duty of upholding the flag.

In the later years of the conflict the main propaganda themes moved away from recruitment to denigration of the enemy and sustenance of corporate morale. In Britain the Central Committee for National Patriotic Organization was founded with private money, and led by the Earl of Rosebery with an emphasis on academic pamphlets such as *Why We Are at War*, but since the press was dominated by long casualty lists, the themes of 1914 increasingly became inappropriate. The fashion for atrocity themes also came and went:

> Wounded and a prisoner our soldier cries for water
> The German sister pours it on the ground before his eyes
> There is no woman in Britain who would do it,
> There is no woman in Britain who will forget it.

Late 1914 saw the totally fictitious story of the Dumfries nurse who had her breasts cut off. Endless stories of rape and severed limbs became steadily less credible. *The Times* produced a story that the Germans were recycling dead soldiers as pig food. When David Lloyd George (1863–1945) succeeded Asquith as Prime Minister he appointed the accomplished newspaper owner Alfred Harmsworth (later Lord Northcliffe, 1865–1922) as head of the enemy propaganda department of the Ministry of Information. The writer H.G. Wells (1866–1946) was in charge of the German section and produced the useful slogans 'the hour of victory' and 'the war to end war' as well as popular stories like *Mr Britling sees it through*. Another able writer John Buchan (1875–1940) was seconded to the department and organized a campaign of leaflets dropped from balloons to the German troops, attacking the Kaiser so vigorously that they had to be withdrawn because of a threat by the Germans to retaliate in kind. Among other writers added to the team were C.F.G. Masterman and Lovell Thomas who orchestrated the hero image of Lawrence of Arabia. It also included J.M. Barrie, Arnold Bennett, G.K. Chesterton, Arthur Conan Doyle, Thomas Hardy, John Galsworthy and Masefield. Bennett, Kipling and H.G. Wells were sent out to France while Gilbert Parker (1862–1932), a novelist born in Canada, was sent to co-ordinate British propaganda in the United States. Meanwhile, the private sector continued to feed the very fast-growing cinema circuit with suitable films like a remake of *The Four Feathers* and *Our Empire's fight for Freedom* –

by 1917 there were 4,000 cinemas in Britain with a weekly audience of 20 million. Masterman became the propaganda film co-ordinator. As head of information Lord Beaverbrook took over a film company, Topical Budget, specializing in newsreels, but it also produced films like *Once a Hun always a Hun*. Morale was fed with a succession of sentimental songs culminating in Ivor Novello's (1893–1951) 'Keep the home fires burning'.

These campaigns may have had some modest effect and certainly this was the view in retrospect of Adolf Hitler who perhaps exaggerated the undermining effect of Allied propaganda on the Germans. Ludendorff had commented 'We were hypnotized by the enemy propaganda like a rabbit by a snake', so that this theme was later used as an excuse for the surrender in 1918 and a stimulus for Germany to make better use of propaganda in the 1940s. One of the few leaflet campaigns from the Allies which is known to have reduced German morale was that on the sinking of 150 U-boats, but in general it could be argued that no propaganda was capable of papering over serious cracks when a war was going badly, and truths spread by enemies were likely to have arrived very soon afterwards without assistance.

AUSTRIA-HUNGARY

With the possible exception of tsarist Russia, the empire least competent in the techniques of propaganda was without question the Austro-Hungarian. The last Habsburg emperors believed they had no need to stoop to make use of such ideas despite the obvious disintegration of their realms; in fact the last of all, Karl I (1887–1992), commented 'ideas cannot be recommended like laxatives, toothpaste or foodstuffs'. The regime also failed to clamp down soon enough on the growing propaganda efforts of the empire's subject nationalities which now bubbled up. Until 1917 Jan Hajsman, leader of the Mafie in Prague, was allowed to project *Ceska Demokratie*. The *Slovenski Narod* stirred up Slovakian nationalism, *Romania* was the equivalent organ of Romanian nationalism and numerous of the other ethnic groups in the Balkans began to found their own media. Significantly it was the Serb radical press which had championed Princip and Crna Ruka as heroes in June/July 1914, thus provoking the Viennese press to retaliate and greatly enhancing the mood for war. The Habsburg empire was broken up because it was on the losing side in the First World War, but even if it had been one of the winners its collapse was only a matter of time.

UNITED STATES

As the war drew to its close there were three men who began to display some real understanding of the potential of well-organized propaganda: President Wilson, Lloyd George and Lenin. Woodrow Wilson (1856–1924), the first US President to hold press conferences, certainly made a substantial effort to build up reasonable worldwide acceptance of the terms of the Treaty of Versailles and it was unfortunate that in the end this was not truly successful. He had appointed George Creel to head a Committee on Public Information which air-dropped some 3 million leaflets on Europe and distributed another 70 million in numerous languages. Creel also organized teams of public speakers and sponsored films like *The Beast of Berlin*. At home in the United States he used newspaper advertising to encourage support for the war effort and a public relations campaign to enlist the moral support of neutral nations. The slogan of making 'the world safe for democracy' was developed by Creel's group, leading up to the promotion of Wilson's Fourteen Points which must rank as one of history's neatest pieces of political packaging. Able communicators like Walter Lippmann (1889–1974) and Norman Angel (1872–1967) were utilized, together with one of the first of the theoretical propagandists, Edward Bernays (1891–1992), nephew of Sigmund Freud and founder of the first public relations business. It was Bernays, for example, who handled the press relations for the birth of Czechoslovakia and Jan Mazaryk's declaration of independence which was one of the more successful exercises.

This was the era in which sauerkraut was tactfully renamed 'liberty cabbage', but the projection of the peace settlement required substantial time and commitment, particularly in Germany and some of the new conglomerate republics. The image of the League of Nations was damaged in the very beginning by the refusal of the American Senate to endorse their own president's treaties and by the over-harsh handling of the defeated Germans. This failure to allow the Germans any possibility of an image of self-respect was probably the most damaging blunder in the history of propaganda.

BRITAIN AFTER 1918

In Britain David Lloyd George, sloganized as the 'Welsh Wizard', was portrayed on film in 1918 as *The Man who saved the British Empire*. He had come to power with the help of Lord Northcliffe whose London *Times* and *Daily Mail* had damned his predecessor Asquith for his conduct of the war in 1916. The support of the two major newspaper barons, Northcliffe and Beaverbrook, plus his cultivation of Scott of the *Guardian*, Riddell of *News of the World* and others had been a crucial part of Lloyd George's power base, but Northcliffe changed sides in 1919 referring now to Lloyd George as a 'prisoner of Tory nincompoops and secret pro-Germans'. The 'Homes fit for heroes' election campaign saw the decimation of the old Liberal Party and Lloyd George still the leader of a Unionist Liberal coalition. The Labour Party made some real headway for the first time, helped slightly by its own well-written newspaper the *Daily Herald*, edited by George Lansbury (1859–1940) with able writers such as Siegfried Sassoon (1886–1967), Osbert Sitwell and G.D.H. Cole.

RUSSIA

Undoubtedly the greatest propagandist to emerge from the wreckage of the First World War was Lenin (1870–1924), born Vladimir Ilyich Ulyanov, whose practical career began in 1894. After five years' study of Marxism he had become leader of the Union for the Liberation of the Working Class in St Petersburg. His early campaigns involved him in the copying out in quadruplicate of leaflets for distribution to the Semyannikov workers and the packing of leaflets in tubes to go to the workers at the Laferne tobacco factory. He soon became involved in the printing of Marxist textbooks disguised in false covers to evade the censor. After arrest and a three-year exile in Siberia he launched his first newspaper the *Iskra* [Spark] from Stuttgart in 1900 with the prophetic metaphor that this 'spark has started a conflagration to which there is still no end'. Though it was to be one of the most historically influential of all propaganda newspapers, *Iskra* was not particularly well-written or appealing to the average Russian reader. Printed in Munich, financed by Struve and edited by Plekhanov it tended to be dull and doctrinaire, intellectual rather than emotively exciting and aimed at an already committed élite rather than the unconverted masses. There were some good correspondents, such as Babushin in St Petersburg and Martov, but the real quality of *Iskra* lay in its distribution. Much of this was due to the painstaking efforts of Lenin's wife Krupskaya who organized the double-bottomed trunks for smuggling it from Switzerland into Russia. She attended to the vast detailed correspondence, sometimes 300 letters a day in invisible ink, which led to the setting up of a substantial mailing list. At its height this created a circulation of 40,000, high readership per copy, and a high level of reader attention. In addition she was able to develop sub-networks like the one at Baku where a committee reprinted the paper and supplied news and extra funds. As yet another aspect of circulation building she organized travelling agents like Radchenko or bulk distribution points like the invaluable railway workers at Pskov and Kiev.

In 1902 Lenin produced one of his most influential pamphlets *Shto Dyelat?* [What to do?] deliberately given the same title as the propagandist novel by Nikolai Tchernyshevsky (1828–89), 'the archbishop of propaganda'. It put across the concept of a cellular élite who would bring about the revolution rather than a dispersed and uncontrolled rising of the whole population. It was because of this obsessive desire to have a totally dedicated minority corps that Lenin and the Bolshevik wing of the party split away from the Mensheviks the year after this pamphlet. Significantly *Shto Dyelat?* was distributed through the *Iskra* network thus to some extent justifying the ideas it preached. However, actual control of *Iskra* was soon lost to the Mensheviks and Lenin was forced to set up a new paper *Vperyod* [Forward] followed by yet another, *Novaya Zhisn* [New Life]. The abortive revolution of 1905 was a non-event in the development of

Communist propaganda, but it did thrust forward one of the most talented writers, Maxim Gorky (1868–1936), and Leon Trotsky (1879–1940) produced the best paper of this period – *Nachenko* – which may have reached 500,000 circulation. Gorky had written a number of emotive short stories, contributed the song 'At the bottom' which was adopted by the 1905 revolutionaries, and now joined Lenin in *Novaya Zhisn* to which, with the poet Nikolai Minsky (1855–1937), composer of 'The Workers' Hymn', he was a major contributor. Two further very able propagandist writers joined the team when Trotsky founded *Pravda* [Truth] in 1912 to offset the Mensheviks' new journal *Luch* [Ray]. Molotov (1890–1986) was its editor. Lenin was contributing daily articles throughout 1913 and his wife devoted herself to updating the circulation lists and distribution network. By 1917 it had reached the level of 100,000 copies per issue.

When war was declared in 1914 Lenin's efforts were temporarily thwarted by the wave of patriotic feeling which even the fast-collapsing tsarist regime could still muster against the Germans. Lenin vainly opposed the war with slogans like 'Turn the guns not against our brothers the wage slaves of other countries but against the bourgeois governments of all countries'. Like so much Communist propaganda it was somewhat long-winded, but Lenin tended to make up for this failing with his dogged repetition and persistence. To the civilian *Pravda* was added *Pravda of the Trenches* aimed at the soldiers at the front and subsidized by the Germans. This effort persisted after the March Revolution, in which the Bolsheviks played no direct part, had toppled the tsarist government. Notably the rebel army made the first recorded use of radio in propaganda history when they broadcast the new status of the Soviets on Tsarskoe Selo radio station, also publishing the same news in *Izvestiya*. During this period Lenin, who had returned to Russia in April, was still perfecting the communication network of his metric pyramid of soviets, each man representing 1,000. The distinctive corporate identity and neat imagery of the Red Flag and the Red Guard were spreading rapidly. Then in June he tried his first test of strength by using *Pravda* to summon a Bolshevik rally. The slogans were the alliterative 'Vsya Vlast Sovietam' [All Power to the Soviets] and variations on the promise of 'bread, peace and land', but the stuttering would-be Bolshevik coup which followed went disastrously wrong. Kerensky and the Provisional Government scored a major propaganda victory over Lenin by releasing forged documents which showed that he had been in German pay. The *Pravda* printing presses in Petrograd were destroyed, leaving only Gorky's *Novaya Zhisn* and the *Kronstadt Pravda* for Lenin to use to try to dampen the scandal.

Lenin's style of speech and writing had a level of personal conviction, a complete contempt for compromisers and a rhythmic build-up of violence and aggression which Trotsky and Stalin both later imitated. Yet he was quite subtle in the use of propaganda. The suburbs of Petrograd were covered with the slogans, 'All Power to the Soviets', which in the early months appeared no more in favour of the Bolsheviks than the rest of the left-wing majority, and 'Down with the Ten Capitalist Ministers', which was more specifically anti-bourgeois. Lenin's event management was also of a high order since he was able to make sure that his slogan-carrying supporters formed the bulk of several major march demonstrations in which they were not really the majority.

The Provisional Government soon lost its propaganda initiative by continuing the war against Germany with disastrous results. As Lenin put it 'peace won't wait, famine won't wait'. He was able to persuade his Bolshevik colleagues that the time was at last ripe for a coup and organized the storming of the Winter Palace. This time the news of the revolution was spread by Trotsky's telegrams – he himself referred to it as 'revolution by telegraph'. The October Revolution also made considerable use of the telephone and significantly Lenin gave special instructions for the capture of the telephone exchange. Once in power the new soviet regime rapidly consolidated its identity and Lenin set up his Plan for Monumental Propaganda. The theme of red worked well and was joined visually by the star symbol and early versions of the hammer and sickle. The pre-revolutionary slogans were now replaced by standard Marxist ones like 'Proletariats of the world unite' and 'Long Live the Third International'; the bands of Russia learned to play the 'Internationale'. Lenin appeared on posters with the strongly alliterative 'Veliki Vozhd Proletarii' [Great Leader of the Proletariat]. The revolution encouraged a number of able poster designers like El Lissitzky and Valentin Serov. Soon there were Agitprop railway trains carrying the hammer and sickle motif, the sides of the wagons painted with slogans and with mobile cinema carriages (see pl. 6). There was even an Agitprop steamboat the 'Red Star' by 1920 and propaganda road floats. Considerable attention was devoted to the development of cinema and short news documentaries like the *Kinopravda*, directed by the remarkable Dziga Vertov, and Pudovkin's *Hammer and Sickle* of 1921 boosting morale. Thousands of commemorative plates, figurines, ornaments and medals projected the image of the revolution. There were large numbers of stylized pictures of its heroes, such as Sergei Ivanov's *March 1905*, which were reproduced for domestic decoration. Lenin had ordered the replacement of all tsarist statues and monuments by April 1918 and he rapidly organized a succession of commemorative events which could be celebrated by public processions. Male literacy camps were being organized by 1920 and female by 1923. Overall, his internal propaganda system after the October Revolution was as thorough as it had been before but with the new objective of consolidation and the defeat of the Whites.

Even more remarkable, however, was the rapidity with which Lenin's regime set about tackling the organization of propaganda abroad. As early as 1917 a section was set up under Karl Radek (1885–1939) for international propaganda and a budget of 2 million roubles was allocated for the worldwide spread of Communist ideas. As a priority it was directed to the lower ranks of the Austrian and German armies so that war pressure on the front would be reduced. *Die Fachel* paid for by the Russians did the same job as *Pravda of the Trenches*, paid for by the Germans, had done. Lenin also used Joffe to organize the Spartacus letter campaign and other efforts to destabilize the Kaiser. Even after the Treaty of Versailles he wrote to Joffe in Berlin saying 'We must publish a hundred times more.'

Soon propaganda in other languages was also being undertaken. There was an aerial leaflet drop on French and English troops on Russian soil. From 1918 a whole range of ethnic propaganda groups were being set up. Trotsky was addressing 'the working people of Europe oppressed and bled white'. Newspapers were printed in Magyar, Serb, Czech and Turkish. Agitators like the Hungarian Bela Kun were trained to return to their own countries to organize revolution. A further school for propaganda was set up at Tashkent to concentrate on India and the Far East. The clause in the Treaty of Brest Litovsk which forbad propaganda across national frontiers was ignored. The Baku Council of Propaganda launched a new paper *People of the East* in four languages and in 1919 the whole concept of a worldwide effort to convert all countries to Marxism was formalized under the title of the Comintern. To mount the campaign at all was a remarkable achievement but its success is not easy to evaluate. Countries like France and Italy soon had active, quite large Communist parties, but were never totally converted. If ultimately the world's most populous country, China, was won over this was more due to the training of ethnic leaders in Moscow and other factors than direct propaganda. Nevertheless the heavy allocation of resource by Lenin and Trotsky to the worldwide spread of Communism was a feature of their policy which was to be largely abandoned by Stalin but was briefly one of the most substantial efforts of its kind in world history since the spread of Islam.

TURKEY

As it had in Russia, Austria and Germany, a great dynasty also came to an end in Turkey with the last Ottoman Sultan. The replacement, who created a new image in the wake of defeat in the First World War, was Mustafa Kemal Ataturk (1881–1938) who developed Turkish nationalism with a new aggressive stance, attacking the existing government as 'a gang of traitors'. Once in power he set about intense promotion of Turkish culture, resurrecting its literature and rewriting its history to present the Turks as separate from both Arabs and Europeans, yet abolishing the fez, dervishes and other relics of the Ottoman past. Turkey also pursued a racist policy of genocide in Armenia and hostility to all things Greek.

ITALY

One other remarkable propagandist belonging more to the ashes of the First World War than to the next generation was the Italian poet-pilot Gabriele D'Annunzio (1863–1938). Author of novels like *Il trionfo della morte* (1894), passionate nationalist and admirer of Nietzsche, he organized his own invasion of Trieste in 1919 and was a pioneer in a number of propaganda techniques, including the use of leaflet bombing, the adoption of intense nationalist postures and language, salutes, intoned crowd responses and black uniforms. His techniques were to be developed by Mussolini and Hitler with appalling results.

Overall, the First World War period had fostered the growth of the unhealthy side of propaganda, coinciding with a period of continued expansion of the media which made the ill effects generally more disastrous.

Dictators

GERMANY

Adolf Hitler (1889–1945) is often put forward as the most obvious example of the misuse of propaganda skill in the modern world. Certainly he had a greater range of media available to him than any predecessor and made the maximum possible use of it, but his techniques were not particularly novel nor was the hypnotic effect which he apparently had over the German nation by any means unique. What is certainly true is that Hitler's entire career was built round his use of propaganda and it was very carefully planned. Joseph Goebbels (1897–1945) who had taken a doctorate in romantic drama and then worked as a publicity man for the Strassers, recognized the quality of Hitler's analysis of propaganda in *Mein Kampf* as:

> a carefully built up erection of statements which whether true or false can be made to undermine quite rigidly held ideas and to construct new ones in their place. It would not be impossible to prove with sufficient repetition and psychological understanding of the people concerned that a square is in fact a circle. They are mere words and words can be moulded until they clothe ideas in disguise.

Hitler indicated in *Mein Kampf,* just as Bolingbroke had done over 200 years before (see p. 201), that it was more effective to appeal to the emotions than to reason, to avoid abstract ideas, constantly criticize the opposition and never appear objective. Vituperation of a succession of scapegoats was the foundation of Hitler's message system, first 'the Versailles traitors', the Germans who had sold out to the Allies in 1918, then the Communists, the same 'spectre rouge' almost which Napoleon had exploited in his move towards power, finally the Jews who were to blame for all Germany's problems.

Hitler's first attempts at propaganda began in 1920 with very limited funds, when he was circulating duplicated sheets to try to induce tiny audiences to attend meetings of the fledgling National Socialist Party in Munich. Soon he was able to afford small advertisements in the *Munchener Beobachter* which were ingenious enough to bring a crowd of 2,000 to the Hofbrauhaus rally. He was helped by a Bavarian writer, secret army funds and the racist poet Dietrich Eckart (1868–1923), inventor of

Deutschland Erwache, who bought the paper *Volkischer Beobachter* for which Hermann Esser (1900–81) specialized in researching scandalous stories about Jews. *Volkischer Beobachter* had a circulation of only 7,000 and no advertising, but Max Amann turned it round and made it the centre of the German press, with circulation up to 30,000 by 1928, 129,000 by 1931 and 1.2 million by 1942. The printer Eher Verlag was responsible for the marketing of Hitler's *Mein Kampf*. Also helpful was Julius Streicher the Nuremberg teacher who founded *Der Sturmer* in 1923 which contained a succession of stories about Jewish ritual murders, sex crimes and the conspiracy foretold in the *Protocols of the Elders of Zion*. Above all there was the massive media empire of Alfred Hugenberg (1865–1951) who supported the right-wing generally from 1919 and Hitler specifically from 1923.

At this stage the Nazi Party was already utilizing the tactics of terror. In August 1921 it was given a Gymnastic and Sports Division and within four months its name was changed to Sturmabteilung – SA – creating a legendary brawl at the Hofbrauhaus which strengthened its reputation. The swastika or hakenkreuz was in use by the party even in 1918. Soon the SA was parading in public with swastika flags; Hitler also at this time recruited a succession of able or well-connected assistants such as Rudolf Hess, Alfred Rosenberg, and Hermann Goering. With additional funds, some from local Bavarian industrialists, some possibly from the White Russians, the party was able to turn the *Volkischer Beobachter* into a daily. Hitler made good progress in uniting the various Bavarian patriotic parties under his wing and attracting Ludendorff as a figurehead. His direct, totally uncompromising stance stood out among less decisive colleagues. As he put it typically in late 1922: 'The Marxists taught – if you will not be my brother I will bash your skull in. Our motto will be – if you will not be a German I will bash your skull in.' The following year, however, his impetuosity in leading the November Munich putsch led to his total humiliation and imprisonment. Yet with remarkable resilience he used his trial to achieve even greater publicity for himself by pouring scorn on the authorities, 'the November criminals', 'the Jew-ridden republic of betrayal', 'the Versailles traitors'. He also used his period in prison to dictate *Mein Kampf*, published by Max Amann, which, though it initially attracted little attention, had sold 6 million copies by 1940.

The next decade saw a gradual build-up to power. He first brought the Rhineland within the scope of his activities by allying with and then taking over the campaign organized by the two Strasser brothers, Gregor the public speaker and Otto editor of their newspapers the *Berliner Arbeiterzeitung* and the fortnightly *Nationalsozialiste Briefe*. One of their writers, Joseph Goebbels, was recruited in this way. To seal the alliance in July 1926 Hitler held his first mass rally at Weimar, where he displayed his superb abilities in event management, with 5,000 men marching past, himself for the first time taking the salute with his arm outstretched. There was also a free distribution of 100,000 copies of the *Volkischer Beobachter*. Three years later he was able to absorb the German National

Party and its wealthy leader Alfred Hugenberg, a former director of Krupps who had bought a chain of newspapers and a film company to project his views. Hitler was also building a closer relationship with the Ruhr industrialists such as Emil Kirdorf (1847–1938) and picked up the support of another newspaper the *Rheinisch-Westfalische Zeitung* edited by Otto Dietrich (1897–1952) who became Hitler's press chief under the newly promoted propaganda supremo Goebbels in 1929. Within five years Goebbels's department, the RMVP, had a staff of 14,000.

By 1930 Hitler thus had a substantial party infrastructure and a substantial proportion of the German press on his side, but his political progress would probably still have been slow but for the catastrophic effects of the Depression on the German economy. By his skilful use of the press, by his clever event management and by his deployment of violence Hitler brought himself to the chancellorship. Once in power his objectives were to change and his range of media widened substantially.

He was the first politician to make major use of radio. He rated highly its employment as a vehicle for propaganda. Goebbels wrote:

> We have a great potential for influencing public opinion. I prophesy the day when every factory, every cinema, theatre, market place and store, railway station and every home will be within range of the Führer's voice.

To make this prophecy come true the Nazis organized the production of cheap new receivers (VE sets – *Volksempfangsanlage*) which could take only one wavelength and 3 million of them were sold. Overall listening rose from 4.5 million to 16 million between 1933 and 1942, helped by a second manoeuvre which was the compulsory installation of radios with loudspeakers in cafés and most public places. In addition the party had radio wardens to check up that people were listening to the right station. The combination of an almost weekly broadcast by Hitler himself as happened in 1933 and an emotive diet of specially chosen music – Strauss marches, Beethoven's 'Eroica' on Hitler's birthday was highly effective. *Forces Favourites* on Sunday had the highest listening figures.

Radio was also used for diplomatic and war propaganda. The most ingenious example was its contribution to the winning of the Saar plebiscite in 1936. Goebbels cunningly subsidized the sale of large numbers of VE sets in the Saar prior to the promised secret ballot organized by the League of Nations. The anti-Nazi leader of the Saar, Max Braun, was smeared as being anti-German and the immediacy of radio was exploited to announce at the last minute that Braun had fled the Saar the day before the plebiscite. It was too late and too difficult to counteract the lie with other media so that even when Braun was driven through the streets he was thought to be an impostor. The German use of Lord Haw-Haw to broadcast to the British was less effective, but Ferdonnet the French traitor broadcasting from Stuttgart had more style.

The French soldiers on the Maginot Line with their *microsoldat* receivers were a vulnerable prey and this was one case where troop demoralization by radio contributed to military success.

The Nazis like the Russian Communists saw cinema as a vital new medium for propaganda. Goebbels in fact was an admirer of Eisenstein's *Battleship Potemkin* and when briefing the director for his new *Victory in the West* suggested that he should imitate the style – odd angles to heighten emotional involvement, powerful music synchronized with the action to emphasize dramatic points and foreshortening of figures to obtain the heroic quality of historical giants. Leni Riefenstahl (1905–) filmed both the Olympic Games and the Nuremberg rally with the same philosophy. The image-building power of film was appreciated, German history and mythology quarried for allegorical material. There was Riefenstahl's use of the Odin myth in Nuremberg for the *Triumph of Will* and a biography of Frederick the Great was a vehicle for boosting Hitler as a great German hero. *Ohn Kruger,* a film about the Boer War, gave plenty of opportunity for vilifying the British and a mass of war films projected the image of German racial superiority, Jewish inferiority and the glories of male comradeship in battle. In the greatest box office success of the Nazi period, a soldier's love story *Grosse Liebe* seen by 28 million people, death in battle was glorified but only enemy casualties were seen on the screen. Thus film was used to raise morale at home, but also at times to do the reverse abroad as when intimidating footage of the Blitzkrieg on Poland was shown to devastating effect in Norwegian cinemas in 1939. Heinrich Hoffman (1885–1957) was Hitler's personal photographer helping him to develop his presence and gestures as well as showing them with appropriate levels of intimidation or benevolence in a series of popular picture books.

Nazi use of poster was also widespread and effective. Red was the standard colour in the early days, mainly to provoke the left. The designs had large crude illustrations or heavy dominating slogans. The anti-Semitic posters combined the swastika and the star of David, hardly needing words. The massive 'Ja' posters in Austria before the Anschluss combined the dominating exposure of Hitler's portrait and hard dramatic slogans like 'Schluss mit der Korruption' ['Fight corruption'], or 'Sieg um jeden Preis' ['Victory at any price'] and 'Ein Kampf, ein Sieg' ['One struggle, one victory']; the massive repetition of swastika displays provided a total outdoor advertising campaign which combined with other media must have been overwhelming. Hitler had a fine range of designers including Paul Hermann, Artur Kampf, Elk Eber and Hohlwein from the earlier period; in fact the poster of Hitler as a knight in shining armour was reminiscent of a similar poster featuring the Kaiser. Numerous illustrative posters idealized the SA, the heroes of the 1923 putsch and later the army. In both qualitative and quantitative terms, therefore, Hitler's use of posters to dominate the urban environment was very substantial.

After 1933 the Nazi press also continued to expand – between 1934 and 1943 newspaper circulations rose from 20 to 26 million. Goebbels launched a new prestige paper, *Das Reich*, which reached a circulation of 1 million and the *Volkischer Beobachter* itself moved even higher. Goebbels's view was that: 'the reader should get the impression that the writer is in fact a speaker standing beside him, an aura of sweat, leather and blood lust.' Similarly Streicher's paper *Der Sturmer* reached a circulation of 500,000 and made use of such classic headlines as 'The Jew Rosenfelder sees reason and hangs himself' or, with reference to the Weimar government, the evocative 'World Champion belly crawlers'. It also used the traditional conspiracy gambit with a clever recycling of the *Protocols of the Elders of Zion*. The Nazi basic technique of frequency, repetition of fairly simple, but very dogmatically confident and extreme concepts with short sharp unadorned words like 'Hate', 'bash', 'kill' was supremely in evidence.

Another prime medium in Hitler's propaganda onslaught, and his own *par excellence*, was spectacle and event management. The examples of Lueger in Vienna and D'Annunzio in Trieste, plus the drill patterns of the old imperial army provided a starting point and rallies were a feature of Nazi ritual from an early stage. The prime setting was spectacular in itself as Nuremberg, like Munich, provided a scenic backdrop full of appropriate historical reminders, enhanced by the illumination of the old castle at night. The organization required split-second timing with the artificially delayed arrival of the Führer a deliberately delayed climax. It required huge camps for the participants and relevant infrastructure, large masses of human beings arranged in patterns with swastikas, eagles, flags and torches. The lighting was dramatic: Sir Neville Henderson described the effect aptly as a 'Cathedral of light'. A neon-lit eagle of huge proportions formed a focal point. The sound effects too were carefully controlled with martial music of proven emotive power. The 1938 Nuremberg rally lasted eight days and its cost was enormous. But as the rhythmic 'Sieg Heils' built up to the personal appearances of Goebbels and Hitler with their carefully studied ability to bring the crowd to hysteria, the total effect must have been so great that dissent was unimaginable. As Aldous Huxley put it 'if exposed long enough to the tom-toms and the singing every one of our philosophers would end by capering and howling like savages'. This was the 'downward transcendence by means of herd intoxication'. There were numerous variations on the theme from Hitler Youth rallies and parades of particular army units to ceremonial entries into fallen capitals like Vienna or Paris, Hindenburg's funeral, major anniversaries and so on, just as there were additional facets to be introduced such as historical pageants or aerial fly-pasts. The resource allocation to this type of propaganda was massive and the artistic thought that went into it from people like the architect and chief event manager Albert Speer (1905–81) was considerable, but the results probably more than justified the effort.

To some extent Hitler's vigorous use of sport as a propaganda medium was an extension of this form of event management and it also suited his racist message. Sporting prowess was regularly used thereafter by dictatorial regimes as a means of projecting their images.

Hitler also developed leaflet bombing, particularly in his 1939 campaign against the French army – the 'guerre de confettis' – when the symbolic autumn leaves were dropped with the metaphor spelt out: 'autumn leaves fall; so fall the Poitous who fight for the English'. This was backed up by megaphone voice-overs and posters carrying the words 'Why die for Danzig?' and similar messages. Hitler's ancillary media included a multiplicity of applications of his corporate identity, an activity in which he was unusually well disciplined. With the black swastika cleverly laid over a red socialist background he was able to achieve massive exposure of his image by coordinating its presentation on flags, uniforms, buildings, vehicles, aircraft, the props for rallies, postage stamps, posters. Then there were the subsidiary images: a whole range of imperial eagles, the brown shirts of the SA, the skull and crossbones of the Gestapo, jackboots, the goose-step, the 'Heil Hitler' all contributed to the visual projection of Nazism. To this could be added the contribution of the visual arts, the quasi-Nordic style of heroic painting, the idealized sculptures of heroes like the wretched Horst Wessel and the massive triumphal architectural projects of Speer, most of which never came to fruition. Painters like Heinrich Knirr produced idealized portraits of Hitler which were replicated in other media.

Music too played a significant part in the build-up of the Nazi mythology, just as it had done since the birth of German nationalism after Napoleon. The 'Horst Wessel Song', 'Deutschland, über alles', the Badenweiler march, 'Lili Marlene', the cult of Wagner, all played their part.

Hitler's understanding of participatory propaganda was acute. For his six plebiscites he encouraged a pro-active attitude, presented voting in favour as a national obligation, scattering the regions with massive 'Ja' posters and where necessary enforced participation in elections by exploiting the open ballot, punishing recalcitrants and then using the large favourable vote as proof of legitimacy. In the same way the annual enforced oath of unlimited loyalty to the Führer was used to endorse the motivation which had suggested it in the first place.

The combination of media frequently and repeatedly deployed by Hitler and his assistants had considerable power. Control was absolute and no aspect of life remained untouched. Even the education of the young, as in Soviet Russia, was geared to the party; the Hitler Youth founded by the anti-Semitic Streicher had its ritual ladder of promotion and regimented adulation of Fascist virtues. The use of short rhythmic and mnemonic phrases echoed the effectiveness of Hitler's own oratorical style based on years of practice in the massive beer halls of Munich. Phrases like Herrenvolk [master race], Lebensraum [usually translated as 'a place in the sun'], the emotive Einkreisung [encirclement], and the apocalyptic idea of Third Reich or Thousand-Year Reich, developed by Moeller van den Bruck in 1923, were all effective. So was

Hitler's well-honed psychological appeal to the basest instincts of the
population: their jealousy of Jewish wealth, their fear of unemployment,
their loss of pride in the First World War. The propaganda was all
underscored by the use of intimidation, the threat of the concentration
camp and by positive inducements such as promotion, medals and
money. This comprehensive motivational system could make the people
of a large and mature nation support violent tyranny for twelve years and
condone, in so far as they knew about it, the Jewish genocide. Hitler's
deep understanding of the latest available media had been crucial. As he
put it 'without the motor car, sound films and wireless there would be no
victory for the National Socialist Party'. David Welch has argued that
Hitler was preaching to the converted: he was, but much of the
conversion had been achieved by earlier German propaganda.

ITALY

In many respects Benito Mussolini (1883–1945) was as able a propagandist
as Hitler and in at least one respect better – as a writer. He had after all
been a professional journalist, editing the socialist *Avanti* in 1914 and
founding his own *Popolo d'Italia* in 1919. As he put it in his autobiography
this 'was the instrument for the making of me'. His style was highly
emotive, full of phrases like 'sacrifice on the altar of patriotism', 'matricide'
to describe lack of patriotism, 'jackals' or 'parasites' for rivals or 'a woman
of saintly courage . . . stood with blazing eyes against a herd of
Communists'. He had his brother Arnoldo, another journalist, and the
poet Filippo Marinetti (1875–1944), who described war as 'the world's only
hygiene', to help him. At the same time he set up his Fascidi
Combatimento, whose first rally he naturally advertized in *Popolo d'Italia*.
He deeply regretted the failure of Italy to win Dalmatia or overseas
colonies, vigorously supported by D'Annunzio whom he called il Duce, in
Fiume (see p. 267). He applied his same emotive style to public speaking,
having commented that his favourite book was Le Bon's *Psychology of the
Crowd* and by 1922 had 300,000 blackshirts for his March on Rome. This
was heralded by a short, evocative proclamation in *Popolo d'Italia* and as a
result of his network of journalists on other papers, received almost blanket
coverage in the Italian press. His son-in-law Galeazzo Ciano was head of his
press department and his brother editor of the *Popolo d'Italia*. His ability to
reincarnate ancient Roman or Italian nationalist images from the past, his
eventual vision of a new Roman Empire gave his propaganda a remarkably
solid base for some years until he was totally overshadowed by Hitler.
    Mussolini like so many tyrants needed overseas victories to offset
economic difficulties at home. He decided on the Muslim world as a soft
target and having first settled on a crusading image of attacking the Arabs
from both Rome and Addis Ababa, then switched to currying favour among
the Arab nations and undermining French influence in the Middle East.

Here he found radio the ideal medium and from Radio Bari, helped by the export of cheap Italian radio receivers many of which were used in restaurants, he began to put out programmes mixing Arab light music with small doses of propaganda; specifically he encouraged Palestinian, Tunisian and Egyptian nationalism, a campaign as irresponsible and potentially dangerous as the efforts of the Russians in the Balkans the previous century. The other potential soft target he identified was in coastal Yugoslavia where he exploited the ethnic divisions, projected Dalmatia as an area historically belonging to Italy, supported the Catholics against the Muslims in the greater Albanian area and generally weakened the Yugoslav nation.

Film was a natural medium to help project his warlike image as shown in *Il grido dell'aquilla* of 1923 with Mussolini portrayed as the new Garibaldi and *Lo Squadrone bianco* of 1936. Mussolini's son directed the production of a film by Rossellini in 1938 to glorify the conquest of Abyssinia (see pl. 7).

SPAIN

There was little originality in the propaganda of General Franco Bahamonde (1892–1975), former commander of the Spanish Foreign Legion in Morocco, who seized power in Spain in 1936 following the model of Mussolini and Hitler. The concept of Falange Española – the Spanish Fascist Party – had been launched three years earlier by Primo de Rivera with his own paper *El Fascio*, and later the FE (Falange Española). The Falangist blueshirts were modelled on the SA and the movement had its own artistic style reflected in every medium, including its own film company, Patria Films founded in Morocco in 1936. Franco positioned himself as the defender of the church and traditional values against Communism. He posed beside pictures of Columbus and other quasi-Spanish heroes. With his propaganda assistant Antonio Bahamonde, Franco encouraged numerous variants on the Viva España theme, for example the ritual of shouting it three times with the crowd response 'Una, grande, libre'. His other propaganda aides were the one-eyed general José Millan Astray, who specialized in terror, Vincente Cadenas, with his new paper *Arriba España*, and his foreign press controller Luis Bolin, whose most significant achievement was the long suppression of the scandal of Guernica. While Franco posed as the new El Cid, hero of the latest Reconquista, defeater of the heretics, the reality of an exceptionally brutal civil war was all too evident.

RUSSIA

Joseph Stalin, born Dzhugashvili (1879–1953), was of the same generation as both Hitler and Mussolini, but the propaganda required to bring him to power was quite different. His problem was not to create a revolution or a coup, but to step into the shoes of a predecessor who had done both and whose image totally overshadowed all else. When Lenin died in 1924 still quite young, there was no obvious successor. The internal battle for power thereafter reveals Stalin's clever understanding of tactical publicity, particularly in his outmanoeuvring of his rival Trotsky.

Stalin was not inexperienced in media control. As early as 1901 he had written for the Georgian nationalist paper *Brdzola*, later ran the *Kavkasky Robochy Listok* in Tiflis and after transferring to Petrograd in 1907 he was co-editor on *Gudok* and *Bakinski Proletarii*. Stalin in 1923/4 projected himself as the self-effacing disciple of Lenin, delivering the prestigious Sverdlov lectures at Moscow to defend Leninist thinking and launching his own new paper *The Bolshevik* for the same purpose. Meanwhile, between February and May 1924 he began a massive recruitment campaign for new young party members and raised membership from 120,000 to 320,000, building himself a personal franchise. One of his major difficulties was Lenin's wife Krupskaya who was circulating *Lenin's Testament* which contained warnings of Stalin's unstable character. Despite this, in Lenin's final months Stalin encouraged hero-worship of the dying man, while Trotsky fell into the trap of criticizing Lenin and making himself out to be superior in *The Lessons of October*. Stalin presented a humbler profile, admitting 'I shared the mistaken position of other comrades' and followed up with a detailed attack on Trotsky to which the latter failed to respond. Stalin was also setting his Moscow power base against the Leningrad group led by Zinoviev, setting the *Moscow Pravda*, with his friend Molotov as editor, against the *Leningrad Pravda* which was still beyond his control. Molotov helped him organize a substantial leaflet drop to 63,000 homes in Leningrad.

While Krupskaya spent her time leaking *Lenin's Testament* to the foreign press, Stalin launched his new strategy of 'Socialism in one country' which appealed to xenophobic nationalism more than did the grandiose world revolution advocated by Trotsky. Stalin published his theme in *Questions of Leninism*, presenting it as adhering to traditional Leninism with all the psychological appeal of faith in Russian character and independence from outside help. Having thus developed his image he set about the final stages of getting rid of his rivals. In 1927 he was strong enough to order the OGPU to seize the pamphlet printing presses of Trotsky and Zinoviev. The following year Trotsky was exiled to Central Asia.

After Stalin's fiftieth birthday there was a shift to a more confident tone in his image projection: massive portraits and statues of him began to appear throughout Russia and the new slogan became 'Stalin is the Lenin of today' or 'Stalin, man of steel', a concept pushed by Lev Mekhlis. Nikolai Bukharin (1888–1938) edited *Pravda* from 1917 to 1928 and *Izvestia* from 1934 to 1937 as written propaganda sank to the level of dull mediocrity. Tribal bards like the Cossack Djabayev and the Caucasian Stalsky were brought in to compose pseudo-epics for Stalin. Radek became his propaganda organizer from 1936 and once Trotsky was expelled from Russian soil Stalin had no rivals. Among his aids was Willi Munzenberg who had remarkable success in spreading fashionable Communism among Western intellectuals and spawning respectable pro-Stalinist literature throughout Europe in the early 1930s.

Once he had disposed of the Trotskyists, Stalin's next propaganda move was the discrediting of the small peasant landowners who had gained from the Revolution but were now regarded as obstacles to further progress. To them was now applied the term 'kulak' which meant a dishonest trader, as Alexander Solzhenitsyn pointed out, and a new word appeared 'podkulachnik' which suggested an even greater contempt. The peasants were blackened as bourgeois small capitalists who must be eliminated to allow the proper collectivization of agriculture. Show trials, public confessions and intimidation were added to the huge media onslaught against the kulaks leading up to their mass eviction, deportation or starvation into submission. Thereafter there had to be the bland promotion of the collective farm, with artists like Aleksandr Gerasimov reduced to painting his *State Stockbreeding Farm*, the kolchoz, with its idealization of tractor output and grain yields.

In the same way much Stalinist propaganda was devoted to the work ethic of industrial productivity, with the packaging of five-year plans and factory targets. Most notable was the image of the eponymous Aleksei Stakhanov, the prize-winning miner who fronted the work ethic public relations campaign of 1935. Numerous films were produced to turn this role model activity into semi-palatable entertainment and acceptable motivation.

Cinema generally was still a major area for Russian propaganda effort. Vertov produced his *Stride Soviet* for the factory work ethic in 1926 and his *Symphony of the Don Basin* for the miners in 1930, then his *Three Songs of Lenin* in 1934. Sergei Eisenstein was the other great cinematic propaganda innovator with his *Battleship Potemkin* in 1925 and *October* in 1928 emphasizing the roles of Lenin and Stalin in the Revolution. The governmental cinema organization changed its name from Goskino to Sovkino in 1924, reflecting its increasing commitment to the leadership and a number of films like *Peter the First* began to home in on the personality cult of Stalin. M.N. Ryatin, a key propaganda organizer who later turned against Stalin was put in charge of the film industry in 1930.

Meanwhile, Stalin also concentrated on the indoctrination of the young, in the same way as Hitler. The Komsomol was given its own youth version of *Pravda* plus a range of ceremonials and motivations.* At the

---

* Stalin orchestrated mass adulation of himself starting with young children reciting his praises each morning.

same time there was a massive output of new children's literature for the new era and replacement textbooks with a Stalinist interpretation of most subjects. Sholokov was considered the acceptable writer while more talented figures like Pasternak were out of favour for straying from the party line. In music there was Shostakovich (1906–75) who initially supported the regime with his First Symphony of 1925 and Khachaturian (1903–78) contributed with *Spartacus*. Mass-produced statues of Lenin and Stalin spread in public places, Sergei Merkurov's *Stalin* was particularly powerful – architecture was massive, sometimes practical like the Dniepropetrovsk dam, sometimes ostentatious like the Moscow underground completed at such cost by Khrushchev. Personified or abstract monuments to the Soviet virtues abounded. Evgeni Vuchetich was the sculptor of numerous Victory monuments from Berlin eastwards, as well as the massive *Motherland* at Volgagrad, and created many apotheoses of Stalin, while Pavel Kovin designed the mosaic propaganda murals for the amazing Moscow underground, Mukhira the idealized image of collective agriculture and Yakovlev an equestrian statue of Marshal Zhukov recalling that of Peter the Great himself.

The Second World War saw the penultimate period of Stalinist propaganda, He proved himself an able motivator of his people during the early setbacks, performing himself on radio from 1941, appointing A.A. Zhdanov as his new head of propaganda (1939–48) and resorting to the old values of patriotism with slogans like 'vsyo dlya pobedy' [all for victory], changing the national anthem from the 'Internationale' to a new warlike tune by the commander of the Red Army choir and encouraging a big expansion of nationalistic war films. The Guards and the Cossack regiments were revived, as was saluting and the officers' mess, while Stalin assumed the rank of marshal. Sergei Gerasimov's war paintings such as *The Rout of the Germans at Kosrun Shevchenkovski* could be compared to the propaganda quality of Goya's *Horrors of War* or Picasso's *Guernica*. Painter Mikhail Khmelko produced *Triumph of the Fatherland* and *Khrushchev in the Trenches* later recycled as *Brezhnev in the Trenches* with the face replaced.

The final period of Stalin's propaganda effort was that of the expanded Soviet empire and confrontation with the West. The Cominform was founded in 1947 to cope with this task and survived until the discrediting of Soviet propaganda caused by crushing of the revolts of Hungary and the rest in 1956. It was responsible for the massive campaign of vilification against Tito's Yugoslav brand of Communism after 1948 and the huge support of radio and other campaigns throughout the rest of the world. If it had a weakness it was its doctrinaire inflexibility which perhaps explains its failure to clinch majorities in many poor and poorly run nations which should theoretically have been ripe for the reception of Communism. By 1951 Russian propaganda was veering back to the tsarist line with Peter the Great and Catherine revived as heroes, Russian inventors discovered for every possible invention, a xenophobic, anti-

Western, anti-Semitic strain coupled with ever less meaningful assertions of Leninist dogma. Stalin took titles like Generalissimo, Father of the People and Shining Son of Humanity while *Pravda* was packed with adulatory letters. The Orders of Suvorov and Kutuzov (medals) were revived. But intimidation on a massive scale remained the prime feature of Stalin's image-broking within Russia.

JAPAN

Since the Meiji revival of Bushido at the end of the nineteenth century Japan had continued to develop its own special form of nationalism. Kita Ikki's (1893–1937) *Outline Plan for the Reconstruction of Japan* had been the main textbook for the right but in 1931 there began a further lurch into xenophobia as the Japanese feared attack in Manchuria from post-revolutionary Russia and revived China. The rebellious Japanese officers of Kwantung took the law into their own hands in the attack on Mukden in 1931, but issued a prior communiqué blaming China. Their aggressive actions received a more favourable press than the efforts at peacemaking by the 'cowardly' Shidehara. The situation took a turn for the worse when Japan was expelled from the League of Nations in 1933 for its intransigence in Manchuria, and from this point onwards until 1945 the military ethos increasingly took over the Japanese mind. It achieved this not so much through public media as by the heavy indoctrination of school children and young territorial conscripts. *Kokutai no Hongi* (Principles of National Policy) became the standard primer which was successfully used to persuade all young Japanese that they should put nation ahead of self. The same theme was used in the Greater Japan Youth Association, founded in 1915. In addition by 1935 there were 11 million reserve soldiers who had passed through the army indoctrination camps. Between 1936 and 1939 Japanese newspapers were either closed down or had to toe the hysterical expansionist line, upholding the 'righteous imperial army' against the 'atrocious Chinese bandits'. Victories were grossly exaggerated and defeats censored out. The image of the holy war in China, of 'revere the Emperor and expel the barbarian', the notion of achieving a 'new order in Asia' by superior commitment and will-power were just steps towards the sado-masochistic war ethic of 1942 to 1945. The need for more space to offset the overpopulated homeland provided a useful excuse, as it had in Germany. The fact that the vast bulk of Japanese professional politicians opposed the war was irrelevant. School textbooks were rewritten so that the young could be educated to their heroic destiny from an early age.

The propagandist writers fomenting rabid nationalism in the lead-up to Pearl Harbor included Okawa Shumei (1886–1957), Matsuoka Yosuke (1880–1946) and Colonel Hashimoto Kingoro (1890–1957). Their language was reminiscent of Hitler's Germany with even more use of metaphor. For example, the statements of Sakurakai, the Cherry Blossom Society, one of a number of militant groups, were laced with phrases like: 'sacred light', 'poisonous sword', 'torrent of corruption', 'wash out the bowels of the decadent politicians' and 'divine soldiers'.

Japan's favourite military song 'Umi Yukaba' used lyrics written in the eighth century. At the same time the state encouraged a revival of Shintoism which it associated with the imperial way, whereas jazz, Hollywood and all things Western were discouraged. Intellectuals were forced to make public confessions of their changes of mind (tenko) and Makiguchi Tsunesaburo (1871–1944) who had led the revival of Buddhism, Soka Gakkai, was interned in a prison camp. The generations of indoctrination in middle-class Bushido were enough to create one of the most paranoically overmotivated populations in modern history. As Bruton put it: 'The official brainwashing which had been directed at the Japanese people for more than a decade had by now taken effect upon the leaders as well.'

Once Japan was committed to war the cinema became a prime propaganda medium as it did in other countries. Military epics like *Chocolate and Soldiers* (1938) and *The Story of Tank Commander Nishizumi* (1942) projected the image of the ideal Japanese soldier. Kamikaze [Divine Wind] of 1944 drew the comparison with the Mongol Hordes and Kurosawa's *The Most Beautiful* (1944) promoted the new virtue of Yase Gaman [emaciated endurance] idealizing the spiritual value of suffering as the consequences of the war bit deep.

The Japanese propaganda managers produced massive numbers of slogans for national solidarity. Variations in the *ichioku* [100 million] were popular: 100 million as a flaming jewel, 100 million as one family, 100 million as a shattered jewel. In 1944/5 the message veered towards collective self-sacrifice and fighting to the end with the martyrdom of the kamikaze airmen as the prime example. Ironically the government war propaganda department known as Domei later transmogrified itself into Dentsu the largest commercial advertising agency in the world and a significant aid to the postwar Japanese economic imperialism.

SOUTH AMERICA

A number of regimes in the West Indies and South America showed propaganda techniques which imitated the style of Mussolini and Franco. Rafael Trujillo took over Dominica in 1930 and used heavy intimidation and media control to maintain his dynasty in power for over thirty years. Getulio Vargas (1883–1954) achieved similar control over Brazil, making heavy use of radio 'fireside chats' and government newsreels at the cinema. Another brilliant propagandist of the war period was Eva Duarte Peròn (1919–1952) who masterminded the rise of her husband Juan to the presidency of Argentina. Evita, as she was known, first developed her career as a radio presenter on Radio Belgrano in 1939 and by the time of the military coup of 1943 she was doing a fifteen-minute weekly propaganda piece with a strong listenership. She had the warmth of personality and good sense to organize a well-planned appeal to the less well-off Argentinian workers, *los doscamisados* [the shirtless], which enabled her somewhat less imaginative husband to leapfrog to the top of the military hierarchy within three years, while she herself achieved real reforms in welfare and women's suffrage. She continued to make very effective use of radio, bought and ran three major newspapers, used massive poster campaigns which exploited her own charismatic appearance, and extended her husband's image with good event management of the various anniversary celebrations in Buenos Aires. Overall, by the time of her early death from leukaemia she had achieved one of the most remarkably penetrating personal images of any twentieth-century figure, albeit this was soon eroded by the later exposure of her private extravagances.

In the long history of propaganda this period of Fascist dictatorships was probably the most damaging in almost every respect. Mass deception and emotive blackmail were used on a huge scale and for the first time in conjunction with the novelty value of new media, radio and the 'talkies'.

Democratic Propaganda

BRITAIN

Britain in the 1920s and '30s showed no particular sense of direction in the deployment of propaganda skills and this was a common feature of most parliamentary democracies. Radio and cinema were both developed during this period and the power of the more successful newspaper groups continued to grow but utilization was fragmented. Andrew Bonar Law (1858–1923) during his brief premiership was notable for the partisan use of film; he used the newsreel company Topical Budget to put across the pro-Tory line in cinemas. In 1921 it had brought out *Farcical Revolution*, a film attacking the Labour Party's handling of the Poplar rates problem.

Stanley Baldwin (1867–1947) became Prime Minister for the first time in 1923. Beaverbrook, who had had a taste of power as Minister of Information under Lloyd George, offered to help Baldwin in return for political access and his newspapers put across a very imperialist message. Northcliffe's brother Harold Harmsworth (1878–1940) still wanted a peerage but fairly consistently attacked Baldwin, as did Grant Morden who supported the right-wing Birkenhead. The *Morning Post* and *Yorkshire Post* were totally behind Baldwin, *The Times* and the *Telegraph* marginally less so. The image of both opposition parties, Labour and Liberal, was certainly damaged by the publication of the Zinoviev letter, a forgery probably developed for propaganda purposes by White Russian exiles, which portrayed British left-wingers as Communist sympathizers and was published by the *Daily Mail* a week before the 1924 election, causing great damage to the Labour Party. Baldwin did have the capacity to create for himself a satisfactory photographic persona, the dependable pipe-smoking image which fitted the media of his day. He was also the first British prime minister to adapt his style to the new medium of radio and one of the first Tory leaders to drape election platforms with Union flags so that the party's patriotic image would be endorsed – he was re-elected in 1929 on a slogan of 'Safety First'. When challenged by the combined might of Beaverbrook, Rothermere and the Empire Free Trade crusade between 1929 and 1931 he made his remarkable appeal over their heads in a speech ghosted by Rudyard Kipling which attacked the idea of 'power without responsibility, the prerogative of the harlot throughout the ages'. It was successful and Beaverbrook backed down.

Neville Chamberlain (1869–1940) resorted to a number of propaganda techniques to damp down concern about German aggression from 1937 to 1939. George Steward had been made the chief Downing Street press officer by Ramsay MacDonald in 1929 to assist him against the serried ranks of the Tory press barons. Steward now joined in the effort to dissuade the British press from undermining the peace process, arguing among other things that bad news had been contributing to falling circulations and lower advertising revenues. The *News Chronicle*, owned by the pacifist Cadbury, needed no urging; the *Daily Herald* and *John Bull*, owned by Southwood, followed suit and even Beaverbrook was at this time dedicated to Hoare. The *Yorkshire Post* was almost unique in its attacks on appeasement. At the same time Sir Joseph Bell, a former intelligence chief who had controlled public relations for the Tory Party in the 1935 election, was running the National Publicity Bureau for Chamberlain with the objective of putting across the ideals of the National government. It had its own magazine *Truth* and contributed to the general playing down of war worries which suited Chamberlain's negotiations but has been seen in hindsight as misplaced.

Winston Churchill (1874–1965) overcame an image of failure and unpopular measures by persistent, truculent chauvinism which in due course came to suit the mood of the country. Like so many potential leaders he had spent time as a journalist – during the Boer War, as editor of the *British Gazette* during the 1926 strike and then as a well-paid freelance for his friends in the press such as Bracken and sometimes Beaverbrook. His fortnightly pieces for the *London Evening Standard* were widely syndicated and his weekly column in the *News of the World* had a substantial readership.

The general revival of the imperialist image in the 1930s had been helped by the foundation of the Imperial Institute, John Grierson's Empire Marketing Programme, the return to fashion of patriotic films like *Cavalcade* in 1933 and the Korda/Balcon productions of imperial classics like Haggard's *She* and *The Four Feathers* again. George V's 1924 Christmas broadcast to the empire was written by Rudyard Kipling. It was the *Daily Telegraph* which took the lead in calling for Churchill's return to office in 1939.

Once in power Churchill, like Baldwin, had a good photographic persona in his old age, including the love of hats and cigars which made him the perfect press photocall and eventually the 'V' sign borrowed from the Belgians. Both as a highly effective live orator and a brilliant user of radio, he was an all-round accomplished public communicator so long as his country was in military mode. Some of his verbal images achieved instant immortality: his 'boneless wonder' for Ramsay MacDonald, his 'some chicken, some neck', 'the soft underbelly of Europe' and his 'Iron Curtain'. His sentences also had a rhythmic resonance both when spoken and on the page.

British propaganda during the Second World War showed both the strengths and weaknesses of more sophisticated use of techniques. The Ministry of Information reappeared with a heavy requirement to sustain

domestic morale against protracted bombing. John Reith, former first
general manager of the British Broadcasting Corporation, served briefly
as minister but was regarded as too weak, as were various contributors
whose public school background made it hard for them to communicate
at street level and who lacked the emotive imagination to combat the
near hysteria which hit towns like Coventry. Similarly the Empire Crusade
of 1940 was ineffective – research showed that only half the population
noticed it and only one in twenty remembered it. Mass Observation had
been founded in 1937 to monitor attitudes, so at least the government
was made conscious of its failure. The massive poster campaign 'Freedom
is in peril – we're going to see it through' was put up on more than
50,000 sites on the railways and other government buildings. Lord
Bracken (1901–58), Churchill's friendly press baron took over the
ministry with a more open and positive attitude to press relations while
Stephen Tallent who had organized the publicity for the Empire
Marketing Board also contributed. The author J.B. Priestley proved to be
one of the few effective radio broadcasters with genuine emotive power
other than Churchill himself, and Herbert Morrison brought an earthier
touch to the chauvinist sloganizing with his 'go for it' campaign. By 1940
the overall public relations output was enormous with over 700 press
releases and photographs generated every week. There were frequent
leaflet drops like *Make your home safe* which went out to 7 million homes
and *If the Invader Comes*, written by the rather too up-market team of
Kenneth Clark and Harold Nicholson. Poster campaigns were legion,
many of them quite futile like the 'Mightier Yet' battleship poster which
lost all credibility when the *Prince of Wales* was sunk. There were the
alliterative slogans like 'Careless Talk Costs Lives' and 'Faith in the Fight'
or repetitive half-rhymes like 'Dig for Victory'.

UNITED STATES

In the United States Franklin Roosevelt (1884–1945) did not found his
career on original propaganda ideas but stands out as one of
propaganda's great packagers. As Governor of New York State he was a
very bland campaigner, borrowing slogans like 'bread not booze' from
the Temperance movement. He had the financial resources to hire huge
letter-writing teams to give every opinion-influencer the feeling of
personal attention. His 'New Deal', borrowed from Mark Twain, and his
uncle's 'Fair Deal' came in his acceptance speech at the democratic
convention in Chicago in 1932. Soon afterwards he borrowed Napoleon's
'Hundred Days'. His 'Looking Forward', his 'Lend Lease', and his
postwar 'Four Freedoms' were all simple concepts, neatly put together
and then well delivered. Like Churchill and Stalin he was an excellent
broadcaster and achieved particular success with his 'fireside chats' which
evolved from his earlier use of radio as a state governor who had to buy

time on regional radio for a monthly broadcast, as the local press was dominated by the Republicans. He was also a prolific user of the whistle-stop train technique of electioneering and he was the first presidential candidate to use the aeroplane. Starting his presidency with very little support from the press he set about winning them over as much as possible by well-organized press conferences in which he went to great pains to explain the detail of his policies. His secretary Stephen Early was extremely able at handling press relations and he was also helped by the fact that his wife Eleanor was an excellent communicator in her own right who ran press conferences for women correspondents and wrote a regular column herself.

In general the Second World War was a period of technical rather than strategic innovation in terms of propaganda history. Radio became of major significance as the medium able to cross frontiers and achieve high penetration of neutral or enemy territory. Not only was the power of transmitters increased to give longer ranges but there was now work done to enhance radio's credibility as an invading medium with the use of more subtle stories, authentic background material and the selection of voices which were acceptable in the reception area concerned. The BBC, for example, conducted some remarkably effective campaigns in the Indian subcontinent, where the loyalty of the people, given their wish for freedom from colonial rule, was achieved to a surprising extent. With rather less subtlety but very great resources Robert E. Sherwood launched The Voice of America radio network in 1941, which was for two decades to be the major medium for projecting the American point of view in all parts of the world, eventually in straightforward competition with Radio Moscow when Berlin and Tokyo ceased to be the enemy.

The other cross-frontier medium which reached full maturity at this time was leaflet bombing, a much more extravagant and wasteful form of propaganda but one which could be very effective. Percy Winner, who became field propaganda aide to General Eisenhower, organized the dropping of 30 million leaflets over North Africa and France before the Allied landings. In 1942 the Office of War Information (OWI) produced a tabloid newspaper *L'Amerique en guerre* and was dropping 7 million copies a week on France by 1944, with similar projects in Norway, Spain, Holland and in due course Germany itself with the *Sternebanner*. More devious extensions of this idea, such as the dropping of safe conduct passes for surrendering German soldiers, helped offset the efforts of Goebbels: he had encouraged the deliberate misinterpretation of the concept of unconditional surrender in Germany, so that it was perceived as the route to total slavery, thus encouraging more troops to fight to the last. Similarly the OWI had organized an effective surrender campaign for the Italian army and later a useful leak on surrender talks with Japan in July 1945. In total by 1945 the OWI had a staff of 130,000 and a budget of $110 million per year.

Elsewhere President Roosevelt recognized the importance of propaganda generally in a number of neutral areas: he appointed Nelson

Rockefeller to organize a campaign to counteract the effects of Nazi propaganda in South America. The poet Archibald MacLeish (1892–1986) had been brought in to run the Office of Facts and Figures in 1941. Gradually the United States acknowledged a greatly increased need to project what it perceived as the rightness of its stance and superiority of its way of life in every part of the world.

SOUTH AFRICA

One of the least savoury aspects of propaganda in a supposedly democratic state was the range of racist themes developed after the late 1930s by the Afrikaners in South Africa. The ethnic jealousy of the National Party and its racist wing Ossewa Brandwag was greatly stimulated by the centenary re-enactment of the Great Trek in 1938; the event management of this impressive display, the decorated wagons, the monument put up at Blood River, the singing of 'Die Sten van Suid Afrika' [The Journey of South Africa], all helped develop a new mythology of Boer heroics which was turned into a philosophy by Dr Geoff Cronje, author of *Afrika in Apartheid* (1943). This book was publicized and used by the party leader Daniel Malan (1874–1959) who since 1915 had been editor of the Nationalist newspaper *Die Burger*. Malan, a long-term fomenter of a deeply prejudiced, scaremongering policy based on the perceived 'Black Peril – swaart gevaar' sought to win power in the 1948 election so that he could implement the apartheid legislation. His policies were projected in the extreme right-wing *Die Kruithoring* and in the election he resorted to slogans like 'A vote for Smuts is a vote for Stalin'. Thus one of the world's more long-term and pernicious regimes achieved a power which it was to use to impose forty years of racial tyranny.

Decolonization and the Cold War

The history of propaganda in the late 1940s belongs to two uniquely talented propagandists, who had both been building up their images during the previous three decades but now each achieved their major breakthrough, Mahatma Gandhi and Mao Zedong.

INDIA

Mohandas Karamchand Gandhi (1869–1948) abandoned a successful legal practice in Bombay to devote twenty-one years to supporting the Indian population of South Africa against discrimination. During this period he developed many of the communication techniques which were to enable him to dominate when he returned to India. Certainly he paid attention to the development of press, founding his *Indian Opinion* in South Africa in 1902 and later the weekly *Harijan*, which became the organ of his South African Harijan Serah Sangh, the organization to uphold the rights of the untouchables, but he also clearly understood the need for specially vivid messages to penetrate large semi-literate or illiterate masses. His influential pamphlet *Hind Swaraj* (Indian Independence) drew on traditional Indian folklore for its authenticity, his vivid use of simile – 'Satya graha is like a banyan tree with innumerable branches' – owed much to Jain and Buddhist models, yet he was as much at home with occidental catchphrases as when he referred to the Cripps proposal in 1942 for a constituent assembly as 'a post-dated cheque on a crashing bank'. Above all, however, his image making was physical – his simple monkish clothing and bare feet, his visible preference for old-fashioned tools rather than modern machines, his well-thought-out symbolic acts like the emptying of chamber pots for untouchables at Phoenix Farm, which led to a fall-out with his wife. His equally dramatic march of 200 miles to collect salt in 1930 was clever defiance of a government exploiting a commodity, a technique similar to the Boston Tea Party. Above all his development of the Jain concept of passive resistance and his unflinching public application of it ensured substantial publicity and huge moral authority even when his political skills were suspect. Most effective of all were his well-publicized fasts intended to be to the death, acts of deliberate self-martyrdom which could outmanoeuvre much more powerful opponents and won him superhuman status. Mahatma, the Great Soul, in the epic fasts of Yeravada gaol and in 1944 in the Muslim slums of Calcutta had a power reminiscent of that achieved by Christ through his acts of sacrifice. As he wrote himself in his *The Story of my Experiment with Truth*: 'Truth embodied in the living example is far more potent than tons of propaganda based on falsehood. . . . Truth is self-propagating.' His concept of the living example was in fact an outstandingly successful deployment of propaganda technique which gave him a unique influence over both Hindus and Muslims which no subsequent Indian politician was able to emulate.

CHINA AND NORTH KOREA

Like Gandhi, Mao Zedong (1893–1976) had to overcome a relatively weak media system in a large country with a low level of literacy. Admittedly China had a rich tradition of contribution to media development – the inventions of both paper and printing – but its vast peasant population, during the 1920s to '50s, presented the would-be political propagandist with immense problems.

Mao and many of his colleagues had had the benefit of some Russian training in propaganda techniques when Communism first looked East in 1919, but he contributed a special panache, sense of imagery and feeling for the communication needs of a large population which owed nothing to the Russian example. As early as 1919 he became editor of the *Hsiang Kiang Review* and was an addicted writer for the rest of his career. Early on he understood like Gandhi the need for images which could transcend media weakness. In 1927 he wrote an article on peasant associations in Hunan which used a mixture of slogans, pictures and group activity to attack exploiting landlords. Mao and the others developed techniques of local public interrogation, demonstrations, dressing bullies in paper hats and petty bourgeois in tails which could be cut off, a formula of intimidating rituals which could be replicated in one village after another as Communism was made to spread. Then he added to the heroic quality of his own image with the Great March of 1934, giving it larger than life stature. The crossing of the Liutung bridge over the raging Taku River in 1935 was to provide one of the classic visual images of Communist determination, recorded in the heroic-style paintings of Li Tsing Tsin. Significantly it was to be the re-enactment of the Great March at the time of the Cultural Revolution over thirty years later, plus Mao's pseudo-heroic swim down the Yangtze, which were to revive his fading career when he had lost the initiative in the 1960s.

Meanwhile, Mao worked on the development of his 'mass line' conversion campaigns which extended the effectiveness of print matter by encouraging communal reading, wall-posting and literacy classes. He announced: 'Our people are poor and blank but the most beautiful poem can be written on a blank sheet of paper.' To some extent at least it was a two-way process and in 1925 an official wrote 'In our propaganda we must know and examine the opinion of the masses which is necessary in guiding them'. This slow process of building up membership in the face of heavy odds was inadvertently supported by the Japanese invasion which forced Chiang Kai Chek's regime to reward Mao's help with greater media freedom. The New China News Agency founded in 1937 produced material which won the Chinese Communists some international support and in 1938 Mao's help against Japan was so significant that Chiang Kai Chek could not prevent the major Communist paper *New China Daily* from being circulated in Nationalist areas. The relative success of Mao's troops against Japan compared with the Kuomintang laid the foundation of the Communists' political victory in 1949, as did the increasingly obvious corruption of the Kuomintang ministries. Mao's propaganda remained infinitely more competent than Chiang's and he was helped by some gifted practitioners. Teng To, for instance, the poet and satirist, was editor of the influential *Peking People's Daily*, organ of the Central Committee and supported Mao strongly from 1938 to 1949 though he was later to attack Mao's policy of overseas aggression.

Once Mao had achieved power in 1949 the objectives of his propaganda changed; as he put it 'the Chinese people, one quarter of the human race, have now stood up'. The avoidance of counter-revolution due to his poor economic performance, the stirring up of hatred against the Americans to justify his foreign policy and the stimulation of a new work ethic were now what mattered. In 1949 Mao supporter Lo Jui Ch'ing launched 'the campaign for the suppression of anti-revolutionaries with fanfare' aimed at five targets: bribery, tax evasion, cheating, theft and spying. This was to be the kind of neat packaging, a specific target and an imaginative title, which were to become characteristic of Maoist China. In 1951 a new association was set up with 1,550,000 propaganda workers organizing groups for the production of wall newspapers, communal readings and poster sticking; this was mainly directed towards anti-American feeling as Mao undertook expansion into Korea and Indo-China. In Shantung by 1952 there were 450,000 propagandist newspaper reading groups, which together with the wall newspapers greatly increased message penetration. The replacement of classical Chinese by the vernacular in a simplified alphabet helped the process. The importance of radio was also recognized and in 1956, since there were only about 1.5 million sets for a population of 600 million, loudspeakers were organized for collective listening in factories, dormitories and other public buildings. Similarly with the very small number of proper cinemas, great attention was given to the build-up of mobile film projector units so that during the 1950s film attendance rose from 50 million to 1.39 billion, the most widely shown film being *Resist America, Aid Korea.*

In 1957 came the imaginative Hundred Flowers Campaign – 'let a hundred flowers blossom, a hundred schools of thought' – though in fact it was only a series of minor variations on one school of thought, the

moulding of Chinese mass personality to industrial survival and renewed
war effort orchestrated by propaganda chief Lu Dingyi. Armies of
students were employed to put up vast numbers of posters, often
handwritten, the Tatzepao; the shipyard workers put up over 500,000
posters in seven days. The following year came the 'Great Leap Forward',
a campaign to project the new economic expansion and technological
revolution. In this period Peng Chen was controlling propaganda for
Mao with the help of Chow Yang, editor of the *Literary Gazette*. They
organized the output of popular parables based on the themes of good
peasants against bad landlords. Typical was 'Support for the three red
banners: party line, Great People's Communes and the 'Great Leap
Forward.' To film was added the encouragement of live theatre; during
the 1950s the number of actors increased from around 50,000 to around
five times that number as professional street theatre was encouraged to
reinforce the messages of press, radio and cinema. Living news playlets
like *Truman dreams of Hitler* were supplied by authors like Liu Chang Lee.
Writers such as Lu Hsun were employed to produce little parables to
illustrate specific points such as the conscientiousness of the People's
Liberation Army 'uncles' in replacing broken water jars for reluctant old
peasants. Overall, as Mao put it at this time 'art is neither more nor less
than a major weapon in the revolutionary class struggle'.

As the economic benefits of the Great Leap Forward were slow to
materialize so Mao's career in the early 1960s went into a period of
eclipse. The three main Maoist papers, *Red Flag*, *People's Daily* and
Liberation Army, vied with those controlled by the Peking Committee, the
Peking Daily, *Peking Evening News* and *Front Line*; Mao appeared to be
sidelined. From this stalemate Mao started stirring up communal
paranoia by encouraging complaints about the play *Hai Rui Dismissed from
Office*, which he could suggest was a capitalist attack on himself in 1961.
This was allowed to build up slowly to a pitch of youthful hysteria as the
new generation were encouraged to find fault with their parents. This
turned in 1966 into his propagandist *tour de force*, the Cultural Revolution,
with himself playing the leading role as he sought to regain the initiative.
After a six-month media silence he orchestrated his most spectacular
stunt, his famous Yangtze swim of 9 miles in 75 minutes at the age of
seventy-three, followed by 5,000 other swimmers pulling rafts decorated
with red Mao slogans such as 'Follow Chairman Mao in the teeth of the
waves'. It not only demonstrated his continued physical vigour, but his
almost superhuman charisma. It was followed by the re-enactment of the
Long March and a string of goodwill tours.

Having appealed to the masses of disaffected young over the heads of
his colleagues Mao mobilized them into the new Red Guard which was to
become the infrastructure of his assault on the middle classes, his route
to resumption of supreme power from the Central Committee. It was a
time for mass hysteria based on idolization of the magical old swimmer
and a cacophony of simplistic new red images. Red plastic copies of the

Chairman's thoughts were issued in vast numbers with a campaign to 'sweep away all monsters'. In a typical piece of Maoist packaging it was a campaign 'to eliminate the four olds: old habits, old ideas, old customs, old culture'. It was anti-middle class and anti-middle age, so it could embrace all the hysteria of a popular youth culture, fired by a series of well-written popular songs: 'The East is Red', 'Sailing the Seas we depend on the Helmsman' and 'Battle Song of the Red Guards'. Massive crowds were collected to chant 'Mao Zedong' in unison and 'Mao is the red, red sun in our hearts'. Huge red banners and portraits dominated the scene. Intellectuals and bureaucrats were humiliated in public to create a hysterical mob atmosphere of rhythmic chanting, victimization and violence towards the perceived enemy. Symbolic acts of violence, such as the burning of galleries or the public humbling of university professors and bank managers, and the orgy of public confessions were all part of the controlled process of discrediting Mao's colleagues such as Liu Shao Chi and Deng Xiaoping who had veered towards a marginally more capitalist policy than suited Mao. The shuffling of the order in the Politburo was now reflected in the priorities of the new mega-posters in Tiananmen Square. Mao had won back his supremacy. The Red Guard was successfully demobilized before it got totally out of control and in 1968 its duties passed over to the more reliable new Workers' Propaganda Teams, party workers trained as 'a transmission belt between party and population', reading aloud Mao's thoughts to still illiterate villagers.

In the visual arts for some years Mao rejected the great Chinese tradition of painting, which he thought of as reactionary, and he favoured slavish imitation of Soviet propaganda art. A typical example was the painting *The East Grows Crimson* by Li Chang Ching which was modelled on Feodor Shurpin's *Morning of our Fatherland*, with Mao in the centre instead of Stalin. This trend lasted until the late 1950s when there was a return to the *go hua* style of Chinese painting, though Soviet realism still dominated the major mural sites of Peking.

Given the huge obstacles which he faced, Mao's overall performance as a propagandist was substantial. He created for his own reasons a huge lift in literacy and newspaper penetration, but had even pre-empted it with his organization of public readings. He orchestrated a huge deployment of radio, mobile cinema and live theatre to project his image. The musical *The White-Haired Girl* achieved great popularity projecting the Maoist theme. He also harnessed popular music most effectively and created a highly visible corporate identity with his own face and the vast multiplicity of red ephemera. He cultivated a most vivid use of metaphor, perhaps particularly suited to the Chinese, and a succession of memorable idea packages. Like Hitler he had successfully moved the hatred of the people from one figure to another – landlords, nationalists, Japanese, Americans, capitalists, petty bourgeois intellectuals; for each period he was able to pick a popular scapegoat, useful in the protection of his own infallibility. This, allied with the element of terror which the accompanying torture induced, was an important reinforcement of his propaganda.

There can be little doubt that Mao played a considerable part in formulating the ideas of his own campaigns; he was certainly a competent writer and his poetic thoughts had a simplicity and sincerity which made them a useful tool. Harder to judge is the contribution of his fourth wife, Jiang Qing (1914–91), a former actress who certainly organized opera, theatre and ballet as propaganda media for her husband, but was perhaps less relevant to the cruder forms of mass communication. Certainly her production of the opera *Taking Tiger Mountain by Stratagem* was a significant step in the build-up to the Cultural Revolution and she may well have been responsible for the element of paranoia which entered Mao's propaganda from this period. Also important, was Lu T'ngi, chief propaganda organizer for Mao from 1966, but his precise contribution is hard to evaluate.

In terms of overseas propaganda the Chinese variety travelled no better than most others. From 1948 the Chinese were serious international broadcasters, starting in Yemen and eventually stretching to twenty-four different languages, but their greatest successes were probably in Africa where the competition was weak and their own Third World image perhaps closer to that of their audiences. From the Russians they learned and then developed the concept of massive gymnastic performances which turned into huge pictorial or word messages and this too they passed on to Africa, but to only marginal effect.

The dictator Kim Il Sung (1912–94), 'the great leader', used intimidation and a strong personality cult with a code of hysterical self-reliance to sustain a regime creating widespread impoverishment. Formerly a guerrilla leader against the Japanese, he took refuge and was trained in Russia from 1942 and was then installed by the Russians as leader of his country with a remit to take over all of Korea. When he invaded the South in 1950 he used Pyonyang Radio to announce that it was the South which had invaded the North.

AFRICA

The decolonization process in Africa produced a number of remarkable propagandists. Johnstone Kamau, renamed more charismatically Jomo Kenyatta – Kikuyu word for the belt of beads he always wore – (1889–1965) showed a remarkable ability to combine the techniques of European propaganda with a deep understanding of tribal motivations. Brought up as a Kikuyu warrior/farmer and educated in a Church of Scotland mission he could see the distorting effect of one culture superimposing its attitudes on another. In 1922 he joined the Kikuyu Central Association and supported an anti-slave labour campaign in the Indian-financed *East African Chronicle*. Six years later he played a part in the foundation of the first Kikuyu newspaper *Muiginthania* before a seven-year period abroad, mainly in Britain, where he wrote his *Facing Mount Kenya*, an encapsulation of the nation's folk culture. On his return in 1946 he advocated extreme nationalism through his Kenya African Union, and earned himself a six-year period of hard labour, which as with so many potential African leaders, gave him massive credibility among his own people. His almost superhuman image as Mzee, his style of hats and ever-present fly whisk, his rhythmic calls for Uhuru (freedom) and the emotive Swahili exhortation 'Harambee' provided a basis for crowd control. His ability to enthuse his people and create a new mythology round himself gave him a firmer base for his political career than many of his contemporaries in their emergent African states.

Shallower, for example, was Kwame Nkrumah (1909–72) who similarly spent several years in Britain, returned to his native Gold Coast in 1947 as secretary of the United Gold Coast Convention, had a spell in prison, founded his own Positive Action campaign and after a further period in prison became the first leader of an independent Ghana in 1957. Thereafter, however, he allowed his image to be developed more on the European model, styling himself President from 1960, erecting his own statue in numerous public places and fostering a personality cult which left him overexposed when his actual performance became suspect. Most of the more successful African leaders followed a slightly more cautious path, many using a spell in a European prison as the foundation for their images, retaining some level of ethnic individuality in their presentation and not pushing the personality cult to the point of counter-productivity.

Another example of African skill in propaganda was the effort of the underdog Biafran state in the Nigerian civil war of 1967. General Emeka Ojukwu told the rest of the world that genocide was being perpetrated against his Igbo nation by the Muslim-dominated northern establishment, employing public relations professionals in Europe to make sure that the story was covered. Nigerian protest literature had grown rapidly from around 1946 with the Onitsha market selling cheap chap books and plays like Hubert Ogunde's *Tiger's Empire* attacked British colonialism.

The Portuguese were the most reluctant Europeans to give up possession in Africa and it required a radical change at home before this could be contemplated. The Portuguese revolution of 1961 started with the novel idea of hi-jacking a luxury liner, the *Santa Maria*, now renamed *Santa Liberdade*, which was then used as a propaganda base for contacting the world's media and obtaining international support. The revolutionary government replaced the semi-Fascist regime of Salazar which had been based on the slogan 'God, Fatherland and Authority' and which had retained its colonial objectives when elsewhere empire went out of fashion.

Especially bitter was the propaganda battle between Frelimo and the Portuguese colonial government from 1965, not only within Mozambique but to win over world opinion. Latterly it focused on the major dam project at Cabora Basso, a piece of industrialization wanted by the Portuguese but not Frelimo. Here as elsewhere in Africa there was a rich vein of popular protest song in many local languages.

THE CARIBBEAN

Particularly remarkable was the image creation of Fidel Castro (1927–) who also gained credibility by spells in prison and created his own legend as a guerrilla leader, clad in fatigues and beard for the rest of his career. In 1955 he met the charismatic Che Guevara (1928–67) in Mexico, one of many who were to assist in the campaign to oust the Batista dictatorship from Cuba. Castro packaged his movement as '26th July' and achieved reasonable media coverage with his writings in *La Calle* as well as support outside Cuba from the *New York Times*. His 1957 attack on Ubero heightened his military image, which was further developed in the *Zig Zag* magazine and his own small radio station the Voice of Sierra Maestra set up in 1958. He put out leaflets drawing attention to its frequency and also ran his own news-sheets. His use of the not exactly original slogan 'Liberty or death' struck the right note and the kidnapping of the racing driver Fangio during a Grand Prix race was a further device to grab world headlines. Once in power after 1959 he became addicted to mass rallies and very long speeches and with the help of Russian subsidies laid the foundations for an extended period of personal dictatorship, packaged still in the image of old fatigues and guerrilla glory.

Substantially less savoury were the propaganda techniques of the Haitian dictator Papa Doc Duvalier, founder of Action Nationale. A poet and journalist he pushed pure black nationalism at the expense of the mulatto and founded a journal *Les Griots* in 1938 on his way to power.

RUSSIA AND AMERICA

The two major and slightly reluctant protagonists of the Cold War in the 1950s were Dwight D. Eisenhower (1890–1969) and Nikita Khrushchev (1894–1971). Both came to prominence because of their Second World War records; both inherited from their predecessors an atmosphere of extreme confrontation. In Russia Stalin had built up a formidable propaganda network which switched its attention to the new enemy as soon as the Germans surrendered. A staff of some 140,000 was employed worldwide to attack the Americans as wagers of germ warfare and ruthless pro-Semitic exploiters. Russian radio stations increased their output to 3,000 hours per week in sixty languages often concentrating on areas like Greece or Portugal, where Communist revolutions were expected, or

Yugoslavia, which had switched to a deviant form. The output of print too was massive, with, for example, some 10 million print items being sent from Russia to the United States in a single year. The effectiveness of all this Russian propaganda, except on peoples like the Cubans or Angolans who saw a vested interest, was limited. Stalin's assistants were too inflexible, too doctrinaire in presenting the Communist case in a welter of antagonistic clichés – the imperialist Fascist lackey syndrome – or in unintelligible Marxist dogma.

The Americans, meanwhile, retaliated in kind. Full advantage was taken of the Berlin Airlift in 1948 as a visible demonstration against Communism and the anti-Russian theme was developed heavily by Ed W. Barrett for *Newsweek* and extended in 1950 into President Truman's 'Campaign of Truth'. This whole effort was raised to the level of hysteria when Senator Joseph McCarthy (1909–57) exploited television to indulge in a massive spread of innuendo against even the mildest of left-wing sympathizers in the United States. His clever use of the media and totally unscrupulous resort to slander achieved massive if short-lived exposure for a brief essay in propaganda which was close to the style of Hitler or Stalin until his true personality was clearly exposed on television in an interview with Ed Murrow. Meanwhile, the war in Korea provided the focus for mutual vituperation between the two superpowers.

The American presidential campaigns of 1952 and 1956 which resulted in Eisenhower's double term were the first in which television and the new techniques of consumer advertising played a major part. His advertising adviser Kevin McCann wrote the hagiographic *The Man from Abilene*. The 'I like Ike' campaign of 1952 was devised by the advertising agency BBDO and a network of Ike Clubs was set up throughout the country. The 1956 Republican convention was stage-managed by MGM, and the $48 million democratic campaign for Adlai Stevenson was organized by another advertising agency, Norman Craig and Kummel, previously most famous for the Maidenform Bra. As another Eisenhower publicity aide, Rosser Reeves, remarked, the two parties 'were just like two competing brands of toothpaste'.

All this was seen as a downward drift not just into the commercialization of politics and later religion, but also as the development of new seduction techniques to mislead the masses. Vance Packard was one of several popular writers who were worried about what they regarded as the new symbol manipulation with the result that inferior politicians and policies might be made to look better than superior alternatives. Such commentators were also concerned at the escalation in campaign budgets and this was to come to a head during Richard Nixon's second term. Meanwhile, even the liberal Adlai Stevenson was resorting to the new techniques in 1966 as film adviser Charles Guggenheim developed the *cinema verité* technique of filming candidates on 'walkabout' and his campaign managers pushed the 'Nervous about Nixon?' line.

The multinational campaign to boost America's image also continued to escalate under Eisenhower. His adviser in this sector Abbot Washburn mounted a massive worldwide anti-Communism campaign, with 244 US libraries in 84 countries, an increase in the Voice of America output and 24 new American TV stations in 19 countries. Cecil B. De Mille was commissioned to film *The Korea Story*. The opinion poll fashion was extended so that the US image could be monitored in other countries and Nelson Rockefeller was brought back into the government to run Eisenhower's 'Open Skies' campaign. Egypt, one example of the countries hovering between the influence of East and West, was deluged with a million American leaflets boasting about the US-backed Aswan dam scheme. It had little effect, but more serious may have been the results of anti-Russian propaganda in Hungary where the campaign contributed to the premature Hungarian rebellion of 1956. Certainly in terms of the balance of image building between America and Russia, the harshness of Russian reprisals in 1956/7 did Communism irreparable harm, but equally the US was damaged badly by its own Little Rock racial prejudice scandal and the shooting down of its U2 spy plane in 1956.

In many respects Nikita Khrushchev was different in his attitude to propaganda both from his international contemporaries and other Soviet leaders. He only emerged gradually as the leader of the collective leadership of 1953 and his huge attack on his dead predecessor Stalin included criticism of his personality cult, by definition, therefore, a disavowal of the techniques of personal propaganda. In addition this speech was supposedly secret, delivered to the Twentieth Congress of the Communist Party in 1956 and only unofficially leaked thereafter. He even allowed Solzhenitsyn's *One Day in the Life of Ivan Denisovich* to appear in *Novi Mir* with devastating effects. He closed down the discredited Cominform in 1956 but appointed his son-in-law Aleksei Adzhubei to run the new APN Novosti to cultivate the world's press in its place. Using the Russian successes in space travel, rather than political dogma he showed the Third World in particular how Communism could help underdeveloped countries make rapid technological progress. His gradual destruction of Stalin's image and his isolation of the police chief Beria were relatively subtle. He also avoided the development of a personality cult based on himself. The odd result of this was that he thus laid himself open to being harmed by any campaign which did focus on him, so that the efforts of Brezhnev and Podgorny to unseat him incorporated the unusually devious ploy of promoting a Khrushchev personality cult. It was they, not Khrushchev himself, who promoted the big portraits of the party secretary, the constant quotations from his speeches in the press, the publication of adulatory books, the production of the film *Our Nikita Sergeyevich*. Thus Brezhnev outmanoeuvred Khrushchev, making him appear a hypocrite and making possible his deposition on the grounds of excessive personality cult.

Khrushchev had certainly made this more possible by his flamboyant behaviour on the international scene, where he was much more interested in promoting his own image than at home. His use of the famous third shoe to emphasize points in a United Nations speech, his relish both of the successful Sputnik flights and the shooting down of the U2, his vivid phrases such as calling Mao 'a living corpse', his obvious awareness of his capacity to win headlines in Western media, reveal him as a very able propagandist. As the career of Mikhail Gorbachev was to demonstrate thirty years later it was easier in some respects for a Soviet leader to achieve media success abroad, where charisma was the main asset, than to get it right with the captive media of native Russia.

BRITAIN

Other world leaders of this period who showed marginal developments in the use of propaganda technique included Harold Macmillan (1894–1980). Macmillan was the first British party leader to exploit the new techniques of advertising and television, spending £468,000 through Colman Prentice and Varley on the 'Never had it so good' campaign of 1959. The party vice-chairman had even been sent across to the US to study campaign techniques there and Ed Murrow had conducted a well-planned TV interview with Macmillan in 1958 which hugely helped his Gallup rating. He perceived the value of visual imagery and photocalls by donning fur hats on his visits to Moscow. He packaged his policies alliteratively as 'prosperity and peace', attacked his opponent Gaitskell as the 'desiccated calculating machine', spoke at seventy-four meetings to a total of 150,000 people and did his final party political broadcast lasting fifteen minutes straight to camera. His 'wind of change' speech of 1960 was probably his most enduring international metaphor, but by 1962 his image was overexposed and fading.

FRANCE

The seeds of Charles de Gaulle's (1890–1970) image had been sown in two world wars. His consciousness of the value of propaganda was shown as early as 1940 when he chose to publish his *The Army of the Future* as his means of provoking improvements in the French military. During the Second World War and immediately after 1945 he developed an image of uncompromising obstinacy which relegated him, rather as it had done Churchill, to apparently long-term political unemployment. Discontented with the level of performance after all the efforts of the war, he became the figurehead of a group looking for greater international standing for France. This became focused on his new party, Rassemblement du Peuple Français (RPF) for which he employed the gifted writer and former resistance hero André Malraux (1901–76) as leading propaganda organizer. Malraux had worked both in China in Mao's early period and in Spain. It was Malraux who planned the impressive launch of RPF in 1947 with a period of three months' intensive press activity concentrating on the threat of Communism and exploiting the fact that the Chamber was in summer recess. There was a ceremonial re-enactment of the cliff-top fight of Bruneval, attended by a crowd of 50,000. This image protection was extended into an even larger mass meeting in October with tricolours in evidence, the cross of Lorraine, de Gaulle's corporate symbol, on blue banners, and frequent use of Gaullist idioms like 'the abyss of Communism'. The RPF, however, still did badly in the elections of 1951 and de Gaulle retired again ostentatiously to Colombée les deux Eglises. He produced his war memoirs which proved a best-seller and it was the Algerian crisis and the humiliation of Suez which finally created the right climate for the virtual military takeover of 1958. Once in power de Gaulle inaugurated the Fifth Republic with a pomp suited to international pre-eminence, backed by the Republican Guard, the 'Marseillaise', the Arc de Triomphe and his own inimitably monolithic style of press conference. He maintained an Olympian detachment which went with his consistent efforts to build up France's international image by well-orchestrated state visits to Russia and elsewhere. He might occasionally be mocked at home, as when he was depicted as the Sun King in the satirical magazine *Le Canard Enchaînée* or as Charlot de Sous by the students of 1963, but for some time he ensured that the French mass media, television in particular, were fairly well muzzled and dissatisfaction muted. His use of frequent referenda endorsed his image until he tried it once too often and had to resign in 1969.

YUGOSLAVIA

In 1937 Vaso Cubrilovic had published *Iseljavanje Avnauta*, a proposal for the ethnic cleansing of Albanians in Kosovo, a step in the century-long Serbian propaganda campaign which finally exploded in 1990. However, a self-made leader of the Second World War years with a natural flair for image creation of the highest order, Joseph Broz Tito (1892–1980), had the strength of will to restrain ethnic minorities. Tito had been in Russia as a prisoner of war during the 1917 Revolution and saw Communism in action. He developed his persona with a spell in prison in Yugoslavia in 1928 for sedition and then a dramatic career as a resistance leader from 1941 to 1945. For the first three years of his prime ministership he was little different from other satellite leaders within the Soviet bloc, but once expelled from the Comintern by Stalin in 1948 he had to forge an image on a larger scale. He based this on two concepts: on the one hand the residual romanticism of the People's Liberation War which he had led against the Nazis and rival Yugoslav groups, and on the other the idea of Tito's Yugoslavia, himself as the supreme unifying factor of a diverse nation riven with petty ethnic and religious differences and a long tradition of conflict. He boosted this by exploiting his unique position as a buffer between the Soviet and Western blocs, creating the concept of non-alignment. He encouraged a substantial personality cult which could be justified as genuinely necessary to offset the barely submerged rumblings of the minorities. His agitprop section, run by men like Vladimir Dedijer, former *Politika* journalist and later author of *Sarajevo 1914*, worked hard to extinguish nationalisms, particularly Croat, Bosnian and Kosovo Albanian. He was helped by several public trials of his opponents, and a fair level of intimidation, washed down with Western subsidies to ease his economic difficulties. As he aged and as, in the way of other Communist countries, the populations bored with economic stagnation, the ethnic problem began to revive, particularly in Kosovo in 1968. By self-rehabilitation the Croats emerged from their Nazi stigma aided by a revival of their Catholic Church, just as the Serb persona was revitalized by a gentle resurgence in the Greek Orthodox, both of which in turn could make the Bosnian Muslims feel threatened. After Tito's death his name and shrine continued to have some influence but it soon gave way to new pressure groups like Nasa Rec which provided a focus for rival ethnic groups.

CHURCHES AND CULTS

The postwar decade or two was a period of spiritual uncertainty in Italy in which a number of religious propaganda efforts were relatively successful. Not the least of these was yet another remarkable rescue of the image of the papacy achieved by Cardinal Roncalli (1881–1963) who became Pope John XXIII in 1958. His was a mixture of personal saintliness which worked well on television and a willingness to tackle updating – aggiornamento – of the papacy. His eight encyclicals and his calling of the Second Vatican Council marked a new period of papal extroversion which was to be maintained by his successors as they adapted to the new need for worldwide media exposure.

Several fringe religious leaders showed remarkable propaganda skills. Sun Myung Moon (1920–) a Korean Christian founded his new church in New York in 1954, adapting the traditional techniques of emotive conversion to the new environment. His style concentrated on event management, particularly the massive multiple wedding ceremonies which were a dominant feature of his ethos, his use of the *Washington Times* and his own book *New Vision of World Peace*, his Japanese-style marketing expertise, training and street salesmen, his Korean Folk Ballet Troupes and his integrated conversion follow-up programme which led to the cult's reputation for brainwashing. Certainly conversion techniques involved disguised approach, deprivation, isolation and heavy indoctrination, alliance with the subject against his or her parents and authority. Yet despite this Moon was very right-wing in his political sympathies, thriving on his anti-red stance, using all the tools of book and video publishing on a substantial budget fed by his commercial activities.

The same year as Moon launched his church Ron Hubbard (1911–86) founded his Church of Scientology. Hubbard was a former science fiction writer who invented his own war record and showed remarkable creativity in the packaging of his movement with large sales of his books on Dianetics, a remarkable cell network created to aid expansion and strangely successful concepts like Thetan for soul, Engrams and meters, all based on the idioms of science fiction. He enhanced his propaganda by using the endorsement of film stars and other celebrities, then tied his close followers with a mixture of hypnosis, mental programming and intimidation.

The peak year of the mass rallies organized by the revivalist preacher Billy Graham (1918–) was also 1954. He too took advantage of the latest advertising techniques, of large football stadia, of well-organized music, of television, including satellite, and of traditional revivalist preaching techniques to mastermind a substantial worldwide act of evangelism. He used a number of crowd manipulation techniques including deliberate late arrival in the arena. He also used the old crusader and Wesleyan ploy of persuading individual members of the crowd to get up from their seats and come down to make a commitment.

The 1950s were primarily a period in which the images of the traditional empires finally lost all credibility, while the two superpowers Russia and the United States devoted huge resources to their own mutual struggle for image dominance. The greatest propaganda failure was almost inevitably the United Nations which despite all the ideal qualities lacked the emotive charisma and personality to put across the attractions of peace or racial harmony.

It was also a period in which the traditional forms of the mainstream religions were struggling for credibility though the more extreme sects could exploit their very eccentricity to attract media attention. This coincided with a massive escalation in the volume and influence of commercial advertising, extended on to television, cinema and radio as well as to the more traditional media of press and posters. Because advertising began to focus on lifestyles and highly competitive materialism, it now played a role in the formation of worldwide attitudes on a broader front than the mere choice of goods. The criteria of commercial selection were proceeding to take over from the old ideologies as arbiters of behaviour. The new cultural empires were run by businesses rather than religious or political parties.

Drift to Left and Right

UNITED STATES

During the 1960s and '70s the most obvious continuing products of propaganda were the American presidents, partly because in the nature of that office there was no obvious career structure to weed out candidates and partly because the gladiatorial nature both of the party selection process and actual election meant that image was crucial. John F. Kennedy (1917–63) was the first postwar example of this, since his predecessor Eisenhower had come to the White House as a successful wartime commander. Kennedy's war memoirs *Profiles in Courage* (1956) won a Pulitzer prize (helped by ghostwriter Sorensen and probably some favours to the judges from his father) and this contributed to his developing war hero image. He won the senatorial seat for Massachusetts in 1950 with the slogan 'he can do more for Massachusetts' and a well-directed appeal to the woman voter. With the aid of the family fortune he could afford a long build-up of his presidential aspirations, which he set about rather like Lenin by developing a massive mailing list of some 70,000 names which he could reach using the free congressional franking facility. The issuing of mailers like his *Strategy of Peace* was to be a key part of his build-up. He took full advantage of his family's relationship with the Hearsts and their media empire. Pierre Salinger had become his media organizer and still pushed the war hero image – Kennedy wore a clasp in the shape of his old PT boat. Slogans started to position him – 'Let's put a new John in the White House', 'Dollars for Democracy', 'Citizens for Kennedy', 'Baptists for Kennedy'. Apparently spontaneous banners with all the different ethnic and religious slogans appeared at all his rallies, with badges, buttons and all the other paraphernalia. Kennedy also had a highly professional approach to telephone marketing; the 'Calling for Kennedy' campaign inaugurated by his wife Jacqueline was highly effective. The combination of his youthful charisma on television, his concept of 'The New Frontier' and 'It's time to get America moving again' led up to the climax of his campaign, the single combat with Nixon in front of a television audience of 70 million, where Nixon's sallow complexion was reckoned to have cost him the debate. Kennedy's oratory had the right note of enthusiasm, the regular alliteration, the rhyming of key words and the use of poetic cadences.

Once in the White House Kennedy extended his public relations skills to the wider stage, appointing the well-known broadcaster Ed Murrow (1908–65) as head of USIA to mastermind America's international image. Murrow had become deeply unhappy about the ability of glib performers, such as McCarthy, to establish a power base through television. Kennedy's visit to Berlin was managed to maximize on media coverage, exploiting the new Berlin Wall, with 750 foreign journalists brought into the city to witness his 'Ich bin ein Berliner' speech, and strip cartoon material sent to 1,200 foreign newspapers with a collective readership of 100 million. How effective Kennedy's image would have remained had he not been assassinated cannot be estimated and there has been a subsequent grand opera mixture of posthumous scandal and family martyrdom. However, it was probably enough to help Lyndon Johnson defeat Barry Goldwater in the 1964 election. The Republicans were pilloried by a fear-based TV campaign, with commercials including images of a little girl plucking daisies against a nuclear countdown, a model of the eastern seaboard being bombed and an ice-cream shown with a voice-over about strontium-90, the tearing up of social security cards and the metaphor of Goldwater wavering like a weather vane. It was very negative but suited the campaign to defeat such an extreme candidate.

Four years later the 1968 election witnessed the remarkable resuscitation of Richard Nixon (1913–93), whose career seemed to have collapsed after his failure even to capture the governorship of California in 1963. He had worked for five years to counteract the 'would you buy a second hand car from this man' image and his presidency was to become a classic example of the strengths and weaknesses of the new style of political propaganda. His faults had been analysed by Murray Chotiner who joined him as a public relations adviser in 1964 and the advertising space salesman Roy Day. Nixon was good with large audiences or small groups, bad with reporters and bad on television. H.R. (Bob) Haldeman, the television advertising specialist, orchestrated his performance so that his message was directed either to small groups of a dozen questioners with whom he could be friendly and natural – the so called Hillsboro approach later copied by John Major – or mass audiences of over 1,000, nothing in between. He avoided direct TV debate with Hubert Humphrey the Democratic candidate, despite being taunted as 'Richard the chicken-hearted' and 'Richard the Silent'. He used his contacts with publishers like the Reader's Digest to put out a series of articles attacking President Johnson, mainly for being soft on Russia and on North Vietnam. He used words like 'appeasement' and 'retreat', emotive phrases like 'roll back the Communist tide in Vietnam' and in one of his major television broadcasts rounded on Johnson's reduction of American bombing in Vietnam as being 'at the expense of American boys', even going so far as to fabricate a report of thousands of tons of supplies being brought down the Ho Chi Minh trail. Helped by speech writers like Pat Buchanan he was all for hawkish patriotism and a return to traditional moral values. He won the election and the policies he then followed were often quite different from his pre-election rhetoric.

His second campaign of 1972 was really much easier, though it was to represent a nadir in the long-term history of political manipulation with the huge scandal of Watergate. Ironically this subsequently discovered cheating, which was to ruin Nixon's career, was not even remotely necessary. He had a reasonable record and his campaign run by Bob Haldeman and Peter H. Dailey defeated the Democrat George McGovern quite easily despite being outspent in media terms by $42 million to $30 million. One of the results of Watergate was that for future elections promotional budgets for presidential elections were to be restricted well beneath both sums to $20 million in the hope of reducing the corrupting effect of campaign fund-raising.

Inevitably the post-Watergate election saw a swing to the Democrats. The replacement President Ford was initially lacking in media presence, whereas the candidate Jimmy Carter had a fresh, apparently untainted rustic image which suited the moment. Peter H. Dailey handled Ford's campaign but was replaced halfway through by Browning McDougall who made a last failing effort to turn the tide by producing television commercials attacking Carter direct. Carter's own campaign was handled with some style by Gerald Rafshoon, with confident television advertisement showing the stone faces of Mount Rushmore with the slogan 'Why not the best?', while posters showed Carter and Mondale with the effective double meaning 'Leaders for a change'.

RUSSIA

With the fall of Khrushchev Russian political propaganda took a step backwards. Leonid Brezhnev (1906–85) took over with most of the orthodox image trappings of a traditional Soviet leader. With the hagiolatry of captive media, the Kremlin event management teams with their May Day parades and other sacred rites, generals with medals down almost to their waists, the propaganda of Communism was becoming increasingly monolithic and sterile. In 1976 on his seventieth birthday Brezhnev adopted the title of 'Vozhd', or leader, with all the trappings of equality to Lenin. He had already dismissed the more liberal Aleksandr Yakovlev (1923–), who was later to reappear under Gorbachev and Yeltsin as his propaganda chief, and the Soviet media suffered from steadily decreasing credibility. The nadir came with the adulation which greeted the publication of Brezhnev's heavily ghosted war memoirs, *Little Hand*, in 1978. Without fresh thinking or adaptation to a younger generation the image of Soviet Communism looked dull and uninspiring.

BRITAIN

Political propaganda in Britain was moving into a more sophisticated mode. Edward Heath and Harold Wilson slugged it out in relatively traditional terms with only minor swings, traditional, mainly head-on use of television and a fairly banal exchange of slogans. The dominant propaganda journalist of the period was Hugh Cudlipp (1913–98) who ran the *Daily Mirror* campaigns in favour of Harold Wilson and advised James Callaghan on anti-inflation propaganda in the 1970s while Joe Haines was Wilson's main slogan writer. The one novelty was the uncharacteristic British use of referenda – one in 1975 on entry to the EEC and the second in 1978 on Scottish and Welsh devolution – but both were conducted with fairly low media budgets and lack of real campaign energy on both sides. It was Margaret Thatcher's campaign against James Callaghan in 1979 which took Britain into a new era of propaganda sophistication which, to some extent like Watergate, left a feeling later of subtle deception. Her Director of Publicity, Gordon Reece, an ex-television producer, orchestrated her new hairstyle and voice, concentrating her television appearances on lightweight entertainment programmes rather than direct confrontation with opposing politicians. He also organized the numerous newsreel shots of her doing housework and shopping, all part of an attempt to put her across as a practical, sympathetic person as opposed to a combative politician. It helped to make some inroads for her against the personal lead in the opinion polls enjoyed by her avuncular rival, James Callaghan. For not even the constant repetition of 'the winter of discontent' (Shakespeare: *Richard III*) theme had had much effect. What was more concerning, however, at least in hindsight, was the use of Tim Bell at the highly fashionable advertising agency Saatchi and Saatchi. He organized party political broadcasts and poster campaigns, specifically the notorious pun 'Labour isn't working' showing a dole queue. Subsequent complaints that the queue image was a fake photograph using Conservative students as models were really irrelevant; what was more concerning was the blatant hypocrisy of the message in that Conservative policies as such were never likely to deliver a short-term fall in unemployment. The very slickness of the Saatchi and Saatchi approach was to bring a professional artificiality to British electioneering which soon also spread to the Labour Party.

Meanwhile, Margaret Thatcher once in power was able to carve a totally new image based on her uncompromising conviction of her own rightness and her aggressive determination. She acquired the 'iron lady', Boadicea, TINA (There Is No Alternative) profile, decked out with a few phrases from her speech writers, such as the misquotation 'the lady's not for turning' after the endless expectation of a U-turn on economic policy, or the Jacques Delors–back-door pun. Overall, this image took her through three successful elections and in the process many significant reforms. Bernard Ingham acted as a proficient, almost domineering press organizer, carefully orchestrating her appearances.

The dominance of British press media by a small number of press barons, such as Rupert Murdoch and Robert Maxwell, contributed to upsetting the balance of party propaganda. Throughout the world the fashion for longer periods of television news had spread after the late

1960s when the visual version of radio newsreading was replaced by more film and video actuality as techniques improved. This led specifically to the greater in-action coverage of politicians and the reduction of the less entertaining head-on policy statements to 'sound bites', suitable for an audience with a very short attention span. It also meant that outside factors played a more important role than logical delivery in deciding the overall charisma quotient of politicians heading for the top. It was increasingly a world in which democracies constantly referred to the mirror of opinion polls and often oversteered their images by reacting to minor changes in statistics. Advisedly a number of countries outlawed the publication of opinion polls in election periods yet in Britain the habit remained one of the major applications of commercial marketing techniques to political propaganda, the exploitation of existing forward momentum to create extra momentum, made more false by the use of biased questionnaires. American presidential primaries worked on the same principle.

MIDDLE EAST AND AFRICA

The resurgence of Islam in the 1960s and '70s was both assisted by and in its turn assisted a number of leaders who showed real propaganda flair. They tended to display a common anti-Western, particularly anti-American, tone, a revival of Arab ethnic style, drawing on the Koran for familiar themes and a deep anti-Israeli strain. The resurgence was given a massive stimulus by the powerful Voice of the Arabs radio station in Cairo.

Not untypical of the leaders who drew on this theme was Mua'mmer Gaddafi (1942–), who organized the army coup in Libya in 1969. His 'Communiqué No. 1' for Benghazi Radio put across the image of Turkish domination, followed by Italian, followed by a decadent monarchy. Gaddafi targeted his appeal to the poorer end of Libyan society and deliberately fostered the Bedouin image, himself wearing traditional dress and living in a tent, while he encouraged ethnic art and lifestyles such as desert horsemanship. His new Tripoli Radio took over as the most aggressive source of pan-Arab broadcasting, with highly charged anti-Semitic, anti-American programme material. Meanwhile, domestically he embarked on a period of cultural revolution, using mass rallies packed with students to support his anti-middle-class, anti-private property programme. This was all packaged as the 'Third Universal Theory' or the 'Third Way', incorporated in his *Green Book* under his green flag. He used radio and his main official paper *al Fajr al Jadid* to put across his creed and maintained a very high, if at times apparently eccentric, profile both at home and abroad. Since particularly his international image thrived on extremes of hate, this meant that, like the Egyptians before him, his bluff was occasionally called – the problem with bombastic militant propaganda as discovered by a number of aggressive regimes was that if the army was not as invincible as claimed there was an acute loss of credibility.

The propaganda achievement of the Ayatollah Ruhollah Khomeini (1900–89) was even more impressive. His reputation as a preacher and an ascetic priest who slept on the floor and supported traditional Shi'ite views without compromise, initially grew quite slowly. Tape cassettes of his speeches were circulated and he was part of the general protest movement against the virtual dictatorship wielded by the Shah since 1953. Then during the brutally suppressed riots of Qom in 1963 which followed the Shah's so-called white revolution, Khomeini was arrested, one of his sons died in mysterious circumstances and his picture began to be put up in the bazaars. He had written a book *Secrets Revealed* attacking the Shah as far back as 1941; now he began a series of open letters and organized bigger rallies which condemned the Shah for atrocities and attacked the brutality of his secret police the Savat. In addition he expressed alarm when the Shah tried to swamp Islam with a new breed of modernizing mullahs. Khomeini was adept at using high points in the Shi'ite calendar – Ramadan, the fortieth day of mourning of the imam Husayn's martyrdom (see p. 125)) and the Haj – to exploit the additional fanaticism of the crowds. In 1978 he was exiled to France, where he continued the international development of his image. Meanwhile, the Shah's position became untenable; his brutalities were welcomed as martyrdom by a people for whom martyrdom was especially venerable. His spectacular coronation ceremony had done more harm than good and when he put out a press release attempting to smear Khomeini, it backfired disastrously. His regime crumbled and Khomeini returned to take over in 1974.

Khomeini's image was based on a highly conservative interpretation of Shi'ite tradition, strict adherence to traditional Muslim ethics and customs, and a highly emotive veneration for ascetics and martyrs. The yearly cycle revolved round daily prayer, now shown on television, the ten days of Muharram, Ramadan, the Haj and the birthdays of the twelve imams. Automatically the new government became virulently xenophobic, particularly against the Americans, who had supported the Shah, and against the Iraqis, who had a Shi'ite minority. Khomeini's manipulation of the media was impressive. Papers like *Ittilaat* supported him, others disappeared and in 1980 200 journalists were sacked for being too soft on the mujahidin. Television and radio, wall posters and Shia-based event management were all well utilized to back up Khomeini's hierocratic theme and his Reconstruction Crusade aided by his huge workforce of local imams. But the Shia medium *par excellence* was the Passion play, where vast crowds were brought in to watch traditional Shia works with subtle contemporary additions.

Propaganda became even more important when the quarrel with Iraq came to a head. The rival radio stations of Baghdad and Teheran bombarded each other with insults, and as Saddam Hussein's superior army threatened to engulf them the Iranians could only hold out by sheer fanaticism and self-sacrifice, the virtues most often projected in Khomeini's propaganda system. The Iranian film industry was also revived with strongly Islamic films like the popular *Safeer* (1983).

Among other able Arab self-propagandists of this period Yasser Arafat (1929–)was one of the most remarkable. Again he cultivated the visual image of an ascetic wandering warrior in traditional dress, symbol of the martyrdom of his own people, constantly surviving attacks on his own life, frequently, until he mellowed, making attacks on others. Given his lack of any home base or stable media, radio was the medium which above all made his remarkable political career possible, keeping up the morale and momentum of the Palestine Liberation Organization over many years of disappointment. The powerful Voice of Palestine, broadcasting from various borrowed capitals, could reach all his far-flung adherents. Ultimately he had to soften his image somewhat to reach agreement for the new Palestinian state in 1993–5. The mantle of extremism was then taken over by high-profile terrorist groups such as Hamas and Izbollah.

Among African nationalist propagandists of the second generation of the decolonizing period two in particular stand out. Robert Mugabe (1924–) was leader of the underground ZANU faction in the struggle for Rhodesian independence. ZANU's corporate symbol was a cock, whose stance was uncompromising and its primary medium was radio transmitted from across the border in Zambia. The four-times-weekly programme *Mirror of Zimbabwe* from Zambia Radio played a key role in fostering Mugabe's power base until his takeover from white rule was successful. In general in the southern half of Africa radio as a medium which could cross frontiers and dispense with literacy played a great part in the remaining liberation movements. Chinese transmitters given to Tanzania were the main source of a number of key services leading to the victory of Frelimo in Mozambique and the strength of SWAPO in Namibia. Despite the heavy racist content of its domestic propaganda the Voice of South Africa radio station tended to adopt a much softer tone for external broadcasts, and even encouraged a strong ethnic content in its own regionalized Bantu stations.

Nelson Mandela (1918–), the South African lawyer and opponent of apartheid, won an international image and regional hero status by, like so many potential leaders of African liberation movements, spending time in prison, in his case a particularly long time on Robben Island. By his uncompromising stance he acquired a unique authority, matched by his genuine integrity and sincerity. His early speeches had been recorded on long-playing records, so that these helped preserve awareness of his ideas during his long imprisonment. He subsequently displayed a natural ability to project an extremely disciplined, understated image. From 1992 the ANC used Reg Lascaris as its advertising adviser and in Mandela's presidential campaign of 1994 mounted a massive multilingual radio campaign to back it.

Regrettably in 1993 Africa produced a particularly vicious trend in racist propaganda when the Hutu regime in Rwanda decided to get rid of the rural Tutsi tribe. With Radio-Television Libre des Milles Collines financed by Felicien Kabuga as their prime medium the Hutu called for the extermination of the *inyenzi* or cockroaches – 'Look at the size of the person and how small the nose and then take out your machete.' The popular singer Simon Bikundi made use of the anti-Tutsi interpretation of Rwanda history and Hassan Ngezera ran the *Kangura*, the newspaper of the radically racist Hutu CDR party. The fact that so many tribal animosities revived after years of suppression by colonial regimes demonstrates the depth of earlier inculcation.

Other examples of regional propaganda skills in Africa include the remarkable case of Somalia. This area had a fine tradition of living poetry with professional reciters known as *hafidayad*. Highly effective propaganda poetry, developed over centuries of tribal panegyric, was used to arouse nationalist feeling in the 1970s, with tape recordings of it for playing in cassettes produced in bulk and the broadcasting of poetry on Mogadishu Radio.

PHILIPPINES

To the East this period saw the career of another of those typically mendacious self-made propagandist dictators, Ferdinand Marcos (1917–89). He built his career on a fictitious record of war heroics against the Japanese; Benjamin Gray helped him to embroider it for the magazine *Bannawag* in 1949 and this was further extended in the epic film *Maharlika – Marked by Fate*. Journalists were bribed to use pictures of Marcos and his glamorous wife Imelde in their papers. In the year of his second presidential election in 1969 he published his *Rendezvous with Destiny* and used the standard ruse, defence against the red peril, to help his image abroad. He invented a new ancestry for himself with his real father thrust into the background, a new image of descent from a famous pirate, and before that the original Filipino man who sprang from a bamboo stick. Imelde also played with new mythologies, reviving the legend of the Golden Salacot as she and her husband wove a fiction of respectability round a particularly corrupt regime, one which so mismanaged its economy that among other things it came to condone, if not encourage, child prostitution as a way of earning foreign currency.

The revolution which eventually overturned the corrupt regime of Ferdinand Marcos in 1986 was greatly assisted by the martyrdom of Benigno Aquino, the charisma of his widow and the overt megalomania of Marcos and his wife. Significantly one of the few mass media which assisted Mrs Cory Aquino in her bid for power was Radio Veritas, a station managed by the Catholic Church. Thereafter the church continued to sponsor advertising programmes to help build up national self-respect.

CAMBODIA

Perhaps even less savoury was the propaganda orchestrated by the Cambodian leader Pol Pot (1926–98) whose *Black Paper* of 1978 was a racist attack on the Vietnamese in which the Khmer were depicted as suffering five centuries of unfair struggle. The nationalist obsession of the Khmer Rouge produced publicity campaigns as facile as the imitation Mao 'Super Great Leap Forward': it was used, however, to legitimize one of the most brutal acts of genocide in the second half of the twentieth century.

JAPAN

On an altogether different plane was the remarkable way in which postwar Japanese opinion leaders refashioned the indoctrination processes previously used to foster military nationalism to create an almost fanatical drive to economic supremacy. The technique of *seishin*, the drills of the peaceful samurai, involved the combination of physical exercises that reduced the individual to a tired, unquestioningly obedient automaton. Chanting for twenty-four hours without break, kneeling in submission to blows, marathon running and drill were all used to instil a self-sacrificial, submissive ethos which suited Japanese industry. The continued myth of a race undiluted by ethnic minorities and with superior will-power, the re-exposure by television to the mythology of the selfless though now peaceful warrior, the ever popular *Chushingura* epic and other neo-samurai material projected the ideals of a new economic imperialism. Japan also developed the mass aerobics pioneered by the totalitarian regimes as a metaphor of bulk motivation and obedience.

CULTS AND RELIGION

While Islamic propaganda thrived on the new wave of Arabic nationalism, there was significant development in the propaganda of other great religions. Father Charles Coughlin, with his shrine of the Little Flower in Detroit, was one of the first to base his efforts on the successful use of radio, using The Radio Church of God. Then in the 1950s came the upsurge of television evangelism with Bishop Fulton Sheen, Billy Graham and Oral Roberts. There were, however, several spectacular examples of the way in which an able communicator working even in a sophisticated urban environment in the 1970s could successfully put across the most eccentric of messages.

Jim Jones (1931–78), who had raised money by selling pet monkeys door-to-door, founded his own church, the People's Temple in Indianapolis. His main targets were ex-drug addicts and down-and-outs, his main attacks were on colour prejudice and the risk of nuclear war. He appointed his own twelve angels and had a violent strain to his preaching which gradually helped increase his flock. After a brief move to Brazil he returned to California where with some support from the local press by 1971 he had acquired 2,000 followers and branches in both Los Angeles and San Francisco. Two years later he was delivering his first sermons on mass suicide and even rehearsing a communion-type ritual for drinking poison. Despite adverse publicity in the *San Francisco Chronicle* he was still able to move with 800 followers to a new base in Guyana in 1977 where a year later under the threat of Congressional investigation he succeeded in inducing 912 people to drink cyanide. This remains a classic example of the capacity of a persuasive leader to motivate a vulnerable target group to behave irrationally.

Other evangelists, particularly in the United States, also used television and radio to achieve remarkable results with surprisingly obscurantist and old-fashioned messages, though none were as damaging as the disaster of Jonestown. Another millennialist cult was that of David Koresh (1960–93) which ended in the disastrous siege of Waco and had clearly used similar brainwashing techniques on susceptible disciples. In addition in 1969 David Moses Berg (1919–) founded his offshoot of the Jesus People known as the Children of God, announcing that he had heard voices. He promoted with some success a creed which allowed unlimited sexual licence and a form of religious prostitution. His message medium tended to be pamphlets and stories illustrated in comic book style known as *Mo's Letters* with titles like *God's Whore* and the *Dying Dollar*.

Jimmy Swaggart was typical of a group of very able television evangelists of this period who could build up substantial incomes for their churches and in some cases themselves, obtain high credence with relatively shallow material. Bill McCartney (1940–), a Colorado football coach, adapted the event management skills of the sports stadium to organize mass rallies of his Promise Keepers, one of a number of rather right-wing, male-dominated Christian sects reacting against the liberal faction. Their platform was based on the typical packaging of a list of the popular number of seven promises.

Exotic Eastern cults also appealed to jaded Western audiences. Bhagwan Rajneesh had begun meditation camps in 1969 which were soon attracting 2,000 visitors a day in Poonah where frenzy and hysteria led to a rationalization of promiscuity as a vehicle for holiness, always a popular stance at least in the short term. When the cult moved to the United States, Big Muddy Ranch, Oregon had its own weekly paper (1974–8). The popularity of the Eastern cults in the 1960s was enhanced by their adaptation to the propaganda techniques of the period and recognition of a vulnerable target audience in the disorientated youth of the Western cities. ISKCON, the International Society of Krishna Consciousness, originally arrived in Europe in the 1930s but came in real strength to New York with Swami Prabhupata (1896–1977) in 1965. With the charisma of ascetic self-deprivation and the exotic quality of a Hindu background, he achieved fashion status for the cult, appealing successfully to a generation which had largely rejected Christianity but not found any real alternative. The repetition of the endless mantra 'Hare Krishna' was given even greater popular appeal when it was issued as a record by the Beatle George Harrison, currently at the peak of his popularity. Thereafter, the distinguishing yellow robes and haircuts, the drums, the training programmes and communal semi-mendicant existence drew adherents, many of whom were clearly exploited for the financial benefit of the senior people in the cult.

Maharishi Mehesh Yogi was another Indian guru who found he could be more successful outside his native country. Packaging his version of a fairly traditional yogi concept as transcendental meditation he brought this to the West in 1961 and steadily recruited new members for his courses which promised significant emotional rewards and attitudinal improvement. By contrast the Siv Sena sect of extreme Hindus led by an ex-cartoonist Bal Thaceray took an aggressive stance recommending deportation of 100 million Muslims and focusing on ancient grievances.

Japan became particularly prone to the rise of new cults in the last quarter of the twentieth century, partly because of the discrediting of Shinto after the Second World War and partly because of the stresses caused by its acutely competitive economy. In 1984 Shoko Asahara founded the Aum Shinri Kyo (Supreme Truth), one of the many millennialist cults similar to Christian versions based on the same end-of-the-world beliefs but with a Buddhist infrastructure. In 1995 the cult was involved in a release of poisoned gas apparently in the belief that mass murder would speed up the approach of the millennium.

To some extent all the cults, both Christian and non-Christian, had a number of elements in common from the propaganda point of view. They all had at least a figurehead who was an ascetic charismatic figure with a well-packaged answer to the problems of life. All targeted the disillusioned postwar generation which had loose or non-existent spiritual allegiances. All had an emotional technique for recruitment and a ritualized subsequent indoctrination with the added benefits to the member of a form of communal existence. All were initially quite successful, but tended to suffer eventually, like the medieval monastic orders, from a sudden increase in cash income which eroded their ascetic image and sometimes corrupted their leaders to the point of self-destruction.

Propaganda and the Fall of Communism

Without question the most remarkable developments in propaganda history in the 1980s occurred in the Soviet bloc. In different ways three figures were outstanding, Lech Walesa, Mikhail Gorbachev and Boris Yeltsin, but there were also a significant number of other major contributors. While there were similarities in the movements which gripped Russia's satellites and led to the disintegration of the Soviet bloc, there were also marked differences.

POLAND

In Poland there were four strands which provided the basis for opposition propaganda: Poland's long patriotic tradition and special dislike for the Russians, the strong residual imagery of the Catholic Church, a middle-class intellectual groundswell and the protest articulacy of organized labour. The revival of Polish patriotism took the form of a new fashion for their great nineteenth-century writers, the singing of songs like 'God protect Poland' and 'Rota', huge attention to the memories of the resistance and the Warsaw Uprising, with a shift of hate from the Germans to the Russians for its failure. The Catholic Church produced a number of charismatic leaders, notably Cardinal Karol Wojtyla (1920–) of Krakow, a poet and playwright, who returned to his native country in 1979 as Pope John Paul II and conducted his famous mass in Victory Square, a major piece of event management. This was followed two years later by the massive funeral of his colleague Cardinal Wyszinski (1901–81). At the other end of the clerical spectrum there were notable parish priests like Henri Jankowski of Gdansk whose church became a patriotic shrine and museum, offering substantial support to Solidarność (Solidarity), and the martyred Jerzy Popieluszko whose church also became a shrine and he himself a role model for the patriotic virtues.

Among the intellectuals the key figures in propaganda terms were Jacek Kuron who had helped found the KOR in 1976. He was of major importance in ensuring that news of the 1980 strikes reached the international press as well as radio stations which beamed it back into Poland. Jan Litynski who later ran the Solidarity election campaign was an early key figure in running the underground newspaper *Robotnik* which by

1980 had a circulation of 45,000. Bronislav Geremek was a major originator of material which helped bridge the gap between the patriotic socialism of Gdansk and the democratic aspirations of the Polish middle class.

Lech Walesa (1943–) developed Solidarity in 1980, very much in the mould of a traditional European trade union, in the Gdansk shipyards which were an ideal breeding ground for it. But it had an excitement and determination, a good graphic image, good slogans and a remarkable ability to obtain access to the media, even in Communist Poland, peaking with the well-managed sit-in. Significantly the Gdansk agreements of 1981 included demands for fair media coverage and an end to censorship. Solidarity also by this time had 40 per cent of all Polish journalists in its membership and 60 per cent of all television crews. It was producing its own paper *Jednosc*, had a column in *Dziennik Baltyski*, the Gdansk daily and its own national magazine *Tygodnik Solidarność* with a circulation of 500,000. It peaked with a membership of 8 million.

Walesa had been helped by his image as a genuinely staunch Roman Catholic and as a real shipyard worker. His original paper *Gazeta Wyborcza* had supported the action plans and recruitment drives of Solidarity. The persecution of Father Jankowski and other government errors played into his hands and Professor Geremek proved an excellent television broadcaster.

In contrast, there was General Jaruzelski; his main concessions to image were his dark glasses, required since he was snow-blinded during his Siberian exile, but somehow it did not work, nor did his revival of traditional four-cornered hats for the Polish army. Otherwise it was just a question of whether he would resort to bullets or water cannon, and when force was no longer practicable he stood little chance in a free election even against a divided Solidarity. Such was the change in mood of the electorate that Litynski could run the witty poster campaign just before the election with a photograph of Gary Cooper and the Polish for *High Noon* as its challenging slogan.

RUSSIA

Mikhail Gorbachev (1931–) was the first Soviet leader since Lenin to appeal directly to the Russian people over the heads of the army and in doing so showed a substantial understanding of public relations technique which he was later to develop for a world audience. Having risen through the ranks as a Soviet *apparatchik* he was already close to the top in Russian politics before he had any need to use propaganda skills, though he did get excellent coverage in *Pravda* in 1977 for his experiments in winter harvesting techniques in Stavropol. He was employed by Andropov, the KGB chief, in 1982 to mount a small attack on Brezhnev in the *Aurora* magazine. This was followed much later by a more extensive attack on the whole Brezhnev entourage with the help of Viktor Afansyev, the editor of *Pravda* who was friendly with both Andropov and Gorbachev. This gradually developed into a general attack on political corruption in 1984, the most significant change in Russia since Khrushchev's attack on Stalin in 1957, and more far reaching because it was the beginning of the self-destruction of Soviet Communism. The Andropov interregnum (1982–4) saw the image of Soviet leadership in transition, facing both ways, balancing between a sufficiently hard line to keep the old guard military happy and a hint of liberalism to encourage the rest. In late 1984 Gorbachev announced a change in the approach to propaganda methods in *Pravda* and then when he assumed the leadership made his highly symbolic speech at the Smolni Institute, where Lenin had spoken, with a new style of open oratory which heralded glasnost. He disposed of his closest rival for power – Romanov, who had appeared the worse for drink on television – following this up with a campaign organized by Ligachev against alcohol abuse in high places, using slogans like 'for sober leadership and a sober population'. This was followed by a major launch of glasnost in December 1985 and fifteen months later the first 'perestroika' campaign in February 1987, managed by Aleksandr Yakovlev (1923–), Gorbachev's experienced head of propaganda. He was succeeded by Vadim Medvedev (1929–) who had been his deputy in the Brezhnev days and now supervised Gorbachev's propaganda in the key period 1988–90. The novelist Anatoly Rybakov (1917–98) was rehabilitated and his previously banned *Children of Arbat* sold 7 million copies. Other authors like Yevtushenko and Andre Vozneshensky followed as well as the film maker Natasha Borchevsky, as the arts were gradually released from their requirement to defend Communism.

Gorbachev's massive switch of emphasis internally was matched by his ability to catch the imagination of the rest of the world with the abandonment of the costly Afghan War and a promise of the end of the Cold War. He had softened up the Russian public by encouraging satirical pieces about the Afghan War in the magazine *Ogonek*. His state visits abroad and successful disarmament negotiations boosted his international image to very great heights, but there were poor practical results from perestroika at home. With no more censorship or easy propaganda network to rely on, his reputation in Russia itself began to move into a steep decline. It was Gorbachev's misfortune that he chose to unleash the Soviet media to assist him in his own battles against the old guard but this very act was in due course to leave him vulnerable to his own decensorship. Anton Borovich, one of the new breed of investigative reporters, was encouraged in 1987 to produce major articles and television documentaries which showed the dreadful sufferings of Soviet troops in Afghanistan, creating an emotive reaction against the Afghan War which would help give Gorbachev the moral authority to pull out. The ending of the Afghan War in 1988 was one of Gorbachev's triumphs, a major help too in Soviet rehabilitation abroad, but the free press unleashed in the process could not be entirely retamed. The protest songs of Vladimir Vysotski (1938–80), copied on thousands of illicit cassettes while Brezhnev was alive, now came into the open, as did many of the samizdat newspapers. *Isvestia* which followed the fashion doubled in circulation to 10 million between 1985 and 1989 while the readership of the more traditional *Pravda* fell steadily. The new popular paper of glasnost was *Moskovski Novosti* edited by Gregor Yakovlev (1930–), author of some twenty books and thirty film scripts, a key figure in the ability of the new media to withstand Kremlin pressure – he had been in Prague from 1972 to 1975. The magazine *Ogonek*, pioneer in uncovering scandals, rose sixfold and, most startling, the new title *Argumenti i Fakti* topped 20 million. *Rasputin* even began the revival of the cult of the good old days of the tsars. On the literary side Pasternak's *Dr Zhivago* appeared at last in its native country, Yuri Trigonov's *House on the Embankment* had already been decensored as both novel and play by Andropov and in 1988, after protests from Yakovlev, Solzhenitsyn's *Gulag Archipelago* was sponsored by *Novi Mir* which had also taken the first steps to attack Lenin the year before.

Cinema was also unleashed, most notably with the film *Repentance* which significantly had been shot in Georgia, before Gorbachev's promotion, under the auspices of Edvard Shevardnadze. Its strong attack on Stalin attracted huge audiences in 1986. There had long been a flourishing underground film industry with men like Arkady Ruderman who shot the Minsk demonstrations of 1980 and took round his reels for secret showings, so the infrastructure for anti-establishment film was well in place. The same applied to television where a number of hard-hitting documentaries led the way with Gorbachev's blessing; *Protsess* in 1988 was a highly successful attack on Stalinism. But if Gorbachev had encouraged the realistic coverage of Afghanistan in 1987 it did not suit him quite so well that the crushing of riots in Tblisi in 1989 was filmed by the Georgian network or that there was wide coverage of Soviet troop brutality in Baku the year after. Most ironically it was the television coverage of the nineteenth plenary conference in 1989, which had been orchestrated by Gorbachev, that included footage, shown after eight hours' hesitation, of the dramatic flare-up between Ligachev and Boris Yeltsin, which was to lead to a massive surge in the latter's popularity with disastrous long-term consequences for Gorbachev.

Boris Yeltsin (1931–), promoted to the Politburo by Gorbachev in 1985 and ejected two years later for excessive criticism, was able to fight his way back into power partly because his personality and appearance made him an ideal opposition focal point and partly because by this time the media in Russia were too open for politicians to continue to 'disappear'. Gorbachev was now vulnerable because of the patent lack of economic improvement. Cartoon images had him moving from one unfinished construction site (*stroika*) to another. Button badges were on sale with the message 'Perestroika 2+2=5'. Yeltsin accused Gorbachev of the cult of personality, the most cutting jibe possible and the one which had been used before against Khrushchev. In the March 1989 regional elections Yeltsin won his way back in as a Moscow deputy with a remarkable 89 per cent of the vote after a very astute campaign, exploiting the classic underdog stance. When exposed to a rigged television press conference he had bypassed it to organize his own, showing excellent understanding of and contacts in the television industry. His act of flying to Riga after the January putsch to show solidarity, followed by his speech which was shown on television throughout the Baltic states and pasted on the lampposts of Riga was a rehearsal for his later defiance of the August coup in Moscow. When one of his rallies was broken up by the police he made sure his followers were carrying 'Hands off Yeltsin' banners and tricolours so that television coverage would help him rather than the government. It was this mastery of quick preparation and seizing of photo opportunities, combined with his very distinctive appearance and manner which were to enable him with one single act to overcome the military coup of 1991; his symbolic climbing on top of a tank to make his speech against the short-lived military junta must rank as one of the most dramatic examples of spontaneous seizure of media centre stage in modern history. In addition great importance must be attached to the fact that under Yakovlev and Medvedev many Russian journalists now became accustomed to show they had minds of their own and did not cave in to the junta's pressure. Even the junta-controlled television and radio stations appeared a little half-hearted; *Pravda* supported President Yanaev, but *Izvestia* insisted on printing both sides, while *Argumenti i Fakti* under Vladislav Starkov and *Moskovski Novosti* even resorted to samizdat editions to support Yeltsin. Also with great ingenuity the staff at the Russian parliament rigged up a makeshift short-wave radio transmitter which was enough to establish some kind of contact with the outside world. This plus the call by Shevardnadze and Yakovlev for human cordons round the parliament and the imaginative use of a 100-yard long tricolour, along with poor junta-imposed censorship, all helped Yeltsin to win. Later, as he followed Gorbachev in being unable to deliver economic improvement his image too went into rapid decline.

CZECHOSLOVAKIA, HUNGARY AND ROMANIA

The propaganda development of the Czech liberal movement was quite different from that in Poland and Russia. Certainly, as in those two countries, the image projection of the Communist regime had become stale and unconvincing. In 1988 the big neon sign in Wenceslas Square still read 'With the Soviet Union for ever', and in the window of the party office there was a dusty bust of Lenin with some dried flowers. However, the Czech opposition was more middle class and less xenophobic than in Poland and Russia. Its underground media such as *Lidove Noviny* had only small circulations. The Charter 77 movement and the Mazaryk Society, both of which counted Vaclav Havel (1936–) as a member, were linked with the Jazz Section and later the Democratic Institute rather than organized labour.

The spectacular suicide of Jan Palak, the brutal suppression of student rallies in 1988 and two spells of imprisonment for the playwright Vaclav

Havel began to give the movement against Communism more cohesion and fire. Havel showed real ingenuity as an image developer when he wrote a petition *Just a few sentences*, and then organized the signing of it by as many well-known people as he could, releasing news of this in chunks over a period so that he would obtain optimum exposure. In this he was helped by a press office run by Peter Uhl, but Havel was now well on his way to the orchestration of the mass rallies and outmanoeuvring of the old regime which would make the revolution unstoppable.

In Hungary the transition from Communism to democracy was led by Karoly Grosz who had risen from being a printer and country newspaper editor to be deputy head of the party's propaganda division in 1968 with special control over television and radio.

The downfall of the Ceauşescu regime in Romania had an even more unlikely propaganda origin, though as elsewhere the common factors of martyrs, crowd rallies, and exposure of police brutality on the media appeared. In this case the initial focus was on the remarkable success of the Hungarian protestant priest Laszlo Tokes who attracted large crowds to his church at Timisoara, where his sermons were critical of the Ceauşescu repressions, particularly the destruction of thousands of small peasant villages. There then followed the usual cycle of suppression, rallies, police brutality and heightened crowd response. The rallies became even better organized, with men like the writer Claudius Jordache taking charge; there followed the symbolic excision of the hammer and sickle from hundreds of Romanian flags, the songs and the rhythmic chant 'Ole, ole, ole Ceauşescu Nu mai e' [Down with Ceauşescu], and banners with 'Romania Libera'.

AFGHANISTAN

Versatility in coping with poor resources characterized the propaganda aspects of the anti-Communist rebellion in Afghanistan. Some techniques were borrowed from revolutionary Iran, such as the mass production of tapes for broadcast in the village bazaars. As the Kabul government had control over radio, television and such newspapers as existed, the mujahidin had to create its own media. This included a makeshift postal service which proved excellent in the transmission of news and leaflets for reading aloud to the mainly illiterate population. In a country where the tradition of poetic epics learned by heart still persisted there were new mujahed epics glorifying the rebel army. Loud hailers were used to taunt Russian troops with slogans like 'Allah o Akbar'. International broadcasters like the BBC and VOA assisted, but most effective were new lightweight radio transmitters donated by the West and using the technology developed by the FM pirate stations. As Safi commented 'a radio transmitter was worth more than a thousand Kalashnikovs'. Generally the propaganda ability of leaders like Ahmed Shah Massoud was considerable and Afghanistan a good example of the effective use of mini-media winning against government-controlled mass media.

The Decade of Spin

POLAND AND RUSSIA

As Lech Walesa was the first major anti-Communist to rise to power he was also the first to fall. Surprisingly in this and similar events elsewhere in Eastern Europe the failed propagandists of the Communist regimes came back with revitalized skills to win back credibility. In Poland the classic example was Jerzy Urban, a propagandist hack under Jaruzelski who became a virulent satirist against Walesa using his weekly magazine *Nie*, scatological, sensational and hugely successful. He supported the ex-journalist and Communist revival candidate Aleksandr Kwasniewski.

Throughout the former satellite nations the political skills of the Communists began to re-emerge. Boris Yeltsin himself suffered a massive decline in popularity during 1994/5 and in his re-election campaign of 1996. He had to respond by using all the techniques of Western propaganda as well as some borrowed clichés from the old Soviet Union. With the help of his daughter Tatyana Dyachenko, a computer expert, he exploited the capacity of new software to target large numbers of individuals by name, so that, for example, he could mail a 'personal' letter to 3 million female veterans thanking them for their heroism. He also sacked the management of the main television channels so that he could control his own propaganda in the broadcast media and put out a six-page newspaper supplement entitled *God Forbid*, warning of the dangers of a victory for Gennadi Zyuganov. He used focus groups and professional hecklers, exploited the red terror, issued ultra-emotive advertising and rigged opinion polls. He even subsidized the advertising cost of one of his rivals, General Lebed, to cut out other more extreme candidates. He was helped by the new breed of Russian publicists like Anatoli Chubais, campaign manager, Valentin Yameshev, his assistant, and Sergei Lisovsky, advertising executive. In addition he used advice given by Dick Morris, the planner employed by Bill Clinton to help him win Arkansas, with an ad hoc team of experienced US electoral campaigners and PR men to focus the election totally on the evils of Stalinist Communism and the possibility of civil war. For the first time since Russian mass media were privatized, millionaire owners like Boris Berezovsky could control both a major television station and newspapers so that he could wield significant political power, particularly when he fell out with Yeltsin and gave massive if deviously motivated support to General Lebed. In late 1997 Russian television was used to try to build confidence in the revalued rouble, a classic example of economic propaganda used to protect the suspect credibility of paper money. However, the economic tide was too strong and Yeltsin's image went into another period of acute decline, with little attempt to hide his problems of health and alcohol.

The later 1990s saw many of the professional propagandists who had failed to defend old-style Communism, re-emerging as successful leaders of the repositioned Communist or right-wing elements in each area.

YUGOSLAVIA

Media-led revival of historic glories played its part in the disastrous upsurge of Serbian nationalism in 1990. The novels of Vuk Draskovic and Dobrica Cosic, later president of the rump Yugoslavia, resurrected the myths of the Blackbird Field when the Turks drove the Serbs out of Kosovo in the fourteenth century with the Serbs seeing themselves as perpetually victimized. These ideas were developed and exploited by Slobodan Milošević (1941–), using unemployed youngsters to form 'demo networks' so that impressive rallies could be staged, for instance on the 600th anniversary of the Battle of Kosovo in 1989. He purged the main media to gain control and began projecting the myth of the Greater Serbia on television. In 1991 there was an exhibition in Belgrade of films showing the massacres of Serbs by Croats from 1914 to 1944 and Draskovic's book *The Knife* reminded the Serbs of the Croats' traditional obsession with knives. Then significantly it was a Serbian nationalist psychiatrist and gusla-playing poet Radovan Karadžić who became leader of the Bosnian enclave. The Muslim lawyer Alija Izetbegovic, who had himself helped to write the *Islamic Declaration* of 1970, emerged as his Islamic opposite number. Obsessive racism by the Serbs was fanned into mass criminality to claim more land from Croats, Bosnians, Albanians and all other minorities. Serb nationalist propaganda, some of it funded by Western business, contributed directly to an extremely violent civil war and to the genocide which went with it. Milošević's tight control over the RTS state broadcasting service was crucial and his exploitation of conspiracy myths to form the paranoia of the Serbs was a clear derivation from Hitler while Karadžić stole BBC equipment to set up *Kanal S*, a makeshift racist television station in Pale. Among other ruses this staged a massive human shield mock-up for the benefit of the West in 1995.

Equally the Muslims of Bosnia like those of Afghanistan and Southern Russia all gained confidence from the example of Iran. The Russians had indulged in fierce anti-Muslim propaganda in Uzbekistan and Kazakhstan in the 1930s and '40s souring their relationship so that the Muslim minorities became a real problem after the fall of the Soviet Union. This culminated in the extremely bitter rebellion in Chechnya, which itself did much to damage Boris Yeltsin.

CHINA

The only Communist country where the idea of mass rallies of the people achieving moral victories over brutal police forces did not work was in China. In the Tiananmen Square riots of June 1989 the authorities stood their ground. The brutalities there were not allowed to foster an escalation of demonstrations, just total suppression. The regime of Deng Xiaoping (1904–96) concentrated on socio-economic propaganda with particular emphasis on population control and its material benefits. However, Chinese propaganda remained ambivalent with the two senior controllers Wang Renzhi and Ding Guan'gen preaching Maoist Marxism and economic reform in the same breath. In 1992 the major personality cult of Deng Xiaoping as the new helmsman and father of the nation began, spearheaded by his daughter Deng Rong, while Jiang Zemin took over all real executive powers. In due course this led to the propaganda triumph of the reoccupation of Hong Kong by the new president Jiang Zemin, and the revival of the Opium Wars scandal to cast a slur over the departing British.

INDIA

In 1998 Sonia Gandhi, the Cinderella of Orbassano, made clever use of the reluctant queen concept, achieving popularity by disguising any political ambition under a cloak of humility and the Indian equivalent of apple pie to revive the Congress Party and the Gandhi dynasty against the nationalist BJP. It failed to win a majority and Atal Vajpayee of the BJP Hindu Nationalist Party inaugurated a period of frenzied confrontation with Pakistan which involved competitive demonstrations of nuclear arms. However, it was remarkable to what extent the new Asian democracies, particularly on the Indian sub-continent, produced dynastic rulers despite the huge political incorrectness of hereditary power.

UNITED STATES

Meanwhile, the significance of image, specifically television image, was becoming even more critical in the choice of American leaders. Ronald Reagan (1911–) had the presence and voice control of an experienced if not totally successful Hollywood actor. He had made his first political impact in 1964 with a television speech in favour of Barry Goldwater. He built up his career with an image of arch-conservatism, attacking youth culture and preaching hawkish patriotism on Vietnam. He used phrases like 'clean up the mess at Berkeley' (university) and 'sexual orgies so vile I cannot describe them to you' with an anti-intellectual, anti-liberal stance that for whatever reason struck a more acceptable note among Americans than Jimmy Carter's somewhat more humane but damaged integrity. His slogan was the meaningless 'The Time is Now'. Nixon's campaign adviser Peter H. Dailey was recalled to run Reagan's campaign for the presidency in 1980 on a budget of $25 million. It exploited Carter's misfortunes in the Iran hostage affair and exuded confidence without offering rational debate. Its most memorable slogan was 'You ain't seen nothin' yet'. Reagan won a second term against Mondale in 1984 despite a strong attack on his handling of the economy which in television commercials was shown in the metaphor of a roller-coaster. His ad hoc 'Tuesday Teams' of advertising professionals including Tom Messner and Barry Vetere worked on the Reagan/Bush campaign. In 1988 George Bush continued the Republican safely conservative mood, outmanoeuvring the Democrat Michael Dukakis (see pl. 5), as John Major later did Neil Kinnock in Britain, with the spectre of increased taxation – 'Read my lips'.

His successor Bill Clinton (1946–) demonstrated even more obviously the fluke effects of media usage in achieving political power which had little real foundation other than loss of faith in the previous regime. His original climb to power in Arkansas was masterminded by Dick Morris and Richard Dresner, paid for by chicken tycoon, Don Tyson. Using a mixture of aggressive fund-raising and tactical television advertising, he won the governorship in 1978. He lost it in 1980 but won it again in 1982 by repositioning himself further to the right on the advice of Morris and his own wife, Hillary. In 1990 he demonstrated his skill by responding to negative television coverage on the Friday before the state election by raising a bank loan and launching his own heavy television campaign on the Sunday. He exploited this ability to communicate an 'I feel your pain' empathy in the presidential campaign in 1992 and again in 1996, so that large numbers of voters who believed he was insincere still 'went with the glitz'. This was helped by the 'triangulation' of Clinton by Morris in the centre ground so that he would lose his dangerous liberal image and following a simplistic formula of '4 Es' – Education, Environment, Economy and Extremism – he was adept at using satellite facilities to appear in several areas at the same time. Morris himself was brought down by scandal, but Clinton survived to face further allegations of corruption and later sexual harassment. These were spearheaded by the *American Spectator*, which pioneered the Whitewater story and the Moonie-owned *Washington Times*.

The efforts to smear Clinton included a foundation set up by members of the Mellon media family with stories of murder and drug smuggling as well as adultery. The response was led by George Stephanopoulos. Partly the press attacks on Clinton were provoked by his cultivation of satellite and cable broadcasters at the expense of the press, but this coincided with the fast growth of real national papers in the US helped by new transmission technology. Technically novel was the use of the Internet by Clinton's opponents to trickle-leak substantial quantities of low-life allegations. However, Clinton's personal popularity seemed almost to thrive on adversity and in 1998 the Republicans snatched virtual defeat from the jaws of victory, perhaps mainly through concentrating entirely on negative propaganda.

IRAQ AND IRAN

Saddam Hussein (1937–) became leader of the ruling Bathist party in Iraq in 1973 developing a propaganda theme initiated by Michel Aflaq (1910–89) who produced his *Fi Sabil al Bath* in 1959 including 'the creative function of mass violence' and the motto 'one Arab nation with an eternal mission'. Iraqi nationalism generally was sustained by a significant living tradition of poetry in Iraq with popular propagandist poets like al Jawahiri and novelists such as Dhunin Ayyub. Another major propaganda writer who assisted Saddam's image projection was Abdul-Amir Malla (1942–97), a poet, novelist and journalist, who switched from projecting the Shi'ite cause to helping the dictator. Saddam cultivated a khaki image and as he built up his huge army had himself depicted first as the new Hammurabi of Babylon, then the Emperor Sargon of Agade. Then, like so many self-made monarchs before him, he had his ancestry traced back to the most respectable possible source, Ali, the Fourth Caliph of Baghdad. To back up this imperial image he rebuilt Babylon itself, decorated the streets of Baghdad – with triumphal arches based on his hands holding scimitars modelled on a vast scale – and he constructed eighty-three palaces. As warlord he failed to reduce Iran and took an even bigger risk with his attack on Kuwait which led to the Gulf War.

Saddam was highly proficient in his use of television and radio within his own country, but above all a master of diplomatic propaganda in which he often outmanoeuvred the Iranians, the Americans and the United Nations and might well have succeeded in isolating Kuwait, which he claimed as a province of Iraq. His ability to dominate world media was remarkable, as was his hold over his own people.

The blackening of his name by most of the rest of the world's media was not totally effective, particularly when it relied on unconvincing testimonials from Kuwait, but his genocide of the Kurds stretched his credibility to breaking point. Yet in 1995 a well-organized plebiscite showed him winning 99 per cent of popular support in Iraq and his deeply damaging regime continued to survive. The fanaticism of his army was enhanced by gory rituals such as the sacrifice of dogs. Again in 1998 he positioned himself as the undeserving victim of US/UK attack.

In the late 1990s Iran remained one of the most heavily propagandized countries in the world with policed exclusion of Western media and continued heavy extreme Shi'ite indoctrination of the entire population. However, under President Khatami, elected in 1997, there came the first signs of relaxation, and he was supported against the conservative mullahs by Mohsen Sazegara and the newspaper *Jameyeh.*

BRAZIL

An example of a media-made ruler was Fernando Collor of Brazil whose power base was built on the regional television network of Allagoas run by his brother Roberto. This in turn was extended into national coverage for Collor's promotion by the patronage of the larger national television and press empire, Globo, run by Dr Robert Marino who dominated Brazilian media. He orchestrated Collor's presidential campaign in 1989, using such techniques as a doctored television debate between the presidential candidates, in which parts unfavourable to Collor were cut out, and artificial opinion polls charting Collor's imagined popularity, which thus in due course briefly became real. Once elected to the presidency Collor soon allowed his corruption to become more obvious and made the serious error of falling out with his television executive brother. After launching a damning indictment of the President, the Globo empire also decided to change sides and to undermine him with skills even sharper than they had used to build him up. Most originally they chose to include very hard-hitting satire against him in their weekly soap opera *Body and Soul,* a programme with a vast and faithful following throughout the country. With 80 million viewers nightly, a third of them illiterate, a television company like Globo, especially when under the same ownership as a major newspaper, wielded an extremely unhealthy level of power.

WESTERN EUROPE

In 1994 Italy followed much the same pattern as Brazil in that a media magnate, Silvio Berlusconi (1937–) used his control of the mass media to build such a dominating image for himself that he was able to create an election-winning new party, Forza Italia. With three television networks taking 90 per cent of all Italian television advertising revenue, the former nightclub singer Berlusconi also had the Mondadori publishing house as part of his Fininvest empire, and was able to use PR and advertising techniques to build a quite false image of freedom from corruption, which did not for long stand the test of power.

It was France that had essentially pioneered the new shift of socialist party image to the centre ground. After years in opposition François Mitterrand (1916–95) sanitized his socialist platform and managed to defeat the somewhat divided Gaullists under Giscard d'Estaing in 1981. This was to some extent to be a model for other left-wing parties to present a softer, more appealing image, which was paralleled by Bill Clinton in the USA, Tony Blair in Britain and Gerhard Schröder (1944–) in Germany. All three hired public relations specialist James Carville to help smooth out their images.

In general the 1990s witnessed the wide application of computer technology to message management and the rise of 'spin doctors' like Dick Morris and Peter Mandelson. The techniques here included unattributed leaks of misleading information, keeping media waiting to the last minute before releasing stories (thus preventing opposition comment for twenty-four hours), the idea of blocking out an unfavourable story by interposing something more dramatic as, for example, when UK Conservatives took attention away from an anti-European rebellion with an attack on grant aid for lesbian and gay groups. There was a battle for initiative between increasingly powerful government information controllers, who could try to starve media which refused to be 'on message', and increasingly powerful media owners who could retaliate by digging for dirt. This was the high period for 'sound-bites', short, sharp comments that fitted the tabloid headline or abbreviated newscast. The appetite for attention-grabbing pictures was met by the construction of artificial 'photo opportunities'. Computer combing of old speeches provided pre-researched rebuttals for any combination of questions. Tony Blair's (1953–) election victory in 1997 was built on highly professional repackaging of the 'New' Labour Party image by Peter Mandelson (1953–), a former TV presenter, and disciplined use of these new techniques, helped by the very tarnished image of his opponents. One perhaps crucial additional factor was Blair's persuasion of Rupert Murdoch and his highly influential *Sun* newspaper to change sides from Conservative to Labour in the final years of John Major's government. Once in power the government's image was very tightly controlled by Mandelson and the chief press aide Alastair Campbell.

As the millennium approached, the doctrine of rights preached since Paine and Rousseau by the articulate liberal majority had spawned numerous plangent minorities, each propagandizing its own self-asserted sets of values: minority races, sects, sexual and lifestyle preference groups, and groups with numerous other teleological obsessions.

At the same time there were unprecedented levels of economic propaganda, with advertising as its backbone, geared to maintain international industry by encouraging increasing material wastage through accelerated obsolescence and the competitive worship of luxury or taste. All this was projected as the only way of avoiding worldwide economic catastrophe. Unless a country's GDP was growing then it was perceived as in danger of slump. Unless international business was left free to exploit the media to create artificial worldwide demand for its products and worldwide wastage, then it was expected that no form of media manipulation would be strong enough to stop the loss of confidence, so the spectre of recession had become the ruling phobia of the world, and with the end of Communism there was no alternative system on offer.

The last quarter of the twentieth century saw a huge worldwide escalation in the use of social propaganda, typically in the efforts to discourage tobacco smoking and Third World population growth. Numerous health, addiction, public safety and behavioural topics were addressed, with the propaganda fights against the spread of AIDS and the use of drugs achieving varied results. But all such examples of the use of propaganda to improve the human condition were minuscule compared with the commercial juggernaut promoting massive waste of the world's resources.

At the risk of oversimplification, just as a potential template for categorization it may be possible to put tentative scores against the contrasting spectra of mindsets visibly fostered by various propaganda recipes at the end of this century. Giving a notional score from 1 (low) to 10 (high) against the selected criteria it might look like this:

Criteria	Typical European Middle Class	Iranian Shi'ite	Young US Black	Left-Bank Israeli	Hutu Activist
Work ethic	7	6	3	8	2
Material aspirations	9	4	6	6	5
Respect for life	8	5	6	4	2
National consciousness	6	9	2	10	10
Belief in God	3	10	3	10	3
Sexual equality	7	4	6	5	4
Marital ethics	4	9	3	8	5
Care for young	6	7	3	7	4
Environment	5	4	2	4	3
Tolerance of deviations	6	1	7	2	4

Throughout the world there have been many examples of flimsy political regimes and flimsy religions pushed above the limits of their inherent strength by the foibles of media projection. Yet the major international groupings such as the EEC and the UN remain essentially propaganda failures, lacking popular appeal despite their self-evident worthiness and one multinational grouping, the Soviet Union, disappeared almost overnight. The British Commonwealth, a clever piece of repackaging, was one of the more successful examples of a group of countries with some elements of an image, but even it was badly damaged. All across the world it seemed as the millennium approached that people got more of the propaganda they wanted than the propaganda they needed. Many more were physically free than in previous centuries but the minds of the masses were still often bound by the silken chains of emotional management.

Epilogue

Historical generalizations are always potentially dangerous, but even a cursory review of the world's propaganda history points to a number of almost foolproof suggestions. Firstly, propaganda, the use of communication skills to create or maintain power and influence, is one of the oldest techniques in the world. The human species is a natural propagandist. Those to the fore of the pack wish to assert their images and their ideas with a will that is as innate as a peacock's display of its feathers. The basic instinct to propagandize is a factor of vanity and the lust for power.

Secondly, there is clear evidence of the considerable role which propaganda skills, used consciously or unconsciously, have played in the rise of most regimes and religions throughout history. Propaganda is the catalyst for group activity leading to mass manipulation, leading in turn to the imposition of the ideas and objectives of the few on the many. Thirdly, though there is a level of judgement here, it can be suggested that these successful regimes and religions were not always by any means the most efficient or benign that were available at the time. Many regimes and religions which achieved power and influence as a result of their propaganda skills went on to cause unnecessary wars, persecutions and hardships which their less charismatic rivals might have avoided.

Fourthly, because propaganda is never a totally efficient process it produces deviations and extremes in its results, over-indoctrination and mis-indoctrination, which lead to divisiveness, persecution or mass-masochism. Fifthly, we have seen that powerful or novel ideas often surface and win through, whatever the problems of censorship, lack of media access or lack of funds, whereas even with the advantages of censorship, vast budgets and unimpeded access to all media, weak or stale ideas will still eventually lose support. Sixthly, because propaganda by its nature tends to be combative, competitive and often intimidating it induces a quite unnecessary level of mass neurosis with consequential ill effects for ordinary people. Finally, despite all these disadvantages and portents of disaster, the propaganda function does play an essential and useful part in the control of human behaviour, the encouragement of human cooperation and the spread of improved standards.

Having considered the inherent dangers it is important to attempt an explanation of propaganda's unreliability. This lies firstly in the rule of the line of least resistance, dictated by the balance of message appeal, media facility and audience receptivity. For instance, propaganda usually chooses to flatter – its tells its audience that it is racially or ethnically superior, religiously superior, militarily superior; the master race, God's chosen people, the invincible. Such flattery has been the prelude to many of history's great disasters; it is dangerous because on the one hand it creates aggressive overconfidence, while on the other it encourages contempt for lesser mortals who can therefore be disposed of. This has resulted in thousands of examples of racial intolerance, war, religious persecution, witch-hunting, gypsy-baiting and genocide. From flattery of the present, propaganda extends itself both forwards and backwards. It nearly always promises a future which it may not be able to deliver. False futures, victory in war, triumph over disasters, escape from economic ills, everlasting life, heaven and hell, a golden millennium round the corner or the Second Coming, are the bait of behaviour. Inversely flattery of the past, sentimental reverence for a previous era presented as if without blemish, is used to provide false credibility for the present: the Third Reich reviving the Second, the Second Empire reviving the First, the tsars reviving the caesars, the Second Coming even better than the original Messiah.

The second line of least resistance which propaganda tends to follow is its appetite for high drama, for conflict, its love of heroics and martyrdom, of masochistic self-denial, of fights and fairy tales, of exotic visual themes, performances that appeal to the senses. Because of its requirement to entertain and motivate it sensationalizes, it thrives on extremes and helps extremes to thrive.

In reviewing the overall history of propaganda certain unpleasant traits keep recurring. There seems to have been little let-up from Nebuchadnezzar to Saddam Hussein, from Caesar to Hitler, in the creation of highly destructive over-geared tyrannies based essentially on mass intimidation, on the delusion of dangers, imaginary third-party enemies, the *spectre rouge* for Napoleon and Hitler, the black peril for Jefferson Davies and Malan, the white peril for Lenin, the yellow peril for Kaiser Wilhelm and General Tojo. The conspiracy theory has been used again and again to cow opposition with the promise of strong rule, national solidarity, efficiency and glory.

The second most dangerously exploited delusion has been the myth of ethnic individuality, the exaggerated nationalism of groups who often barely had a language of their own, let alone a special colour, special facial structure or uniquely sacrosanct way of life. Whether it was would-be master races like the Romans, the French, the British, the Germans, the Americans, Confederate Americans, Afrikaners, Japanese, or paranoid minor races like the Basques, the Irish, the Cossacks, the Bosnian Serbs, the Armenians and the Palestinians, the propagandized exaggeration of differences, the heightened perception of uniqueness has caused vast multiplication of human misery.

The third great delusion has been the myth of inspiration, the conviction that the vision of one should be the vision of everyone, that legend repeated often enough becomes fact, the pseudo-scholasticism of texts and relics, the incestuous self-rationalization of innumerable strata of repeated aphorisms, all resolved into a fanatical sense of infallibility which takes the right to destroy opposition. Mass sacrifice by the Aztecs, mass burning by the Inquisition, mass persecution of the Jews, the propaganda of cumulatively fictitious precedents has been one of the three great causes of man-made misery. From the stone tablets of Sinai to the golden plates of the Mormons, from the *Will of Constantine* to the *Protocols of the Elders of Zion* or the *Malleus Maleficarum*, enhanced or fake credentials have been among the least praiseworthy elements of propaganda. The delusions of religious superiority, the insidious propaganda which portrayed the Muslims as filth, Catholics as anti-Christ, Jews as murderers of Christ, are as illogical as the mythologies of master races, master castes or the master sex.

The fourth great delusion, one of the most actively fostered for many millennia, is the delusion of rank, the hereditary right to acquire deference, power, property and wealth, a concept deeply inculcated by a vast array of primitive media, which have given visual charisma and emotive credibility to an otherwise illogical concept.

In the final years of the twentieth century it is interesting to review the general trends in propaganda and their effects. It is clear that for those who have the power of access to the mass media by whatever means there is a general tendency towards increased blandness, for political and religious leaders close to the top to avoid controversy, to avoid too much logic or specific policies or beliefs, to rely rather on style and presentation, good appearance and a broadly acceptable norm, safety not risk. On the other hand for those who do not have such ready access there is a tendency towards eccentricity, the need for sensation, for the raw material of a variant mythology to stand out from the crowd.

Linking these two concepts from the media point of view is the fact that in some respects the new technology of the mass media, the increased sophistication of presentation and distribution, mean that it is much harder for any but establishment figures to make any real impact. At the same time, however, the new technology has also had mini-media implications, and the 1990/1 anti-Communist revolutions showed in particular the importance of home-made newspapers on small machines, amateur copying of tape cassettes, smuggled film shows, and makeshift radio transmitters. Another factor is that audiences throughout the world are constantly becoming more exposed to the latest in international mass media entertainment, they are better trained, more aware, often more cynical. Despite all this, though, they do still have the capacity to be moved by the most unexpected, illogical, far-fetched ideas, both new and old. There is nothing to show that audiences under pressure are any less responsive to manic calls for ethnic violence, minority baiting, hysterical intolerance, mass indulgence in vanity, masochism and self-destructive hedonism, than they were in the Middle Ages. Similarly in a world full of dangers it is not necessarily much easier for those worthy propagandists who seek to persuade their fellows to save the environment, to avoid unpleasant diseases, to give up poisonous drugs, to have fewer children or adopt any of the other changes of attitude agreed by the majority to be desirable. One of the difficulties of the modern world is the need to promote middle-of-the-road moralities and compromise policies which lack the charisma of the old-fashioned absolutes.

As the Roman Empire went down on a diet of gladiatorial shows, free bread and circuses, so the modern world buries itself understandably in soap operas and obscure sporting contests rather than heeding the preachers of doom. If there is a lesson to be learned from any history then certainly the history of propaganda is a candidate for pointing out pitfalls which are highly likely to recur in the future. To help avoid them it is reasonable to suggest that there should be continuous research into and explanations at all levels, old and young, of the mechanics of racialist indoctrination and nationalism so that groups are not falsely led into impractical rebellions or unnecessary persecutions. There should be the same activity with regard to the techniques of religious propaganda to prevent dangerous, over-fanatical cult propagation. These two assertions do not ascribe the right for any individual to condemn any nationalist movement or any religious cult, only to be provided with immunization training so that he or she can make a balanced judgement as to whether to join such movements.

Peoples should be encouraged to be alert to the techniques adopted by all potential leaders, religious and political, in the build-up of their personal images and following. There should be training and understanding of the way in which moral standards are propagated, both out of the past and out of the present, both out of dominant majorities and minority groups. In the same way there should be a full recognition of the methods used for communal health and social education, the use of propaganda to prevent the spread of disease, overpopulation, pollution, road accidents and so on. In parallel we need to be aware of the manipulation of attitudes in economic matters, the persuasion to save or spend, work hard or have a relaxed worth ethic, to beg, lend, invest or buy. This also applies to the adjustment of moral standards undertaken by self-appointed opinion leaders, some good, some not so good, but certainly with no divine right to dictate new attitudes on sex, marriage, temperance or any other matter.

In the final decade of the twentieth century the academic fashion remained in the Chomsky pattern of being concerned about mass manipulation by the forces of the right, by the establishment and by capital. But equally there were signs of widespread massive destabilization due to the loss of credibility in authority itself. The declining image of objective standards, the reduced respect for the concept of government, for parental or geriatric authority, for religious or ethical prescripts, left material wealth as the only undamaged icon with resultant wide swathes of anarchy and class polarization.

There should now be a greater consciousness of the wider role of the arts and the propaganda element in almost every form of creative communication, but particularly in the management of events and the emotional range of conversion processes. We can accept the utility of propaganda, much of it undirected and anonymous, the settled beckoning to the unsettled, which helps the human to feel part of a group, sane, secure, integrated, possibly cooperative, caring and even quite altruistic. But we ought to know how it works and realize that when it fails to work chaos can ensue.

Man, as we have seen, has been manipulated by his fellows from the beginning of time and has in turn often been manipulative. We do not mind being manipulated. We often benefit from it, but equally there have been numerous occasions when we have been quite easily led into the most preposterously dangerous behaviour. We have been motivated to genocide, human sacrifice, war, witch-hunting, racist hysteria, religious intolerance and many other forms of irrational behaviour. The media we use to do this to each other have developed. But the type of images and messages which sway us have changed very little.

The problem of propaganda throughout the ages is that it has almost always failed to deliver what it promised. Frequently it has led to the physical or emotional damaging of its recipients. In the past much of the harm has related to the overselling of religious dogma or the promotion of glorious war, but the last few centuries have seen the steady accretion also of commercial propaganda which glorifies physical appearance and worldly success leading to mass feelings of competitiveness and often inadequacy which are almost as harmful.

Bibliography

PART ONE

CHAPTER 1

Abelson, H.I., and Karlins, M., *Persuasion: how Opinion and Attitudes are changed*, New York, 1970.
Aranguren, J.L., *Human Communication*, transl., London, 1967.
Barthes, Raymond, *Mythologies*, transl. London, 1973.
Bernays, E.L., *The Engineering of Consent*, New York, 1955.
Carpenter, E. and McLuhan M., *Explorations in Communications*, Boston, 1966.
Chomsky, Noam, *Deterring Democracy*, London, 1991.
Doob, Leonard, *Public Opinion and Propaganda*, London, 1949.
Driencourt, J., *La Propagande*, Paris, 1950.
Ellul, Jacques, *Propaganda:the Formation of Men's Attitudes*, transl., New York, 1973.
Fraser, L., *Propaganda*, London, 1959.
Gans, H.J., in McQuail, D., ed., *Sociology of Mass Communications*, London, 1972.
Herman, E.S., and Chomsky, N. , *Manufacturing Consent*, New York, 1988.
Hoggart, Richard, *The Uses of Literacy*, London, 1958.
Hovland, C., *Communication and Persuasion*, Yale, 1965.
Innis, Harold, *The Bias of Communication*, Toronto, 1951.
Jackall, Robert, (ed.), *Propaganda*, Basingstoke, 1995.
Jowett, Garth S. and O'Donnell V., *Propaganda and Persuasion*, London, 1986.
Katz, D. (ed.), *Public Opinion and Propaganda*, New York, 1954.
Lasswell, H.D., Casey, R.D. and Smith, B.L., *Propaganda and Promotional Activities*, Chicago, 1969.
Lippmann, Walter, *Public Opinion*, New York, 1922.
McLuhan, Marshall, *Understanding Media*, London, 1964.
Packard, Vance, *The Hidden Persuaders*, New York, 1957.
Plato, *Republic*, transl., London, 1960.
Schramm, W., ed., *Mass Communications*, Chicago, 1960.
Walter, J., *The Propaganda Gap*, New York, 1963.
Williams, Raymond, *Communications*, London, 1962.
Wright, C.R., *Mass Communications*, London, 1959.

CHAPTER 2

Barbu, Z., *Society, Culture and Personality*, London, 1971.
Davison, W. Philip, *International Communications*, New York, 1968.

Dexter, L.A., and White, D.M., (eds), *People, Society and Mass Communications*, London, 1964.
Lull, J., *Media, Communication and Culture*, London, 1994.
McQuail, D., (ed.), *Sociology of Mass Communications*, London, 1972.
Praktanis, A.R. and Aranson, E., *The Age of Propaganda*, New York, 1992.
Thompson, J.B., *Media and Modernity*, Cambridge, 1995.

CHAPTER 3

Atkinson, R.F., *Moral Indoctrination*, London, 1975.
Bantock, G.H., *Freedom and Authority in Education*, London, 1952.
Bartlett, F.C., *Political Propaganda*, Cambridge, 1940.
Berlin, Isaiah, *The Crooked Timber of Humanity*, London, 1990.
Black, J.B., *The Coordination and Control of Propaganda*, London, 1969.
Blumler, J., *Political Effects of Mass Communication*, London, 1977.
Davison, W. Philip, *Mass Communications and Conflict Resolution*, New York, 1974.
Domenach, J.M., *La Propagande Politique*, Paris, 1973.
Fagen, R., *Politics and Communication*, Boston, 1966.
Hart, Henry O., *Mass Communication and Social Change*, Munich, 1979.
Hawthorn, Jeremy (ed.), *Propaganda, Persuasion and Polemics*, London, 1987.
Hudson, M., and Stanier, J. *War and the Media*, Stroud, 1998.
Huntford, R., *The New Totalitarianism*, London, 1972.
Jackall, R., and Vidich, A. (eds), *Propaganda*, London, 1995.
Keane, John, *The Media and Democracy*, Cambridge, 1991.
Lazarsfield, P.F., and Merton, R.K., *Mass Communication, Popular Taste and Organized Social Action*, New York, 1969.
McQuail, D., *Towards a Sociology of Mass Communications*, London, 1972.
Mitchell, M.G., *Propaganda, Polls and Public Opinion*, New York, 1970.
Negrine, Ralph M., *Politics and the Mass Media in Britain*, London, 1989.
Pye, L., *Communications and Political Development*, New York, 1963.
——, *Political Personality and Nation Building*, New York, 1961.
Rose, R., *Influencing Voters*, London, 1957.
Schramm, W., *Mass Media and National Development*, Stanford, 1963.
Seymore-Ure, Colin K., *Political Impact of Mass Media*, London, 1974.
Taylor, Philip M., *Munitions of the Mind:War Propaganda*, Wellingborough, 1990.
Thomson, Oliver, *History of Sin*, Edinburgh, 1993.
Whale, John, *The Politics of the Media*, Manchester, 1989.
Winkler, Allan M., *The Politics of Propaganda: the Office of War Information*, New Haven, 1978.

CHAPTER 4

Abercrombie, Nicholas, *Television and Society*, Cambridge, 1996.
Apel, P.H., *The Message of Music*, London, 1958.
Black, Jeremy, *Maps and Politics*, London, 1998.
Blumler, J., and McQuail, D., *Television in Politics*, London, 1968.
Borzello, Frances, *Civilizing Caliban: the Misuse of Art*, London, 1987.
Boyce D. George, Curran, J. and Wingate, P. (eds), *Newspaper History*, London, 1978.
Bradby, David (ed.), *Performance and Politics in Popular Drama*, Cambridge, 1980.
Briggs, Asa, *History of Broadcasting in the United Kingdom*, London, 1961.
Carter, D., *The Fourth Branch of Government*, New York, 1959.

Casey, R.D., *The Press, Propaganda and Pressure Groups*, New York, 1950.

Crampton, W.G., *The World of Flags*, London, 1990.

Curran, J. and Gurevitch, M. (eds), *Mass Media and Society*, London, 1991.

——, and Seaton, J., *Power without Responsibility: Press and Broadcasting in Britain*, London, 1988.

——, (ed.), *Impacts and Influences: essays on media power in the twentieth century*, London, 1987.

Daiches, David, (ed.), *Literature and Western Civilization*, London, 1975.

Etzkorn, K.P., (ed.), *Music and Society*, London, 1973.

Foulkes, A.P., *Literature and Propaganda*, London, 1983.

Gage, John, *Colour and Culture*, London, 1993.

Gallo, Max, *The Poster in History*, transl., London, 1974.

Gamboni, D.G., *Emblemes de la Liberté*, Berne, 1991.

Gay, P., *Art and Action: Causes in History*, London, 1976.

Getlein, F. and D., *The Bite of Print: satire and irony in woodcuts*, London, 1964.

Giddings, R. (ed.), *Literature and Imperialism*, London, 1991.

Gombrich, E.H., *Norm and Form*, London, 1966.

Grierson, J., *On Documentary*, (ed.) Forsyth Hardy, London, 1966.

Hale, Julian, *Radio, Power and International Broadcasting*, London, 1975.

Halloran, J.D. (ed.), *The Effects of Television*, London, 1966.

Isaacs, H.R., *The Idols of the Tribe: Group Identity and Political Change*, London, 1975.

Isaakson, F. and Furhammar, L., *Politics in Film*, transl., London, 1971

Kamenetsky, C., *Children's Literature*, Athens, 1984.

Kiernan, V.G., *Poets, Politics and the People*, London, 1989.

Koss, Stephen, *The Rise and Fall of Political Press in Britain*, London, 1981.

Kracauer, S., *The Nature of Film*, New York, 1961.

Lindahl, R., *Broadcasting across Borders: a study in the role of propaganda*, London, 1976.

Metzl, E., *The Poster*, London, 1963.

Oinas, F.J., *Heroic Epic and Saga*, Indiana, 1978.

Paulin, Tom (ed.), *Faber Book of Political Verse*, London, 1986.

Perris, Arnold, *Music as Propaganda*, Westpoint, 1985.

Philippe, Robert, *Political Graphics: art as weapon*, Oxford, 1982.

Poster, Mark, *The Second Media Age*, London, 1995.

Pronay, Nicholas (ed.), *Propaganda and Politics in Film 1918–45*, London, 1982.

Quint, D., *Epic and Empire*, Princeton, 1992.

Ranney, Austin, *Channels of Power – the impact of television*, New York, 1983.

Reynolds, K., *Children's Literature in 1890 and 1990*, Plymouth, 1994.

Rhode, E., *A History of Cinema*, London, 1966.

Rickards, Maud, *Posters of Protest and Revolution*, Bath, 1970.

Ryan, James, *Picturing Empire*, London, 1998.

Salmon, Lucy M., *The Newspaper and Authority*, New York, 1923.

Smith, A. (ed.), *Television and Political Life*, London, 1979.

Suleiman, S., *Authoritarian Fiction*, New York, 1983.

Thomson, F.P., *Tapestry: Mirror of History*, London, 1980.

Tracey, Michael, *Production of Political Television*, London, 1978.

Trenaman, J., *Television and Political Image*, London, 1959.

Weill, Alain, *The Poster: a worldwide survey*, New York, 1985.

Westrup, J., *Introduction to Musical History*, London, 1957.

Von Volborth, C-A., *The Art of Heraldry*, Poole, 1987.

Young, Robert, *White Mythologies*, London, 1990.

Zipes, Jack, *Fairy Tales and the Art of Subversion*, London, 1983.

CHAPTER 5

Barbu, Zevedei, *Problems of Historical Psychology*, transl., Cambridge, 1960.
Brown, J.A.C., *Techniques of Persuasion*, London, 1963.
Canetti, E., *Crowds and Power*, transl., London, 1962.
Castles, F.G., *Pressure Groups*, London, 1967.
Cohen, Stanley, *Folk Devils and Moral Panics*, London, 1980.
Crowley, D. and Mitchell, D., *Communication Theory Today*, Cambridge, 1994.
——, *National Style and the Nation State: design in politics*, London, 1992.
Czitrom, D., *Media and the American Mind*, North Carolina, 1982.
Doob, L.W., *Propaganda: its Psychology and Techniques*, New York, 1935.
Douglas, Tom, *Scapegoats*, London, 1995.
Freud, Sigmund, *Group Psychology and the Analysis of the Ego*, New York, 1930.
Halloran, J.D. Eliot, P. and Murdoch, G., *Demonstrations in Communications*, London, 1972.
Huxley, Aldous, *The Devils of Loudun*, London, 1952.
Knox, Ronald, *Enthusiasm*, Oxford, 1950.
Koestler, Arthur, *Arrow in the Blue*, London, 1958.
Miller, G., *The Psychology of Communications*, London, 1970.
Moscovici, Serge, *Social Influence and Social Control*, transl. London, 1976.
Pritchett, V.S., *The Mythmakers*, London, 1979.
Quatter, T.H., *Propaganda and Psychological Warfare*, London, 1952.
Rosnow, R.L. and Robinson, E.J., *Experiments in Persuasion*, New York, 1969.
Sargant, W., *The Battle for the Mind*, London, 1957.
Snook, I.A. (ed.), *Concepts of Indoctrination*, London, 1972.
Sorokin, P.A., *see* Rosnow above.
Temple, R., *Open to Suggestion*, London, 1985.
Vernon, M.D., *Human Motivation*, London, 1968.
Zimbardo, P.G., *see* Rosnow above.

CHAPTER 6

Boorstin, D.J., *The Image*, New York, 1962.
Friedberg, David, *The Power of Images*, Chicago, 1989.
Rees, Nigel, *Slogans*, London, 1982.
Sox, H. David, *Relics and Shrines*, London, 1985.

CHAPTER 7

Bettelheim, Bruno, *The Uses of Enchantment, the meaning and importance of fairy tales*, London, 1977.
Bourdieu, Pierre, *Language and Symbolic Power*, transl., Cambridge, 1992.
Frazer, J.G., *The Golden Bough*, London, 1922.
Raglan, Lord, *The Hero: a Study in Tradition, Myth and Drama*, London, 1936.
Samuel, Raphael, (ed.), *The Myths We Live By*, London, 1990
Vovelle, Michel, *Ideologies and Mentalities*, transl., Cambridge, 1990.
Warner, Marina, *From the Beast to the Blonde*, London, 1995.

CHAPTER 8

Doob, L.W., *Propaganda: Its Psychology and Techniques*, New York, 1935.
Crowley, D. and Mitchell, D., *Communication Theory Today*, Cambridge, 1994.

Curran, J. and Gurevitch, M. (eds), *Mass Media Society*, London, 1986.
Hawthorn, J. (ed.), *Propaganda, Persuasion and Polemics*, London, 1985.
Schramm, W., *The Process and Effects of Mass Communication*, Chicago, 1971.

CHAPTER 9

Brown, J.A.C., *Techniques of Persuasion*, London, 1963.
Hovland, C., *Communication and Persuasion*, Yale, 1965.
Le Bon, Gustave, *The Crowd*, London, 1896.
Moscovici, Serge, *The Age of the Crowd*, transl., Cambridge, 1985.
Ransat, R., *Smear*, London, 1991.
Scheflin, Alan, *Mind Manipulation*, London, 1978.

CHAPTER 10

Bryant, J. and Zillman, Dolf, *Perspective on Media Effectiveness*, Hillsdale, 1986.
Dawkins, Richard, *Climbing Mount Improbable*, London, 1996.
Klapper, J.T., *The Effects of Mass Communication*, New York, 1960.
MacLean, Eleanor, *Between the Lines: how to detect bias and propaganda in the News*, Montreal, 1981.
Schramm, W., *The Process and Effects of Mass Communication*, Chicago, 1971.
Smith, B.L., and Casey, R.D., *Propaganda, Communications and Public Opinion*, Princeton, 1946.
UNESCO, *Many Voices in One World*, New York, 1980.

PART TWO

CHAPTER 11

Atkinson, R.J.C., *Stonehenge*, London, 1960.
Barrett, J.C., *Fragments from Antiquity*, Oxford, 1994.
Childe, V.G., *The Dawn of European Civilization*, London, 1957.
Clark, G. and Piggott, S., *Prehistoric Societies*, London, 1970.
Daniel, G.E., *Megalith Builders of Western Europe*, London, 1958.
Hallstrom, G., *Monumental Art of Northern Europe*, Stockholm, 1960.
Megaw, J.V.S., *Art of the European Iron Age*, Bath, 1970.

CHAPTER 12

Aldred, C., *The Egyptians*, London, 1984.
——, *Egyptian Art*, London, 1980.
Baron, S.W., *Social and Religious History of the Jews*, New York, 1962.
Black, J.A., and Green, A.R. (eds), *Gods, Demons and Symbols of Ancient Mesopotamia*, London, 1990.
Gardiner, Alan H., *Egypt of the Pharaohs*, Oxford, 1964.
Grimal, N.A., *History of Ancient Egypt*, transl., Oxford, 1992.
Kaniel, M., *Judaism*, London, 1979.
Koch, Klaus, *The Prophets*, London, 1982.

Larsen, Mogens T. (ed.), *Power and Propaganda, a Symposium on Ancient Empires*, Copenhagen, 1979.

Lasswell, H.D., Lerner, D. and Speier, H. (eds). *Propaganda and Communications in World History*, Honolulu, 1979.

Mason, Rex, *Propaganda and Subversion in the Old Testament*, London, 1987.

Olmstead, A.T.E., *History of the Persian Empire*, Chicago, 1948.

Reade, J.E., *Assyrian Sculpture*, London, 1983.

Saggs, H.W.F., *The Might that was Assyria*, London, 1984.

Stacey, W.P., *Prophetic Drama in the Old Testament*, London, 1990.

Thapar, Romila, *History of India*, London, 1966.

Wiseman D.J., *Nebuchadnezzar and Babylon*, Oxford, 1988.

CHAPTER 13

Arnold, B. and Gibson, D.G., *Celtic Chiefdoms*, Cambridge, 1995.

Boardman, John (ed.), *Oxford History of Classical Art*, Oxford, 1993.

Bury, J.B., Cook, S.A. and Adcock, F.E., *Cambridge Ancient History: Athens*, Cambridge, 1953.

Cook, S.A., Adcock, F.E. and Charlesworth, M.P., *Cambridge Ancient History: Roman Republic*, Cambridge, 1951.

Donan, Rob, *Temple Propaganda*, Washington, 1981.

Evans, Jane D., *The Art of Persuasion from Aeneas to Brutus*, Michigan, 1992.

Grant, Michael, *Roman Coins*, London, 1946.

Hammond, N.G.L., *History of Greece*, Oxford, 1986.

——, *Alexander the Great*, London, 1981.

——, *History of Macedonia*, London, 1979

Jones, C.E., *Speech and Persuasion in Fifth Century Athens*, London, 1988.

Kautilya's *Arthashastra*, R. Shamasastri (transl.), T.G. Sastri (ed.), Mysore, 1958.

Meier, Christian, *The Political Art of Greek Tragedy*, transl., Cambridge, 1993.

Piccivilli, Luigi, *Temistocle etc.*, Genova, 1987.

Powell, Anton (ed.), *Roman Poetry and Propaganda in the Age of Augustus*, London, 1992.

——, ed., *Classical Sparta*, London, 1989.

Scullard, H.H., *From the Gracchi to Nero*, London, 1976.

Smarczyck, B., *Untersuchungen zur Religionspolitike . . . Athens*, Munich, 1990.

Sordi, M., *Propaganda e Persuasione nell'Antichita*, Milan, 1974.

Syme, Ronald, *The Roman Revolution*, Oxford, 1939.

Thapar, R., *Asoka and the Decline of the Mauryas*, Oxford, 1961.

Twitchett, D. and Loewe, M., *Cambridge History of China: Ch'in and Han*, Cambridge, 1986.

Wallman, Peter, *Triumviri reipublicae constituendae*, Frankfurt, 1980

Yavetz, Zvi, *Julius Caesar and his Public Image*, transl., London, 1983.

CHAPTER 14

Baharal, D., *Victory of Propaganda . . . 193–235 AD*, Oxford, 1996.

Barclay, William, *Communicating the Gospel*, London, 1962.

Blurton, T.R., *Hindu Art*, London, 1992.

Borman, Lukas, *et al. Religious Propaganda and Missionary Competition in the New Testament Period*, Leiden, 1994.

Cameron, Alan, *Claudian: Poetry and Propaganda at the Court of Honorius*, Oxford, 1970.

Child, H. and Cobles, D., *Christian Symbols*, London, 1960.

Fiorenza, Eliz S. (ed.), *Aspects of Religious Propaganda in Judaism and Early Christianity*, Notre Dame, 1976.
Frend, W.H.C., *The Rise of Christianity*, London, 1984.
Grabar, André, *Christian Iconography*, London, 1969
Grant, Michael, *The Emperor Constantine*, London, 1993.
Green, M., *Evangelism and the Early Church*, London, 1964.
Grunewald, T., *Constantinus Maximus Augustus: Herrschafts-propaganda*, Stuttgart, 1990.
Heather, Peter, *Goths and Normans*, Oxford, 1991.
Howarth, P., *Attila, King of the Huns*, London, 1994.
Huskinson, Janet M., *Concordia Apostolorum: Christian Propaganda Art in Rome in the 4th and 5th Centuries*, Oxford, 1982.
MacMullen, R., *Christians in the Roman Empire*, Yale, 1984.
Rhys David, T.W., *Buddhism, its History and Literature*, London, 1923.
Schulz, H., *Jesus*, Philadelphia, 1971.
Seckel, Dietrich, *The Art of Buddhism*, transl., London, 1964.
Trillmich, W., *Familien Propaganda der Kaiser Kaligula*, Frankfurt, 1978.

CHAPTER 15

Billington, James H., *The Icon and the Axe*, London, 1966.
Chamberlin, Russell, *Charlemagne*, London, 1986.
Cormack, Robin, *Writing in Gold: Byzantine Society and its Icons*, London, 1985.
Franke, H. and Twitchett, D., *Cambridge History of China: Alien Regimes*, Cambridge, 1994.
Gibb, A.R. Hamilton, *Arabic Literature*, Oxford, 1963.
Guillaume, Alfred, *Islam*, London, 1963.
——, *Life of Muhammad*, Oxford, 1978.
Haldon, J.F., *Byzantium in the Seventh Century*, Cambridge, 1990.
Head, Thomas, *Hagiography and the Cult of Saints*, Cambridge, 1990.
Hourani, Albert, *History of the Arab Peoples*, London, 1991.
Kubler, G., *The Art and Architecture of Ancient America*, London, 1954.
Lings, Martin, *Muhammad*, London, 1983.
McKitterick, R., *New Cambridge Medieval History*, Vol. 2, Cambridge, 1995.
Page, R.I., *Chronicles of the Vikings*, London, 1995.
Papadopoulos, A., *Islam and Muslim Art*, London, 1980.
Rodley, Lynn, *Byzantine Art and Architecture*, Cambridge, 1994.
Sharon, M., *Black Banners: The Establishment of the Abbasid State*, Jerusalem, 1983.
Smyth, A.P. *King Alfred the Great*, Oxford, 1995.
Ullman, Walter, *History of Political Thought in the Middle Ages*, London, 1965.
Ure, P.N., *Justinian and his Age*, London, 1951.
Yamamura, K., *Cambridge History of Japan: Medieval Japan*, Cambridge, 1990.
Zarnecki, G., *English Romanesque Art*, New York, 1984.

CHAPTER 16

Biller, Peter (ed.), *Heresy and Literacy 1000–1530*, Cambridge, 1996.
Borsook, Eve, *Messages and Mosaics in Sicily 1130–87*, Oxford, 1990.
Brown, R. Allen, *Norman Conquest*, London, 1984.
Camille, Michael, *The Gothic Idol*, Cambridge, 1989.
Cohn, Norman, *The Pursuit of the Millennium*, London, 1957.
Daniel, Norman, *Islam and the West: the Making of an Image*, London, 1992.

Folda, Jaroslav, *The Art of the Crusader in the Holy Land*, Cambridge, 1995.
Hassig, Debra, *Medieval Bestiaries*, Cambridge, 1996.
Jordan, K., *Henry the Lion*, Oxford, 1986.
Lloyd, Simon, *English Society and the Crusades*, Oxford, 1988.
Mâle, Emil, *Religious Art in France*, Princeton, 1958.
Moorman, J.R.H., *History of the Franciscan Order*, Oxford, 1974.
Muir, L.R., *The Biblical Drama of Medieval Europe*, Cambridge, 1929.
Munstenburg, Hugo, *The Japanese Print*, New York, 1982.
Nelson, Janet, *Politics and Ritual in Early Medieval Europe*, London, 1986.
Oldenbourg, Zoë, *The Crusades*, transl., London, 1966.
Paterson, L.M., *The World of the Troubadours*, Cambridge, 1993.
Pochoda, Elizabeth T., *Arthurian Propaganda*, Chapel Hill, 1971.
Richard, Jean, *Saint Louis*, Oxford, 1992.
Rossabi, Morris, *Khubilai Khan*, Berkeley, 1987.
Runcieman, J.C.S., *The History of the Crusades*, London, 1965.
Throop, P.A., *Criticism of the Crusade: Public Opinion and Crusade Propaganda*, Philadelphia, 1975.
Tipton, C. (ed.), *Nationalism in the Middle Ages*, New York, 1977.
Tobins, S., *Cistercians*, London, 1995.
Turville, Peter T., *England and Nationality: Language, Literature and the National Identity 1290–1340*, Oxford, 1996.
Tyerman, Chris, *England and the Crusades*, Chicago, 1988.
Ullman, Walter, *Principles of Government and Politics in the Middle Ages*, Cambridge, 1961.
Wilson, Stephen, *Saints and their Cults*, Cambridge, 1983.

CHAPTER 17

Abulafia, D., *Frederick II*, London, 1988.
Aston, Margaret, *Lollards and Reformers and Imagined Literacy in Late Medieval Religion*, London, 1984.
Babinger, Franz, *Mehmed the Conqueror*, Princeton, 1978.
Borst, Arno, *Medieval Worlds: Barbarians, Heretics and Artists in the Middle Ages*, transl., Cambridge, 1991.
Brooke, Rosalind and C., *Popular Religion in the Middle Ages*, London, 1984.
Brown, C.J., *The Shaping of History and Poetry in Late Medieval France*, Birmingham, 1985.
Burke, Peter, *Popular Culture in Medieval Europe*, London, 1978.
Burman, Edward, *The Templars*, London, 1986.
Castedo, Leopoldo, *History of Latin American Art and Architecture*, transl., London, 1969.
Cobo, B., *History of the Inca Empire*, transl., Austin, 1979.
Conrad, G.W. and Demarest, A.A., *Religion and Empire: the Dynamics of Aztec and Inca Expansion*, Cambridge, 1984.
Ellenius, Allen (ed.), *Iconography, Propaganda and Legitimation*, Oxford, 1948.
Goodman, Anthony, *The Wars of the Roses*, London, 1990.
Green, R.F., *Poets and Prince-pleasers: Literature and the English Court in the late Middle Ages*, Toronto, 1980.
Huizinga, J., *The Waning of the Middle Ages*, London, 1924.
Ianziti, G., *Humanistic Historiography under the Sforzas: Politics and Propaganda in 15th Century Milan*, Oxford, 1988.
Kemp, Wolfgang, *The Narrative of Gothic Stained Glass*, Cambridge, 1997.
Jordan, Karl, *Henry the Lion*, Oxford, 1986.
Joyce, Marcus, *Mezoamerican Writing Systems*, Princeton, 1992.

Justice, S., *Writing and Rebellion: England 1381*, Berkeley, 1994.
Labarge, Margaret, *Saint Louis*, London, 1968.
——, *Henry V*, London, 1975.
Maier, Christoph, *Preaching the Crusades*, Cambridge, 1994.
Meiss, Millard, *Great Age of Fresco*, London, 1970.
Nedlands, Robin, *The Hundred Years War*, London, 1990.
Rosenberg, Charles M. (ed.), *Art and Politics in the Late Medieval and Early Renaissance*, Paris, 1990.
Russell, J.B., *Witchcraft in the Middle Ages*, New York, 1972.
Sabloff, J.A., *Cities of Ancient Mexico*, London, 1989.
Strayer, Joseph R., *The Reign of Philip the Fair*, Princeton 1980.
Sumption, Jonathan, *The Hundred Years War*, London, 1990.
Swaan, Wim, *The Later Middle Ages, Art and Architecture*, London, 1977.
Taylor, John, *English Historical Literature in the Fourteenth Century*, Oxford, 1987.
Warner, Marina, *Alone of all her Sex: The Myth and Cult of the Virgin Mary*, London 1976.
——, *Joan of Arc: the Image of female Heroine*, London, 1987.
Yamanura, K. (ed.), *Cambridge History of Medieval Japan*, Cambridge, 1990.

CHAPTER 18

Barstow, Anne L., *Witchcraze*, New York, 1994.
Burckhardt, J., *The Civilization of the Renaissance in Italy*, transl., London, 1944.
Burke, Peter, *Culture and Society in Renaissance Italy*, London, 1972.
Chambers, D.S., *Patrons and Artists in the Italian Renaissance Europe*, London, 1970.
Cox-Rearick, Janet, *Dynasty and Destiny in Medici Art*, Princeton, 1984.
Dunlop, I., *The Royal Palaces of France*, London, 1985.
Goffen, Rena, *Piety and Patronage in Renaissance Venice*, Yale, 1986.
Goodman, Anthony, *The Wars of the Roses*, London, 1990.
Hale, J.R., *Machiavelli*, London, 1961.
——, *Civilization of the Renaissance in Italy*, London, 1992.
Hollingsworth, Mary, *Patronage in Renaissance Italy*, London, 1994.
Knecht, R.J., *The Rise and Fall of Renaissance France*, London, 1996.
Martineau, Jane (ed.), *The Genius of Venice*, London, 1987.
Mumfrey, Peter, *Painting in Renaissance Venice*, Yale, 1995.
Purkiss, Diane, *The Witch in History*, London, 1996.
Strong, Roy, *Art and Power: Renaissance Festivals 1450–1650*, London, 1984.
Townsend, R.F., *Aztecs*, London, 1992.
Trevor Roper, Hugh, *Princes and Artists: Patronage and Ideology in Four Habsburg Courts*, London, 1976.
Welch, E., *Art and Society in Italy 1350–1500*, Oxford, 1997.
Yates, Francis A., *The Valois Tapestries*, London, 1959.

CHAPTER 19

Andersson, C. and Talbot, C., *From A Mighty Fortress: Prints, Drawings and Books from the Age of Luther*, Detroit, 1983.
Anglo, Sydney, *The Image of Tudor Kingship*, London, 1992.
——, *Spectacle and Pageantry and Early Tudor Policy*, Oxford, 1969.
Brown, Jonathan and Elliott, J.H., *A Palace for a King*, Yale, 1980.
Camporesi, Piero, *The Fear of Hell: Images of Damnation and Salvation in Early Modern Europe*, transl., Cambridge, 1991.

Dickens, A.G., *The German Nation and Luther*, London, 1974
——, *The Courts of Europe: Patronage and Royalty 1400–1800*, London, 1977.
Geyl, Pieter, *The Revolt in the Netherlands*, London, 1958.
Griffiths, Ralph A., and Thomas, R.S., *The Making of the Tudor Dynasty*, Gloucester, 1985.
Guy, J., *Reign of Elizabeth I*, London, 1990.
Hearn, Karen, *Dynasties and Painting in Tudor and Jacobean England*, London, 1995.
Hickman, M.L., *Japan's Golden Age*, Yale, 1996.
Hoak, D. (ed.), *The Tudor Political Culture*, Cambridge, 1995.
Hosking, Geoffrey, *Russia: People and Empire*, London, 1992.
Hsia, Ronnie, *Social Discipline in the Reformation*, London, 1989.
Israel, J., *The Dutch Republic*, Oxford, 1995.
Kingdon, R.M., *Myths about St Bartholemew's Massacre*, Harvard, 1988.
Klaniczay, G., *Uses of Supernatural Power*, Cambridge, 1990.
Loades, D., *Tudor Court*, London, 1986.
McGrath, Alister, *Life of John Calvin*, Oxford, 1990.
Mitchell, D., *History of the Jesuits*, London, 1980.
Neale, J.E., *Elizabeth*, London, 1934.
Ozment, S.E., *Reformation in the Cities*, Yale, 1975.
Robinson-Hammerstein, H., *Transmission of Ideas in the Lutheran Reformation*, Blackrock, 1987.
Schama, Simon, *Embarrassment of Riches*, London, 1987.
——, *Patriots and Liberators*, London, 1957.
Scribner, R.W., *For the Sake of the Simple Folk: Popular Propaganda for the German Reformation*, Cambridge, 1989.
Strong, Roy, *The English Icon*, London, 1969.
——, *The Cult of Elizabeth*, London, 1977.
Tawney, R.W., *Religion and the Rise of Capitalism*, London, 1955.
Watt, Tessa, *Cheap Print and Popular Piety 1550–1640*, London, 1991.
Yates, Francis, *Astraea*, London, 1975.
Zagorin, P., *Rebels and Rulers 1500–1660*, Cambridge, 1982.

CHAPTER 20

Anglo, Sydney (ed.), *The damned art: essays in the literature of witchcraft*, London, 1977.
Beller, E.A., *Propaganda in the Thirty Years War*, Princeton, 1940.
Cressy, David, *Bonfires and Bells*, London, 1989.
Eisenstein, Elizabeth, *The Printing Press as an Agent of Change: Communication and Cultural Transformation in Early Modern Europe*, Cambridge, 1979.
Elliott, J.H., *Imperial Spain*, London, 1963.
Fraser, Antonia, *Cromwell*, London, 1974.
Hall, J.W. (ed.), *Cambridge History of Japan: Early Modern*, Cambridge, 1991.
Howarth, David, *Art and Patronage in the Caroline Court*, Cambridge, 1993.
Hutton, R., *The British Republic*, London, 1990.
Loomie, A.J., *The Ceremonies of Charles I*, New York, 1987.
Mann, R.G., *El Greco and his Patrons*, Cambridge, 1986.
Sawyer, Jeffrey K., *Printed Poison: pamphlet propaganda in seventeenth-century France*, Berkeley, 1990.
Sharp, K., *The Personal Rule of Charles I*, Yale, 1992.
Smith, N., *Literature in Revolutionary England 1640–60*, London, 1994.
Strong, Roy, *Britannia Triumphans*, London, 1980.
Wedgewood, C.V., *The Thirty Years War*, London, 1956.

CHAPTER 21

Atherton, H.M., *Political Prints in the Age of Hogarth*, London, 1974.
Censer, J.R. and Popki, J.D. (eds), *Press and Politics in pre-revolutionary France*, Berkeley, 1987.
Claydon, Tony, *William III and the Godly Revolution*, Cambridge, 1996.
Colley, Linda, *Britons: the Forging of a Nation 1707–1837*, London, 1993.
Crankshaw, David, *The Habsburgs*, London, 1971.
Downie, J.A., *Robert Harley and the Press*, London, 1979.
Erickson, Carolly, *Great Catherine*, London, 1994.
Gawthrop, Richard, *Pietism and the Making of 18th Century Prussia*, Cambridge, 1993.
George, M.D., *English Political Caricatures*, London, 1961.
Goldgar, Bertrand, *Walpole and the Wits*, London, 1960.
Hall, H. Gaston, *Richelieu's Desmarets and the Century of Louis XIV*, Oxford, 1990.
Harris, Tim, *London Crowds and Popular Politics in the Reign of Charles II*, Cambridge, 1987.
Hastie, P.J.P., *Dryden's Tory Propaganda*, Princeton, 1993.
Innis, H.A., *The Empire and Communications*, Toronto, 1952.
Kantorowicz, E., *Frederick II*, London, 1957.
Klaits, Joseph, *Printed Propaganda under Louis XIV*, Princeton, 1977.
Knecht, R.J., *Richelieu*, London, 1991.
Monod, Paul, *Jacobitism and the English People*, Cambridge, 1989.
Murray, J.T., *George I, the Baltic and the Whig Split of 1717; a study in diplomacy and propaganda*, London, 1969.
Newman, Gerald, *The Rise of English Nationalism 1740–1830*, London, 1987.
Perry, T.W., *Public Opinion, Propaganda and Politics in 18th Century Britain*, London, 1961.
Plumb, J.H., *Sir Robert Walpole*, Oxford, 1973.
Richards, J.O., *Party Propaganda under Queen Anne*, Athens, 1972.
Ritter, Gerhard, *The Sword and the Sceptre: The Problem of Militarism in Germany*, transl., London, 1973.
Spector, R., *The English Literary Periodical and the Climate of Opinion during the Seven Years War*, London, 1959.
Troyat, H., *Peter the Great*, transl., London, 1988.

CHAPTER 22

Agulhon, Maurice, *Marianne into Battle: Republican Imagery and Symbolism in France*, transl., Cambridge, 1981.
Berger, C., *Broadsides and Bayonets*, Philadelphia, 1961.
Brookner, Anita, *Jacques Louis David*, London, 1980.
Clark, R.N., *Benjamin Franklin*, London, 1983.
Cobban, R., *History of France*, London, 1957.
Crow, T.E., *Emulation: Making Artists for Revolutionary France*, Yale, 1995.
Darnton, R. and Roche, D., *Revolution in Print: the Press in France, 1775–1800*, Berkeley, 1989.
Davidson, Philip, *Propaganda and the American Revolution*, North Carolina, 1941.
Fischer, David H., *Paul Revere's Ride*, Oxford, 1994.
Farge, Arlette, *Subversive Words: Public Opinion in 18th Century France*, transl., Cambridge, 1994.
Gilchrist, J. and Chiswick, H., *The Press in the French Revolution*, Oxford, 1991.
Gough, Hugh, *The Newspaper Press in the French Revolution*, London, 1988.
Jones, C. (ed.), *Britain and Revolutionary France*, Exeter, 1983.
Kennedy, Emmet, *Cultural History of the French Revolution*, Yale, 1989.
Leith, J., *The Idea of Art as Propaganda in France 1750–99*, Toronto, 1965.

Ozouf, M., *Festivals and the French Revolution*, transl., London, 1988.
Paulson, Ronald, *Representation of Revolution*, Yale, 1983.
Reilly, B.F., *American Political Prints 1766–1870*, Boston, 1991.
Robriquet, J., *Daily Life in the French Revolution*, transl., London, 1950.
Schama, Simon, *Citizens*, London, 1985.
Schlesinger, A.M., *Prelude to Independence*, New York, 1958.
Smith, Culver S., *The Press, Politics and Patronage*, Athens, 1977.

CHAPTER 23

Ascherson, Neal, *The Struggles for Poland*, London, 1987.
Davies, N., *History of Poland*, London, 1981.
Field, G. Wallis, *A Literary History of Germany: The Nineteenth Century*, London, 1975.
Garvin, Tom, *The Evolution of Irish National Politics*, Dublin, 1981.
Hertz, Fred, *The Development of the German Mind*, London, 1957.
Holtman, Robert B., *Napoleonic Propaganda*, Baton Rouge, 1950.
Legge, James Granville, *Rhyme and Revolution in Germany: a Study in German History, Life, Literature and Character*, London, 1918.
Mack Smith, D., *Cavour and Garibaldi*, Cambridge, 1953.
Rudorff, R., *The Myth of France*, transl., London, 1970.
Schulze, H., *The Course of German Nationalism 1763–1867*, Cambridge, 1991.
Thompson, J.M., *Napoleon*, London, 1952.
Woolf, S.J., *Napoleon's Integration of Europe*, London, 1991.
——, *The Italian Risorgimento*, London, 1969.

CHAPTER 24

Briggs, Asa, *Public Opinion and Public Health in the Age of Chadwick*, London, 1948.
Edsall, N.C., *Cobden*, Harvard, 1986.
Jenkins, Roy, *Gladstone*, London, 1995.
Johannsen, R.W., *The Halls of Montezuma*, New York, 1985.
Ward, John T., *Chartism*, London, 1973.

CHAPTER 25

August, Thomas G., *The Selling of Empire: British and French Propaganda, 1890–1940*, London, 1985.
Balfour, M., *The Kaiser and his Times*, London, 1964.
Beringer, R.E., *Why the South lost the Civil War*, Princeton, 1986.
Boaahem, A. Adu (ed.), *General History of Africa*, Paris, 1985.
Coetzee, Marilyn, *The German Army League*, New York, 1990.
Donald, D.H., *Lincoln*, London, 1995.
Eri, Gyongyi and Jobbagyi, Z., *Great Age of Art and Society in Hungary, 1896–1904*, London, 1990.
Gall, Lothar, *Bismarck*, transl., London, 1986.
Heiberg, Marianne, *The Making of the Basque Nation*, Cambridge, 1989.
Hichberger, J.W.M., *The Images of the Army 1815–1914*, Manchester, 1988.
Hobsbawm, Eric and Ranger, T. (eds), *The Invention of Tradition*, Cambridge, 1983.
Jelavich, C., *Tsarist Russia and Balkan Nationalism*, Berkeley, 1958.
Keyserlingk, Robert H., *Media and Manipulation (Bismarck)*, Montreal, 1977.

Knightley, P., *The First Casualty: From Crimea to Vietnam: the War Correspondent as Hero, Propagandist and Myth Maker*, New York, 1975.
Kulstein, P., *Napoleon III and the Working Class*, Los Angeles, 1969.
Layton, Susan, *Russian Literature and Empire*, Cambridge, 1994.
Mackenzie, John M., *Propaganda and Empire 1880–1900*, Manchester, 1983.
Metcalf, Thomas R., *Ideologies of the Raj*, Cambridge, 1994.
Meyer, Jurg, *Die Propaganda der Deutscher Flottenbewegung, 1897–1900*, Bern, 1967.
Morris, Andrew, *Scaremongers: Advocacy of War and Rearmament 1856–1914*, London, 1984.
Mose, George L., *Nationalization of the Masses*, New York, 1975.
Parker, Peter, *The Old Lie: The Great War and the Public School Ethos*, London, 1987.
Pollard, James E., *The Presidents and the Press*, New York, 1947.
Raffalovitch, *L'Abominable Venalité de la Presse 1897–1917*, Paris, 1931.
Rosenberg, E., *Spreading the American Dream 1890–1945*, New York, 1982.
Seal, Anil, *The Emergence of the Indian Nation*, London, 1968.
Tebbel, J.W., *The American Great Patriotic War against Spain*, Manchester, 1996.
Wilson, D., *Life and Times of Vuk Stefanovic Karadzic*, Oxford, 1970.
Wittke, Carl, *German Language Press in America*, Kentucky, 1957.

CHAPTER 26

Berlin, Isaiah, *Karl Marx*, London, 1948.
Collier, R., *The General next to God: William Booth*, London, 1956.
Harrison, S., *Cults*, London, 1994.
Mitchell, David, *Queen Christabel*, London, 1977.

CHAPTER 27

Bruitz, George, *Allied Propaganda and the Collapse of the German Empire*, Stanford, 1938.
Buitenhuis, Peter, *The Great War of Words, Literature as Propaganda 1914–18*, London, 1989.
Carr, E.H., *The Bolshevik Revolution*, London, 1950–64.
Chennault, Libby, *Battle-lines: World War I Posters*, Chapel Hill, 1988.
Cornwall, M. (ed.), *The Last Year of Austria-Hungary*, Exeter, 1990.
Ferguson, Neil, *The Pity of War*, London, 1998.
Figes, Orlando, *People's Tragedy: Russian Revolution 1891–1924*, London, 1996.
Haste, Cate, *Keep the Home Fires Burning: Propaganda in the First World War*, London, 1979.
Kushner, David, *The Rise of Turkish Nationalism*, London, 1977.
Lasswell, H.D., *Propaganda Techniques of the First World War*, New York, 1927.
Mackenzie, J.A., *The Propaganda Boom*, London, 1938.
Massie, R.K., *Dreadnought*, London, 1992.
Messinger, G.S., *British Propaganda and the State in the First World War*, Manchester, 1992.
Osley, Anthony, *Persuading the People*, London, 1995.
Peterson, H.C., *Propaganda for War: Campaign against American Neutrality*, London, 1995.
Ramsaur, E.E., *The Young Turks*, Princeton, 1957.
Read, J.M., *Atrocity Propaganda 1914–18*, New Haven, 1941.
Ross, Stewart H., *Propaganda for War: How the US was . . .* , London, 1996.
Sanders, M.L., and Taylor, P.M. (eds), *British Propaganda in World War I*, London, 1982.
Schlinder, C., *Hollywood goes to War*, London, 1979.

Sillars, Stuart, *Art and Survival in First World War Britain*, London, 1987.
Squires, J.D., *British Propaganda at home and in the USA 1914–17*, Harvard, 1987.
Ulam, A., *Lenin*, London, 1959.

CHAPTER 28

Adam, P., *The Arts of the Third Reich*, London, 1992.
Ades, D., Benton, T. et al. (eds), *Art and Power in Europe under the Dictators 1930–1945*, London, 1995.
Allen, W.S., *The Nazi Seizure of Power*, London, 1966.
Baghorn, F.C., *Soviet Foreign Propaganda*, Princeton, 1964.
Benn, D. Wedgwood, *Persuasion and Soviet Politics*, Oxford, 1989.
Bransted, E.K., *Goebbels and National Socialist Propaganda*, London, 1968.
Brown, M.C. and Taylor, B., *Art of the Soviets*, Manchester, 1993.
Bullock, A., *Hitler: A Study in Tyranny*, London, 1952.
Calman, D., *The Nature and Origin of Japanese Imperialism*, London, 1992.
Clews, John C., *Communist Propaganda Techniques*, London, 1964.
Davis, Sarah, *Public Opinion in Stalin's Russia*, Cambridge, 1997.
Dower, J., *Japan in Peace and War*, London, 1995.
Ellwood, Sheelagh, *Spanish Fascism*, London, 1987.
Grosshans, H., *Hitler and the Artists*, New York, 1983.
Golomstock, Igor, *Totalitarian Art*, London, 1990.
Gombrich, E.H., *Myth and Reality in German Wartime Broadcasting*, London, 1970.
Grunberger, R., *Social History of the Third Reich*, London, 1964.
Hale, O.J., *Captive Press in the Third Reich*, Princeton, 1964.
Hitler, Adolf, *Mein Kampf*, transl., London, 1939.
Hollander, G.P., *Soviet Political Indoctrination*, New York, 1972.
Irving, D., *Goebbels*, London, 1996.
Kenez, Peter, *The Birth of the Propaganda State: Soviet Methods of Mobilization 1917–29*, Cambridge, 1985.
Laurence, J., *The Seeds of Disaster: South African Propaganda*, London, 1968.
Leiser, Erwin, *Nazi Cinema*, London, 1974.
Nolletti, Arthur (ed.), *Reframing Japanese Cinema*, Indiana, 1992.
Redlich, S., *Propaganda and Nationalism in Wartime Russia*, Boulder, 1982.
Shillony, B., *Politics and Culture in Wartime Japan*, Oxford, 1987.
Speer, Albert, *Inside the Third Reich*, transl., London, 1955.
Taylor, Richard, *Film Propaganda: Soviet Russia and Nazi Germany*, London, 1979.
Taylor, Robert, *The Word in Stone: the Role of Architecture in National Socialist Ideology*, Berkeley, 1974.
Tucker, Robert C., *Stalin in Power*, New York, 1990.
Welch, David, *Propaganda and German Cinema*, Oxford, 1983.
——, *Third Reich: Politics and Propaganda*, London, 1993.
White, S., *The Bolshevik Poster*, London, 1988.
Wolferen, K.V., *The Enigma of Japanese Power*, London, 1989.
Wykes, A., *The Nuremberg Rallies*, London, 1970.
Zeman, Z.A.B., *Nazi Propaganda*, London, 1973.
——, *Selling the War: Art and Propaganda in World War Two*, London, 1978.

CHAPTER 29

Alderman, G., *British Elections: Myth and Reality*, London, 1978.
Balfour, M., *Propaganda in War, 1939–45*, London, 1979.
Burk, R.F., *Dwight D. Eisenhower*, Boston, 1986.

Calder, Angus, *The People's War, 1939–45*, London, 1970.
Chapman, J., *The British at War: cinema, state & politics 1939–45*, London, 1998.
Chisholm, Anne and Davie, M., *Beaverbrook*, London, 1992.
Cockett, R., *Twilight of Truth: Chamberlain's Appeasement and the Manipulation of Public Opinion*, London, 1989.
Cole, Robert, *Britain and the War of Words in Neutral Europe, 1939–45*, London, 1990.
Cormack, Michael, *Ideology and Cinematography in Hollywood 1930–9*, London, 1994.
Cull, N.J., *Selling War: the British Propaganda Campaign against American Neutrality in World War II*, Oxford, 1995.
Freidel, F., *F.D. Roosevelt*, Boston, 1990.
Fulbright, J.W., *The Pentagon Propaganda Machine*, Washington, 1970.
Gilbert, Martin, *Churchill*, London, 1991.
Grant, Mariel, *Propaganda and the Role of the State in Post-war Britain*, Oxford, 1994.
Hachten, W.A., *The Press and Apartheid*, London, 1984.
Honey, M., *Creating Rosie the Riveter*, Amhurst, 1984.
Jenkins, Roy, *Baldwin*, London, 1987.
Judd, David, *Posters of World War II*, London, 1972.
Mclaine, Ian, *Ministry of Morale*, London, 1979.
Nicholas, S., *The Echo of the War*, Manchester, 1996.
Rhodes, A., *Propaganda: the Art of Persuasion: World War II*, New York, 1975.
Schiller, H., *Mass Communication and the American Empire*, New York, 1958.
Short, K.R.M. (ed.), *Film and Radio Propaganda in World War II*, London, 1983.
Smith, David, *Socialist Propaganda in the Twentieth Century British Novel*, London, 1978.
Smith, A.C.H., *Paper Voices: the Popular Press and Social Change 1935–65*, London, 1969.
Tallent, Stephen, *Projection of England*, London, 1932.
Taylor, Philip M., *The Projection of Britain 1919–31*, London, 1986.
——, *British Cinema during the Second World War*, Basingstoke, 1988.
Yass, M., *This is Your War. Home Front Propaganda in the Second World War*, London, 1983.

CHAPTER 30

Asia Research Centre, *The Great Cultural Revolution*, Hong Kong, 1967.
Balfour, Sebastian, *Castro*, London, 1995.
Copley, A., *Gandhi: against the tide*, Oxford, 1987.
Crofts, William, *Coercion or Persuasion: Propaganda in Britain after 1945*, London, 1989.
Crozier, R., *Art and Revolution in Modern China*, Berkeley, 1988.
Elegant, R.S., *Mao's Great Revolution*, London, 1970.
Gittings, John, *China Changes Face*, Oxford, 1989.
Howkins, J.M., *Mass Communication in China*, New York, 1982.
Lacouture, Jean, *De Gaulle*, transl., London, 1990.
Page, C., *US Propaganda during the Vietnam War*, London, 1996.
Taylor, J.M., *Evita Perón*, Oxford, 1979.
Thompson, Leonard, *The Political Mythology of Apartheid*, New Haven, 1985.
Yu, Frederick T.C., *The Establishment Propaganda Networks in China*, Dallas, 1952.
——, *Mass Persuasion in China*, London, 1957.

CHAPTER 31

Ambrose, S.E., *Nixon,* New York, 1987.
Bogart, J., *Premises for Propaganda: the United States Information Agency,* Washington, 1976.
Boyd, Douglas A., *Broadcasting in the Arab World,* Philadelphia, 1982.
Czitrom, Daniel, *Media and the American Mind,* North Carolina, 1982.
Dallek, R., *Ronald Reagan: the politics of symbolism,* Harvard, 1984.
Davis, J.H., *The Kennedy Clan,* London, 1985.
Erickson, G.M., *Anti-Communism: the politics of manipulation,* London, 1987.
Ferguson, James, *Papa Doc,* Oxford, 1987.
Hatem, M.A.K., *Information and the Arab Cause,* London, 1974.
Hickson, W., *The Parting of the Curtains 1945–61,* London, 1997.
Hiro, Dilip, *Iran under the Ayatollahs,* London, 1985.
Jansen, G.H., *Militant Islam,* London, 1979.
Lashmar, Paul and Oliver, James, *Britain's Secret Propaganda War 1948–77,* Stroud, 1998.
Noriega, L.A. de, *Broadcasting in Mexico,* London, 1979.
Seymour Ure, Colin, *The American Presidents: power and communication,* London, 1982.
Spitzer, H.M., *Presenting America in American Propaganda,* New York, 1984.
Whitton, J.B., *Propaganda and the Cold War,* London, 1986.

CHAPTER 32

Catis, Liz, *Ireland: the Propaganda War,* London, 1984.
Doder, D. and Branson, L., *Gorbachev: heretic in the Kremlin,* London, 1990.
Galloway, George and Wylke, B., *Downfall: the Ceauşescus and the Romanian Revolution,* London, 1991.
Graffy, J. and Hoskings, G. (eds), *Culture and the Media in the USSR Today,* London, 1989.
Gustainis, J.J., *American Rhetoric and the Vietnam War,* London, 1993.
Holmes, Leslie, *The End of Communist Power,* London, 1993.
Mason, David S., *Public Opinion and Political Change in Poland,* Cambridge, 1985.
Powell, D.E., *Anti-Religious Propaganda in the Soviet Union,* Cambridge, 1975.
Prittie, T., *The Fourth Arab Israeli War – Propaganda,* London, 1974.
Riddell, Peter, *The Thatcher Decade,* London, 1989.
Roxburgh, A., *Second Russian Revolution,* London, 1991.
Sheehy, G., *Gorbachev,* London, 1991.

CHAPTER 33

Almond, Mark, *Europe's Backyard War,* London, 1984.
Bennigse, Alexander, and Wimburn, W., *Muslims in the Soviet Empire,* London, 1989.
Glenny, Misha, *The Fall of Yugoslavia,* London, 1992.
Hampson, Françoise, *Incitement and the Media in the former Yugoslavia,* Colchester, 1993.
Hollingsworth, M., *The Ultimate Spin Doctor (Tim Bell),* London, 1997.
Jones, Nicholas, *Soundbites and Spin Doctors,* London, 1996.
Judah, Tim, *The Serbs: history, myth and the destruction of Yugoslavia,* Yale, 1996.

Karsh, E. and Rautsi, I., *Saddam Hussein*, London, 1991.
Latin, D.D. and Samatar, S.S., *Somalia*, Boulder, 1987.
Malcolm, N., *Bosnia*, London, 1994.
Taylor, Philip M., *War and the Media: Propaganda and Persuasion in the Gulf War*, Manchester, 1992.

Index